Presented to:

_____

By:

_____

God's
Promises
for Women of Faith

WOMEN OF FAITH®

THOMAS NELSON
Since 1798

NASHVILLE DALLAS MEXICO CITY RIO DE JANEIRO

God's Promises for Women of Faith
© 2010 by Women of Faith

Original © 1999 by J. Countryman, a division of Thomas Nelson, Inc., Nashville, TN 37214.

Published in Nashville, Tennessee, by Thomas Nelson. Thomas Nelson is a trademark of Thomas Nelson, Inc.

Thomas Nelson, Inc., titles may be purchased in bulk for educational, business, fund-raising, or sales promotional use. For information, please e-mail SpecialMarkets@ThomasNelson.com.

ISBN-10: 1-4041-8961-0
ISBN-13: 978-1-4041-8961-4

Printed in the United States of America

10 11 12 13 14 [RRD] 5 4 3 2

INTRODUCTION

Over the years, Gloria Gaither has written many wonderful songs. One of my personal favorites is a children's song that goes like this: "I am a promise. I am a possibility. I am a promise with a capital *P*. I am a great big bundle of potentiality." The delight in that verse is not just its musicality, but its truth. It's what the Bible teaches about you and me. We are all a promise . . . because of the promises of God.

Scripture is full of the promises of God. Promises about all He gives us, creates in us, causes for us, and does on our behalf all of our lives on this earth. The problem is we forget! We go through life as though we have nothing but what we can accomplish on our own or work hard to provide for ourselves. We are daughters of the King who live like scavengers, who live as though our resources are limited when, in fact, His resources for us are unlimited.

What we need is a reminder, which I trust you'll find (every time you need one!) in this little book of God's enormous promises.

Mary Graham

CONTENTS

God Encourages Each Woman to...

God Teaches a Woman How to...

God Blesses Women When They...

God Comforts Women as They Learn to...

God Gives Freely to Women...

God Helps Women to Grow by...

God Rejoices with Women When They...

Dynamic Women of Faith

God's Plan
for Women Is to . . .

WORSHIP HIM

Give unto the Lord, O you mighty ones,
Give unto the Lord glory and strength.
Give unto the Lord the glory due to
    His name;
Worship the Lord in the beauty of holiness.

PSALM 29:1–2

Oh come, let us worship and bow down;
Let us kneel before the Lord our Maker.
For He is our God,
And we are the people of His pasture,
And the sheep of His hand.

PSALM 95:6–7

The hour is coming, and now is, when the true worshipers will worship the Father in spirit and truth; for the Father is seeking such to worship Him. God is Spirit, and those who worship Him must worship in spirit and truth.

JOHN 4:23–24

Oh, worship the Lord in the beauty of
    holiness!
Tremble before Him, all the earth.

PSALM 96:9

Then you will call upon Me and go and pray to Me, and I will listen to you. And you will seek Me and find Me, when you search for Me with all your heart.

JEREMIAH 29:12–13

Seek the LORD and His strength;
Seek His face evermore!
Remember His marvelous works which
    He has done,
His wonders, and the judgments of
    His mouth.

1 CHRONICLES 16:11–12

Blessed are those who keep His testimonies,
Who seek Him with the whole heart! . . .
With my whole heart I have sought You;
Oh, let me not wander from Your
    commandments!

PSALM 119:2, 10

Thus I will bless You while I live;
I will lift up my hands in Your name.
My soul shall be satisfied as with marrow
    and fatness,
And my mouth shall praise You with
    joyful lips.

PSALM 63:4–5

 OBEY HIM

But be doers of the word, and not hearers only, deceiving yourselves.

JAMES 1:22

If you love Me, keep My commandments.

JOHN 14:15

Peter and the other apostles answered and said: "We ought to obey God rather than men."

ACTS 5:29

Whoever comes to Me, and hears My sayings and does them, I will show you whom he is like: He is like a man building a house, who dug deep and laid the foundation on the rock. And when the flood arose, the stream beat vehemently against that house, and could not shake it, for it was founded on the rock. But he who heard and did nothing is like a man who built a house on the earth without a foundation, against which the stream beat vehemently; and immediately it fell. And the ruin of that house was great.

LUKE 6:47–49

He who is faithful in what is least is faithful also in much; and he who is unjust in what is least is unjust also in much.

LUKE 16:10

We have had human fathers who corrected us, and we paid them respect. Shall we not much more readily be in subjection to the Father of spirits and live? For they indeed for a few days chastened us as seemed best to them, but He for our profit, that we may be partakers of His holiness.

HEBREWS 12:9–10

The world is passing away, and the lust of it; but he who does the will of God abides forever.

1 JOHN 2:17

Now the just shall live by faith;
But if anyone draws back,
My soul has no pleasure in him.

HEBREWS 10:38

COME TO HIM
IN PRAYER

Let us therefore come boldly to the throne of grace, that we may obtain mercy and find grace to help in time of need.

HEBREWS 4:16

Evening and morning and at noon
I will pray, and cry aloud,
And He shall hear my voice.

PSALM 55:17

Give ear, O LORD, to my prayer;
And attend to the voice of my supplications.
In the day of my trouble I will call upon You,
For You will answer me.

PSALM 86:6–7

For the eyes of the LORD are on the
    righteous,
And His ears are open to their prayers;
But the face of the LORD is against those
    who do evil.

1 PETER 3:12

Then He spoke a parable to them, that men always ought to pray and not lose heart.

LUKE 18:1

When you pray, you shall not be like the hypocrites. For they love to pray standing in the synagogues and on the corners of the streets, that they may be seen by men. Assuredly, I say to you, they have their reward. But you, when you pray, go into your room, and when you have shut your door, pray to your Father who is in the secret place; and your Father who sees in secret will reward you openly.

MATTHEW 6:5–6

You will make your prayer to Him,
He will hear you,
And you will pay your vows.
You will also declare a thing,
And it will be established for you;
So light will shine on your ways.

JOB 22:27–28

Let him ask in faith, with no doubting, for he who doubts is like a wave of the sea driven and tossed by the wind.

JAMES 1:6

LISTEN TO THE HOLY SPIRIT

For what man knows the things of a man except the spirit of the man which is in him? Even so no one knows the things of God except the Spirit of God. Now we have received, not the spirit of the world, but the Spirit who is from God, that we might know the things that have been freely given to us by God.

These things we also speak, not in words which man's wisdom teaches but which the Holy Spirit teaches, comparing spiritual things with spiritual.

1 CORINTHIANS 2:11–13

Speaking the truth in love, may [we] grow up in all things into Him who is the head—Christ—from whom the whole body, joined and knit together by what every joint supplies, according to the effective working by which every part does its share, causes growth of the body for the edifying of itself in love. . . .

Do not grieve the Holy Spirit of God, by whom you were sealed for the day of redemption.

EPHESIANS 4:15–16, 30

For the Holy Spirit will teach you in that very hour what you ought to say.

LUKE 12:12

You, beloved, building yourselves up on your most holy faith, praying in the Holy Spirit, keep yourselves in the love of God, looking for the mercy of our Lord Jesus Christ unto eternal life.

JUDE 20–21

Nevertheless I tell you the truth. It is to your advantage that I go away; for if I do not go away, the Helper will not come to you; but if I depart, I will send Him to you. And when He has come, He will convict the world of sin, and of righteousness, and of judgment: of sin, because they do not believe in Me; of righteousness, because I go to My Father and you see Me no more; of judgment, because the ruler of this world is judged. I still have many things to say to you, but you cannot bear them now.

JOHN 16:7–12

Knowing this first, that no prophecy of Scripture is of any private interpretation, for prophecy never came by the will of man, but holy men of God spoke as they were moved by the Holy Spirit.

2 PETER 1:20–21

If the Spirit of Him who raised Jesus from the dead dwells in you, He who raised Christ from the dead will also give life to your mortal bodies through His Spirit who dwells in you. . . .

The Spirit Himself bears witness with our spirit that we are children of God, and if children, then heirs—heirs of God and joint heirs with Christ, if indeed we suffer with Him, that we may also be glorified together.

For I consider that the sufferings of this present time are not worthy to be compared with the glory which shall be revealed in us. . . .

Likewise the Spirit also helps in our weaknesses. For we do not know what we should pray for as we ought, but the Spirit Himself makes intercession for us with groanings which cannot be uttered. Now He who searches the hearts knows what the mind of the Spirit is, because He makes intercession for the saints according to the will of God.

ROMANS 8:11, 16–18, 26–27

But the Helper, the Holy Spirit, whom the Father will send in My name, He will teach you all things, and bring to your remembrance all things that I said to you.

JOHN 14:26

Being assembled together with them, He commanded them not to depart from Jerusalem, but to wait for the Promise of the Father, "which," He said, "you have heard from Me; for John truly baptized with water, but you shall be baptized with the Holy Spirit not many days from now" . . .

And He said to them, "It is not for you to know times or seasons which the Father has put in His own authority. But you shall receive power when the Holy Spirit has come upon you; and you shall be witnesses to Me in Jerusalem, and in all Judea and Samaria, and to the end of the earth."

ACTS 1:4–5, 7–8

Not that we are sufficient of ourselves to think of anything as being from ourselves, but our sufficiency is from God, who also made us sufficient as ministers of the new covenant, not of the letter but of the Spirit; for the letter kills, but the Spirit gives life. . . .

Now the Lord is the Spirit; and where the Spirit of the Lord is, there is liberty. But we all, with unveiled face, beholding as in a mirror the glory of the Lord, are being transformed into the same image from glory to glory, just as by the Spirit of the Lord.

2 CORINTHIANS 3:5–6, 17–18

God Teaches Women
to Walk in His Word by . . .

PRAISING HIS MIGHT

Praise the LORD!
Sing to the LORD a new song,
And His praise in the assembly of saints.

PSALM 149:1

Praise the LORD!
Oh, give thanks to the LORD, for He is good!
For His mercy endures forever.
Who can utter the mighty acts of the LORD?
Who can declare all His praise?

PSALM 106:1–2

Praise the LORD!
Praise, O servants of the LORD,
Praise the name of the LORD!
Blessed be the name of the LORD
From this time forth and forevermore!
From the rising of the sun to its going down
The LORD's name is to be praised.

PSALM 113:1–3

I will praise the name of God with a song,
And will magnify Him with thanksgiving.

PSALM 69:30

My heart is steadfast, O God, my heart
    is steadfast;
I will sing and give praise.
Awake, my glory!
Awake, lute and harp!
I will awaken the dawn.
I will praise You, O Lord, among the peoples;
I will sing to You among the nations.

PSALM 57:7–9

Praise the LORD!
Praise the LORD, O my soul!
While I live I will praise the LORD;
I will sing praises to my God while I have
    my being.

PSALM 146:1–2

Great is the LORD, and greatly to be praised
In the city of our God,
In His holy mountain.

PSALM 48:1

Every good gift and every perfect gift is from above,
and comes down from the Father of lights.

JAMES 1:17

Because Your lovingkindness is better
      than life,
My lips shall praise You.
Thus I will bless You while I live;
I will lift up my hands in Your name.
My soul shall be satisfied as with marrow
      and fatness,
And my mouth shall praise You with
      joyful lips.

PSALM 63:3–5

TRUSTING HIS POWER

It shall come to pass
That before they call, I will answer;
And while they are still speaking, I will hear.

ISAIAH 65:24

You will keep him in perfect peace,
Whose mind is stayed on You,
Because he trusts in You.
Trust in the LORD forever,
For in YAH, the LORD, is everlasting strength.

ISAIAH 26:3–4

Behold, God is my salvation,
I will trust and not be afraid;
For YAH, the LORD, is my strength and song;
He also has become my salvation.

ISAIAH 12:2

The LORD is on my side;
I will not fear.
What can man do to me?
It is better to trust in the LORD
Than to put confidence in man.

PSALM 118:6, 8

In You, O LORD, I put my trust;
Let me never be put to shame. . . .
For You are my hope, O Lord GOD;
You are my trust from my youth. . . .
Let my mouth be filled with Your praise
And with Your glory all the day.

PSALM 71:1, 5, 8

Yes, we had the sentence of death in ourselves, that we should not trust in ourselves but in God who raises the dead, who delivered us from so great a death, and does deliver us; in whom we trust that He will still deliver us.

2 CORINTHIANS 1:9–10

He will not be afraid of evil tidings;
His heart is steadfast, trusting in the LORD.
His heart is established;
He will not be afraid,
Until he sees his desire upon his enemies.

PSALM 112:7–8

The salvation of the righteous is from the LORD;
He is their strength in the time of trouble.
And the LORD shall help them and deliver them;
He shall deliver them from the wicked,
And save them,
Because they trust in Him.

PSALM 37:39–40

FOCUSING ON HIS LOVE

For thus says the Lord GOD, the Holy
      One of Israel:
"In returning and rest you shall be saved;
In quietness and confidence shall be
      your strength."

ISAIAH 30:15

His work is honorable and glorious,
And His righteousness endures forever.
He has made His wonderful works to
      be remembered;
The LORD is gracious and full of
      compassion.

PSALM 111:3–4

We are always confident, knowing that while we are
at home in the body we are absent from the Lord. For we
walk by faith, not by sight.

2 CORINTHIANS 5:6–7

For He Himself has said, "I will never leave you nor
forsake you."

HEBREWS 13:5

Fear not, for I am with you;
Be not dismayed, for I am your God.
I will strengthen you,
Yes, I will help you,
I will uphold you with My righteous
      right hand.

ISAIAH 41:10

God is our refuge and strength,
A very present help in trouble.
Therefore we will not fear,
Even though the earth be removed,
And though the mountains be carried
      into the midst of the sea;
Though its waters roar and be troubled,
Though the mountains shake with
      its swelling.

PSALM 46:1–3

God has not given us a spirit of fear, but of power and of love and of a sound mind....

[He] has saved us and called us with a holy calling, not according to our works, but according to His own purpose and grace which was given to us in Christ Jesus before time began.

2 TIMOTHY 1:7, 9

Hungry and thirsty,
Their soul fainted in them.
Then they cried out to the LORD in
    their trouble,
And He delivered them out of their
    distresses.
And He led them forth by the right way,
That they might go to a city for a
    dwelling place.

PSALM 107:5–7

Come to Me, all you who labor and are heavy laden, and I will give you rest. Take My yoke upon you and learn from Me, for I am gentle and lowly in heart, and you will find rest for your souls. For My yoke is easy and My burden is light.

MATTHEW 11:28–30

I am the God of your father Abraham; do not fear, for I am with you.

GENESIS 26:24

PRAYING FOR HIS WILL

Evening and morning and at noon
I will pray, and cry aloud,
And He shall hear my voice.

PSALM 55:17

Now when Daniel knew that the writing was signed, he went home. And in his upper room, with his windows open toward Jerusalem, he knelt down on his knees three times that day, and prayed and gave thanks before his God, as was his custom since early days.

DANIEL 6:10

Seven times a day I praise You,
Because of Your righteous judgments.

PSALM 119:164

I will meditate on Your precepts,
And contemplate Your ways.
I will delight myself in Your statutes;
I will not forget Your word.

PSALM 119:15–16

Your word is a lamp to my feet
And a light to my path.

PSALM 119:105

So then faith comes by hearing, and hearing by the word of God.

ROMANS 10:17

These are the [seeds] sown on good ground, those who hear the word, accept it, and bear fruit: some thirty-fold, some sixty, and some a hundred.

MARK 4:20

The LORD is far from the wicked,
But He hears the prayer of the righteous.

PROVERBS 15:29

Pray without ceasing.

1 THESSALONIANS 5:17

FOLLOWING HIS LIGHT

For the commandment is a lamp,
And the law a light;
Reproofs of instruction are the way of life.

PROVERBS 6:23

Be diligent to present yourself approved to God, a worker who does not need to be ashamed, rightly dividing the word of truth.

2 TIMOTHY 2:15

Your word I have hidden in my heart,
That I might not sin against You.
Blessed are You, O LORD!
Teach me Your statutes!

PSALM 119:11–12

For in Him we live and move and have our being, as also some of your own poets have said, "For we are also His offspring."

ACTS 17:28

Whoever transgresses and does not abide in the doctrine of Christ does not have God. He who abides in the doctrine of Christ has both the Father and the Son.

2 JOHN 1:9

Draw near to God and He will draw near to you. Cleanse your hands, you sinners; and purify your hearts, you double-minded.

JAMES 4:8

Jesus said to him, "If you can believe, all things are possible to him who believes."

MARK 9:23

Those who are Christ's have crucified the flesh with its passions and desires. If we live in the Spirit, let us also walk in the Spirit.

GALATIANS 5:24–25

REJOICING DAY AND NIGHT

How sweet are Your words to my taste,
Sweeter than honey to my mouth!

PSALM 119:103

The law of the LORD is perfect,
    converting the soul;
The testimony of the LORD is sure,
    making wise the simple;
The statutes of the LORD are right,
    rejoicing the heart;
The commandment of the LORD is pure,
    enlightening the eyes;
More to be desired are they than gold,
Yea, than much fine gold;
Sweeter also than honey and the honeycomb.

PSALM 19:7–8, 10

This Book of the Law shall not depart from your mouth, but you shall meditate in it day and night, that you may observe to do according to all that is written in it. For then you will make your way prosperous, and then you will have good success.

JOSHUA 1:8

I will meditate on Your precepts,
And contemplate Your ways.
I will delight myself in Your statutes;
I will not forget Your word.

PSALM 119:15–16

Put off, concerning your former conduct, the old man which grows corrupt according to the deceitful lusts, and be renewed in the spirit of your mind, and . . . put on the new man which was created according to God, in true righteousness and holiness.

EPHESIANS 4:22–24

We do not lose heart. Even though our outward man is perishing, yet the inward man is being renewed day by day.

2 CORINTHIANS 4:16

The LORD will command His lovingkindness
        in the daytime,
And in the night His song shall be
        with me—
A prayer to the God of my life.

PSALM 42:8

God Delights in
Women Who Are . . .

SEEKING HIM

When my father and my mother forsake me,
Then the Lord will take care of me.

PSALM 27:10

O God, You are my God;
Early will I seek You;
My soul thirsts for You;
My flesh longs for You
In a dry and thirsty land
Where there is no water.

PSALM 63:1

Seek the Lord and His strength;
Seek His face evermore!
Remember His marvelous works which
He has done,
His wonders, and the judgments of
His mouth.

1 CHRONICLES 16:11–12

If you confess with your mouth the Lord Jesus and
believe in your heart that God has raised Him from the
dead, you will be saved.

ROMANS 10:9

I love those who love me,
And those who seek me diligently will
find me.

PROVERBS 8:17

Till I come, give attention to reading, to exhortation,
to doctrine.

1 TIMOTHY 4:13

There is a way that seems right to a man,
But its end is the way of death.

PROVERBS 14:12

I sought the LORD, and He heard me,
And delivered me from all my fears.

PSALM 34:4

Always pursue what is good both for yourselves and
for all.

1 THESSALONIANS 5:15

CONFIDENT
IN HIM

I will not leave you orphans; I will come to you.

JOHN 14:18

I thank my God upon every remembrance of you.

PHILIPPIANS 1:3

In You, O LORD, I put my trust;
Let me never be put to shame.
Deliver me in Your righteousness, and
 cause me to escape;
Incline Your ear to me, and save me. . . .
For You are my hope, O Lord GOD;
You are my trust from my youth.

PSALM 71:1– 2, 5

The LORD shall preserve you from all evil;
He shall preserve your soul.
The LORD shall preserve your going out
 and your coming in
From this time forth, and even forevermore.

PSALM 121:7–8

It is better to trust in the LORD
Than to put confidence in man.

PSALM 118:8

Therefore submit to God. Resist the devil and he will flee from you.

JAMES 4:7

Grace and peace be multiplied to you in the knowledge of God and of Jesus our Lord, as His divine power has given to us all things that pertain to life and godliness, through the knowledge of Him who called us by glory and virtue, by which have been given to us exceedingly great and precious promises, that through these you may be partakers of the divine nature, having escaped the corruption that is in the world through lust.

2 PETER 1:2–4

Who is he who overcomes the world, but he who believes that Jesus is the Son of God?

1 JOHN 5:5

With men this is impossible, but with God all things are possible.

MATTHEW 19:26

FORGIVEN
BY HIM

Now to Him who is able to keep you
    from stumbling,
And to present you faultless
Before the presence of His glory with
    exceeding joy,
To God our Savior,
Who alone is wise,
Be glory and majesty,
Dominion and power,
Both now and forever.

JUDE 24–25

There is therefore now no condemnation to those who are in Christ Jesus, who do not walk according to the flesh, but according to the Spirit. For the law of the Spirit of life in Christ Jesus has made me free from the law of sin and death.

ROMANS 8:1–2

If we confess our sins, He is faithful and just to forgive us our sins and to cleanse us from all unrighteousness.

1 JOHN 1:9

You have forgiven the iniquity of
    Your people;
You have covered all their sin.

Psalm 85:2

Now whom you forgive anything, I also forgive. For if indeed I have forgiven anything, I have forgiven that one for your sakes in the presence of Christ, lest Satan should take advantage of us; for we are not ignorant of his devices.

2 Corinthians 2:10–11

To him who overcomes I will grant to sit with Me on My throne, as I also overcame and sat down with My Father on His throne.

Revelation 3:21

The Lord will deliver me from every evil work and preserve me for His heavenly kingdom. To Him be glory forever and ever. Amen!

2 Timothy 4:18

GROWING IN HIM

I will instruct you and teach you in the
way you should go;
I will guide you with My eye.

PSALM **32**:8

This Book of the Law shall not depart from your mouth, but you shall meditate in it day and night, that you may observe to do according to all that is written in it. For then you will make your way prosperous, and then you will have good success.

JOSHUA **1**:8

That we should no longer be children, tossed to and fro and carried about with every wind of doctrine, by the trickery of men, in the cunning craftiness of deceitful plotting, but, speaking the truth in love, may grow up in all things into Him who is the head—Christ.

EPHESIANS **4**:14–15

Be doers of the word, and not hearers only, deceiving yourselves.

JAMES **1**:22

I am the vine, you are the branches. He who abides in Me, and I in him, bears much fruit; for without Me you can do nothing.

JOHN **15**:5

O God, You are my God;
Early will I seek You;
My soul thirsts for You;
My flesh longs for You
In a dry and thirsty land
Where there is no water.
So I have looked for You in the sanctuary,
To see Your power and Your glory....
My soul shall be satisfied as with marrow
    and fatness,
And my mouth shall praise You with joyful lips.
When I remember You on my bed,
I meditate on You in the night watches.
Because You have been my help,
Therefore in the shadow of Your wings I will rejoice.

PSALM 63:1–2, 5–7

You did not choose Me, but I chose you and appointed you that you should go and bear fruit, and that your fruit should remain, that whatever you ask the Father in My name He may give you.

JOHN 15:16

For in Him we live and move and have our being, as also some of your own poets have said, "For we are also His offspring."

ACTS 17:28

SERVING HIM

If it seems evil to you to serve the Lord, choose for yourselves this day whom you will serve, whether the gods which your fathers served that were on the other side of the River, or the gods of the Amorites, in whose land you dwell. But as for me and my house, we will serve the Lord.

Joshua 24:15

If anyone serves Me, let him follow Me; and where I am, there My servant will be also. If anyone serves Me, him My Father will honor.

John 12:26

Then Jesus said to him, "Away with you, Satan! For it is written, 'You shall worship the Lord your God, and Him only you shall serve.'"

Matthew 4:10

So the people asked him, saying, "What shall we do then?"

He answered and said to them, "He who has two tunics, let him give to him who has none; and he who has food, let him do likewise."

Luke 3:10–11

By this all will know that you are My disciples, if you have love for one another.

JOHN 13:35

Command those who are rich in this present age not to be haughty, nor to trust in uncertain riches but in the living God, who gives us richly all things to enjoy. Let them do good, that they be rich in good works, ready to give, willing to share, storing up for themselves a good foundation for the time to come, that they may lay hold on eternal life.

1 TIMOTHY 6:17–19

Let each one examine his own work, and then he will have rejoicing in himself alone, and not in another. For each one shall bear his own load.

Let him who is taught the word share in all good things with him who teaches. . . .

Let us not grow weary while doing good, for in due season we shall reap if we do not lose heart.

GALATIANS 6:4–6, 9

The people said to Joshua, "The LORD our God we will serve, and His voice we will obey!"

JOSHUA 24:24

SHOWING HIM TO OTHERS

Now by this we know that we know Him, if we keep His commandments. . . . Whoever keeps His word, truly the love of God is perfected in him. By this we know that we are in Him.

1 JOHN 2:3, 5

Having been justified by faith, we have peace with God through our Lord Jesus Christ, through whom also we have access by faith into this grace in which we stand, and rejoice in hope of the glory of God. And not only that, but we also glory in tribulations, knowing that tribulation produces perseverance; and perseverance, character; and character, hope.

ROMANS 5:1–4

That which we have seen and heard we declare to you, that you also may have fellowship with us; and truly our fellowship is with the Father and with His Son Jesus Christ.

1 JOHN 1:3

Someone will say, "You have faith, and I have works." Show me your faith without your works, and I will show you my faith by my works. . . .

Do you see that faith was working together with his works, and by works faith was made perfect?

JAMES 2:18, 22

"Woe to the rebellious children," says the
  LORD,
"Who take counsel, but not of Me,
And who devise plans, but not of My Spirit,
That they may add sin to sin."

ISAIAH 30:1

My beloved brethren, let every man be swift to hear, slow to speak, slow to wrath; for the wrath of man does not produce the righteousness of God.

Therefore lay aside all filthiness and overflow of wickedness, and receive with meekness the implanted word, which is able to save your souls. . . .

Pure and undefiled religion before God and the Father is this: to visit orphans and widows in their trouble, and to keep oneself unspotted from the world.

JAMES 1:19–21, 27

Though now you do not see Him, yet believing, you rejoice with joy inexpressible and full of glory.

1 PETER 1:8

Now these are the [seeds] sown among thorns; they are the ones who hear the word, and the cares of this world, the deceitfulness of riches, and the desires for other things entering in choke the word, and it becomes unfruitful. But these are the [seeds] sown on good ground, those who hear the word, accept it, and bear fruit: some thirty-fold, some sixty, and some a hundred.

MARK 4:18–20

We speak, not as pleasing men, but God who tests our hearts.

1 THESSALONIANS 2:4

Finally, my brethren, be strong in the Lord and in the power of His might. Put on the whole armor of God, that you may be able to stand against the wiles of the devil.

EPHESIANS 6:10–11

God Walks with
Women . . .

THROUGH HEARTACHE

He heals the brokenhearted
And binds up their wounds.

PSALM 147:3

A man's heart plans his way,
But the LORD directs his steps. . . .
The lot is cast into the lap,
But its every decision is from the LORD.

PROVERBS 16:9, 33

The LORD is near to those who have a
broken heart,
And saves such as have a contrite spirit.
Many are the afflictions of the righteous,
But the LORD delivers him out of them all.

PSALM 34:18–19

Come to Me, all you who labor and are heavy laden, and I will give you rest. Take My yoke upon you and learn from Me, for I am gentle and lowly in heart, and you will find rest for your souls.

MATTHEW 11:28–29

44

"Now I will rise," says the LORD;
"Now I will be exalted,
Now I will lift Myself up."

ISAIAH 33:10

The LORD also will be a refuge for
    the oppressed,
A refuge in times of trouble.
And those who know Your name will
    put their trust in You;
For You, LORD, have not forsaken those
    who seek You.

PSALM 9:9–10

In the day when I cried out, You
    answered me,
And made me bold with strength in my soul.

PSALM 138:3

The LORD will guide you continually,
And satisfy your soul in drought,
And strengthen your bones;
You shall be like a watered garden,
And like a spring of water, whose waters
    do not fail.

ISAIAH 58:11

THROUGH
ADVERSITY

The fear of man brings a snare,
But whoever trusts in the LORD shall be safe.

PROVERBS 29:25

Through God we will do valiantly,
For it is He who shall tread down our enemies.

PSALM 60:12

Beloved, do not think it strange concerning the fiery trial which is to try you, as though some strange thing happened to you; but rejoice to the extent that you partake of Christ's sufferings, that when His glory is revealed, you may also be glad with exceeding joy.

1 PETER 4:12–13

Yes, may you see your children's children.
Peace be upon Israel!

PSALM 128:6

Now thanks be to God who always leads us in triumph in Christ, and through us diffuses the fragrance of His knowledge in every place.

2 CORINTHIANS 2:14

My heart is steadfast, O God, my heart
    is steadfast;
I will sing and give praise.

PSALM 57:7

He said to me, "My grace is sufficient for you, for My strength is made perfect in weakness." Therefore most gladly I will rather boast in my infirmities, that the power of Christ may rest upon me.

2 CORINTHIANS 12:9

The LORD will perfect that which
    concerns me;
Your mercy, O LORD, endures forever;
Do not forsake the works of Your hands.

PSALM 138:8

THROUGH DANGER

My soul, wait silently for God alone,
For my expectation is from Him.
He only is my rock and my salvation;
He is my defense;
I shall not be moved.
In God is my salvation and my glory;
The rock of my strength,
And my refuge, is in God.

PSALM 62:5–7

Do not be a terror to me;
You are my hope in the day of doom.

JEREMIAH 17:17

When you pass through the waters, I will be with you;
And through the rivers, they shall not overflow you.
When you walk through the fire, you
shall not be burned,
Nor shall the flame scorch you.

ISAIAH 43:2

Keep me as the apple of Your eye;
Hide me under the shadow of Your wings.

PSALM 17:8

Yea, though I walk through the valley of
    the shadow of death,
I will fear no evil;
For You are with me;
Your rod and Your staff, they comfort me.

PSALM 23:4

You number my wanderings;
Put my tears into Your bottle;
Are they not in Your book?
In God I have put my trust;
I will not be afraid.
What can man do to me?

PSALM 56:8, 11

He raises the poor out of the dust,
And lifts the needy out of the ash heap . . .
He grants the barren woman a home,
Like a joyful mother of children.
Praise the LORD!

PSALM 113:7, 9

For in the time of trouble
He shall hide me in His pavilion;
In the secret place of His tabernacle
He shall hide me;
He shall set me high upon a rock.

PSALM 27:5

THROUGH
IMPATIENCE

My soul waits for the Lord
More than those who watch for the
    morning—
Yes, more than those who watch for
    the morning.

PSALM 130:6

My brethren, count it all joy when you fall into various trials, knowing that the testing of your faith produces patience. But let patience have its perfect work, that you may be perfect and complete, lacking nothing.

JAMES 1:2–4

Be patient, brethren, until the coming of the Lord. See how the farmer waits for the precious fruit of the earth, waiting patiently for it until it receives the early and latter rain. You also be patient. Establish your hearts, for the coming of the Lord is at hand.

JAMES 5:7–8

He said, "My Presence will go with you, and I will give you rest."

EXODUS 33:14

Wait on the LORD;
Be of good courage,
And He shall strengthen your heart;
Wait, I say, on the LORD!

PSALM 27:14

Those who wait on the LORD
Shall renew their strength;
They shall mount up with wings like eagles,
They shall run and not be weary,
They shall walk and not faint.

ISAIAH 40:31

I cried to the LORD with my voice,
And He heard me from His holy hill.
I lay down and slept;
I awoke, for the LORD sustained me.

PSALM 3:4–5

So, after [Abraham] had patiently endured, he obtained the promise.

HEBREWS 6:15

THROUGH
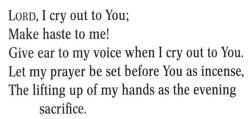
DISAPPOINTMENT

LORD, I cry out to You;
Make haste to me!
Give ear to my voice when I cry out to You.
Let my prayer be set before You as incense,
The lifting up of my hands as the evening
     sacrifice.

PSALM 141:1–2

Many people shall come and say,
"Come, and let us go up to the mountain
     of the LORD,
To the house of the God of Jacob;
He will teach us His ways,
And we shall walk in His paths."
For out of Zion shall go forth the law,
And the word of the LORD from Jerusalem.

ISAIAH 2:3

Fight the good fight of faith, lay hold on eternal life,
to which you were also called and have confessed the good
confession in the presence of many witnesses.

1 TIMOTHY 6:12

Though He was a Son, yet He learned obedience by the things which He suffered.

HEBREWS 5:8

I have fought the good fight, I have finished the race, I have kept the faith. Finally, there is laid up for me the crown of righteousness, which the Lord, the righteous Judge, will give to me on that Day, and not to me only but also to all who have loved His appearing.

2 TIMOTHY 4:7–8

Now godliness with contentment is great gain. For we brought nothing into this world, and it is certain we can carry nothing out. And having food and clothing, with these we shall be content.

1 TIMOTHY 6:6–8

I know that whatever God does,
It shall be forever.
Nothing can be added to it,
And nothing taken from it.
God does it, that men should fear before Him.

ECCLESIASTES 3:14

The wisdom that is from above is first pure, then peaceable, gentle, willing to yield, full of mercy and good fruits, without partiality and without hypocrisy.

JAMES 3:17

For this is commendable, if because of conscience toward God one endures grief, suffering wrongfully. For what credit is it if, when you are beaten for your faults, you take it patiently? But when you do good and suffer, if you take it patiently, this is commendable before God.

1 PETER 2:19–20

May our Lord Jesus Christ . . . comfort your hearts and establish you in every good word and work.

2 THESSALONIANS 2:16–17

[Love] bears all things, believes all things, hopes all things, endures all things.

1 CORINTHIANS 13:7

THROUGH FAILURE

He who loves his life will lose it, and he who hates his life in this world will keep it for eternal life.

JOHN 12:25

Set your mind on things above, not on things on the earth.

COLOSSIANS 3:2

Command those who are rich in this present age not to be haughty, nor to trust in uncertain riches but in the living God, who gives us richly all things to enjoy. Let them do good, that they be rich in good works, ready to give, willing to share, storing up for themselves a good foundation for the time to come, that they may lay hold on eternal life.

1 TIMOTHY 6:17–19

Listen to counsel and receive instruction,
That you may be wise in your latter days.

PROVERBS 19:20

For I considered all this in my heart, so that I could declare it all: that the righteous and the wise and their works are in the hand of God. People know neither love nor hatred by anything they see before them.

ECCLESIASTES 9:1

You are a chosen generation, a royal priesthood, a holy nation, His own special people, that you may proclaim the praises of Him who called you out of darkness into His marvelous light.

1 PETER 2:9

He has not dealt with us according to
    our sins,
Nor punished us according to our iniquities.
For as the heavens are high above the earth,
So great is His mercy toward those who
    fear Him;
As far as the east is from the west,
So far has He removed our transgressions
    from us.

PSALM 103:10–12

Cast your burden on the LORD,
And He shall sustain you;
He shall never permit the righteous to
    be moved.

PSALM 55:22

God Encourages Each
Woman to . . .

CHERISH BEING A FRIEND

Let brotherly love continue. Do not forget to entertain strangers, for by so doing some have unwittingly entertained angels.

HEBREWS 13:1–2

A friend loves at all times,
And a brother is born for adversity.

PROVERBS 17:17

This is My commandment, that you love one another as I have loved you. Greater love has no one than this, than to lay down one's life for his friends.

JOHN 15:12–13

If one member suffers, all the members suffer with it; or if one member is honored, all the members rejoice with it.

1 CORINTHIANS 12:26

Two are better than one,
Because they have a good reward for
their labor.

ECCLESIASTES 4:9

Everyone helped his neighbor,
And said to his brother,
"Be of good courage!"

ISAIAH 41:6

For whoever does the will of My Father in heaven is My brother and sister and mother.

MATTHEW 12:50

For as the body is one and has many members, but all the members of that one body, being many, are one body, so also is Christ.

1 CORINTHIANS 12:12

Through love serve one another.

GALATIANS 5:13

Let all that you do be done with love.

1 CORINTHIANS 16:14

GIVE TO OTHERS WITH GRACE

Let us not grow weary while doing good, for in due season we shall reap if we do not lose heart.

GALATIANS 6:9

Give, and it will be given to you: good measure, pressed down, shaken together, and running over will be put into your bosom. For with the same measure that you use, it will be measured back to you.

LUKE 6:38

She extends her hand to the poor,
Yes, she reaches out her hands to the needy.

PROVERBS 31:20

He who gives to the poor will not lack,
But he who hides his eyes will have many curses.

PROVERBS 28:27

Defend the poor and fatherless;
Do justice to the afflicted and needy.
Deliver the poor and needy;
Free them from the hand of the wicked.

PSALM 82:3–4

By this we know love, because He laid down His life for us. And we also ought to lay down our lives for the brethren. But whoever has this world's goods, and sees his brother in need, and shuts up his heart from him, how does the love of God abide in him?

1 John 3:16–17

Whoever gives one of these little ones only a cup of cold water in the name of a disciple, assuredly, I say to you, he shall by no means lose his reward.

Matthew 10:42

What does the Lord require of you
But to do justly,
To love mercy,
And to walk humbly with your God?

Micah 6:8

Be tenderhearted, be courteous . . . that you may inherit a blessing.

1 Peter 3:8–9

LIVE A LIFE
OF SERVICE

He who does not love does not know God, for God is love.

1 JOHN 4:8

Now, little children, abide in Him, that when He appears, we may have confidence and not be ashamed before Him at His coming.

1 JOHN 2:28

A new commandment I give to you, that you love one another; as I have loved you, that you also love one another. By this all will know that you are My disciples, if you have love for one another.

JOHN 13:34–35

Whoever desires to be first among you, let him be your slave—just as the Son of Man did not come to be served, but to serve, and to give His life a ransom for many.

MATTHEW 20:27–28

For you, brethren, have been called to liberty; only do not use liberty as an opportunity for the flesh, but through love serve one another.

GALATIANS 5:13

As each one has received a gift, minister it to one another, as good stewards of the manifold grace of God. If anyone speaks, let him speak as the oracles of God. If anyone ministers, let him do it as with the ability which God supplies, that in all things God may be glorified through Jesus Christ, to whom belong the glory and the dominion forever and ever.

1 PETER 4:10–11

Whatever you do, do it heartily, as to the Lord and not to men, knowing that from the Lord you will receive the reward of the inheritance; for you serve the Lord Christ. But he who does wrong will be repaid for what he has done, and there is no partiality.

COLOSSIANS 3:23–25

He who is faithful in what is least is faithful also in much; and he who is unjust in what is least is unjust also in much. Therefore if you have not been faithful in the unrighteous mammon, who will commit to your trust the true riches? And if you have not been faithful in what is another man's, who will give you what is your own?

No servant can serve two masters; for either he will hate the one and love the other, or else he will be loyal to the one and despise the other. You cannot serve God and mammon.

LUKE 16:10–13

OFFER
ENCOURAGEMENT

Rejoice with those who rejoice, and weep with those who weep. Be of the same mind toward one another. Do not set your mind on high things, but associate with the humble. Do not be wise in your own opinion.

ROMANS 12:15–16

Therefore comfort each other and edify one another, just as you also are doing.

1 THESSALONIANS 5:11

Therefore let us pursue the things which make for peace and the things by which one may edify another.

ROMANS 14:19

Let us consider one another in order to stir up love and good works, not forsaking the assembling of ourselves together, as is the manner of some, but exhorting one another, and so much the more as you see the Day approaching.

HEBREWS 10:24–25

If we walk in the light as He is in the light, we have fellowship with one another, and the blood of Jesus Christ His Son cleanses us from all sin.

1 JOHN 1:7

If then you were raised with Christ, seek those things which are above, where Christ is, sitting at the right hand of God. Set your mind on things above, not on things on the earth.

COLOSSIANS 3:1–2

You are my hiding place;
You shall preserve me from trouble;
You shall surround me with songs of deliverance.

PSALM 32:7

Do not fear, little flock, for it is your Father's good pleasure to give you the kingdom.

LUKE 12:32

May the Lord of peace Himself give you peace always in every way.

2 THESSALONIANS 3:16

God has sent His only begotten Son into the world, that we might live through Him.

1 JOHN 4:9

GOD ENCOURAGES EACH WOMAN TO . . .

PRAY FOR
ONE ANOTHER

Behold, I am the LORD, the God of all flesh. Is there anything too hard for Me?

JEREMIAH **32:27**

Let this mind be in you which was also in Christ Jesus.

PHILIPPIANS **2:5**

For the eyes of the LORD are on the
    righteous,
And His ears are open to their prayers;
But the face of the LORD is against those
    who do evil.
And who is he who will harm you if you become followers of what is good?

1 PETER **3:12–13**

Rejoice always, pray without ceasing, in everything give thanks; for this is the will of God in Christ Jesus for you.

1 THESSALONIANS **5:16–18**

Take the helmet of salvation, and the sword of the Spirit, which is the word of God; praying always with all prayer and supplication in the Spirit, being watchful to this end with all perseverance and supplication for all the saints.

EPHESIANS 6:17–18

You are of God, little children, and have overcome [false prophets], because He who is in you is greater than he who is in the world.

1 JOHN 4:4

Depart from me, all you workers of iniquity;
For the LORD has heard the voice of my weeping.
The LORD has heard my supplication;
The LORD will receive my prayer.

PSALM 6:8–9

Give ear, O LORD, to my prayer;
And attend to the voice of my supplications.
In the day of my trouble I will call upon You,
For You will answer me.

PSALM 86:6–7

Now this is the confidence that we have in Him, that if we ask anything according to His will, He hears us. And if we know that He hears us, whatever we ask, we know that we have the petitions that we have asked of Him.

1 JOHN 5:14–15

CELEBRATE
WITH JOY

I will praise You, O LORD, with my whole heart;
I will tell of all Your marvelous works.
I will be glad and rejoice in You;
I will sing praise to Your name,
    O Most High.

PSALM 9:1–2

It will be said in that day:
"Behold, this is our God;
We have waited for Him, and He will save us.
This is the LORD;
We have waited for Him;
We will be glad and rejoice in His salvation."

ISAIAH 25:9

I will sing of the mercies of the LORD forever;
With my mouth will I make known
    Your faithfulness to all generations.

PSALM 89:1

A merry heart makes a cheerful countenance,
But by sorrow of the heart the spirit is broken.

PROVERBS 15:13

I will delight myself in Your statutes;
I will not forget Your word.
Make me understand the way of Your precepts;
So shall I meditate on Your wonderful works.

PSALM 119:16, 27

Thus says the LORD: "Again there shall be heard in this place—of which you say, 'It is desolate, without man and without beast'—in the cities of Judah, in the streets of Jerusalem that are desolate, without man and without inhabitant and without beast, the voice of joy and the voice of gladness, the voice of the bridegroom and the voice of the bride, the voice of those who will say:

'Praise the LORD of hosts,
For the LORD is good,
For His mercy endures forever'—

and of those who will bring the sacrifice of praise into the house of the LORD. For I will cause the captives of the land to return as at the first," says the LORD.

JEREMIAH 33:10–11

King Hezekiah and the leaders commanded the Levites to sing praise to the LORD with the words of David and of Asaph the seer. So they sang praises with gladness, and they bowed their heads and worshiped.

2 CHRONICLES 29:30

Blessed are the people who know the joyful sound!

PSALM 89:15

The LORD your God in your midst,
The Mighty One, will save;
He will rejoice over you with gladness,
He will quiet you with His love,
He will rejoice over you with singing.

ZEPHANIAH 3:17

Let them shout for joy and be glad,
Who favor my righteous cause;
And let them say continually,
"Let the LORD be magnified,
Who has pleasure in the prosperity of His servant."
And my tongue shall speak of Your righteousness
And of Your praise all the day long.

PSALM 35:27–28

God Teaches a
Woman How to . . .

TRUST HIM COMPLETELY

Beloved, do not believe every spirit, but test the spirits, whether they are of God; because many false prophets have gone out into the world.

1 JOHN 4:1

The LORD is your keeper;
The LORD is your shade at your right hand. . . .
The LORD shall preserve you from all evil;
He shall preserve your soul.
The LORD shall preserve your going out
    and your coming in
From this time forth, and even forevermore.

PSALM 121:5, 7–8

We have such trust through Christ toward God. Not that we are sufficient of ourselves to think of anything as being from ourselves, but our sufficiency is from God.

2 CORINTHIANS 3:4–5

When I saw Him, I fell at His feet as dead. But He laid His right hand on me, saying to me, "Do not be afraid; I am the First and the Last. I am He who lives, and was dead, and behold, I am alive forevermore. Amen. And I have the keys of Hades and of Death."

REVELATION 1:17–18

The LORD is my shepherd;
I shall not want.
He makes me to lie down in green pastures;
He leads me beside the still waters.
He restores my soul;
He leads me in the paths of righteousness
For His name's sake.
Yea, though I walk through the valley of
    the shadow of death,
I will fear no evil;
For You are with me;
Your rod and Your staff, they comfort me.

PSALM 23:1–4

My help comes from the LORD,
Who made heaven and earth.
He will not allow your foot to be moved;
He who keeps you will not slumber.

PSALM 121:2–3

I will say of the LORD, "He is my refuge
    and my fortress;
My God, in Him I will trust."
Surely He shall deliver you from the snare
    of the fowler
And from the perilous pestilence.
He shall cover you with His feathers,
And under His wings you shall take refuge;
His truth shall be your shield and buckler.

PSALM 91:2–4

HOLD ON
TO FAITH

Let us hold fast the confession of our hope without wavering, for He who promised is faithful.

HEBREWS 10:23

Have I not commanded you? Be strong and of good courage; do not be afraid, nor be dismayed, for the LORD your God is with you wherever you go.

JOSHUA 1:9

For with God nothing will be impossible.

LUKE 1:37

Beloved, while I was very diligent to write to you concerning our common salvation, I found it necessary to write to you exhorting you to contend earnestly for the faith which was once for all delivered to the saints.

JUDE 3

For we walk by faith, not by sight.

2 CORINTHIANS 5:7

[Take] the shield of faith with which you will be able to quench all the fiery darts of the wicked one.

EPHESIANS 6:15–16

You, beloved, building yourselves up on your most holy faith, praying in the Holy Spirit, keep yourselves in the love of God, looking for the mercy of our Lord Jesus Christ unto eternal life.

JUDE 20–21

Be steadfast, immovable, always abounding in the work of the Lord.

1 CORINTHIANS 15:58

To Him who is able to keep you from stumbling . . . be glory and majesty.

JUDE 24–25

HAVE JOY IN HIM

I say to you that likewise there will be more joy in heaven over one sinner who repents than over ninety-nine just persons who need no repentance.

LUKE 15:7

This is the day the LORD has made;
We will rejoice and be glad in it.

PSALM 118:24

These things I have spoken to you, that My joy may remain in you, and that your joy may be full. This is My commandment, that you love one another as I have loved you.

JOHN 15:11–12

Create in me a clean heart, O God,
And renew a steadfast spirit within me.
Do not cast me away from Your presence,
And do not take Your Holy Spirit from me.
Restore to me the joy of Your salvation,
And uphold me by Your generous Spirit.

PSALM 51:10–12

Let us come before His presence
    with thanksgiving;
Let us shout joyfully to Him with psalms.

PSALM 95:2

Because Your lovingkindness is better
    than life,
My lips shall praise You.
Thus I will bless You while I live;
I will lift up my hands in Your name.
My soul shall be satisfied as with marrow
    and fatness,
And my mouth shall praise You with
    joyful lips.

PSALM 63:3–5

The kingdom of God is not eating and drinking, but
righteousness and peace and joy in the Holy Spirit.

ROMANS 14:17

A merry heart makes a cheerful countenance,
But by sorrow of the heart the spirit is
    broken.

PROVERBS 15:13

Oh, satisfy us early with Your mercy,
That we may rejoice and be glad all our days!

PSALM 90:14

CENTER HER LIFE IN HIM

Behold, all those who were incensed against you
Shall be ashamed and disgraced;
They shall be as nothing,
And those who strive with you shall perish.
You shall seek them and not find them—
Those who contended with you.
Those who war against you
Shall be as nothing,
As a nonexistent thing.
For I, the LORD your God, will hold your right hand,
Saying to you, "Fear not, I will help you."

ISAIAH 41:11–13

Let the word of Christ dwell in you richly in all wisdom, teaching and admonishing one another in psalms and hymns and spiritual songs, singing with grace in your hearts to the Lord.

COLOSSIANS 3:16

I sought the LORD, and He heard me,
And delivered me from all my fears.

PSALM 34:4

There is therefore now no condemnation to those who are in Christ Jesus, who do not walk according to the flesh, but according to the Spirit. For the law of the Spirit of life in Christ Jesus has made me free from the law of sin and death.

ROMANS 8:1–2

I will sing to the LORD as long as I live;
I will sing praise to my God while I have my being.
May my meditation be sweet to Him;
I will be glad in the LORD.

PSALM 104:33–34

Denying ungodliness and worldly lusts, we should live soberly, righteously, and godly in the present age, looking for the blessed hope and glorious appearing of our great God and Savior Jesus Christ.

TITUS 2:12–13

I have been crucified with Christ; it is no longer I who live, but Christ lives in me; and the life which I now live in the flesh I live by faith in the Son of God, who loved me and gave Himself for me.

GALATIANS 2:20

My voice You shall hear in the morning, O LORD;
In the morning I will direct it to You,
And I will look up.

PSALM 5:3

REST IN HIS PROTECTION

The LORD is my light and my salvation;
Whom shall I fear?
The LORD is the strength of my life;
Of whom shall I be afraid?
When the wicked came against me
To eat up my flesh,
My enemies and foes,
They stumbled and fell.
Though an army may encamp against me,
My heart shall not fear;
Though war may rise against me,
In this I will be confident.
One thing I have desired of the LORD,
That will I seek:
That I may dwell in the house of the LORD
All the days of my life,
To behold the beauty of the LORD,
And to inquire in His temple.
For in the time of trouble
He shall hide me in His pavilion;
In the secret place of His tabernacle
He shall hide me;
He shall set me high upon a rock.

PSALM 27:1–5

Whoever listens to me will dwell safely,
And will be secure, without fear of evil.

PROVERBS 1:33

I cry out to the LORD with my voice;
With my voice to the LORD I make my supplication.
I pour out my complaint before Him;
I declare before Him my trouble.

PSALM 142:1–2

The LORD is your keeper;
The LORD is your shade at your right hand.
The sun shall not strike you by day,
Nor the moon by night.
The LORD shall preserve you from all evil;
He shall preserve your soul.
The LORD shall preserve your going out
        and your coming in
From this time forth, and even forevermore.

PSALM 121:5–8

"No weapon formed against you shall prosper,
And every tongue which rises against you
        in judgment
You shall condemn.
This is the heritage of the servants of the LORD,
And their righteousness is from Me,"
Says the LORD.

ISAIAH 54:17

I will both lie down in peace, and sleep;
For You alone, O LORD, make me dwell
in safety.

PSALM 4:8

When you pass through the waters, I will
be with you;
And through the rivers, they shall not
overflow you.
When you walk through the fire, you
shall not be burned,
Nor shall the flame scorch you.

ISAIAH 43:2

May He send you help from the sanctuary,
And strengthen you out of Zion.

PSALM 20:2

The Lord is faithful, who will establish you and
guard you from the evil one.

2 THESSALONIANS 3:3

OBTAIN HIS PROMISES

Now this is the confidence that we have in Him, that if we ask anything according to His will, He hears us. And if we know that He hears us, whatever we ask, we know that we have the petitions that we have asked of Him.

1 JOHN 5:14–15

If you diligently heed the voice of the LORD your God and do what is right in His sight, give ear to His commandments and keep all His statutes, I will put none of the diseases on you which I have brought on the Egyptians. For I am the LORD who heals you.

EXODUS 15:26

Seek first the kingdom of God and His righteousness, and all these things shall be added to you.

MATTHEW 6:33

Do not become sluggish, but imitate those who through faith and patience inherit the promises.

HEBREWS 6:12

Let us hold fast the confession of our hope without wavering, for He who promised is faithful.

HEBREWS 10:23

By which have been given to us exceedingly great and precious promises, that through these you may be partakers of the divine nature, having escaped the corruption that is in the world through lust.

But also for this very reason, giving all diligence, add to your faith virtue, to virtue knowledge, to knowledge self-control, to self-control perseverance, to perseverance godliness, to godliness brotherly kindness, and to brotherly kindness love. For if these things are yours and abound, you will be neither barren nor unfruitful in the knowledge of our Lord Jesus Christ.

2 PETER 1:4–8

Now faith is the substance of things hoped for, the evidence of things not seen. . . .

Without faith it is impossible to please Him, for he who comes to God must believe that He is, and that He is a rewarder of those who diligently seek Him. . . .

By faith Sarah herself also received strength to conceive seed, and she bore a child when she was past the age, because she judged Him faithful who had promised.

HEBREWS 11:1, 6, 11

For with God nothing will be impossible.

LUKE 1:37

God Blesses Women
When They . . .

TRUST IN
HIS POWER

In the LORD I put my trust;
How can you say to my soul,
"Flee as a bird to your mountain"?
For look! The wicked bend their bow,
They make ready their arrow on the string,
That they may shoot secretly at the upright
        in heart.
If the foundations are destroyed,
What can the righteous do?
The LORD is in His holy temple,
The LORD's throne is in heaven;
His eyes behold,
His eyelids test the sons of men.
The LORD tests the righteous,
But the wicked and the one who loves
        violence His soul hates.
Upon the wicked He will rain coals;
Fire and brimstone and a burning wind
Shall be the portion of their cup.
For the LORD is righteous,
He loves righteousness;
His countenance beholds the upright.

PSALM 11:1–7

Those who trust in the Lord
Are like Mount Zion,
Which cannot be moved, but abides forever.
As the mountains surround Jerusalem,
So the Lord surrounds His people
From this time forth and forever.
For the scepter of wickedness shall not rest
On the land allotted to the righteous,
Lest the righteous reach out their hands
      to iniquity.
Do good, O Lord, to those who are good,
And to those who are upright in their hearts.
As for such as turn aside to their crooked ways,
The Lord shall lead them away
With the workers of iniquity.
Peace be upon Israel!

PSALM 125:1–5

For You will light my lamp;
The Lord my God will enlighten my darkness.
For by You I can run against a troop,
By my God I can leap over a wall.
As for God, His way is perfect;
The word of the Lord is proven;
He is a shield to all who trust in Him.

PSALM 18:28–30

Whenever I am afraid,
I will trust in You.
In God (I will praise His word),
In God I have put my trust;
I will not fear.
What can flesh do to me?

PSALM 56:3–4

LORD, how they have increased who trouble me!
Many are they who rise up against me.
Many are they who say of me,
"There is no help for him in God."
But You, O LORD, are a shield for me,
My glory and the One who lifts up my head.
I cried to the LORD with my voice,
And He heard me from His holy hill.
I lay down and slept;
I awoke, for the LORD sustained me.
I will not be afraid of ten thousands of people
Who have set themselves against me all around.
Arise, O LORD;
Save me, O my God!
For You have struck all my enemies on
        the cheekbone;
You have broken the teeth of the ungodly.
Salvation belongs to the LORD.
Your blessing is upon Your people.

PSALM 3:1–8

Trust in Him at all times, you people;
Pour out your heart before Him;
God is a refuge for us.

PSALM 62:8

In God I have put my trust;
I will not be afraid.
What can man do to me?
Vows made to You are binding upon me, O God;
I will render praises to You.

PSALM 56:11–12

But You are holy,
Enthroned in the praises of Israel.
Our fathers trusted in You;
They trusted, and You delivered them.

PSALM 22:3–4

He shall cover you with His feathers,
And under His wings you shall take refuge.

PSALM 91:4

PRAISE HIS GOODNESS

Let the saints be joyful in glory;
Let them sing aloud on their beds.
Let the high praises of God be in
their mouth,
And a two-edged sword in their hand.

PSALM 149:5–6

My heart is steadfast, O God, my heart
is steadfast;
I will sing and give praise.
Awake, my glory!
Awake, lute and harp!
I will awaken the dawn.
I will praise You, O Lord, among the peoples;
I will sing to You among the nations.

PSALM 57:7–9

Praise Him with loud cymbals;
Praise Him with clashing cymbals!
Let everything that has breath praise the LORD.
Praise the LORD!

PSALM 150:5–6

Because Your lovingkindness is better than life,
My lips shall praise You.
Thus I will bless You while I live;
I will lift up my hands in Your name.

PSALM 63:3–4

Oh, give thanks to the LORD, for He is good!
For His mercy endures forever.
Oh, give thanks to the God of gods!
For His mercy endures forever.
Oh, give thanks to the Lord of lords!
For His mercy endures forever:
To Him who alone does great wonders,
For His mercy endures forever.

PSALM 136:1–4

In God (I will praise His word),
In the LORD (I will praise His word).

PSALM 56:10

I will bless the LORD at all times;
His praise shall continually be in my mouth.

PSALM 34:1

Whoever offers praise glorifies Me;
And to him who orders his conduct aright
I will show the salvation of God.

PSALM 50:23

HOPE IN HIS FAITHFULNESS

We are hard—pressed on every side, yet not crushed; we are perplexed, but not in despair; persecuted, but not forsaken; struck down, but not destroyed—always carrying about in the body the dying of the Lord Jesus, that the life of Jesus also may be manifested in our body. For we who live are always delivered to death for Jesus' sake, that the life of Jesus also may be manifested in our mortal flesh.

2 CORINTHIANS 4:8–11

For our light affliction, which is but for a moment, is working for us a far more exceeding and eternal weight of glory, while we do not look at the things which are seen, but at the things which are not seen. For the things which are seen are temporary, but the things which are not seen are eternal.

2 CORINTHIANS 4:17–18

Therefore do not cast away your confidence, which has great reward. For you have need of endurance, so that after you have done the will of God, you may receive the promise.

HEBREWS 10:35–36

92

Through the LORD's mercies we are not consumed,
Because His compassions fail not.
They are new every morning;
Great is Your faithfulness.
"The LORD is my portion," says my soul,
"Therefore I hope in Him!"
The LORD is good to those who wait for Him,
To the soul who seeks Him.

LAMENTATIONS 3:22–25

For we know that if our earthly house, this tent, is destroyed, we have a building from God, a house not made with hands, eternal in the heavens.

2 CORINTHIANS 5:1

I would have lost heart, unless I had believed
That I would see the goodness of the LORD
In the land of the living.
Wait on the LORD;
Be of good courage,
And He shall strengthen your heart;
Wait, I say, on the LORD!

PSALM 27:13–14

This hope [set before us] we have as an anchor of the soul, both sure and steadfast.

HEBREWS 6:19

I wait for the LORD, my soul waits,
And in His word I do hope.
My soul waits for the Lord
More than those who watch for the morning—
Yes, more than those who watch for
     the morning.

PSALM 130:5–6

Every morning He brings His justice to light
He never fails.

ZEPHANIAH 3:5

Let us hold fast the confession of our hope without wavering, for He who promised is faithful.

HEBREWS 10:23

REST IN HIS PEACE

For in the time of trouble
He shall hide me in His pavilion;
In the secret place of His tabernacle
He shall hide me;
He shall set me high upon a rock.

PSALM 27:5

Give us help from trouble,
For the help of man is useless.
Through God we will do valiantly,
For it is He who shall tread down our enemies.

PSALM 60:11–12

All your children shall be taught by
      the LORD,
And great shall be the peace of your children.
In righteousness you shall be established;
You shall be far from oppression, for
      you shall not fear;
And from terror, for it shall not come
      near you.

ISAIAH 54:13–14

The LORD will guide you continually,
And satisfy your soul in drought,
And strengthen your bones;
You shall be like a watered garden,
And like a spring of water, whose waters
      do not fail.

ISAIAH 58:11

The Spirit of the Lord GOD is upon Me,
Because the LORD has anointed Me
To preach good tidings to the poor;
He has sent Me to heal the brokenhearted,
To proclaim liberty to the captives,
And the opening of the prison to those
      who are bound.

ISAIAH 61:1

When my father and my mother forsake me,
Then the LORD will take care of me.
I would have lost heart, unless I had believed
That I would see the goodness of the LORD
In the land of the living.
Wait on the LORD;
Be of good courage,
And He shall strengthen your heart;
Wait, I say, on the LORD!

PSALM 27:10, 13, 14

Come to Me, all you who labor . . . and I will give you rest.

MATTHEW 11:28

Let, I pray, Your merciful kindness be for
     my comfort,
According to Your word to Your servant.
Let Your tender mercies come to me, that
     I may live;
For Your law is my delight.

PSALM 119:76–77

Let the words of my mouth and the
     meditation of my heart
Be acceptable in Your sight,
O LORD, my strength and my Redeemer.

PSALM 19:14

Anxiety in the heart . . . causes depression
But a good word makes it glad.

PROVERBS 12:25

STAND STRONG
IN FAITH

You, beloved, building yourselves up on your most holy faith, praying in the Holy Spirit, keep yourselves in the love of God, looking for the mercy of our Lord Jesus Christ unto eternal life.

JUDE 20–21

Be anxious for nothing, but in everything by prayer and supplication, with thanksgiving, let your requests be made known to God; and the peace of God, which surpasses all understanding, will guard your hearts and minds through Christ Jesus.

PHILIPPIANS 4:6–7

Therefore, having been justified by faith, we have peace with God through our Lord Jesus Christ, through whom also we have access by faith into this grace in which we stand, and rejoice in hope of the glory of God.

ROMANS 5:1–2

The Lord is faithful, who will establish you and guard you from the evil one.

2 THESSALONIANS 3:3

My soul, wait silently for God alone,
For my expectation is from Him.
He only is my rock and my salvation;
He is my defense;
I shall not be moved.
In God is my salvation and my glory;
The rock of my strength,
And my refuge, is in God.

PSALM 62:5–7

Without faith it is impossible to please Him, for he who comes to God must believe that He is, and that He is a rewarder of those who diligently seek Him.

HEBREWS 11:6

As Moses lifted up the serpent in the wilderness, even so must the Son of Man be lifted up, that whoever believes in Him should not perish but have eternal life.

JOHN 3:14–15

Now faith is the substance of things hoped for, the evidence of things not seen. For by it the elders obtained a good testimony.

By faith we understand that the worlds were framed by the word of God, so that the things which are seen were not made of things which are visible.

HEBREWS 11:1–3

CLAIM
HIS VICTORY

He has put a new song in my mouth—
Praise to our God;
Many will see it and fear,
And will trust in the LORD.

PSALM 40:3

The LORD is near to those who have a broken heart,
And saves such as have a contrite spirit.
Many are the afflictions of the righteous,
But the LORD delivers him out of them all.

PSALM 34:18–19

The Spirit Himself bears witness with our spirit that
we are children of God, and if children, then heirs—heirs
of God and joint heirs with Christ, if indeed we suffer with
Him, that we may also be glorified together.

For I consider that the sufferings of this present time
are not worthy to be compared with the glory which shall
be revealed in us.

ROMANS 8:16–18

All that the Father gives Me will come to Me, and the
one who comes to Me I will by no means cast out.

JOHN 6:37

The earth is the LORD's, and all its fullness,
The world and those who dwell therein.
For He has founded it upon the seas,
And established it upon the waters.
Who may ascend into the hill of the LORD?
Or who may stand in His holy place?
He who has clean hands and a pure heart,
Who has not lifted up his soul to an idol,
Nor sworn deceitfully.
He shall receive blessing from the LORD,
And righteousness from the God of his salvation.
This is Jacob, the generation of those who seek Him,
Who seek Your face.
Lift up your heads, O you gates!
And be lifted up, you everlasting doors!
And the King of glory shall come in.
Who is this King of glory?
The LORD strong and mighty,
The LORD mighty in battle.
Lift up your heads, O you gates!
Lift up, you everlasting doors!
And the King of glory shall come in.
Who is this King of glory?
The LORD of hosts,
He is the King of glory.

PSALM 24:1–10

Great is the LORD, and greatly to be praised
In the city of our God,
In His holy mountain.

PSALM 48:1

The LORD is your keeper;
The LORD is your shade at your right hand.
The sun shall not strike you by day,
Nor the moon by night.
The LORD shall preserve you from all evil;
He shall preserve your soul.
The LORD shall preserve your going out
        and your coming in
From this time forth, and even forevermore.

PSALM 121:5–8

For God is the King of all the earth;
Sing praises with understanding.
God reigns over the nations;
God sits on His holy throne.
The princes of the people have gathered
        together,
The people of the God of Abraham.
For the shields of the earth belong to God;
He is greatly exalted.

PSALM 47:7–9

God Comforts Women as They Learn to . . .

HANDLE SPIRITUAL
TRIALS

Beloved, do not forget this one thing, that with the Lord one day is as a thousand years, and a thousand years as one day. The Lord is not slack concerning His promise, as some count slackness, but is longsuffering toward us, not willing that any should perish but that all should come to repentance.

2 PETER 3:8–9

Cast your burden on the LORD,
And He shall sustain you;
He shall never permit the righteous to
be moved.

PSALM 55:22

Blessed is the man who endures temptation; for when he has been approved, he will receive the crown of life which the Lord has promised to those who love Him.

For if anyone is a hearer of the word and not a doer, he is like a man observing his natural face in a mirror; for he observes himself, goes away, and immediately forgets what kind of man he was.

JAMES 1:12, 23–24

But He knows the way that I take;
When He has tested me, I shall come forth
    as gold.
My foot has held fast to His steps;
I have kept His way and not turned aside.

JOB 23:10–11

Why are you cast down, O my soul?
And why are you disquieted within me?
Hope in God;
For I shall yet praise Him,
The help of my countenance and my God.

PSALM 43:5

Beloved, do not think it strange concerning the fiery trial which is to try you, as though some strange thing happened to you; but rejoice to the extent that you partake of Christ's sufferings, that when His glory is revealed, you may also be glad with exceeding joy. . . . Yet if anyone suffers as a Christian, let him not be ashamed, but let him glorify God in this matter.

1 PETER 4:12–13, 16

I command you today to love the LORD your God, to walk in His ways, and to keep His commandments.

DEUTERONOMY 30:16

Hear me, O LORD, for Your lovingkindness
    is good;
Turn to me according to the multitude of
    Your tender mercies.
And do not hide Your face from Your servant,
For I am in trouble;
Hear me speedily.
Draw near to my soul, and redeem it;
Deliver me because of my enemies.

PSALM 69:16–18

He who covers his sins will not prosper,
But whoever confesses and forsakes them
    will have mercy.

PROVERBS 28:13

Blessed are those who keep His testimonies,
Who seek Him with the whole heart!

PSALM 119:2

Be doers of the word, and not hearers only, deceiving
yourselves.

JAMES 1:22

GOD COMFORTS WOMEN AS THEY LEARN TO . . .

CONFRONT SERIOUS ILLNESS

Heal me, O Lord, and I shall be healed;
Save me, and I shall be saved,
For You are my praise.

JEREMIAH 17:14

I said, "This is my anguish;
But I will remember the years of the
    right hand of the Most High."
I will remember the works of the Lord;
Surely I will remember Your wonders of old.
I will also meditate on all Your work,
And talk of Your deeds.
Your way, O God, is in the sanctuary;
Who is so great a God as our God?
You are the God who does wonders;
You have declared Your strength among the peoples.

PSALM 77:10–14

For this is God,
Our God forever and ever;
He will be our guide
Even to death.

PSALM 48:14

God will redeem my soul from the power
of the grave,
For He shall receive me.

PSALM 49:15

Yea, though I walk through the valley of the
shadow of death,
I will fear no evil;
For You are with me;
Your rod and Your staff, they comfort me.

PSALM 23:4

For we know that if our earthly house, this tent, is destroyed, we have a building from God, a house not made with hands, eternal in the heavens.

2 CORINTHIANS 5:1

While I live I will praise the LORD;
I will sing praises to my God while I have my
being.

PSALM 146:2

Before I was afflicted I went astray,
But now I keep Your word.
You are good, and do good;
Teach me Your statutes.

PSALM 119:67–68

HANDLE FINANCIAL PROBLEMS

The Lord said, "Who then is that faithful and wise steward, whom his master will make ruler over his household, to give them their portion of food in due season? Blessed is that servant whom his master will find so doing when he comes. Truly, I say to you that he will make him ruler over all that he has."

LUKE 12:42–44

When He had fasted forty days and forty nights, afterward He was hungry. Now when the tempter came to Him, he said, "If You are the Son of God, command that these stones become bread."

But He answered and said, "It is written, 'Man shall not live by bread alone, but by every word that proceeds from the mouth of God.'"

MATTHEW 4:2–4

My God shall supply all your need according to His riches in glory by Christ Jesus.

PHILIPPIANS 4:19

Listen, my beloved brethren: Has God not chosen the poor of this world to be rich in faith and heirs of the kingdom which He promised to those who love Him?

JAMES 2:5

He who trusts in his riches will fall,
But the righteous will flourish like foliage.

PROVERBS 11:28

Then He said to His disciples, "Therefore I say to you, do not worry about your life, what you will eat; nor about the body, what you will put on. Life is more than food, and the body is more than clothing. Consider the ravens, for they neither sow nor reap, which have neither storehouse nor barn; and God feeds them. Of how much more value are you than the birds?"

LUKE 12:22–24

Poverty and shame will come to him who
disdains correction,
But he who regards a rebuke will be honored.

PROVERBS 13:18

FACE THE
YEARS AHEAD

For now we see in a mirror, dimly, but then face to face. Now I know in part, but then I shall know just as I also am known.

1 CORINTHIANS 13:12

The righteous shall flourish like a palm tree,
He shall grow like a cedar in Lebanon.
Those who are planted in the house of the LORD
Shall flourish in the courts of our God.
They shall still bear fruit in old age;
They shall be fresh and flourishing,
To declare that the LORD is upright;
He is my rock, and there is no
       unrighteousness in Him.

PSALM 92:12–15

For none of us lives to himself, and no one dies to himself. For if we live, we live to the Lord; and if we die, we die to the Lord. Therefore, whether we live or die, we are the Lord's.

ROMANS 14:7–8

The fear of the LORD prolongs days,
But the years of the wicked will be shortened.

PROVERBS 10:27

The days of our lives are seventy years;
And if by reason of strength they are eighty years,
Yet their boast is only labor and sorrow;
For it is soon cut off, and we fly away.
So teach us to number our days,
That we may gain a heart of wisdom.
Oh, satisfy us early with Your mercy,
That we may rejoice and be glad all our days!

PSALM 90:10, 12, 14

Older men be sober, reverent, temperate, sound in faith, in love, in patience; the older women likewise, that they be reverent in behavior, not slanderers, not given to much wine, teachers of good things—that they admonish the young women to love their husbands, to love their children.

TITUS 2:2–4

But as for me, I trust in You, O LORD;
I say, "You are my God."
My times are in Your hand;
Deliver me from the hand of my enemies,
And from those who persecute me.

PSALM 31:14–15

For I know that my Redeemer lives,
And He shall stand at last on the earth;
And after my skin is destroyed, this I know,
That in my flesh I shall see God.

JOB 19:25–26

CALL ON GOD'S DIVINE PROTECTION

I will both lie down in peace, and sleep;
For You alone, O Lord, make me dwell in safety.

PSALM 4:8

The angel of the Lord encamps all around
    those who fear Him,
And delivers them.

PSALM 34:7

He who dwells in the secret place of the Most High
Shall abide under the shadow of the Almighty.
I will say of the Lord, "He is my refuge and
    my fortress;
My God, in Him I will trust."

PSALM 91:1–2

So shall they fear
The name of the Lord from the west,
And His glory from the rising of the sun;
When the enemy comes in like a flood,
The Spirit of the Lord will lift up a standard
    against him.

ISAIAH 59:19

The LORD is my light and my salvation;
Whom shall I fear?
The LORD is the strength of my life;
Of whom shall I be afraid? . . .
For in the time of trouble
He shall hide me in His pavilion;
In the secret place of His tabernacle
He shall hide me;
He shall set me high upon a rock.

PSALM 27:1, 5

Are not two sparrows sold for a copper coin? And not one of them falls to the ground apart from your Father's will. But the very hairs of your head are all numbered. Do not fear therefore; you are of more value than many sparrows.

MATTHEW 10:29–31

The eternal God is your refuge,
And underneath are the everlasting arms;
He will thrust out the enemy from
     before you,
And will say, "Destroy!"

DEUTERONOMY 33:27

Whoever listens to me will dwell safely,
And will be secure, without fear of evil.

PROVERBS 1:33

BE CONTENT

"For the mountains shall depart
And the hills be removed,
But My kindness shall not depart from you,
Nor shall My covenant of peace be
     removed,"
Says the LORD, who has mercy on you. . . .
"All your children shall be taught by the
     LORD,
And great shall be the peace of your children. . . .
No weapon formed against you shall prosper,
And every tongue which rises against you in
     judgment
You shall condemn.
This is the heritage of the servants of the LORD,
And their righteousness is from Me,"
Says the LORD.

ISAIAH 54:10, 13, 17

Not that I speak in regard to need, for I have learned in whatever state I am, to be content: I know how to be abased, and I know how to abound. Everywhere and in all things I have learned both to be full and to be hungry, both to abound and to suffer need.

PHILIPPIANS 4:11–12

There is therefore now no condemnation to those who are in Christ Jesus, who do not walk according to the flesh, but according to the Spirit. For the law of the Spirit of life in Christ Jesus has made me free from the law of sin and death. . . . For those who live according to the flesh set their minds on the things of the flesh, but those who live according to the Spirit, the things of the Spirit. For to be carnally minded is death, but to be spiritually minded is life and peace.

ROMANS 8:1–2, 5–6

Now godliness with contentment is great gain. For we brought nothing into this world, and it is certain we can carry nothing out. And having food and clothing, with these we shall be content.

1 TIMOTHY 6:6–8

The LORD is my shepherd;
I shall not want.

PSALM 23:1

The LORD will guide you continually,
And satisfy your soul in drought,
And strengthen your bones;
You shall be like a watered garden,
And like a spring of water, whose waters
        do not fail.

ISAIAH 58:11

116

Not that we are sufficient of ourselves to think of anything as being from ourselves, but our sufficiency is from God.

2 CORINTHIANS 3:5

The LORD is your keeper;
The LORD is your shade at your right hand.
The LORD shall preserve your going out
    and your coming in
From this time forth, and even forevermore.

PSALM 121:5, 8

Eye has not seen, nor ear heard . . .
The things which God has prepared for
    those who love Him.

1 CORINTHIANS 2:9

You are complete in Him, who is the head of all principality and power.

COLOSSIANS 2:10

God Gives Freely
to Women . . .

HOPE FOR ETERNAL LIFE

Sing to the LORD with thanksgiving;
Sing praises on the harp to our God,
Who covers the heavens with clouds,
Who prepares rain for the earth,
Who makes grass to grow on the mountains.
He gives to the beast its food,
And to the young ravens that cry.
He does not delight in the strength of the horse;
He takes no pleasure in the legs of a man.
The LORD takes pleasure in those who fear Him,
In those who hope in His mercy.
Praise the LORD, O Jerusalem!
Praise your God, O Zion!
For He has strengthened the bars of your gates;
He has blessed your children within you.

PSALM 147:7–13

If then you were raised with Christ, seek those things which are above, where Christ is, sitting at the right hand of God. Set your mind on things above, not on things on the earth. For you died, and your life is hidden with Christ in God. When Christ who is our life appears, then you also will appear with Him in glory.

COLOSSIANS 3:1–4

Let us who are of the day be sober, putting on the breastplate of faith and love, and as a helmet the hope of salvation. For God did not appoint us to wrath, but to obtain salvation through our Lord Jesus Christ, who died for us, that whether we wake or sleep, we should live together with Him. Therefore comfort each other and edify one another, just as you also are doing.

1 THESSALONIANS 5:8–11

God, who is rich in mercy, because of His great love with which He loved us, even when we were dead in trespasses, made us alive together with Christ (by grace you have been saved), and raised us up together, and made us sit together in the heavenly places in Christ Jesus, that in the ages to come He might show the exceeding riches of His grace in His kindness toward us in Christ Jesus.

EPHESIANS 2:4–7

I have fought the good fight, I have finished the race, I have kept the faith. Finally, there is laid up for me the crown of righteousness, which the Lord, the righteous Judge, will give to me on that Day, and not to me only but also to all who have loved His appearing.

2 TIMOTHY 4:7–8

Knowing that a man is not justified by the works of the law but by faith in Jesus Christ, even we have believed in Christ Jesus, that we might be justified by faith in Christ and not by the works of the law; for by the works of the law no flesh shall be justified. . . .

I have been crucified with Christ; it is no longer I who live, but Christ lives in me; and the life which I now live in the flesh I live by faith in the Son of God, who loved me and gave Himself for me.

GALATIANS 2:16, 20

For as many as are led by the Spirit of God, these are sons of God. For you did not receive the spirit of bondage again to fear, but you received the Spirit of adoption by whom we cry out, "Abba, Father." The Spirit Himself bears witness with our spirit that we are children of God, and if children, then heirs—heirs of God and joint heirs with Christ, if indeed we suffer with Him, that we may also be glorified together.

For I consider that the sufferings of this present time are not worthy to be compared with the glory which shall be revealed in us. . . . For we were saved in this hope, but hope that is seen is not hope; for why does one still hope for what he sees? But if we hope for what we do not see, we eagerly wait for it with perseverance.

ROMANS 8:14–18, 24–25

Blessed be the God and Father of our Lord Jesus Christ, who according to His abundant mercy has begotten us again to a living hope through the resurrection of Jesus Christ from the dead, to an inheritance incorruptible and undefiled and that does not fade away, reserved in heaven for you, who are kept by the power of God through faith for salvation ready to be revealed in the last time.

In this you greatly rejoice, though now for a little while, if need be, you have been grieved by various trials, that the genuineness of your faith, being much more precious than gold that perishes, though it is tested by fire, may be found to praise, honor, and glory at the revelation of Jesus Christ, whom having not seen you love. Though now you do not see Him, yet believing, you rejoice with joy inexpressible and full of glory, receiving the end of your faith—the salvation of your souls.

1 PETER 1:3–9

Because of the hope which is laid up for you in heaven, of which you heard before in the word of the truth of the gospel, which has come to you, as it has also in all the world, and is bringing forth fruit, as it is also among you since the day you heard and knew the grace of God in truth.

COLOSSIANS 1:5–6

WISDOM FOR DAILY LIVING

My son, pay attention to my wisdom;
Lend your ear to my understanding,
That you may preserve discretion,
And your lips may keep knowledge.

PROVERBS 5:1–2

The fear of the LORD is the beginning of wisdom;
A good understanding have all those who do
      His commandments.
His praise endures forever.

PSALM 111:10

The days of our lives are seventy years;
And if by reason of strength they are eighty years,
Yet their boast is only labor and sorrow;
For it is soon cut off, and we fly away.
Who knows the power of Your anger?
For as the fear of You, so is Your wrath.
So teach us to number our days,
That we may gain a heart of wisdom.

PSALM 90:10–12

How much better to get wisdom than gold!
And to get understanding is to be
    chosen rather than silver.

PROVERBS 16:16

Happy is the man who finds wisdom,
And the man who gains understanding;
For her proceeds are better than the profits
    of silver,
And her gain than fine gold.
She is more precious than rubies,
And all the things you may desire cannot
    compare with her.
Length of days is in her right hand,
In her left hand riches and honor.
Her ways are ways of pleasantness,
And all her paths are peace.
She is a tree of life to those who take hold of her,
And happy are all who retain her.
The LORD by wisdom founded the earth;
By understanding He established the heavens;
By His knowledge the depths were broken up,
And clouds drop down the dew.
My son, let them not depart from your eyes—
Keep sound wisdom and discretion;
So they will be life to your soul
And grace to your neck.

PROVERBS 3:13–22

A wise man fears and departs from evil,
But a fool rages and is self-confident.

PROVERBS 14:16

If any of you lacks wisdom, let him ask of God, who gives to all liberally and without reproach, and it will be given to him. But let him ask in faith, with no doubting, for he who doubts is like a wave of the sea driven and tossed by the wind.

JAMES 1:5–6

"Get wisdom! Get understanding!
Do not forget, nor turn away from the
    words of my mouth.
Do not forsake her, and she will preserve you;
Love her, and she will keep you.
Wisdom is the principal thing;
Therefore get wisdom.
And in all your getting, get understanding.
Exalt her, and she will promote you;
She will bring you honor, when you embrace her.
She will place on your head an ornament
    of grace;
A crown of glory she will deliver to you.
Hear, my son, and receive my sayings,
And the years of your life will be many.
I have taught you in the way of wisdom;
I have led you in right paths."

PROVERBS 4:5–11

My son, keep my words,
And treasure my commands within you.
Keep my commands and live,
And my law as the apple of your eye.
Bind them on your fingers;
Write them on the tablet of your heart.
Say to wisdom, "You are my sister,"
And call understanding your nearest kin,
That they may keep you from the immoral woman,
From the seductress who flatters with her words.

PROVERBS 7:1–5

The fear of the LORD is the beginning of wisdom,
And the knowledge of the Holy One is
    understanding.
For by me your days will be multiplied,
And years of life will be added to you.
If you are wise, you are wise for yourself,
And if you scoff, you will bear it alone.

PROVERBS 9:10–12

The wisdom that is from above is first pure, then peaceable, gentle, willing to yield, full of mercy and good fruits, without partiality and without hypocrisy.

JAMES 3:17

VICTORY OVER SIN

Therefore, if anyone is in Christ, he is a new creation; old things have passed away; behold, all things have become new. Now all things are of God, who has reconciled us to Himself through Jesus Christ, and has given us the ministry of reconciliation, that is, that God was in Christ reconciling the world to Himself, not imputing their trespasses to them, and has committed to us the word of reconciliation.

Now then, we are ambassadors for Christ, as though God were pleading through us: we implore you on Christ's behalf, be reconciled to God. For He made Him who knew no sin to be sin for us, that we might become the righteousness of God in Him.

2 CORINTHIANS 5:17–21

O God, You know my foolishness;
And my sins are not hidden from You.

PSALM 69:5

For as many as are of the works of the law are under the curse; for it is written, "Cursed is everyone who does not continue in all things which are written in the book of the law, to do them." But that no one is justified by the law in the sight of God is evident, for "the just shall live by faith."

GALATIANS 3:10–11

Stand fast therefore in the liberty by which Christ has made us free, and do not be entangled again with a yoke of bondage.

GALATIANS 5:1

This is the message which we have heard from Him and declare to you, that God is light and in Him is no darkness at all. If we say that we have fellowship with Him, and walk in darkness, we lie and do not practice the truth. But if we walk in the light as He is in the light, we have fellowship with one another, and the blood of Jesus Christ His Son cleanses us from all sin.

If we say that we have no sin, we deceive ourselves, and the truth is not in us. If we confess our sins, He is faithful and just to forgive us our sins and to cleanse us from all unrighteousness. If we say that we have not sinned, we make Him a liar, and His word is not in us.

1 JOHN 1:5–10

It is no longer I who live, but Christ lives in me.

GALATIANS 2:20

Create in me a clean heart, O God,
And renew a steadfast spirit within me.

PSALM 51:10

"Wash yourselves, make yourselves clean;
Put away the evil of your doings from
　　before My eyes.
Cease to do evil,
Learn to do good;
Seek justice,
Rebuke the oppressor;
Defend the fatherless,
Plead for the widow.
Come now, and let us reason together,"
Says the LORD,
"Though your sins are like scarlet,
They shall be as white as snow;
Though they are red like crimson,
They shall be as wool.
If you are willing and obedient,
You shall eat the good of the land."

ISAIAH 1:16–19

You know that He was manifested to take away our sins, and in Him there is no sin. Whoever abides in Him does not sin. Whoever sins has neither seen Him nor known Him. Little children, let no one deceive you. He who practices righteousness is righteous, just as He is righteous.

1 JOHN 3:5–7

I have taught you in the way of wisdom;
I have led you in right paths.

PROVERBS 4:11

Therefore, since we have this ministry, as we have received mercy, we do not lose heart. But we have renounced the hidden things of shame, not walking in craftiness nor handling the word of God deceitfully, but by manifestation of the truth commending ourselves to every man's conscience in the sight of God. But even if our gospel is veiled, it is veiled to those who are perishing, whose minds the god of this age has blinded, who do not believe, lest the light of the gospel of the glory of Christ, who is the image of God, should shine on them. For we do not preach ourselves, but Christ Jesus the Lord, and ourselves your bondservants for Jesus' sake. For it is the God who commanded light to shine out of darkness, who has shone in our hearts to give the light of the knowledge of the glory of God in the face of Jesus Christ.

2 CORINTHIANS 4:1–6

COMFORT IN

TROUBLED TIMES

The LORD builds up Jerusalem;
He gathers together the outcasts of Israel.
He heals the brokenhearted
And binds up their wounds. . . .
Great is our Lord, and mighty in power;
His understanding is infinite.
The LORD lifts up the humble;
He casts the wicked down to the ground. . . .
For He has strengthened the bars of your gates;
He has blessed your children within you.
He makes peace in your borders,
And fills you with the finest wheat.

PSALM 147:2–3, 5–6, 13–14

Peace I leave with you, My peace I give to you; not as the world gives do I give to you. Let not your heart be troubled, neither let it be afraid.

JOHN 14:27

For none of us lives to himself, and no one dies to himself.

ROMANS 14:7

Casting all your care upon Him, for He cares for you.

Be sober, be vigilant; because your adversary the devil walks about like a roaring lion, seeking whom he may devour. Resist him, steadfast in the faith, knowing that the same sufferings are experienced by your brotherhood in the world. But may the God of all grace, who called us to His eternal glory by Christ Jesus, after you have suffered a while, perfect, establish, strengthen, and settle you. To Him be the glory and the dominion forever and ever. Amen.

1 PETER 5:7–11

A horse is a vain hope for safety;
Neither shall it deliver any by its
    great strength.
Behold, the eye of the LORD is on those
    who fear Him,
On those who hope in His mercy,
To deliver their soul from death,
And to keep them alive in famine.
Our soul waits for the LORD;
He is our help and our shield.
For our heart shall rejoice in Him,
Because we have trusted in His holy name.
Let Your mercy, O LORD, be upon us,
Just as we hope in You.

PSALM 33:17–22

Turn Yourself to me, and have mercy on me,
For I am desolate and afflicted.
The troubles of my heart have enlarged;
Bring me out of my distresses!

PSALM 25:16–18

I will bless the LORD at all times;
His praise shall continually be in my mouth.
My soul shall make its boast in the LORD;
The humble shall hear of it and be glad.
Oh, magnify the LORD with me,
And let us exalt His name together.
I sought the LORD, and He heard me,
And delivered me from all my fears.
They looked to Him and were radiant,
And their faces were not ashamed.
This poor man cried out, and the LORD heard him,
And saved him out of all his troubles.
The angel of the LORD encamps all
          around those who fear Him,
And delivers them.
Oh, taste and see that the LORD is good;
Blessed is the man who trusts in Him!

PSALM 34:1–8

I will be glad and rejoice in Your mercy,
For You have considered my trouble;
You have known my soul in adversities.

PSALM 31:7

POWER TO
DEFEAT FEAR

Yet in all these things we are more than conquerors through Him who loved us. For I am persuaded that neither death nor life, nor angels nor principalities nor powers, nor things present nor things to come, nor height nor depth, nor any other created thing, shall be able to separate us from the love of God which is in Christ Jesus our Lord.

ROMANS 8:37–39

For You will light my lamp;
The LORD my God will enlighten my darkness.
For by You I can run against a troop,
By my God I can leap over a wall.
As for God, His way is perfect;
The word of the LORD is proven;
He is a shield to all who trust in Him.

PSALM 18:28–30

Then Jesus spoke to them again, saying, "I am the light of the world. He who follows Me shall not walk in darkness, but have the light of life."

JOHN 8:12

The LORD is my light and my salvation;
Whom shall I fear?
The LORD is the strength of my life;
Of whom shall I be afraid?
When the wicked came against me
To eat up my flesh,
My enemies and foes,
They stumbled and fell.
Though an army may encamp against me,
My heart shall not fear;
Though war may rise against me,
In this I will be confident.
One thing I have desired of the LORD,
That will I seek:
That I may dwell in the house of the LORD
All the days of my life,
To behold the beauty of the LORD,
And to inquire in His temple.
For in the time of trouble
He shall hide me in His pavilion;
In the secret place of His tabernacle
He shall hide me;
He shall set me high upon a rock.
And now my head shall be lifted up above
    my enemies all around me;
Therefore I will offer sacrifices of joy in His
    tabernacle;
I will sing, yes, I will sing praises to the LORD.
Hear, O LORD, when I cry with my voice!
Have mercy also upon me, and answer me.

PSALM 27:1–7

Do not be afraid of sudden terror,
Nor of trouble from the wicked when
        it comes;
For the LORD will be your confidence,
And will keep your foot from being caught.

PROVERBS 3:25–26

Delight yourself also in the LORD,
And He shall give you the desires of your heart.
Commit your way to the LORD,
Trust also in Him,
And He shall bring it to pass.
He shall bring forth your righteousness
        as the light,
And your justice as the noonday.

PSALM 37:4–6

I will love You, O LORD, my strength.
The LORD is my rock and my fortress and
        my deliverer;
My God, my strength, in whom I will trust;
My shield and the horn of my salvation, my
        stronghold.
I will call upon the LORD, who is worthy to
        be praised;
So shall I be saved from my enemies.

PSALM 18:1–3

The LORD your God Himself crosses over before you . . . He will be with you, He will not leave you nor forsake you.

DEUTERONOMY 31:3, 8

Your ears shall hear a voice behind you saying, "This is the way; walk in it."

ISAIAH 30:21

Let us therefore come boldly to the throne of grace, that we may obtain mercy and find grace to help in time of need.

HEBREWS 4:16

COURAGE TO BE WOMEN OF INTEGRITY

Blessed is the man
Who walks not in the counsel of the ungodly,
Nor stands in the path of sinners,
Nor sits in the seat of the scornful;
But his delight is in the law of the LORD,
And in His law he meditates day and night.
He shall be like a tree
Planted by the rivers of water,
That brings forth its fruit in its season,
Whose leaf also shall not wither;
And whatever he does shall prosper.
The ungodly are not so,
But are like the chaff which the wind drives away.
Therefore the ungodly shall not stand in
        the judgment,
Nor sinners in the congregation of the righteous.
For the LORD knows the way of the righteous,
But the way of the ungodly shall perish.

PSALM 1:1–6

The LORD shall judge the peoples;
Judge me, O LORD, according to my righteousness,
And according to my integrity within me.

PSALM 7:8

The righteous man walks in his integrity;
His children are blessed after him.

PROVERBS 20:7

I will behave wisely in a perfect way.
Oh, when will You come to me?
I will walk within my house with a perfect heart.
I will set nothing wicked before my eyes;
I hate the work of those who fall away;
It shall not cling to me.
A perverse heart shall depart from me;
I will not know wickedness.
Whoever secretly slanders his neighbor,
Him I will destroy;
The one who has a haughty look and a proud heart,
Him I will not endure.
My eyes shall be on the faithful of the land,
That they may dwell with me;
He who walks in a perfect way,
He shall serve me.
He who works deceit shall not dwell within
    my house;
He who tells lies shall not continue in my
    presence.
Early I will destroy all the wicked of the land,
That I may cut off all the evildoers from the
    city of the LORD.

PSALM 101:2–8

He who speaks truth declares righteousness,
But a false witness, deceit.
There is one who speaks like the piercings
    of a sword,
But the tongue of the wise promotes health.
The truthful lip shall be established forever,
But a lying tongue is but for a moment.

PROVERBS 12:17–19

A good man deals graciously and lends;
He will guide his affairs with discretion.
Surely he will never be shaken;
The righteous will be in everlasting
    remembrance.
He will not be afraid of evil tidings;
His heart is steadfast, trusting in the LORD.

PSALM 112:5–7

The LORD shall judge the peoples;
Judge me, O LORD, according to my righteousness,
And according to my integrity within me.

PSALM 7:8

If I have walked with falsehood,
Or if my foot has hastened to deceit,
Let me be weighed on honest scales,
That God may know my integrity.

JOB 31:5–6

Far be it from me
That I should say you are right;
Till I die I will not put away my integrity
    from me.
My righteousness I hold fast, and will not let
    it go;
My heart shall not reproach me as long as
    I live.

JOB 27:5–6

Blessed are the undefiled in the way,
Who walk in the law of the LORD!
Blessed are those who keep His testimonies,
Who seek Him with the whole heart!
They also do no iniquity;
They walk in His ways.
You have commanded us
To keep Your precepts diligently.
Oh, that my ways were directed
To keep Your statutes!
Then I would not be ashamed,
When I look into all Your commandments.
I will praise You with uprightness of heart,
When I learn Your righteous judgments.
I will keep Your statutes;
Oh, do not forsake me utterly!

PSALM 119:1–8

God Helps Women
to Grow by . . .

RECOGNIZING
EVIL

There is a way that seems right to a man,
But its end is the way of death.

PROVERBS 14:12

Beware of false prophets, who come to you in sheep's clothing, but inwardly they are ravenous wolves. You will know them by their fruits. Do men gather grapes from thornbushes or figs from thistles?

MATTHEW 7:15–16

By this you know the Spirit of God: Every spirit that confesses that Jesus Christ has come in the flesh is of God, and every spirit that does not confess that Jesus Christ has come in the flesh is not of God. And this is the spirit of the Antichrist, which you have heard was coming, and is now already in the world.

1 JOHN 4:2–3

They profess to know God, but in works they deny Him, being abominable, disobedient, and disqualified for every good work.

TITUS 1:16

For God is not the author of confusion but of peace, as in all the churches of the saints.

1 CORINTHIANS 14:33

For God has not given us a spirit of fear, but of power and of love and of a sound mind.

2 TIMOTHY 1:7

For certain men have crept in unnoticed, who long ago were marked out for this condemnation, ungodly men, who turn the grace of our God into lewdness and deny the only Lord God and our Lord Jesus Christ.

JUDE 4

For many deceivers have gone out into the world who do not confess Jesus Christ as coming in the flesh. This is a deceiver and an antichrist. . . .

Whoever transgresses and does not abide in the doctrine of Christ does not have God. He who abides in the doctrine of Christ has both the Father and the Son. If anyone comes to you and does not bring this doctrine, do not receive him into your house nor greet him; for he who greets him shares in his evil deeds.

2 JOHN 7, 9–11

Your word is a lamp to my feet
And a light to my path.

PSALM 119:105

CONTROLLING THE TONGUE

Let no corrupt word proceed out of your mouth, but what is good for necessary edification, that it may impart grace to the hearers.

EPHESIANS 4:29

As long as my breath is in me,
And the breath of God in my nostrils,
My lips will not speak wickedness,
Nor my tongue utter deceit.

JOB 27:3–4

He who would love life
And see good days,
Let him refrain his tongue from evil,
And his lips from speaking deceit.

1 PETER 3:10

Do not be a witness against your
neighbor without cause,
For would you deceive with your lips?

PROVERBS 24:28

Whoever guards his mouth and tongue
Keeps his soul from troubles.

PROVERBS 21:23

A good man out of the good treasure of his heart brings forth good; and an evil man out of the evil treasure of his heart brings forth evil. For out of the abundance of the heart his mouth speaks.

LUKE 6:45

A wholesome tongue is a tree of life,
But perverseness in it breaks the spirit.

PROVERBS 15:4

If anyone among you thinks he is religious, and does not bridle his tongue but deceives his own heart, this one's religion is useless.

JAMES 1:26

Whoever offers praise glorifies Me;
And to him who orders his conduct aright
I will show the salvation of God.

PSALM 50:23

Set a guard, O LORD, over my mouth;
Keep watch over the door of my lips.

PSALM 141:3

DEALING WITH LUST

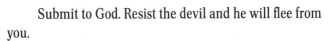

Submit to God. Resist the devil and he will flee from you.

JAMES **4:7**

I say then: Walk in the Spirit, and you shall not fulfill the lust of the flesh. For the flesh lusts against the Spirit, and the Spirit against the flesh; and these are contrary to one another, so that you do not do the things that you wish.

GALATIANS **5:16–17**

Each one is tempted when he is drawn away by his own desires and enticed. Then, when desire has conceived, it gives birth to sin; and sin, when it is full-grown, brings forth death.

Do not be deceived, my beloved brethren.

JAMES **1:14–16**

Then the Lord knows how to deliver the godly out of temptations and to reserve the unjust under punishment for the day of judgment.

2 PETER **2:9**

A man with an evil eye hastens after riches,
And does not consider that poverty will come upon him.

PROVERBS **28:22**

The LORD is far from the wicked,
But He hears the prayer of the righteous.

PROVERBS 15:29

For this you know, that no fornicator, unclean person, nor covetous man, who is an idolater, has any inheritance in the kingdom of Christ and God. . . . Therefore do not be partakers with them.

For you were once darkness, but now you are light in the Lord. Walk as children of light (for the fruit of the Spirit is in all goodness, righteousness, and truth).

And do not be drunk with wine, in which is dissipation; but be filled with the Spirit.

EPHESIANS 5:5, 7–9, 18

Put off, concerning your former conduct, the old man which grows corrupt according to the deceitful lusts, and be renewed in the spirit of your mind, and . . . put on the new man which was created according to God, in true righteousness and holiness.

Nor give place to the devil.

EPHESIANS 4:22–24, 27

Likewise you also, reckon yourselves to be dead indeed to sin, but alive to God in Christ Jesus our Lord.

Therefore do not let sin reign in your mortal body, that you should obey it in its lusts.

ROMANS 6:11–12

OVERCOMING WORDLINESS

Do not be conformed to this world, but be transformed by the renewing of your mind, that you may prove what is that good and acceptable and perfect will of God.

ROMANS 12:2

Then He said to them all, "If anyone desires to come after Me, let him deny himself, and take up his cross daily, and follow Me. For whoever desires to save his life will lose it, but whoever loses his life for My sake will save it. For what profit is it to a man if he gains the whole world, and is himself destroyed or lost?"

LUKE 9:23–25

Do not love the world or the things in the world. If anyone loves the world, the love of the Father is not in him. For all that is in the world—the lust of the flesh, the lust of the eyes, and the pride of life—is not of the Father but is of the world. And the world is passing away, and the lust of it; but he who does the will of God abides forever.

1 JOHN 2:15–17

Have no fellowship with the unfruitful works of darkness, but rather expose them.

EPHESIANS 5:11

We have renounced the hidden things of shame, not walking in craftiness nor handling the word of God deceitfully, but by manifestation of the truth commending ourselves to every man's conscience in the sight of God.

2 CORINTHIANS 4:2

Set your mind on things above, not on things on the earth.

Do not lie to one another, since you have put off the old man with his deeds, and have put on the new man who is renewed in knowledge according to the image of Him who created him.

COLOSSIANS 3:2, 9–10

Denying ungodliness and worldly lusts, we should live soberly, righteously, and godly in the present age, looking for the blessed hope and glorious appearing of our great God and Savior Jesus Christ.

TITUS 2:12–13

These things I have spoken to you, that in Me you may have peace. In the world you will have tribulation; but be of good cheer, I have overcome the world.

JOHN 16:33

He said to them, "Take heed and beware of covetousness, for one's life does not consist in the abundance of the things he possesses."

LUKE 12:15

Do not be unequally yoked together with unbelievers. For what fellowship has righteousness with lawlessness? And what communion has light with darkness? . . .
"Come out from among them
And be separate, says the Lord.
Do not touch what is unclean,
And I will receive you."

2 CORINTHIANS 6:14, 17

But you are a chosen generation, a royal priesthood, a holy nation, His own special people.

1 PETER 2:9

PUTTING
ASIDE PRIDE

Yet it shall not be so among you; but whoever desires to become great among you, let him be your servant. And whoever desires to be first among you, let him be your slave.

MATTHEW 20:26–27

Likewise you younger people, submit yourselves to your elders. Yes, all of you be submissive to one another, and be clothed with humility, for
"God resists the proud,
But gives grace to the humble."
Therefore humble yourselves under the mighty hand of God, that He may exalt you in due time.

1 PETER 5:5–6

A man's pride will bring him low,
But the humble in spirit will retain honor.

PROVERBS 29:23

By humility and the fear of the LORD
Are riches and honor and life.

PROVERBS 22:4

Though the LORD is on high,
Yet He regards the lowly;
But the proud He knows from afar.

PSALM 138:6

The Pharisee stood and prayed thus with himself, "God, I thank You that I am not like other men—extortioners, unjust, adulterers, or even as this tax collector. I fast twice a week; I give tithes of all that I possess." And the tax collector, standing afar off, would not so much as raise his eyes to heaven, but beat his breast, saying, "God, be merciful to me a sinner!" I tell you, this man went down to his house justified rather than the other; for everyone who exalts himself will be humbled, and he who humbles himself will be exalted.

LUKE 18:11–14

"He who glories, let him glory in the LORD." For not he who commends himself is approved, but whom the Lord commends.

2 CORINTHIANS 10:17–18

Submit to God. Resist the devil and he will flee from you.... Humble yourselves in the sight of the Lord, and He will lift you up.

JAMES 4:7, 10

Pride goes before destruction,
And a haughty spirit before a fall.
Better to be of a humble spirit with the lowly,
Than to divide the spoil with the proud.
He who heeds the word wisely will
    find good,
And whoever trusts in the LORD, happy is he.

PROVERBS 16:18–20

As the elect of God, holy and beloved, put on tender mercies, kindness, humility, meekness, longsuffering.

COLOSSIANS 3:12

Walk worthy of the calling with which you were called, with all lowliness and gentleness.

EPHESIANS 4:1–2

REJOICING IN THE LORD

Let the word of Christ dwell in you richly in all wisdom, teaching and admonishing one another in psalms and hymns and spiritual songs, singing with grace in your hearts to the Lord.

COLOSSIANS 3:16

Then he said to them, "Go your way, eat the fat, drink the sweet, and send portions to those for whom nothing is prepared; for this day is holy to our Lord. Do not sorrow, for the joy of the LORD is your strength."

NEHEMIAH 8:10

Those who sow in tears
Shall reap in joy.
He who continually goes forth weeping,
Bearing seed for sowing,
Shall doubtless come again with rejoicing,
Bringing his sheaves with him.

PSALM 126:5–6

This is the day the LORD has made;
We will rejoice and be glad in it.

PSALM 118:24

Restore to me the joy of Your salvation,
And uphold me by Your generous Spirit.
Then I will teach transgressors Your ways,
And sinners shall be converted to You.

PSALM 51:12–13

His lord said to him, "Well done, good and faithful servant; you were faithful over a few things, I will make you ruler over many things. Enter into the joy of your lord."

MATTHEW 25:21

These things I have spoken to you, that My joy may remain in you, and that your joy may be full. This is My commandment, that you love one another as I have loved you.

JOHN 15:11–12

You became followers of us and of the Lord, having received the word in much affliction, with joy of the Holy Spirit.

1 THESSALONIANS 1:6

My lips shall greatly rejoice when I sing to You,
And my soul, which You have redeemed.

PSALM 71:23

God Rejoices with Women When They . . .

JOIN WITH OTHER BELIEVERS

You call me Teacher and Lord, and you say well, for so I am. If I then, your Lord and Teacher, have washed your feet, you also ought to wash one another's feet. For I have given you an example, that you should do as I have done to you. Most assuredly, I say to you, a servant is not greater than his master; nor is he who is sent greater than he who sent him. If you know these things, blessed are you if you do them.

JOHN 13:13–17

God is faithful, by whom you were called into the fellowship of His Son, Jesus Christ our Lord.

Now I plead with you, brethren, by the name of our Lord Jesus Christ, that you all speak the same thing, and that there be no divisions among you, but that you be perfectly joined together in the same mind and in the same judgment.

1 CORINTHIANS 1:9–10

He who says he is in the light, and hates his brother, is in darkness until now. He who loves his brother abides in the light, and there is no cause for stumbling in him. But he who hates his brother is in darkness and walks in darkness, and does not know where he is going, because the darkness has blinded his eyes.

1 JOHN 2:9–11

God, who is rich in mercy, because of His great love with which He loved us, even when we were dead in trespasses, made us alive together with Christ (by grace you have been saved), and raised us up together, and made us sit together in the heavenly places in Christ Jesus.

EPHESIANS 2:4–6

Now John answered Him, saying, "Teacher, we saw someone who does not follow us casting out demons in Your name, and we forbade him because he does not follow us."

But Jesus said, "Do not forbid him, for no one who works a miracle in My name can soon afterward speak evil of Me. For he who is not against us is on our side. For whoever gives you a cup of water to drink in My name, because you belong to Christ, assuredly, I say to you, he will by no means lose his reward.

"But whoever causes one of these little ones who believe in Me to stumble, it would be better for him if a millstone were hung around his neck, and he were thrown into the sea."

MARK 9:38–42

You are a chosen generation, a royal priesthood, a holy nation, His own special people, that you may proclaim the praises of Him who called you out of darkness into His marvelous light.

1 PETER 2:9

Now indeed there are many members, yet one body. And the eye cannot say to the hand, "I have no need of you"; nor again the head to the feet, "I have no need of you." No, much rather, those members of the body which seem to be weaker are necessary. And those members of the body which we think to be less honorable, on these we bestow greater honor; and our unpresentable parts have greater modesty, but our presentable parts have no need. But God composed the body, having given greater honor to that part which lacks it, that there should be no schism in the body, but that the members should have the same care for one another. And if one member suffers, all the members suffer with it; or if one member is honored, all the members rejoice with it.

Now you are the body of Christ, and members individually.

1 CORINTHIANS 12:20–27

If we say that we have fellowship with Him, and walk in darkness, we lie and do not practice the truth. But if we walk in the light as He is in the light, we have fellowship with one another, and the blood of Jesus Christ His Son cleanses us from all sin.

1 JOHN 1:6–7

SEEK TO UNDERSTAND GOD'S WAYS

Forsake foolishness and live,
And go in the way of understanding. . . .
The fear of the LORD is the beginning of wisdom,
And the knowledge of the Holy One
    is understanding.

PROVERBS 9:6, 10

How much better to get wisdom than gold!
And to get understanding is to be
    chosen rather than silver.
The highway of the upright is to depart
    from evil;
He who keeps his way preserves his soul.

PROVERBS 16:16–17

Seek the LORD while He may be found,
Call upon Him while He is near. . . .
"For My thoughts are not your thoughts,
Nor are your ways My ways," says the LORD.
"For as the heavens are higher than the earth,
So are My ways higher than your ways,
And My thoughts than your thoughts."

ISAIAH 55:6, 8–9

If any of you lacks wisdom, let him ask of God, who gives to all liberally and without reproach, and it will be given to him.

JAMES 1:5

Make me understand the way of Your precepts;
So shall I meditate on Your wonderful works....
Give me understanding, and I shall
    keep Your law;
Indeed, I shall observe it with my
    whole heart....
Your hands have made me and fashioned me;
Give me understanding, that I may
    learn Your commandments....
You, through Your commandments,
    make me wiser than my enemies;
For they are ever with me....
Through Your precepts I get understanding;
Therefore I hate every false way.
Your word is a lamp to my feet
And a light to my path....
I am Your servant;
Give me understanding,
That I may know Your testimonies.

PSALM 119:27, 34, 73, 98, 104–105, 125

But there is a spirit in man,
And the breath of the Almighty gives him
understanding.

JOB 32:8

Great is our Lord, and mighty in power;
His understanding is infinite.

PSALM 147:5

For the LORD gives wisdom;
From His mouth come knowledge
and understanding;
He stores up sound wisdom for the upright;
He is a shield to those who walk uprightly.

PROVERBS 2:6–7

Lead me in Your truth and teach me,
For You are the God of my salvation.

PSALM 25:5

I applied my heart to know,
To search and seek out wisdom and the
reason of things.

ECCLESIASTES 7:25

STAND IN AWE
OF THE LORD

If you seek her as silver,
And search for her as for hidden treasures;
Then you will understand the fear of the LORD,
And find the knowledge of God.

PROVERBS 2:4–5

He does not delight in the strength of
    the horse;
He takes no pleasure in the legs of a man.
The LORD takes pleasure in those who
    fear Him,
In those who hope in His mercy.

PSALM 147:10–11

The fear of the LORD is the beginning
    of knowledge,
But fools despise wisdom and instruction.

PROVERBS 1:7

The fear of the LORD leads to life,
And he who has it will abide in satisfaction;
He will not be visited with evil.

PROVERBS 19:23

In the fear of the LORD there is strong confidence,
And His children will have a place of refuge.
The fear of the LORD is a fountain of life,
To turn one away from the snares of death.

PROVERBS 14:26–27

Then those who feared the LORD spoke
     to one another,
And the LORD listened and heard them;
So a book of remembrance was
     written before Him
For those who fear the LORD
And who meditate on His name.
"They shall be Mine," says the LORD of hosts,
"On the day that I make them My jewels.
And I will spare them
As a man spares his own son who
     serves him."

MALACHI 3:16–17

Let us hear the conclusion of the whole matter:
Fear God and keep His commandments,
For this is man's all.
For God will bring every work into
     judgment,
Including every secret thing,
Whether good or evil.

ECCLESIASTES 12:13–14

Praise the LORD!
Blessed is the man who fears the LORD,
Who delights greatly in His commandments.

PSALM 112:1

In mercy and truth
Atonement is provided for iniquity;
And by the fear of the LORD one
     departs from evil.

PROVERBS 16:6

Who is the man that fears the LORD?
Him shall He teach in the way He chooses.
He himself shall dwell in prosperity,
And his descendants shall inherit the earth.
The secret of the LORD is with those who
     fear Him,
And He will show them His covenant.

PSALM 25:12–14

Behold, the fear of the Lord, that is wisdom,
And to depart from evil is understanding.

JOB 28:28

SEEK HIS SOVEREIGNTY

For the LORD is our Judge,
The LORD is our Lawgiver,
The LORD is our King;
He will save us.

ISAIAH **33:22**

Then Moses said to God, "Indeed, when I come to the children of Israel and say to them, 'The God of your fathers has sent me to you,' and they say to me, 'What is His name?' what shall I say to them?"

And God said to Moses, "I AM WHO I AM." And He said, "Thus you shall say to the children of Israel, 'I AM has sent me to you.'"

EXODUS **3:13–14**

For with God nothing will be impossible.

LUKE **1:37**

Whom have I in heaven but You?
And there is none upon earth that I
      desire besides You.

PSALM **73:25**

169

Great is the LORD, and greatly to be praised;
And His greatness is unsearchable.
One generation shall praise Your works to another,
And shall declare Your mighty acts. . . .
Your kingdom is an everlasting kingdom,
And Your dominion endures throughout
     all generations.

PSALM 145:3–4, 13

For thus says the High and Lofty One
Who inhabits eternity, whose name is Holy:
"I dwell in the high and holy place,
With him who has a contrite and
     humble spirit,
To revive the spirit of the humble,
And to revive the heart of the contrite ones."

ISAIAH 57:15

The heavens declare the glory of God;
And the firmament shows His handiwork.

PSALM 19:1

Behold, I am the LORD, the God of all flesh. Is there anything too hard for Me?

JEREMIAH 32:27

In the beginning God created the heavens and the earth. The earth was without form, and void; and darkness was on the face of the deep. And the Spirit of God was hovering over the face of the waters.

Then God said, "Let there be light"; and there was light.

GENESIS 1:1–3

"Am I a God near at hand," says the LORD,
"And not a God afar off?
Can anyone hide himself in secret places,
So I shall not see him?" says the LORD;
"Do I not fill heaven and earth?" says
    the LORD.

JEREMIAH 23:23–24

For of Him and through Him and to Him are all things, to whom be glory forever.

ROMANS 11:36

HOPE FOR REVIVAL

Your light has come!
And the glory of the LORD is risen upon you.
For behold, the darkness shall cover the earth,
And deep darkness the people;
But the LORD will arise over you,
And His glory will be seen upon you.

ISAIAH 60:1–2

All the ends of the world
Shall remember and turn to the LORD,
And all the families of the nations
Shall worship before You.
For the kingdom is the LORD's,
And He rules over the nations.

PSALM 22:27–28

For the earth will be filled
With the knowledge of the glory of the LORD,
As the waters cover the sea.

HABAKKUK 2:14

This gospel of the kingdom will be preached in all
the world as a witness to all the nations, and then the end
will come.

MATTHEW 24:14

The voice of one crying in the wilderness:
"Prepare the way of the LORD;
Make straight in the desert
A highway for our God.
Every valley shall be exalted
And every mountain and hill brought low;
The crooked places shall be made straight
And the rough places smooth;
The glory of the LORD shall be revealed,
And all flesh shall see it together;
For the mouth of the LORD has spoken."

ISAIAH 40:3–5

The LORD has made bare His holy arm
In the eyes of all the nations;
And all the ends of the earth shall see
The salvation of our God....
So shall He sprinkle many nations.
Kings shall shut their mouths at Him;
For what had not been told them they shall see,
And what they had not heard they shall consider.

ISAIAH 52:10, 15

I will seek what was lost and bring back what was driven away, bind up the broken and strengthen what was sick; but I will destroy the fat and the strong, and feed them in judgment.

EZEKIEL 34:16

Indeed the LORD has proclaimed
To the end of the world:
"Say to the daughter of Zion,
'Surely your salvation is coming;
Behold, His reward is with Him,
And His work before Him.'"
And they shall call them The Holy People,
The Redeemed of the LORD;
And you shall be called Sought Out,
A City Not Forsaken.

ISAIAH 62:11–12

I will show wonders in the heavens and in
    the earth:
Blood and fire and pillars of smoke.
The sun shall be turned into darkness,
And the moon into blood,
Before the coming of the great and awesome
    day of the LORD.
And it shall come to pass
That whoever calls on the name of the LORD
Shall be saved.
For in Mount Zion and in Jerusalem
    there shall be deliverance,
As the LORD has said,
Among the remnant whom the LORD calls.

JOEL 2:30–32

SEARCH FOR SIGNS OF ETERNITY

Heaven and earth will pass away, but My words will by no means pass away.

MATTHEW 24:35

The Spirit expressly says that in latter times some will depart from the faith, giving heed to deceiving spirits and doctrines of demons, speaking lies in hypocrisy, having their own conscience seared with a hot iron, forbidding to marry, and commanding to abstain from foods which God created to be received with thanksgiving by those who believe and know the truth.

1 TIMOTHY 4:1–3

Know this, that in the last days perilous times will come: For men will be lovers of themselves, lovers of money, boasters, proud, blasphemers, disobedient to parents, unthankful, unholy, unloving, unforgiving, slanderers, without self-control, brutal, despisers of good, traitors, headstrong, haughty, lovers of pleasure rather than lovers of God, having a form of godliness but denying its power. And from such people turn away!

2 TIMOTHY 3:1–5

For since the beginning of the world
Men have not heard nor perceived by the ear,
Nor has the eye seen any God besides You,
Who acts for the one who waits for Him.

ISAIAH **64:4**

For the wages of sin is death, but the gift of God is eternal life in Christ Jesus our Lord.

ROMANS **6:23**

Jesus answered and said to them: "Take heed that no one deceives you. For many will come in My name, saying, 'I am the Christ,' and will deceive many. And you will hear of wars and rumors of wars. See that you are not troubled; for all these things must come to pass, but the end is not yet. For nation will rise against nation, and kingdom against kingdom. And there will be famines, pestilences, and earthquakes in various places. All these are the beginning of sorrows.

Then they will deliver you up to tribulation and kill you, and you will be hated by all nations for My name's sake. And then many will be offended, will betray one another, and will hate one another. Then many false prophets will rise up and deceive many. And because lawlessness will abound, the love of many will grow cold. But he who endures to the end shall be saved. And this gospel of the kingdom will be preached in all the world as a witness to all the nations, and then the end will come."

MATTHEW **24:4–14**

Then two men will be in the field: one will be taken and the other left. . . . Watch therefore, for you do not know what hour your Lord is coming. . . . Therefore you also be ready, for the Son of Man is coming at an hour you do not expect.

MATTHEW 24:40, 42, 44

And it shall come to pass in the last days, says God,
That I will pour out of My Spirit on all flesh;
Your sons and your daughters shall prophesy,
Your young men shall see visions,
Your old men shall dream dreams.
And on My menservants and on My
     maidservants
I will pour out My Spirit in those days;
And they shall prophesy.
I will show wonders in heaven above
And signs in the earth beneath:
Blood and fire and vapor of smoke.
The sun shall be turned into darkness,
And the moon into blood,
Before the coming of the great and
     awesome day of the LORD.
And it shall come to pass
That whoever calls on the name of the LORD
Shall be saved.

ACTS 2:17–21

There are also celestial bodies and terrestrial bodies; but the glory of the celestial is one, and the glory of the terrestrial is another. . . .

So also is the resurrection of the dead. The body is sown in corruption, it is raised in incorruption. It is sown in dishonor, it is raised in glory. It is sown in weakness, it is raised in power. It is sown a natural body, it is raised a spiritual body. There is a natural body, and there is a spiritual body.

1 CORINTHIANS 15:40, 42–44

Behold, I tell you a mystery: We shall not all sleep, but we shall all be changed—in a moment, in the twinkling of an eye, at the last trumpet. For the trumpet will sound, and the dead will be raised incorruptible, and we shall be changed. For this corruptible must put on incorruption, and this mortal must put on immortality. So when this corruptible has put on incorruption, and this mortal has put on immortality, then shall be brought to pass the saying that is written: "Death is swallowed up in victory."

"O Death, where is your sting?

O Hades, where is your victory?"

The sting of death is sin, and the strength of sin is the law. But thanks be to God, who gives us the victory through our Lord Jesus Christ.

1 CORINTHIANS 15:51–57

Beloved, now we are children of God; and it has not yet been revealed what we shall be, but we know that when He is revealed, we shall be like Him, for we shall see Him as He is. And everyone who has this hope in Him purifies himself, just as He is pure.

1 JOHN 3:2–3

I do not want you to be ignorant, brethren, concerning those who have fallen asleep, lest you sorrow as others who have no hope. For if we believe that Jesus died and rose again, even so God will bring with Him those who sleep in Jesus.

For this we say to you by the word of the Lord, that we who are alive and remain until the coming of the Lord will by no means precede those who are asleep. For the Lord Himself will descend from heaven with a shout, with the voice of an archangel, and with the trumpet of God. And the dead in Christ will rise first. Then we who are alive and remain shall be caught up together with them in the clouds to meet the Lord in the air. And thus we shall always be with the Lord. Therefore comfort one another with these words.

1 THESSALONIANS 4:13–18

Dynamic Women
of Faith

MARY—MOTHER OF JESUS

Now in the sixth month the angel Gabriel was sent by God to a city of Galilee named Nazareth, to a virgin betrothed to a man whose name was Joseph, of the house of David. The virgin's name was Mary. And having come in, the angel said to her, "Rejoice, highly favored one, the Lord is with you; blessed are you among women!"

But when she saw him, she was troubled at his saying, and considered what manner of greeting this was. Then the angel said to her, "Do not be afraid, Mary, for you have found favor with God. And behold, you will conceive in your womb and bring forth a Son, and shall call His name JESUS."

LUKE 1:26–31

Now there stood by the cross of Jesus His mother, and His mother's sister, Mary the wife of Clopas, and Mary Magdalene. When Jesus therefore saw His mother, and the disciple whom He loved standing by, He said to His mother, "Woman, behold your son!" Then He said to the disciple, "Behold your mother!" And from that hour that disciple took her to his own home.

JOHN 19:25–27

And Mary said:
"My soul magnifies the Lord,
And my spirit has rejoiced in God my Savior.
For He has regarded the lowly state of
     His maidservant;
For behold, henceforth all generations
     will call me blessed.
For He who is mighty has done great
     things for me,
And holy is His name.
And His mercy is on those who fear Him
From generation to generation.
He has shown strength with His arm;
He has scattered the proud in the
     imagination of their hearts.
He has put down the mighty from
     their thrones,
And exalted the lowly.
He has filled the hungry with good things,
And the rich He has sent away empty."

LUKE 1:46–53

ELIZABETH—MOTHER OF JOHN THE BAPTIST

There was in the days of Herod, the king of Judea, a certain priest named Zacharias, of the division of Abijah. His wife was of the daughters of Aaron, and her name was Elizabeth. And they were both righteous before God, walking in all the commandments and ordinances of the Lord blameless. But they had no child, because Elizabeth was barren, and they were both well advanced in years.

LUKE 1:5–7

The angel said to him, "Do not be afraid, Zacharias, for your prayer is heard; and your wife Elizabeth will bear you a son, and you shall call his name John."

LUKE 1:13

Now indeed, Elizabeth your relative has also conceived a son in her old age; and this is now the sixth month for her who was called barren. For with God nothing will be impossible.

LUKE 1:36–37

You, child, will be called the prophet of
    the Highest;
For you will go before the face of the Lord
    to prepare His ways,
To give knowledge of salvation to His people
By the remission of their sins.

LUKE 1:76–77

It happened, when Elizabeth heard the greeting of Mary, that the babe leaped in her womb; and Elizabeth was filled with the Holy Spirit. Then she spoke out with a loud voice and said, "Blessed are you among women, and blessed is the fruit of your womb! But why is this granted to me, that the mother of my Lord should come to me? For indeed, as soon as the voice of your greeting sounded in my ears, the babe leaped in my womb for joy. Blessed is she who believed, for there will be a fulfillment of those things which were told her from the Lord."

LUKE 1:41–45

SARAH—WIFE OF ABRAHAM

Then God said to Abraham, "As for Sarai your wife, you shall not call her name Sarai, but Sarah shall be her name. And I will bless her and also give you a son by her; then I will bless her, and she shall be a mother of nations; kings of peoples shall be from her."

GENESIS 17:15–16

Then God said: "No, Sarah your wife shall bear you a son, and you shall call his name Isaac; I will establish My covenant with him for an everlasting covenant, and with his descendants after him."

GENESIS 17:19

The LORD visited Sarah as He had said, and the LORD did for Sarah as He had spoken. For Sarah conceived and bore Abraham a son in his old age, at the set time of which God had spoken to him. And Abraham called the name of his son who was born to him—whom Sarah bore to him—Isaac.

GENESIS 21:1–3

God said to Abraham, "Do not let it be displeasing in your sight because of the lad or because of your bondwoman. Whatever Sarah has said to you, listen to her voice; for in Isaac your seed shall be called."

GENESIS 21:12

By faith Sarah herself also received strength to conceive seed, and she bore a child when she was past the age, because she judged Him faithful who had promised.

HEBREWS 11:11

HANNAH—MOTHER OF SAMUEL

She was in bitterness of soul, and prayed to the LORD and wept in anguish. Then she made a vow and said, "O LORD of hosts, if You will indeed look on the affliction of Your maidservant and remember me, and not forget Your maidservant, but will give Your maidservant a male child, then I will give him to the LORD all the days of his life, and no razor shall come upon his head."

1 SAMUEL 1:10–11

It came to pass in the process of time that Hannah conceived and bore a son, and called his name Samuel, saying, "Because I have asked for him from the LORD."

1 SAMUEL 1:20

"The LORD has granted me my petition which I asked of Him. Therefore I also have lent him to the LORD; as long as he lives he shall be lent to the LORD." So they worshiped the LORD there.

1 SAMUEL 1:27–28

The LORD visited Hannah, so that she conceived and bore three sons and two daughters. Meanwhile the child Samuel grew before the LORD.

1 SAMUEL 2:21

RUTH—GREAT GRANDMOTHER OF DAVID

Boaz answered and said to her, "It has been fully reported to me, all that you have done for your mother-in-law since the death of your husband, and how you have left your father and your mother and the land of your birth, and have come to a people whom you did not know before. The LORD repay your work, and a full reward be given you by the LORD God of Israel, under whose wings you have come for refuge."

Then she said, "Let me find favor in your sight, my lord; for you have comforted me, and have spoken kindly to your maidservant, though I am not like one of your maidservants."

RUTH 2:11–13

Blessed are you of the LORD, my daughter! For you have shown more kindness at the end than at the beginning, in that you did not go after young men, whether poor or rich. And now, my daughter, do not fear. I will do for you all that you request, for all the people of my town know that you are a virtuous woman.

RUTH 3:10–11

So Boaz took Ruth and she became his wife; and when he went in to her, the LORD gave her conception, and she bore a son.

RUTH 4:13

The neighbor women gave him a name, saying, "There is a son born to Naomi." And they called his name Obed. He is the father of Jesse, the father of David.

RUTH 4:17

LYDIA—SELLER OF PURPLE

On the Sabbath day we went out of the city to the riverside, where prayer was customarily made; and we sat down and spoke to the women who met there. Now a certain woman named Lydia heard us. She was a seller of purple from the city of Thyatira, who worshiped God. The Lord opened her heart to heed the things spoken by Paul. And when she and her household were baptized, she begged us, saying, "If you have judged me to be faithful to the Lord, come to my house and stay." So she persuaded us.

ACTS 16:13–15

When it was day, the magistrates sent the officers, saying, "Let [Paul and Silas] go." . . .

So they went out of the prison and entered the house of Lydia; and when they had seen the brethren, they encouraged them and departed.

ACTS 16:35, 40

Verses That Are Special to Me

_____

_____

_____

_____

_____

_____

_____

_____

_____

_____

_____

_____

_____

_____

_____

_____

_____

_____

_____

_____

_____

_____

VERSES THAT ARE SPECIAL TO ME

_____

_____

_____

_____

_____

_____

_____

_____

_____

_____

_____

_____

_____

_____

_____

_____

_____

_____

_____

_____

_____

_____

PRAYER REQUESTS

_____

_____

_____

_____

_____

_____

_____

_____

_____

_____

_____

_____

_____

_____

_____

_____

_____

_____

_____

_____

ANSWERED PRAYERS

NOTES

ANSWERED PRAYERS

NOTES

God's Plan of Salvation

Therefore, just as through one man sin entered the world, and death through sin, and thus death spread to all men, because all sinned.
—ROMANS 5:12

For all have sinned and fall short of the glory of God, being justified freely by His grace through the redemption that is in Christ Jesus.
—ROMANS 3:23–24

For the wages of sin is death, but the gift of God is eternal life in Christ Jesus our Lord.
—ROMANS 6:23

But God demonstrates His own love toward us, in that while we were still sinners, Christ died for us.
—ROMANS 5:8

Moreover, brethren, I declare to you the gospel which I preached to you, which also you received and in which you stand, by which also you are saved, if you hold fast that word which I preached to you—unless you believed in vain.

For I delivered to you first of all that which I also received: that Christ died for our sins according to the Scriptures, and that He was buried, and that He rose again the third day according to the Scriptures.
—1 CORINTHIANS 15:1–4

For God did not send His Son into the world to condemn the world, but that the world through Him might be saved.   —JOHN 3:17

He who believes in the Son has everlasting life; and he who does not believe the Son shall not see life, but the wrath of God abides on him.
—JOHN 3:36

For God so loved the world that He gave His only begotten Son, that whoever believes in Him should not perish but have everlasting life. —JOHN 3:16

But as many as received Him, to them He gave the right to become children of God, to those who believe in His name.
—JOHN 1:12

For by grace you have been saved through faith, and that not of yourselves; it is the gift of God, not of works, lest anyone should boast.
—EPHESIANS 2:8–9

Behold, I stand at the door and knock. If anyone hears My voice and opens the door, I will come in to him and dine with him, and he with Me. —REVELATION 3:20

But what does it say? "The word is near you, in your mouth and in your heart" (that is, the word of faith which we preach): that if you confess with your mouth the Lord Jesus and believe in your heart that God has raised Him from the dead, you will be saved. For with the heart one believes unto righteousness, and with the mouth confession is made unto salvation. —ROMANS 10:8–10

Therefore whoever confesses Me before men, him I will also confess before My Father who is in heaven. —MATTHEW 10:32

And this is the testimony: that God has given us eternal life, and this life is in His Son. He who has the Son has life; he who does not have the Son of God does not have life. These things I have written to you who believe in the name of the Son of God, that you may know that you have eternal life, and that you may continue to believe in the name of the Son of God. —1 JOHN 5:11–13

Executive
Affair

Executive
Affair

BER CARROLL

POOLBEG

Published 2004
by Poolbeg Press Ltd
123 Grange Hill, Baldoyle
Dublin 13, Ireland
E-mail: poolbeg@poolbeg.com

Typesetting, layout, design © Poolbeg Group Services Ltd.

1 3 5 7 9 10 8 6 4 2

A catalogue record for this book is available from the British
Library.

ISBN 1-84223-180-4

Typeset by MAGPIE DESIGNS in Palatino 10/14
Printed by Litografia Rosés S.A. , Spain

www.poolbeg.com

ABOUT THE AUTHOR

Ber Carroll was born in Blarney, Co Cork,
in 1971. She is a qualified accountant
and works as a finance director in the
information technology industry.
She moved to Sydney with her husband
in 1995 and their son was born in 2002.

ACKNOWLEDGEMENTS

Thanks to my parents and my entire family for all their support.

Also to Lynne Stubbs, Peter Gracie and Lyn Atkin who trawled through the manuscript in its earliest form.

To Rob, for being my best friend, a wonderful husband and a ruthless editor. To Conor, even though he was just a twinkle in his dad's eye when this book was written. To Mandy, avid reader, super auntie and nanny supreme.

Thanks also to an unknown assessor at The Manuscript Appraisal Agency who offered me such an enthusiastic response, to my agent Brian Cook and everybody at Poolbeg for getting behind an unknown writer.

And thanks to the many others who touched this book in one way or another, Claire Oaks, Jerry Winfrey, Dick Postman, Tristan Tegroen, Scott Mortimer, Jeanette Martin, Chris Ryan and Ann Marie Forrest.

**For my dad, Donal,
who always believed in me**

CHAPTER ONE

It was one of those Friday nights in Dublin where it seemed as if the whole population was seeking solace from the approaching winter in the crowded pubs. The noise inside Maguire's was deafening. People shouted over each other to be heard. Everybody seemed to have so much to say.

Amtech employees were shoulder to shoulder as they packed the limited floor space. Maguire's, only three doors down from their Ballsbridge plant, was a compulsory stop on the way home from work. Claire was jammed into a corner, surrounded by the newly formed Oracle Upgrade Project Team. It seemed like a good idea to come to Maguire's after their first meeting that afternoon. Reality was that very little team bonding could be done with the overwhelming noise.

Claire saw Susan and Margaret come in and waved at them across the bar, using sign language to indicate

1

she would catch up with them later. Michael was having an intense conversation over to her left. His pint of Guinness was hardly touched as he talked through the project plan with another team member. She tried to make eye contact with him to see if he wanted another pint. He seemed to be oblivious to her presence so she squeezed her way to the bar to order a solitary vodka.

On later reflection, she realised that Michael had become more remote and preoccupied as the evening progressed. She remembered trying to engage him in conversation, talking to the others in the group when he gave monosyllabic answers. More images – kissing him, holding his hand – all without registering his lukewarm response. It was all very obvious with the wisdom of hindsight and without the glow of several vodkas.

She had no idea something was wrong until they were walking home. She was babbling about Paris. They were going there for Christmas. He was walking very fast, holding her hand firmly and she struggled to keep up with him.

"We need to book our tickets . . . we should get up early tomorrow to do it . . ." she said breathlessly. When he stopped suddenly, she bumped into him, giggling.

"I don't think Paris is a good idea . . ." he said quietly.

She giggled again at his serious expression. "Stop

being funny . . . we really need to get our act together or all the flights will be booked out . . . Christmas is a very busy time."

"Claire . . . look . . . I don't know how to say this . . ."

"Say what?" she asked with mild curiosity.

"I don't think we should see each other any more . . ."

"Are you joking?" she asked sharply. "Because if you are, I'm not finding it very amusing."

"I'm sorry . . . I'm not joking . . . it's not anything you've done . . . it's just me," he said awkwardly, playing with her fingers as he spoke.

She stared at him in shock, taking a few seconds to absorb the awfulness of what he was saying.

"You want to break up with me?" she asked stupidly, pulling her hand from his grasp, stepping back from his closeness.

"Yes . . . look, we've been together for three years and the writing's on the wall . . . marriage and kids. I'm not ready for that. I want some fun before I settle down . . ." His voice trailed off, his eyes focussed downwards, away from the hurt on her face.

Another few seconds of silence.

He's serious. He's leaving me.

"Is there someone else?"

She didn't expect a positive answer to the pathetic question.

"I have met someone. Her name is Karen . . . but it's very casual." His voice sounded foreign with insincerity.

More silence, then thankfully anger came to her assistance.

"Well, that's very nice for you. I'd hate to think of you alone without a girlfriend."

"There's no need to be bitchy."

"I think there is . . . I think that I have some excellent reasons to be a bitch."

"I was hoping we could stay friends . . ."

"Oh, for God's sake, don't give me that 'friends' bull- shit!" She was vaguely aware that she was shouting.

"Look, we still work for the same company. I thought it would be easier for both of us if we were on speaking terms . . . but, if this is how you want it . . ."

"Don't you try that . . . it's the way *you* want it, not me . . . you know what?" She glared at him. "I hope you are sure of what you're doing because I really think you're throwing away something special . . . see you around and all that crap!"

Her steps were quick and frantic as she walked away. She turned on her ankle, cursed and looked around to see if he was watching. She saw only his back as he strode in the opposite direction. She was at least ten minutes' walk from home and she was suddenly aware that the residential street was deserted and badly lit. She opened her mouth to yell at him to come back but realised he was too far away to hear.

She reached the flat and let herself in. She didn't turn on the lights, making her way to the bedroom from the streetlight outside. It was a tiny place; she and Fiona had squeezed themselves into it for three years. Claire hadn't bothered to look for a new flatmate when Fiona went to Sydney last year. It seemed pointless when Michael spent so much time there. She sat on the side of the bed and turned on the lamp. His aftershave was on the dresser. His things were all over the flat. She would have to collect them tomorrow, put them in a box.

It's over . . . it's really over . . . but it can't be . . . not after three years . . . not in ten minutes . . . but he's got a girlfriend . . . Karen. He was meeting her behind my back . . . how could he do that? How could I not know he was doing it? When did he meet her? Does she know about me? Does she know that he slept here last night?

* * *

She couldn't find her swipe card to get in. She stood in the cold, her frozen fingers searching through her handbag. It wasn't in there. She would have to wait until someone else came along. She hoped it wouldn't be someone that she knew, someone that she would have to talk to. It turned out to be Mark, her boss.

"You're a security risk, Claire . . . you're always losing that thing." He was only half joking.

She was glad he wasn't in a good mood. He was too preoccupied to ask her about her weekend.

She took the stairs, knowing she wouldn't be able to stand up to the closer scrutiny she might get from Mark in the lift. Most of the workforce were in transit – hanging coats, making coffee, gossiping. She had no choice but to mumble a response to the numerous cheerful "Good mornings" that were bestowed en route to her desk. Margaret and John were huddled around Susan at her desk. They cupped their coffee mugs fervently with both hands, as if trying to extract some energy that would get them through the long week ahead.

Shrugging off her jacket, she switched on her PC, staring impatiently at the screen as she waited for the machine to start up. She typed her password furiously, ignoring the well-established ritual of having a chat with her colleagues before starting the working day. She saw them looking at each other with raised eyebrows, their conversation dying. She could feel their curious looks turn in her direction. She made sure her face had a look of intense concentration that nobody could dare interrupt.

Susan waited a polite thirty minutes before sitting, uninvited, on Claire's visitor's seat.

"Had a good weekend?" she asked conversationally.

"It was OK. How about you?"

"Yeah, it was good, but it just went too quickly. I can't believe it's Monday again."

Claire kept typing, hoping she would go away.

"You seem extraordinarily busy this morning," Susan commented.

"Yes, I am. I need to put some financials together for a tender response that's due today . . ."

"Anything I can help you with?"

"No, I just need to concentrate . . ."

"OK, I can take a hint – talk to you later." Susan went back to her desk.

Claire wasn't brave enough to go down to Michael's office to see if he was there. Her phone taunted her all morning to call his extension. She even picked it up once but put it back down when she remembered it wasn't possible to have a private conversation in the open-plan office. The memory of his face, the unarguable resolve, the unmistakable lack of emotion, should have been enough to make her accept it was over. But she couldn't help thinking that if he rang today, there was still some hope of forgiving him. She had thought the same all day Saturday and Sunday. The only phone call she had received over the weekend was from her mother. She didn't tell her what had happened.

"Do you want to grab some lunch with me?" Susan was back, determined to find out what was wrong.

Claire was prepared for her. "No, I can't. I still haven't finished this."

"Is everything OK? You don't seem yourself today . . ."

"Everything's fine . . . or at least it would be if I could get this done."

"Do you want me to bring you back some lunch?"

Claire didn't feel like eating. "Yeah, thanks. Just pick me up a sandwich, anything will do . . ."

It was a relief to leave at six thirty. Her head was

throbbing from the harsh glare of the computer screen. Engrossed in her work, she had had an ironically productive day, clearing most of her backlog. She had almost managed to keep thoughts of the weekend at bay. Now, as she left, the piercing cold stung her face and images came crashing into her consciousness. It was dark already, a severe frost glistening on the footpath. A miserable evening, matching her mood perfectly.

* * *

She struggled through the week. Michael didn't call. His only attempt at communication was an email, inviting her to the next project meeting. She didn't answer it. It was Mark who forced the issue.

"Aren't you coming to this meeting?" he asked, stopping by her desk on his way.

"I sort of forgot about it . . ." She reddened when she heard how lame her excuse sounded.

"Well, it's not too late – walk down with me."

She hesitated before getting up.

"I didn't know that you were going," she said.

"I asked Michael to invite me to the first few meetings so I can keep abreast of what's going on. This is the most important step forward that we've had in Finance since I joined Amtech. I want to make sure I can at least bluff about it when I need to."

She couldn't help laughing with him.

All the others were there, chatting while they waited. She was glad she had Mark to walk in with.

"OK, let's start," said Michael. "Thanks to everyone for coming along. We'll try to keep this under an hour – I appreciate how busy you all are." He looked and sounded relaxed. "As you all know, the first stage of the plan is the payables module. We've picked this because our current processes in that area are weak. We've already established, at our meeting last week, that we'll get an immediate benefit from implementing the module. I want to have a go at agreeing the roll-out schedule today." He made comfortable eye contact with each of the team members. Claire looked away when his eyes met with hers.

"I'd like to see Ireland first on the list. The project is being driven from here, after all," Mark said, briefly looking at Claire for her agreement. "How long would it take to get it up and running?"

"My best guess is three months, maybe four," Michael answered confidently. "We'd have a full complement of people on site to work on any glitches."

"Any suggestions for the next country after Ireland?" Mark asked. "Claire?"

"Um . . ." She could see him looking at her suspiciously when she reddened for the second time that day. "I dunno . . . maybe Australia . . . they are a medium-sized subsidiary, not too big or too small. And there's no language barriers."

After the meeting, she and Mark walked up the stairs together.

"You seemed preoccupied in there," he remarked.

"Yes, I was."

"Is there something I should know?"

"Can you take me off this project?" she blurted, stopping on the stairs.

"Why? Has something happened between you and Michael?" he asked, his voice suddenly kind.

"It's too close for me to talk about, Mark. I'll tell you at some point – just for now I need to get off the project."

"OK, I'll stand in for you in the interim."

She gave him a grateful smile.

* * *

Friday came with painful slowness and she was faced with being alone with her thoughts for the weekend.

"Are you coming to Maguire's with us?" Susan had her jacket on.

"Thanks, Sue, but I can't. I need to get up early tomorrow morning. I'm going to come to work to catch up on a few things." Working was a better alternative to being alone in the flat, looking at the box she had filled with his things. She had spent too much time already trying to figure out how she was going to return them to him.

"Come on! A drink will do you good. It will cheer you up. You can go home after one . . . that's not such a big deal, is it?" Margaret had joined Susan, bag on shoulder, lipstick gleaming, ready to leave.

"I . . ." Claire tried to resist but relented due to their

10

jointly formidable expressions. "OK so – just one, though."

Just like the previous Friday evening, Maguire's was buzzing with the high-spirited working population. Margaret expertly negotiated their way through the crowds, keeping an experienced eye out until some seats were available.

Claire drank quickly, keeping out of the conversation, anxious to get home before they started to interrogate her. She had her jacket in her hand, ready to leave, when Susan slammed another drink in front of her.

"Susan, I have to go home. I can't drink this . . . have it yourself." She pushed it away, standing up with purpose.

"Relax, for God's sake . . . it's Friday night," Susan said, pushing it back.

Not wanting to appear churlish, Claire sat down again, drinking obediently.

They had trapped her. Like a well-trained relay team, they ran to the bar each time she was ready to leave.

"Michael's dumped me," Claire divulged, several rounds later.

"We guessed. Look, it's an awful thing to happen but you're better off without him."

Claire didn't expect Susan's clumsy hug and spilt some of her drink down her front. When they stopped laughing, she asked, "Why am I better off?"

"He was too . . . well . . . boring." Margaret said and immediately looked as if she regretted being so honest.

"Yeah, he was," Susan agreed. "That would have annoyed the hell out of you if you had got married. There are much more interesting men than Michael out there . . . look around you." She leered at a group of males nearby to prove her point and earned a communal laugh.

"I never knew you thought that about him."

"I know – you'll probably never speak to us again if you get back together with him." Susan made a face.

"I'm never going to get back with him . . . he has a new girlfriend."

"What? Already? Get this girl another drink," Margaret barked at John, the office junior. He jumped up, too scared to question her authority even outside work.

"Do you know her?"

"No, Karen somebody." Claire covered her face with her hands. "How was I so stupid to get involved with somebody I work with?"

Her question was met with damning silence from the group. She became conscious of the roar of voices around them. It occurred to her that Michael might be amongst the crowd.

Margaret saw her looking around and asked, "Have you seen him since last weekend?"

"Just at the project meeting on Wednesday . . . he looked as if he hadn't a bother on him. I've barely moved from my desk in case I bump into him . . . sooner or later I'll run out of luck and I'll meet him . . .

if not at work, then at some pub . . . he might even be with her . . ."

"Yeah, Dublin can be a small place and working with him doesn't help. Hopefully he'll have the good grace to keep a low profile."

"I don't think he sees the need to keep a low profile. He was perfectly calm on Wednesday whereas I was a mess. I've asked Mark to take me off the Oracle Upgrade Project. I know it's not very professional of me to let my personal life affect my business life, and Mark must think I'm pathetic, but I really can't face Michael."

"Don't worry about Mark – he'll understand where you're coming from," Susan said, finishing her drink and wondering where on earth John was.

Claire scanned the crowd again. Michael was tall, he would stand out. She only saw John as he returned with the drinks.

"I bet that Karen will dump him after a few weeks anyway, then he'll be a sorry bastard. But you're not to take him back when he comes crawling." This advice was from John, carrying four glasses in his big hands. Working closely with three females had made him an honorary girl and entitled him to give advice.

"I feel like running away." Claire didn't want to be always on edge like this, always looking for Michael in the crowd.

"Go on a holiday – when you come back you'll be able to cope better," Margaret suggested.

"I need more than a holiday . . . I need a permanent solution. There's no way I can continue to work at Amtech while he's there . . . and I'm sick of Dublin anyway."

"Claire, you're young, the world's at your feet – there's nothing stopping you from going to England or America," Margaret said, her voice now serious.

"You're my supervisor, you're not meant to be trying to get rid of me!"

"True, I forgot myself for a minute," Margaret laughed.

They put her in a taxi, their prolonged goodbyes and hugs annoying the impatient taxi-driver. She collected her mail on the way into the flat. Her credit-card statement, her phone bill and a letter from Fiona. From Australia. She hadn't seen Fiona since she moved to Sydney last year. Claire wondered now why she and Susan hadn't gone with her at the time.

She got into bed and opened the letter. It wasn't eloquent; it was basic and blunt, just like Fiona herself. There was a photograph enclosed, Fiona at Ayers Rock. The red earth looked fake. Fiona's brown hair was tied back in a pony-tail that was blowing in the wind. Her freckled face had an underlying tan. She was laughing.

Claire turned out the light, lying on her back, staring into the darkness.

I'll get through this. A few months and I'll feel normal again. It's only been a week. Her eyes became accustomed to the dark. The faint light seeping in from under the blinds outlined the main objects in the room and it felt eerie and lonely. She turned the light back on, feeling foolish.

He's probably out with her tonight. Sooner or later I'm going to meet them together . . . he'll have his arm around her . . . I need to get out of Dublin ...

She had a fitful sleep, images of Fiona, Michael and outback Australia intertwined.

* * *

Whilst other software companies struggled with the harsh challenges that the 90's presented, Amtech Corporation had significantly increased its market share and was placed fifth largest company in the software industry. In the twenty years since its incorporation, there were just three years it had reported a loss. The company attributed its success to an aggressive acquisition policy and an impressive retention programme for its employees. It boasted a board of directors where the newest member had been on the board eight years.

Donald Skates had been the CEO for almost twelve years. He held the record for the longest-standing CEO in Silicon Valley, the fickle IT capital of the world. He had been with the company when it had only one hundred people. It was now the proud employer of ten thousand people across forty-nine countries. In some ways, the real secret of Amtech's success was Donald's conservative streak. It was a differentiating characteristic in an impulsive industry and it went down well with large Government and Financial Sector customers who felt safe in the hands of a risk-adverse company. Amtech resisted pressure to conform to other popular trends in IT, such as casual dress and flexitime but it still made the grade as an Employer of Choice.

Amtech Ireland, the largest international subsidiary of Amtech Corporation, had a prime location in Ballsbridge, Dublin. It was the only location outside San Jose where software development, manufacturing and user manual translation were all performed on the same site. Reasonable labour costs, generous grants from the Irish government and easy access to Europe were some of the factors that had encouraged the board of directors to open the plant eight years earlier.

It was a modern building, the smooth white walls and black-tinted windows at odds with the old Georgian houses in the district. Most other IT companies in Dublin were located in the outer suburbs and Amtech had the choice of skilled employees due to its convenient location. The current headcount was approximately one thousand but the company expected the number to increase by thirty per cent when it released a significant upgrade to its main product, a human resources information system, at the end of the year.

Claire had been one of two graduate accountants employed in 1997, Susan was the other. In the four years she had progressed from trainee to financial accountant. Amtech Ireland was a fast-moving company and opportunities were frequent, even for those who weren't overly ambitious. Her progress had been easy, cushioned by competent colleagues and 'best practice' standards.

She liked her job and a sizeable portion of her social life was tied up with work. If her world had remained stable, it would never have occurred to her to use Amtech's international presence as a means of travelling overseas. She felt suddenly ashamed that it had taken a personal disaster to make her question the routine of her life.

When she went in on Monday, she turned a blind eye to her brimming in-tray and connected to the *Employee News* section of the Amtech homepage. She got into 'Vacant Positions' and was surprised by the number of roles advertised. There were roles in countries she didn't even recognise. She used the Search function to select Finance Management positions only. Her search yielded three hits: two roles in San Jose and one in Sydney, Australia. She skimmed through the role descriptions, skills and qualifications for each. She knew before doing this that she would choose Sydney.

She felt nervous as she knocked on Mark's door. He beckoned her to enter when she opened the door slightly to see if he was free. His phone rang as she sat down and she studied his boyish face as she waited for him to finish. Only thirty years old, he was well-positioned on the corporate ladder but the undoubted stress that came with his position had left no visible marks on his smooth face. He had been Finance Director for two of the four years she had worked at Amtech Ireland. He was a popular boss with his staff, talented and sharp but with a healthy sense of humour.

"Miss Quinlan, what brings you to my office at such an early hour of the morning?" He grinned at her as he put the phone down.

"I've seen an internal advertisement for this role in Sydney that I want to talk to you about . . ." she said bluntly, putting a printout of the ad on his chaotic desk.

"Oh . . ." He seemed taken aback, the grin slipping from his face.

"Sorry, Mark, I should explain myself," she said as she recognised that she had started at the wrong place. "Look, you probably know by now that Michael and I have split up . . ."

He nodded.

"And, much as I try to be professional and not let it interfere with my job, the fact is that my world has turned upside-down and I don't have the ability to act as if nothing has happened when I see Michael at work."

"I understand," he nodded again. He sat back in his chair as he watched a variety of expressions chase across her face.

"So, either I leave Amtech and go to another company . . . or I see if Amtech are willing to transfer me . . . overseas," she concluded, relieved to notice that

Mark was looking much more receptive than he was earlier. He picked up the role description to read.

"It's undoubtedly a good career move for you, Claire, a promotion," he stated, his tone matter-of-fact.

"I thought you would approve." She smiled to take the edge off the atmosphere. "What do you know about Amtech Australia?"

"Well, they are quite a bit smaller than Dublin as it's obviously a sales and marketing subsidiary and not manufacturing like we are. I think they have about three hundred people. I don't know Dan Fielding, the Finance Director, personally but I have heard only positive things about him and the subsidiary."

"Good. So will you support me if I apply for the role?"

"Yes, I will. I don't want to lose you from our team here but this seems like the lesser of two evils. Send Dan your résumé . . . I have a call with Robert Pozos tomorrow and I'll mention it to him then," he answered, looking tired as he picked up his substantial pile of morning mail.

Robert Pozos, based in San Jose, was the Senior Vice-President of Finance and a member of the Board of Directors. Claire knew that he travelled extensively but she had never met him. He and Mark had a good relationship and they spoke weekly. Claire was confident that Mark would pave the way for her as much as he could. The rest would be up to her.

She went back to her desk but found it hard to

concentrate so she wasted a few minutes surfing the net. She found a site on Bondi Beach and had difficulty suppressing a smile as she studied the vibrant pictures. Fiona lived close to Bondi.

* * *

She shut the door behind her and sat down before dialling the Sydney number. Her interview with Dan was at eight – she had five minutes to go. The screen came alive with the image of the room in Sydney. There was a long board table. The curtains were drawn to block out the sunlight. Her own image was in a small box on the bottom left of the screen. She self-consciously fixed her hair and when she saw how slow and obvious her movements were on screen, she reminded herself not to fidget throughout the interview. While she waited, she read through a copy of the résumé that she had sent to Dan. She looked up to see a blurred male figure move jerkily across the room until he was seated. It was hard to see his features but his hair was white. He was older than she expected.

"Good morning, Claire." His smile was friendly.

"Good evening, Dan."

"It's nice to meet you at last. Thanks for agreeing to this interview at such short notice."

"It's no problem. I'm very keen to pursue the opportunity and thank you for considering me," she said, making an early pitch to show her enthusiasm for the role.

"Claire, I'll start by giving you some background information on the position. The incumbent is leaving at the end of this week to take on a new role in San Jose, under Robert Pozos. We're looking for a good generalist, with proven operational ability in financial accounting, treasury, taxation and customer proposals." He paused deliberately to allow Claire to respond.

"Dan, I believe I can demonstrate effective skills in each of those areas. Tax may be a bit of a challenge, given that I am not familiar with the local legislation – however, income tax principles tend to be fairly standard in most countries these days."

Dan adjusted his position in his seat before speaking. She could see his lips move but it was a few moments before the sound of his voice reached her end.

"I agree, tax should not be an insurmountable problem. We have advertised the role externally. However, it is our preference to have an internal candidate over an external one. It would be a much smoother transition for us if we found an existing employee who would be familiar with Amtech's policies and procedures."

"Have you had many external applicants?" She hadn't considered the possibility of competition for the role she had set her heart on.

"Yes, but none of them jump out at me . . . Claire, I've been through your résumé in detail and have talked to Robert Pozos about your role and performance in Dublin. I am not going to make this interview too laborious as I have a lot of positive and reliable information that most interviewers don't have about the candidate they are interviewing. So, why don't we just have a chat . . . you tell me about you and then I'll tell you about me."

Their chat lasted an hour.

When she turned off the video, she sat down to make some notes:

4 Direct Reports – Financial Accountant, Accounts Payable, Payroll, Credit Control.

General Manager – Steve Ryan.

Sales Director – Frank Williams.

HR Director – David Di Gregario.

20% growth in revenue over last year. Increased opportunities in outsourcing of Application Software Support.

External Auditors – average audit report at year end. Concerns with some balance sheet accruals and accounts payable controls.

* * *

Susan was walking along the corridor when Claire opened the door.

"So, that's where you've been all morning . . . Who did you have the video conference with?" she asked, peering into the room and obviously disappointed to find the video switched off.

"I can't really tell you at the moment, but all will be revealed soon. Do you want to come around for dinner and a glass of wine Saturday night?"

"Only if you tell me what's going on."

"With some luck, I'll have something to tell you by then. Prepare to be shocked."

Claire laughed as she left Susan in the agony of her natural nosiness.

* * *

On Saturday night she opened the door to Susan whose face was red from the icy cold.

"Have I told you that you are a heartless bitch for leaving me in suspense like this?" Susan was bearing a paper-wrapped bottle that was very likely to be white wine.

"Yes, a number of times."

"Stop teasing me. Just tell me, please, before I die of curiosity!"

Claire laughed. "OK, I can't bear to keep it to myself any longer anyway. I'm going to Sydney," she said triumphantly.

"You're what?" Susan was flabbergasted. "How?"

"I applied for a Finance Manager's role there. It was advertised in *Employee News*. I had an interview with Dan Fielding on Wednesday and he called me yesterday to tell me that the job was mine, if I wanted it."

"Really?"

"Yes, really! I'm so *excited!* I'm going to *Sydney!*" She did a little dance around the kitchen.

"Wow, you've knocked me for six. I didn't think you were serious about leaving Dublin . . . and all this since last week – you haven't wasted any time, I'll say that."

Susan hadn't taken off her heavy winter coat. She still hung onto the bottle of wine. She did indeed look stunned.

"I just want to get away from Michael and everybody who knew us as a couple. I know that this might seem a drastic solution but it's perfect. The change will be good for me. It's time for a revolution, Susan!"

"I'm really happy for you but I'm going to be so lonely without you here. And I'll be so jealous of you and Fiona having fun in the sun while I'm stuck at home in the miserable cold . . . where's your damn wine-bottle opener?"

They opened the wine. "Mark and Margaret are going to miss you. We're *all* going to miss you," Susan said, moving cushions to make herself comfortable on the sofa.

"Mark's been great. It's his connections that got me the job. He's pretty close to Robert Pozos and it seems that Robert gave Dan Fielding all the assurances he needed. There was very little for me to do."

"Are they going to pay your relocation costs?"

"They'll pay my airfare and my living expenses for the first four weeks."

"That's a pretty good deal." Susan was looking thoughtful as she swirled the wine in her glass. "You know, I get the impression that Mark might be extending his responsibility outside Ireland and he'll be happy to have you as someone to rely on in Australia."

"What do you mean? Do you know something I don't?"

"Mark's been on a lot of calls with the US lately and he's more involved in the Oracle Upgrade than you would expect. It wouldn't surprise me if they made Ireland some kind of international headquarters for IT and Finance with Mark at the helm. The upgrade will bring a lot of synergies – it would make sense to centralise some of the functions. It would be great if I could somehow wangle a business trip to Sydney . . . I know I'm fantasising, but indulge me."

The wine was an Australian Chardonnay, from the Hunter Valley.

"I'm going to go there," Claire declared, pointing at the wine bottle.

"Where?"

"The Hunter Valley. I remember Fiona saying it's just outside Sydney."

"I bet you and Fiona have been making all sorts of cosy plans for the good times you're going to have without me," Susan retorted with pretend jealousy.

"Actually, I haven't told her yet that I'm coming . . . let's call her now and tell her to start planning my arrival party!"

Grinning, she dialled the number without more ado. It rang and then she heard a muffled "Hello?".

"Fi, it's me, Claire!" she shouted unnecessarily in her excitement.

"Claire?" Fiona sounded disorientated and Claire

remembered the time difference. It was early morning in Sydney.

"Oh, sorry, I didn't mean to get you out of bed. Guess what?" she squealed.

"What?" Fiona asked with a loud yawn.

"I'm coming to Sydney! I'm getting a transfer with Amtech! Isn't it great? Can I stay with you when I get there?"

"Of course you can. Hey, that's really great news ... even worth waking me up for. When are you coming?" Fiona asked, sounding more sprightly.

"January, provided my business visa comes through by then."

"Hey, that's only a few weeks away!"

"As far as I'm concerned, the sooner the better! I can't wait to get out of here," Claire said, a hint of despair seeping into her tone.

"Why? Has something happened?" Fiona asked with immediate concern.

"Yes, but it's a long story and I don't want to ruin my good mood right now. Susan is here. She wants to talk to you."

Claire handed the phone to Susan who had been hovering impatiently. The three of them had been inseparable through their college years. It would be great to see Fiona again.

CHAPTER TWO

Julia's first marriage had been perfect. Perfect until the day Josh announced he wanted out, two years before.

It had been a Sunday morning. She had woken to find him lying on his back, staring at the ceiling.

"What are you thinking so hard about?" She smiled sleepily at him, reaching over to touch his bare chest.

"Just that I can't do this any more . . ." he answered, his eyes squinting slightly but still focussed upwards.

She leaned over him and kissed him lightly on his lips. "Can't do what? Sleep with a woman as sexy as me?"

He didn't laugh. "Live this stale existence." His voice was unmistakably abrupt. She tried to shake off the remaining shreds of sleep so she could catch up with what was happening in his mind. Something was terribly wrong. His face was so grim that she instinc-

27

tively moved away to put some distance between them.

"Is something wrong at work?" she asked, adjusting the pillows so she could sit upright.

He was still lying down. "I'm jacking it in. I've had enough. I want to go to Europe."

"But you love your job . . ."

"I've hated it for years . . . how observant of you to notice." He turned towards her, his eyes accusing. There was something akin to hatred written on his face and it stunned her into silence for a few moments.

"Honey, if going to Europe is important to you, then we'll do that," she said with difficulty. "We can rent the house out for a few months." She had never been outside California for more than a week. She loved their house in Palo Alto and would hate to leave it for an extended time.

"No, Julia, I need to get away from you too," he said coldly.

Her face flushed with shock. "You don't mean that . . ."

He shrugged.

"OK, if you want a holiday without me, I'm disappointed, but I'll support you in whatever you want to do," she said finally.

"You're not getting it," he said bluntly, throwing back the duvet to get out of bed. "It's not a holiday. I'm going to Europe permanently. And I don't want you with me."

She turned her head from his nakedness. She heard

the rattle of his belt as he pulled on his jeans. He opened the door and left her alone in their bedroom.

* * *

He was in the kitchen when she came downstairs, making his breakfast. Her face flamed from crying and she hung her hair so that he wouldn't see as she entered the brightness of the room. The kitchen faced the morning sun.

"You're obviously stressed about something . . . this just isn't like you . . . maybe you're suffering from depression . . . lots of people do without knowing it . . . you should see a doctor," she said, her voice soothing, putting a forgiving hand lightly on his arm.

He pushed it away. "You haven't listened to a word I said, have you? I'll spell it out again!" he yelled, his face red with immediate anger. "I'm out of this country, this marriage . . . I know what I want from life and I don't need any damn doctor telling me different!"

"Please, Josh . . . you can't just throw away ten years like that," she begged, raising her own voice in desperation.

"Just *shut up . . . shut up!* You're making it worse for both of us!"

He slammed the door and the calendar on the back jerked from its hook. She picked it up absently and put it back on the door.

* * *

They didn't speak for a few days. He moved into the

bedroom downstairs. The only place she saw him was in the kitchen. His expression was so ferocious that she couldn't find the courage to start a conversation of any kind. She convinced herself that silence was much better than damning words.

He looked slightly more approachable when she got in from work on Friday. She smiled at him nervously, hoping he had come to his senses.

"We must put the house on the market," he said.

She stared at him, totally bewildered about how this nightmare had started. Josh had been the one who wanted to get married straight after graduation. He had been the one who carefully planned their future. Now he was the one who wanted to sell their beautiful house.

"But I don't want to leave here . . ." Her tears were instantaneous. She let them drip unchecked down her face – they stained the white collar of her shirt.

"Buy me out then," he answered, his voice bursting with impatience.

"I don't have the money . . . you know I don't." She stared at him, her red eyes begging him not to make this final decision.

"Well, then, there's no other option but to sell . . ." He moved away from her stare to the other side of the room.

"That doesn't seem fair. It wasn't my choice to end this relationship so why should I suffer?"

He strode back towards her, his well-toned body

shaking with fury.

"Look . . ." He pointed his finger so it almost touched her face. She stepped back from him and he dropped his hand, clenching it by his side.

"Look . . . I'm trying to be fair . . . but you should think who was working his ass off for the last few years while you dabbled in your nice easy job . . . you don't deserve half of the house so consider yourself lucky that I'm prepared to split the money with you!"

Something awful had happened to the kind generous Josh she had known for ten years. The man standing over her with hatred contorting his handsome face was a stranger.

* * *

Julia would have moved out if she had somewhere to go. It was a harsh way to discover she had no friends she could turn to for help. It took three months to sell the house. At first she prayed for it to take as long as possible so Josh had time to change his mind. At the end, when he started dating other women, each day was more humiliating than the one before. She forced herself to work every morning and didn't venture outside her bedroom from the moment she got home. She found that she couldn't sleep. She tried sleeping tablets but they made her sluggish and even more depressed the next day. A colleague at work suggested she have a glass of wine in the evening to help her sleep. She didn't usually drink but she was desperate. Initially, she found that the wine did help her relax and she was able to get a few hours' sleep.

The house didn't sell for as much as Josh wanted, which gave him one more thing to be angry about. She was glad when a middle-aged man bought it. He was a small balding bachelor. She would have found it harder if it had been a couple. She was suddenly very conscious of being single. Everywhere she went she couldn't help noticing couples holding hands, kissing. She searched for ones that were arguing with each other but couldn't find any. Passing strangers on the street, she obsessively searched their fingers for the taunting gleam of a wedding band. She discovered there were very few single men around.

Josh didn't show the same interest in the furniture as he did in the house. She kept most of it and squeezed it into her new home, a small overpriced apartment in an ordinary suburb of San Jose. Tall miserable trees over-crowded the minuscule yard and kept the unit in perpetual shade. The carpet and walls were in good condition but were a depressing deep green. They made the unit even darker. She missed her bright spacious house where the furniture really belonged. It looked ridiculous in the pokiness of her unit. She wished she had sold it.

San Jose was busy and impersonal next to the sophis-ticated pace of life in Palo Alto and insomnia was still tormenting her. She wanted to escape to the peace that only sleep could offer but it continued to elude her. Thoughts of failure and inadequacy were only dimmed by the wine but each night she had to drink more and more before she finally passed out. Wine made her cry. She often wondered if her neighbours could hear her hysterical sobbing in the early hours of the morning. There was a young couple living in the unit next to hers; the other side was vacant. Julia kept out of their way. The few times she had seen them, they looked as if they were happy together. She resented their happiness.

She never thanked them for calling for help the night she finally broke down.

* * *

She saw him doing his rounds. She knew he was going to come and bother her with stupid questions.

"My name's Chris Duffy. I'm a psychiatrist here at the hospital."

He sat on her bed. His familiarity made her furious.

"I want to have a little talk with you . . . just for thirty minutes or so."

He paused for a moment to give her the opportunity to respond. She stared at him with as much hostility as she could muster. She didn't intend to make it easy for him.

"Right . . . Julia . . . what age are you?"

She sighed, folding her arms. "Thirty-three, if that's relevant."

"Who do you live with?"

"Nobody . . . my husband has left me . . . is that what you need to know?"

"You think he's the only reason you are here today?" His pale face was expressionless.

"Of course it is," she answered, her tone insolently impatient.

"You mixed some pills with liquor . . ." He checked his notes. She didn't comment.

"Do you do that often?" His green eyes were magnified behind his spectacles as they studied her.

"No ... I was trying something new."

"How much alcohol do you usually drink?"

"Just a few glasses of wine a day," she shrugged.

"Is it ever more than a few?"

"Yes, if I'm having a particularly shitty day," she snapped at him.

"So on a bad day, would it be as much as ten drinks?"

"Yes, I suppose it could."

"What's the most you've ever had?"

"I don't remember."

"Do you ever have difficulty remembering what happened the night before?"

"Yes, thankfully – I drink so I can forget. Loss of memory is exactly what I want in my life." She gave him a sarcastic smile.

"Do you drink alone?" His voice was a monotone, his eyes hopping from his notes to her face.

"Let me see . . . I live alone . . . I'm going to be divorced soon . . . how about you take a guess from that?"

He adjusted his position on the bed, crossing his legs.

"Did it ever occur to you that you might have a problem with liquor?" he said earnestly.

"No, it didn't . . . because I don't. I didn't even drink before my husband left me. I only drink wine so I can get some sleep. If there were any decent sleeping pills available I wouldn't need to drink."

"Judging by the alcohol we found in your blood, you must have had a lot of wine that night. We would normally associate that level of consumption with an alcoholic."

His accusation shocked her into a silence that only lasted a few moments.

"I don't really care what you think, Mr Duffy. I don't have any kind of dependency on alcohol. And to prove it, when I get out of here I'm going to give up drinking. Now, get off my bed. There are plenty of other people in this shit-hole that really do need a shrink. I'm not one of them."

He did as she requested.

* * *

"You look dreadful," Eleanor Newbury commented as she leaned across the bed to kiss Julia's cheek.

"Thanks, Mom, that makes me feel a lot better," Julia responded sharply, resisting the urge to tell her that the two-piece suit she was wearing was more suitable for a wedding than a hospital. Her mother looked well for her sixty-five years. She was fortunate enough to have an excess of both money and time to invest in her appearance. The Californian sun hadn't kissed her white skin in more than thirty years. She would never admit to the two face-lifts that kept her looking young.

"I'm just telling you the truth . . . do you want me to lie?" Eleanor pursed her reddened lips and sat down with a long-suffering sigh, resting her large handbag on the tip of her knees.

"One doesn't usually find a beauty parlour in a psychiatric hospital, Mom," Julia said with sarcasm.

"There's no need to be sarcastic! How can you expect to get your life back together if you don't make an effort with your appearance?" Indignation was written all over Eleanor's perfectly made-up face.

"Having a nervous breakdown is traumatic for most people. You don't just hop up and get on with life straight away . . ." Julia started to cry.

Eleanor moved uncomfortably in her seat. "Your psychiatrist says you may be an alcoholic."

"Don't tell me he has been on at you as well!"

"I'm only telling you what he said. I told him that you didn't drink when you lived at home."

"I don't want you talking to him. He's the one that needs a shrink. He's so off the mark with me that it's alarming."

"He said that denial is common in alcoholics."

"Mom, drop it. OK? Just drop it."

Eleanor obediently changed the subject. "Have you heard anything from Josh?"

"No . . . how would he know where to find me? Only

you and Dad know that I'm here . . . anyway, he's probably left the country by now." Julia leaned over to get some tissues and blew her nose loudly to annoy Eleanor.

"You got married too young . . . I always knew he wasn't right for you," Eleanor sniffed, patting her styled hair in fear that a strand had strayed out of place as a result of the unpleasant conversation.

"For God's sake, Mom . . . we had ten great years together . . . I can't help it if he woke up one morning with a premature midlife crisis!" Julia shouted in exasperation.

"People don't just change overnight – I always knew he was unreliable."

"And how exactly did you know that?" Julia asked with gritted teeth.

"Because he works in advertising, a fickle line of business," Eleanor stated with conviction.

Josh's integrity was the one thing Julia had always been sure of. Now it was open to question, just like everything about their life together.

"And you shouldn't have let yourself get into a position like that," Eleanor continued tactlessly. "You sacrificed everything for him . . . you had a good degree and you never used it."

Julia couldn't argue with her on that point. Her career had been making Josh happy, making his home life as undemanding and well-organised as possible so he could succeed at work.

"When I'm well again . . . I'm going to look for a better job . . . something that has potential," she promised, her voice subdued.

"That's wonderful, darling . . . you could meet a nice man in one of those big corporations . . . there's not a lot of suitable men out there, you know . . . and you're not getting any younger."

CHAPTER THREE

Claire's obligatory four weeks' notice flew by in a whirl of packing with the unwelcome interruption of Christmas. She spent it with her parents, her brother, his wife and their two children. She tried hard but couldn't help being depressed, haunted by memories of previous Christmases with Michael that she couldn't get out of her mind. Her mother was depressed because her daughter was leaving to live on the other side of the world with no planned date of return. Her brother was depressed because his children behaved like horrors. She escaped early, using work commitments as the feeble excuse.

* * *

Her last day was busy; she wanted to leave with a clear desk and a clear conscience. It was sometime after lunch when she turned around in her seat to find Michael standing behind her. It was six weeks since she had last seen him. He looked the same.

"Hi." She gave him a brief smile to show she was too busy to talk.

"Hi yourself."

She didn't intend to help him find the right words to fill the silence that followed.

"I just came around to wish you good luck."

"Thanks."

"Are you having a bon voyage party tonight?"

"Maguire's, straight after work. You're more than welcome to come." Her phone started to ring as she delivered the insincere invitation. "Hello, this is Claire speaking."

"Claire, this is Robert Pozos." He spoke slowly. His Californian accent wasn't strong.

"Oh, hello, would you mind holding a minute?" She put the phone down and turned to Michael.

"Sorry, I have to take this call."

"I'll see you later, then."

She picked the phone back up, her hand shaking slightly.

"Sorry about that, Robert. How can I help you?"

"I'm just calling to see if you are all set for the move," he said. She relaxed; he sounded nice.

"Yes, today's my last day. I'm a little nervous but really looking forward to it."

"That's good. And you've received your letter of offer from Dan?"

"Yes," she confirmed. "That came through last week

40

and I sent the signed copy back to him straight away."

"That's good. You were happy with the terms?"

"More than happy. Thank you for being so accommodating."

"It's no trouble. I'm glad that all is in order. I may be in Sydney later this year so I guess I'll see you then. Good luck."

"Thanks for everything." When she put the phone down she felt strangely emotional. Then she remembered Michael and knew why. She was glad that Robert had called when he did.

As she tidied her desk, she warned the girls not to blame all future problems on her as they usually did with other ex-employees.

"Remember, I'll still be working for the same company so any derogatory comments will get back to me," she said, her face stern as she looked at them.

"Who can we blame so? Now Mark will find out for sure how useless we all are," Susan complained.

"I think he knows by now how bad you really are," Claire answered as she skimmed through some paperwork before throwing it in the bin.

"I like your filing system," Margaret remarked.

"It's very liberating, throwing important documents in the bin. You should try it."

"Come on, Claire, finish up. It's party time. You don't work here any more," Susan said as Mark came out of his office.

"Can I have everybody's attention, please?" The hum

of conversation stopped and they gathered around Claire's desk.

"I think you will all agree that Claire is going to be sorely missed," Mark began. "I'm quite heartbroken to lose such a dedicated hardworking employee."

"You're embarrassing me," Claire grinned.

"He's lying through his teeth," someone shouted and everybody laughed.

"The positive side is that Amtech is not losing Claire and Australia is a great move for her, both personally and career-wise . . . Claire, we wish you all the luck in the world. We know you'll succeed with the role in Sydney. Just have fun while you do it and don't forget to stay in touch with us." Mark kissed her on the cheek and handed her a book of Aussie slang words.

"Thanks . . . I'll get great use out of this . . . I'm going to miss you all and of course I'll also miss the unpaid overtime, the bad weather . . ." She laughed even though she was close to tears. The sadness stayed with her as she handed in her security card and left the familiarity of Amtech Ireland behind.

Michael didn't go. She wasn't surprised. They stayed at Maguire's until midnight when they were physically escorted from the premises with the usual threat of being barred forever. They responded with the over-used complaint of not being able to finish their drinks in peace. Neither party meant a word of what they said and it would be all forgotten, only to be repeated again the next week. They huddled on the footpath, collectively shivering in the frosty January night. Susan took control of the indecisive mob by suggesting they go to a nearby club. It was just a short walk but somehow they lost half the crowd on the way. Claire was very drunk, too drunk to dance. She stood watching her good friends let their hair down on the dance floor, thinking how much she was going to miss them. Then she was crying, overcome with uncertainty about leaving Dublin.

"Claire . . . what's wrong?" It was Mark – she hadn't realised he had come to the nightclub.

"I'm making a terrible mistake . . . but I've paid for my flight . . . and given up my job . . . so it's too late."

"Don't be so stupid! Everyone here wishes they had the balls to do what you're doing. Me included," he consoled, squeezing her shoulders with his arm. "And I meant what I said earlier, Claire, about keeping in touch. I know we'll be talking about the Oracle Upgrade in a few months but don't hesitate to call if you need some advice – and it doesn't have to be work-related. Call if you just need to hear a friendly voice . . . or even the latest gossip. OK?"

"Thanks, Mark. That means a lot. Why are all decent men like you married?" she sniffed, wiping her wet mascara-smudged eyes with her hand.

He looked at her. She had lost quite a bit of weight in the last month and her dark blue eyes were too big in her pale face. She was tall, striking in her fitted top and not aware of the looks she got from the other men in the club. She didn't deserve to be hurt and he felt sorry for her.

"I know, we're a rare commodity. Come on, I'll get you a glass of water – that's the most decent thing any man can do for a woman in your condition," he said laughing.

They sat companionably on the floor and Claire fell asleep, oblivious to the grime that would forever ruin her Levis. He shook her awake when the club closed.

"Claire, we have to leave. Can you remember where you live?"

She looked at him blankly, through a sleep-and-alcohol-induced haze. Left with no alternative, he searched her handbag to find her address and her keys. He managed to get her home and left her to fall into bed, where she slept, fully clothed, until ten hours later.

* * *

Streaks of grey rain splattered the window as the plane began its lurching descent into Sydney. She felt cheated. She had left Ireland in a wintry sunshine, and rain was the last thing she had expected at the end of her journey. Her eyes were bloodshot and her face drawn from exhaustion. The emotional goodbyes at Dublin airport and an uncontainable sense of anticipation had prevented her from relaxing enough to sleep.

The pilot impatiently circled Sydney until the early-morning curfew ended. Judging by the queues in customs, several planes must have landed within seconds of each other. Her luggage was amongst the last pieces to be loaded onto the carousel and she was tired and grumpy as she made her way out to the arrivals lounge.

Fiona was the first person she saw. She looked tanned and Claire concluded to herself that the sun must shine in Sydney after all. Excitement beamed across Fiona's face as she waved frantically before barging through the crowds to give her an enthusiastic hug.

"Not too close, Fi – I haven't washed in thirty-six hours!" Claire gave her a weary smile.

"It's great to see you, smelly or not!"

"It's good to see you too! I'm so happy to be here – I'm dog-tired but very happy."

"Come on, Den's parked in a five-minute drop-off zone, so we'd better hurry," Fiona said and picked up Claire's suitcase with enviable energy.

Den was Fiona's ex-boyfriend. He jumped out of the car to greet them, oblivious of the glares of the parking attendant who was pointedly looking at his watch. A huge smile split his red beard in two and his matching hair brightened up the dreary morning. His car was the most ancient vehicle Claire had ever seen, an enormous sickly green Ford Falcon that had to be thirty years old. They drove through the eastern suburbs with Marvin Gaye's "Sexual Healing" blaring from the battered radio. It seemed an inappropriate song for so early in the morning and it didn't help her feel less disorientated.

Fiona and Den shared an apartment in Bondi, located

down a narrow sidestreet where securing a park was an impossible feat. Den dropped them off outside before setting off on 'Mission Impossible'. The apartment was small and bright. The walls were startling white and the timber floors gleaming. The clean smell of polish hinted that Fiona had gone on a cleaning spree in honour of Claire's arrival. There was a large balcony, bigger than the unit itself, and if you leaned right over the left-hand corner you could see the beach. Claire was to sleep in the sun room.

"I didn't realise that you were still living with Den," Claire said as she sat down on the fold-up bed.

"It makes sense at the moment. It's convenient for both of us," Fiona answered, dropping Claire's case with a thud before joining her on the bed.

"But hasn't it been a few months since you broke up?"

"Nearly three. We're still really good friends and I like him staying here. I would miss him terribly if he moved out."

"He seems like a really nice guy. Perfect for you."

"He was perfect in many ways," she said, regret obvious in her voice. "He's great fun and very bright. Would you believe that he's a corporate lawyer?"

"Really?" Claire asked with surprise.

"I know. It's hard to believe when you see how he dresses . . . and his car. It's amazing he's not disbarred for having a car like that," Fiona laughed.

"I don't know how you do it . . . I could never see

myself living with Michael as a friend," Claire said, her expression sombre.

"What happened between you two?" Fiona asked, also becoming serious.

"I don't really know. When we broke up, he was seeing someone else but obviously something wasn't happening for him for some time before that."

"And you had no idea?"

"Absolutely none. We were in Maguire's after work that night and I thought we were having a great time. He waited the whole night, until we were on our way home, before dropping his little bombshell. I was a little bit tipsy and it took a while for what he was saying to sink in."

"Did you see him after that?"

"Only a few times . . . Enough of Michael, tell me about Sydney."

They sat on the bed for a few hours, chatting, laughing, reminiscing. Eventually Claire relaxed enough to feel sleepy and Fiona left to do some grocery shopping.

* * *

When she woke it was dark outside. If it hadn't been for her bed shaking from the stereo vibrations, she suspected she would never have woken again. Dishevelled and still half-asleep, she wandered out to the living-room. Den and Fiona were sitting on the floor, playing cards, surrounded by empty beer bottles and a cloud of smoke.

"Cute pyjamas," Den commented. "I've always liked Mickey Mouse."

"Thought you'd be too tired to go out on the town tonight so we'll have our own little party here instead," Fiona said, standing up unsteadily. "What would you like to drink?"

"I'll have a beer, although my body is telling me that it's morning and it's immoral to start drinking so early in the day," Claire said, shaking her head in bewilderment as she sat down on one of the beanbags.

Den turned the music up louder. "We were keeping it down for your benefit," he explained.

Claire nodded as if she fully agreed the volume had been far too low and took a healthy swig of her drink.

"What's this beer?" she asked, as she looked curiously at the label on the bottle.

"VB, darl. Good old Victoria Bitter, best beer in the world," Den replied in an exaggerated Aussie drawl.

"You know what? It's great to be in Australia! Cheers!" Claire said, raising her beer bottle to clash it noisily with his.

* * *

It was 6.00a.m., a ridiculous hour to be wide awake. Her head was directly under the window and she moved the curtain so she was looking up at a perfect blue sky. She sighed with relief that the torrential rain of the previous day had disappeared. She got up and had a long shower before putting on a pair of shorts and T-shirt. Looking out her window, she could see that their tiny street was stirring with traffic and pedestrians. She wrote Fiona a brief note to tell her that she was going out. The blinding sun forced her back inside after two minutes to get a pair of sunglasses. One didn't have much need for sunglasses in Ireland so it was an understandable oversight.

She walked the whole length of Bondi Beach, breathing in the sea air, letting it clear her cluttered mind. Despite the early hour, the beach was alive with surfers, joggers and even some volleyball players. She drank it all in, the vivacity infectious.

I can't believe I've got all this practically on my doorstep. I can even come here every day after work, she thought as she sat on the beach, toes curled in the sand, looking at the crashing surf. After an hour, feeling stiff from sitting for so long, she walked to the main strip, bought a Sunday paper and had breakfast at one of the multitude of outdoor cafes.

Arriving back at the flat just after nine, she was disappointed that Fiona still wasn't up. Unable to restrain her impatience, she knocked gently on Fiona's bedroom door.

Fiona sat up and grunted something that could have been "Good morning."

"Sorry . . ." Claire said meekly. "I've been awake for ages and I'm dying to get out to see everything. Do you reckon Den will take us out in the car?"

There was a movement in the blankets and Den's head appeared as if from nowhere.

"Sure thing, babe. Just give me a minute," he said and gave a loud unselfconscious yawn.

Thankful she had at least knocked before barging in on them, she quickly backed out of the room, muttering something about them taking their time and not rushing on her account. She wondered if they had got back together or if it had been just a drunken indiscretion.

* * *

Just one hour later, the Ford Falcon was chugging across the magnificent Harbour Bridge. Claire sat in the front and Den, acting as tour guide, answered her constant stream of questions with good humour. Sydney was beautiful. The vast harbour, the protected bushland on the heads and the red rooftops all created a stunning backdrop for the city. They passed beach after beach, leafy suburb after leafy suburb until they reached Palm Beach and couldn't go any further. They went for a rowdy swim, with lots of splashing and squealing, before lying in the sunshine. Fiona had the foresight to pack a picnic and a bottle of wine. As Claire sat on the soft rug, her skin warm from the sun, her face glowing from the wine, she thought that life didn't get much better.

* * *

The following morning she restlessly tossed and turned for over an hour, willing herself to go back to sleep. She reluctantly got up, defeated.

Fiona was in the kitchen having breakfast.

"You're up early for someone who's meant to be on holiday," she said, without sympathy.

"Tell me about it. You look really good," Claire said with admiration. Fiona had always favoured an alternative style of dress and she didn't look like herself in the smart grey suit and the high-heeled court shoes.

"Everyone here gets pretty dressed up for work," she retorted defensively. "I'd better get going . . . here's my business card . . . you can ring me if you get lost."

* * *

It was an idyllic week. She continued to wake up early and used it to her advantage, spending the mornings sightseeing before it got too warm. Returning in the afternoon, she would have a leisurely lunch on the balcony before walking to the beach. By the end of the week she knew the city centre intimately and was an expert on the eastern suburbs public-transport system. Fiona and Den had the privilege of a cooked dinner every evening when they got in from work. She was so relaxed and content with life that she almost didn't mind returning to work.

It was ironic that she found it hard to get up early on Monday morning, the first morning that she had needed to. She spent over an hour getting ready, choosing to wear a dark navy suit, the short sleeves and short skirt showing off a light tan from a week of sunbathing. She brushed her hair back from her face; straight and almost black, it fell to shoulder length. Putting her bag on her shoulder, she gave her reflection one last critical look before leaving.

Rush hour was a new experience. Used to the leisurely pace of midday commuters, she was momentarily stunned by the crowds and how quickly they were moving. She wasn't skilled enough to actually secure a seat on the train and had to stand uncomfortably for the twenty-minute journey. Exiting at the North Sydney Station, she was almost half an hour early. She went for a cup of tea, sipping it nervously as she absently studied the parade of business people as they strode arrogantly past.

She walked into the reception of Amtech Australia at precisely one minute before nine, standing awkwardly as the receptionist answered a series of calls. Employees hurried past, throwing brief curious glances in her direction.

She introduced herself as soon as there was a lull in the incoming calls. "Hi, I'm Claire Quinlan. I'm starting today."

"Nice to meet you, I'm Audrey," the receptionist answered, giving a friendly smile. "Dan told me to expect you. Take a seat while I try to get hold of him."

She was reading the *Sydney Morning Herald* when Dan Fielding hurried out to the reception area. He was out of breath and his freckled face was flushed from exertion. With his shock of white hair and a multitude of soft wrinkles, it was impossible not to like him immediately. He shook her hand vigorously, almost painfully, and she followed him as he weaved his way through the open-plan workstations to arrive at his office. He invited her to sit at the meeting-table that was located in front of his large cluttered desk.

"When did you arrive in Sydney?" he asked, rummaging through the stacks of paperwork on his desk.

"A week ago. I've been sightseeing and sunbathing since. It feels strange to have to go to work – I got used to the good life," she said, smiling.

"Any problems settling in?"

"No, I'm staying with a friend and she's taken good care of me. Sydney is an easy city to get around."

"Well, I'm real glad you're here, Claire. I've been without a Finance Manager for three weeks now and I'm feeling the pressure. I'm sure that the rest of the team is too." He found what he was looking for and sat down across from her. "This is the organisation chart at senior management level only. I report to the General Manager, Steve Ryan," he indicated his name on the chart with his pen, "and this is a more detailed Org Chart for the Finance department. You will be my only direct report – everyone else reports to you. The team is a good one – most of the people have been with Amtech for a few years and know what they're doing."

"That's good to know. How close did you work with the previous Finance Manager?" She was trying to memorise the names on the chart.

"Very closely. In fact, I expect the Finance Manager to be very close to all the senior management team, giving day-to-day operational support while I handle the strategic side. I think Emma has done a reasonable job of getting the right reports to the senior managers but some things have fallen through the cracks and I think they'll all be very happy that you have started."

He showed her to her office. It was on the other side of the building and he introduced her to a few people they met en route.

"Doing this walk a few times a day is what keeps me fit. Well, here you are . . . not very big . . . and I'm afraid you don't have a view of the harbour." He peered out the tiny window to see if there was anything of interest.

"Don't worry. I love it," she said, putting her bag and the few pieces of paper she had acquired on the desk. "Where do the rest of the department sit?" She was impatient to meet her four direct reports.

"Just around the corner. Come on and I'll introduce you to everybody." He stood back to allow her to pass through the door in front of him.

The workstations were only a few steps away, as Dan had promised. Archive boxes were abandoned in every available corner, piles of filing stacked on most desks. The printer area was a total disaster zone with months of homeless printouts. Everybody, including Dan, seemed cheerfully unaware of the mess. He stopped to introduce Claire to a short robust girl who was knee-deep in paperwork.

"This is Emma, our Financial Accountant," Dan said,

casually leaning against one of the nearby filing cabinets as Emma stood up to shake Claire's hand. "Emma was presented with her ten-year service award last month. She started as a filing-clerk back in 1990 and has worked her way up to this position."

Claire guessed she was in her late twenties, but it was difficult to put an age to her serious face. Her eyes were wary and her smile was tight. Claire felt uncomfortable, sensing hostility but not totally sure.

Maybe she's just nervous and I'm being paranoid.

"Claire, meet James, our Accounts Payable Administrator. He gets up at six every morning for a surf and then comes in here for a sleep. Paying our vendors is just about the last thing on his mind!" Dan shook his head in despair.

James laughed, his even teeth perfect in his tanned face. His hair was bleached yellow-blond from the sun, his shoulders muscled under his pristine white shirt. Claire guessed he was very popular with the female contingent of Amtech.

"How could you say that, Dan?" he protested with a hurt expression. "I live for my work!"

Dan shot him a derisive look. "As you know, James, Claire has transferred from Amtech Ireland so she will be a great asset to us when the Oracle Payables upgrade comes around in a few months."

"I was only involved in the upgrade for a few weeks before I left," she said, thinking immediately of Michael.

"But you know all the right people, Claire. Those contacts will mean more than anything when we rip out our current process and implement the upgrade," Dan responded.

"I can't wait until my job is turned upside-down and inside out," James said, his expression not at all enthusiastic.

Faces, names and first impressions were churning in her head. Dan was oblivious to her disorientation, determined to squeeze an impossible number of introductions into fifteen minutes. She followed obediently as he made his way to a tiny woman with titian hair in a childish pony-tail. Her face was busy with light freckles, her youthful look contradicting the thick wedding band on her left hand.

"Now, Claire, this is Stacey, the most important person in the company, our Payroll Officer!" He smiled as he put a friendly arm around the woman. "Stacey is an efficiency freak. We tease her that she's got a Compulsive Obsessive Disorder. Oops!" He deliberately scattered some paperclips on Stacey's immaculate desk, his boyish grin disappearing when she threw her stapler at him. It hit the wall with a crash, leaving a noticeable dent. A few curious heads popped up over the partitions and the office erupted in laughter.

"Nice to meet you, Claire," Stacey said with a wide smile. "Don't take any notice of Dan – he's just a child who needs a firm hand."

"See what I have to put up with, Claire? My staff

have no respect for me. Stacey, make sure you deduct the repair bill for that wall from your salary!"

"Of course, Dan. I pay myself extra anyway so I can afford it."

Dan was laughing as he rested his hand on the shoulder of the middle-aged man who sat opposite Stacey. His back to the commotion, he had continued working despite the noise.

"Last but not least, our Credit Supervisor, Alan Harris. Alan has been with us six years. He has a dotted line of responsibility to Frank Williams the Sales and Marketing Director."

Alan's grey hair needed a cut and his shirt was barely tucked into his trousers. He had a very slight smirk on his face, as if he knew something nasty that she was yet to find out. He extended a limp sweaty hand for her to shake without rising from his seat. Obviously not keen to indulge in small talk, he immediately turned his back and resumed typing, stopping dead any potential conversation.

Maybe he's just very busy and I've caught him at a bad time, thought Claire.

Dan had a meeting to attend and he promised to call around later in the day to see how she was getting on.

She sat in the bare office, pretending to study the organisation chart, feeling like an intruder. It looked like Emma and Alan were going to be difficult and she wasn't sure how to manage them. They were both with the company a long time and she doubted if she could tell them anything they didn't already know. Maybe she was way out of her depth with the position she had taken on. Her negative thoughts were interrupted by a beep from her PC, indicating that there was a new message in her inbox. It was from Susan.

Hi Claire,

Did you get there OK? What's it like? Anybody interesting in the office? Work is boring without you. Mark and Margaret are interviewing for your replacement. We've been checking out the candidates as they've been waiting in reception. There's a gorgeous guy gone through to the second interview stage but Margaret says that a girl is the strongest candidate. I've seen her, she looks like a swot. The weather here is shocking – my car door was frozen with ice this morning. Write soon with all your news. I'm starving for some excitement in my mundane life.

Susan

Susan had perfect timing, even from the other side of the world. Claire typed a reply, happy to have something to do.

Hi there,

Great to hear from you! What are you doing at work at this hour of the night? Don't you have a life? I love Sydney. I did lots of sightseeing last week. Today is my first day in the office and I have just met my team – four people in total and some of them didn't seem too happy to see me. I guess no job is without its challenges. Just to make you jealous, the weather is beautiful and I go for a swim at BONDI BEACH every day (are you green yet?). Fiona hasn't changed a bit. She's still living with Den – he's a really nice guy. Say hello to everybody for me.

Talk to you soon,
Claire

Feeling more confident, she took a steadying breath and went in search of Emma. She looked very busy and Claire felt awkward interrupting her.

"Hello, Emma," she said, seeing the familiar Oracle background on Emma's screen. "Do you use Oracle for all your accounting?"

"Yes, but I don't believe we use it to the same extent as Ireland does. Our payables process is partially manual. I imagine the new upgrade should bring us up to the same level as the other subsidiaries," Emma answered, turning around.

"It will actually put you ahead of the other subsidiaries as Australia is second in line to Ireland for the implementation. I'm keen to get stuck in and have a look at the balance sheet – when would you be free to do a review with me?" She kept her tone light.

Emma checked her electronic calendar and Claire could see over her shoulder that her day was free of appointments.

"Sometime this afternoon?" Emma suggested, with

the slightest hesitation.

"Is two OK?" Claire said quickly, anxious to make a firm time.

"Sure."

Claire went back to her office, relieved that she had organised something to do in the afternoon. She printed off a trial balance from Oracle and spent the next two hours doing a top-level review, preparing a comprehensive list of questions for Emma. When she finished, she sent meeting invitations to each of her reports, setting up one-to-one sessions for that week. She asked each one to come prepared with a summary of their role and what their major issues were. Even though she was a little intimidated by Alan Harris, she decided to meet with him the next day. Once he and Emma were done, the rest would be easy.

She was glad to leave the office at lunch-time. It was almost thirty degrees outside and she took off her jacket. She hadn't been mentally prepared for the stress of starting a new job and was annoyed with herself for being caught off-guard. She sat on a bench in a nearby park with a sandwich and orange juice. The view from the park was spectacular, the blue sky meeting with the even bluer waters of the harbour, the sun making the water sparkle. The beauty of her surroundings calmed her. She was much more composed when she returned to the office.

The balance-sheet review went well. Emma seemed to be competent but she wasn't quite as experienced as

Claire had first thought. She spent three hours with her, shooting rapid questions, scribbling hurried notes. There was a mutual respect by the time the meeting was over. She could understand why Emma would be wary of a new boss, especially as she would work more closely with Claire than the others.

"Do you enjoy your job?" Claire asked, trying to make the meeting less formal.

"Yes, Amtech has been very good to me. I've come a long way here," Emma answered, her tone guarded.

"How long have you been a qualified accountant?" Claire continued, persisting with the conversation after a brief silence. Emma looked uncomfortable.

"Actually, I'm not. I never got around to doing the exams. I could kick myself. I couldn't apply for your job because that was one of the requirements." She gave an embarrassed shrug.

Claire appreciated her honesty and warmed to her.

"Yeah, it's funny how much emphasis companies place on qualifications when ability should be more important. Still though, you should consider doing the exams just to have that piece of paper."

"I guess you're right. What I really need is for someone to put pressure on me – I'm too lazy to motivate myself," Emma admitted, looking thoughtful.

"Why don't you bring in some information on the classes and we'll have a look at it together," Claire suggested.

It was five by the time she finished with Emma and

she was preparing to leave for the day when Dan reappeared.

"How's your day been?" he asked.

"Not too bad for a first day," she lied.

In truth she had found it long and difficult.

"I want to take you on a quick round of the executive area before you go home," he said, his hands in his pockets as he spoke.

The last thing she needed was the stress of meeting even more people. She hesitated for a second before summoning up what she hoped to be a genuine smile.

"OK then."

He waited for her while she shut down her PC and locked her office door.

She followed Dan into the office next to his own after he tapped lightly on the door. The nameplate declared the occupant to be *Steve Ryan, General Manager*. The plush navy carpet and large teak desk were impressive against the backdrop of the city view. Steve looked haggard and grey in the colour-rich room. He shook Claire's hand briskly.

"Good to have you on board, Claire. We've been without a Finance Manager for longer than Dan and I would like." His face was serious and unsmiling. "I was about to treat myself to a drink after a hard day. Would you both care to join me?"

He opened a plain teak door to reveal a well-stocked drinks cabinet and small refrigerator. He took out three crystal glasses without waiting for their consent. She didn't want a drink but didn't know how to say that as he poured a casual measure of bourbon into each glass before adding some ice cubes. His movements were smooth and efficient; he was obviously used to the routine of fixing drinks in his office. He handed the glasses to them and they had an undefined toast. He took a generous drink from his glass before setting it down by his phone so he could dial a number.

"Samantha, tell Frank and Brian we're having drinks in here if they want to come in."

They came within seconds, their eyes immediately questioning her presence.

"Claire, this is Frank Williams, Sales and Marketing Director," Steve said, stepping back to make the introductions. "And this is Brian Brooker, Services Director."

Frank was large, he towered over the others. His height helped disguise the weight he carried. He was obviously a man used to eating and drinking well. He nodded in her direction before going to the drinks cabinet to fix two extra drinks. Brian Brooker was of a smaller and slighter build. His face was a rounded boyish shape but it had deep age and laughter lines.

"Very pleased to meet you," he said, thrusting his hand out. "I've heard really good things about the services organisation in Amtech Ireland. Were you involved with that group when you worked there?"

"Yes, I did all the project accounting," she answered as she sipped the bourbon cautiously. "Our projects weren't very big, though. Largest one we ever had was a prime contract for a local council. It was about two million Irish pounds."

"That's very interesting – we've just signed up a project that sounds quite similar," he said thoughtfully. "It's quite a complex deal – I'd like to meet up with you to go through it as soon as you're settled in."

"No problem," she said with a smile.

Frank Williams joined them, handing Brian his drink.

"Of course, something has to be done about the sales commission that our reps earn for those projects," he said, his black eyes assessing her. "At the moment it's calculated on margin and that's outside the control of the reps. All other IT companies pay commission on revenue."

Claire laughed lightly. "You won't be able to get that one changed. Human Resources in San Jose set the commission plans and they are adamant that the same rules apply worldwide. You must admit that it doesn't make sense to pay commission if a project is losing money."

He didn't seem to like her answer, his eyes narrowing to black slits in his olive face. He terminated the conversation by turning abruptly to speak to Steve Ryan.

Brian Brooker looked as if he was trying to disguise a smile by sipping his drink. "Don't take Frank to heart," he murmured. "He gets upset when he can't manipulate people." Then he added, his voice loud enough for Frank to hear, "So, where are you staying in Sydney?"

"Bondi," she answered, embarrassed by Frank's behaviour. She hoped that Dan and Steve hadn't noticed.

She liked Brian and she stayed for another thirty minutes, speaking mostly to him. When she finally escaped into the fresh evening air, she felt flushed from the bourbon. Exhaustion had made it go straight to her head and it took her a few seconds to remember the direction of the train station. Dan had told her that she had met most of the senior management team with the exception of David Di Gregario, the Human Resources manager. He was away on overseas business for the week.

* * *

Alan Harris declined their first meeting, claiming he didn't have any free time all week. She rescheduled to Monday of the following week. She was furious when he cancelled the second meeting by sending a cowardly email only ten minutes before it was due to start. He obviously believed his schedule took priority over her plans for the day. She stared at his message, trying to decide the best way to handle the situation. If she let him get away with such behaviour now, she would have no hope of managing him in the future. She gave herself five minutes to calm down before striding determinedly to his cubicle.

"Alan, you can't keep cancelling the meeting – I want to do a detailed review of credit." Her voice was hard.

"You obviously don't know that I manage my own area and report directly to Dan," he said, not moving his eyes from his screen, his tone blatantly patronising.

"That's odd. On the organisation chart that Dan gave me, you report to the Finance Manager – not the Finance Director," she said, giving him a cold stare.

"That's just on paper … it doesn't reflect the way things really work," he answered, his voice loaded with hostility.

"Well then, I'll clarify the situation with Dan – just in case there has been a misunderstanding."

She felt several pairs of curious eyes watch her as she walked away. She resisted the temptation to go straight to Dan. She wanted Alan and the others to think that she had more important things to attend to.

She finally caught up with Dan in his office, much later in the day .

"Of course he reports to you. He reported to your predecessor as well … he never seemed to have a problem with that. Maybe he doesn't like having a female boss," he said with a small smile.

"That must be it," she smiled back.

"Do you want me to intervene?" he offered.

"No, thanks. I'll have to get used to dealing with him."

Alan was switching off his PC when she got to his

desk. She stood firmly in the way of his exit, raising her voice so the others could hear.

"I've talked to Dan and he has confirmed that you do indeed report to me. So, let's have the review first thing on Friday. That should give you enough time to get some information together. I want to see a list of the top twenty accounts over 90 days, details of what the issues are and who has been assigned to fix them." Without giving him time to reply, she swung around and returned to her office. Her hands were trembling. It was only her second week, very early to have a confrontation with one of her staff. There was a man she didn't recognise waiting outside her office.

"Claire?"

"Yes."

"Hello, I'm David Di Gregario, Human Resources Manager."

"Hello." She offered him her hand.

"I missed you when you started last week. I was in Asia."

"Yes, Dan mentioned you were away."

"How was your first week with Amtech Australia?"

"Quite challenging."

"I couldn't help overhearing your conversation with Alan," he said, giving her a supportive smile. "I think you handled the situation well."

"Thank you. I'll regard it as a learning experience."

He took a seat in her office.

"Dan said I should see you about these headcount

reports. They don't look right to me." He frowned as he looked at the reports in his hand.

"OK. I'll have a chat with Stacey to see how she extracted them. I'm not familiar with the payroll system yet but I believe she's a whiz. We should be able to sort out what's wrong pretty quick."

"Great," he said, handing her a printed document. "Now, I also wanted to give you this to sign. It's a confidentiality declaration. It's a standard document that all new employees sign."

"I had to sign one of these a few years ago when I started in Dublin. You know, Finance and Sales were regarded as the two groups that had access to the most confidential, and potentially dangerous, information."

"We're considering the possibility of asking staff to sign fresh declarations on an annual basis to remind them of the importance of confidentiality," David said as she scribbled her signature on the page.

He left after a few more minutes of idle chat and she locked up her office with relief.

CHAPTER FOUR

Julia and Robert had been married for over a year now. She had met him shortly after her divorce was finalised. She had secured a position in the legal department of Amtech, based on South Market Street with all the bustle of downtown San Jose. She didn't fully understand Amtech's niche in the IT world, but with over two thousand employees based at head office, she had the potential to meet some friends. She didn't know that she would work in Amtech for only six months.

She had first seen Robert at a company function. He was at the bar, his handsome face creased with an alluring frown. He appeared to be alone. She abruptly terminated her conversation with a balding, hopeful colleague and approached the bar.

"Do you have a light?" she asked, her tone cool. This

man held a position of power in the company. It wasn't only his expensive suit that bespoke an executive salary, there was an impenetrable aura of confidence that could only be possessed by a decision-maker.

He lit her cigarette without speaking. She inhaled, sitting gracefully on the bar stool.

"You look bored."

"My wife couldn't come and everyone seems to be engrossed in conversation with their partners," he replied, a hint of anger in his voice.

"I know what it's like. I'm here on my own too," she said, arching her back seductively as she exhaled the smoke. She smiled at him but didn't meet his eyes. If she looked into his eyes he would know she was flirting, by avoiding them he couldn't be sure. It was a tactic she had used when she was single, before she met Josh.

Robert made a move to walk back to his table.

"Why didn't your wife come?" she asked suddenly, trying to stop him from leaving.

"Well, if you really want to know, we had a huge argument last night and we haven't spoken to each other all day," he said harshly. "I couldn't remind her that this was on because she wouldn't talk to me."

Julia was delighted. She loved to hear about other people who had relationship problems. It made her feel less of a failure.

"Serves her right then," she laughed.

"I guess it does," he agreed with a reluctant grin.

He looked at her properly. She was very attractive. Her black sequinned dress showed off a good figure, too thin by some men's standards but not by his. Her blonde highlights were a refreshing change from his wife's dark hair. He had been sitting with Wayne and Cherie all night, the conversation dominated by tales of their children. Fond as he was of them, he needed a break.

"I haven't seen you around before," he commented, sitting down, his knees brushing hers.

"I've only been with the company two weeks. My name's Julia, by the way." She extended her hand to shake.

"Robert Pozos."

"Nice to meet you, Robert."

"You don't seem to have a drink, Julia. Can I buy you one?"

She hesitated. She hadn't touched an alcoholic drink since the night her neighbours called the ambulance. She could still feel the shock when the shrink at the hospital asked if she had a problem with liquor. That was three months ago now. She had proved the shrink wrong. She had proved she could give up alcohol whenever she wanted. Right now, she wanted a few social drinks with this man. He didn't look like the soft drink type.

"Yes, a vodka and coke, thanks."

An hour passed before he confirmed he was a vice-president of the company. Most men would have gloated about their self-importance within minutes. Robert only revealed his position in answer to a direct question. Her attraction to him was real and tangible. She wasn't good at being single and had been looking for someone like Robert Pozos since the divorce. They stayed at the bar, chatting casually. The vodka tasted very different to wine but she recognised the glow. She was relieved that she was able to drink slowly; there was no urge for a second drink. She was in control. The shrink was wrong.

Robert was embarrassed when Wayne and Cherie came over to say goodnight.

"I've been incredibly rude. I apologise . . . I didn't realise it was this late," he said, jumping to his feet. "Julia, this is Wayne and Cherie, very good friends of mine."

There was a flurry of handshakes and politely murmured greetings. Julia liked Cherie immediately – she looked homely and unthreatening. They exchanged pleasantries for a few minutes before Wayne and Cherie left.

"Nice people," she remarked.

"I've known them for years," he answered, absently looking at his watch.

"I suppose we should make a move too, before we are thrown out."

They drained their glasses in one simultaneous sleek movement.

Julia shivered in the cool night air and he put his

arm around her.

"Would you like to come back to my place for a coffee?" she asked quietly, mentally taking a deep breath while she waited for his answer.

The idea of not going home that night appealed to Robert. It would be a suitable revenge on Dianne.

"Why not?" he said, his tone casual. "The night is still young. Where do you live?"

"It's about a fifteen-minute walk, but we can get a cab if you like," she answered, eager to please him.

"Let's walk – I could do with the fresh air."

They didn't speak as they walked. His arm was still around her, his fingers caressing her bare shoulder. His hand slipped inside her dress. Their pace got faster.

* * *

Shutting the door behind them, she turned to face him in the darkness. He was a shadow as he moved silently towards her. He kissed her roughly, his beard making her face tingle. She stepped backwards until her back was rigid against the door. His hands were in her hair, tilting her head, straining her neck as his lips moved down from hers. She didn't feel him pull the zipper on her dress. It fell smoothly to her ankles. She stepped out of it, giving a delicate kick so it slid across the tiles. She wasn't wearing a bra and her breasts were white in the blackness of the hallway. His hands cupped them, raising them to his mouth. She responded by opening his belt, his trousers falling to the floor. She moved her G-string to one side and the door rattled as he fucked her against it. She smiled when she thought of her neighbours. He wasn't gentle with her but she didn't mind. She sensed she would have to act quickly with Robert if she was going to have any chance at success. She didn't want to give him time to think about the wife he wasn't talking to.

* * *

Donald Skates hosted a dinner party every year for his senior management team. The CEO of Amtech Corporation lived with his second wife, Lisa, in a large, Mediterranean-style house in Palo Alto. A few years ago, Donald's first wife had tragically died of cancer after twenty-five years of marriage. Her death had affected him badly and for a few months he teetered on the edge of a breakdown. He would never know that the board of directors came very close to firing him. He had been more surprised than anybody when he fell in love with Lisa, who had been his loyal PA for almost ten years. She helped him save his sanity and dignity and he soon regained the board's confidence.

Julia didn't tell Robert that she had lived in Palo Alto with Josh. Coming to the party had rattled her new confidence with painful memories. She was nervous as Robert drove slowly up the driveway to the house. The extravagant lights in the garden and in the large open windows screamed opulence. This was the first company function they were going to as a couple. Robert had finally left his wife. Julia had shared him for five months. Five long months of knowing that he was sleeping in the same bed as Dianne every night. She didn't know how well these people knew Dianne or to what extent they would make comparisons. At least Cherie would be there, one kind face in the sea of executives and their intimidating partners. Robert had told her that Cherie and Dianne had never got along. That made Cherie safe, someone to cling to.

Robert was seated on her left, Lisa on her right. Donald sat next to Robert, and Wayne and Cherie were opposite. She counted twenty-four people at the table and was amazed at Lisa's courage to take on such a large dinner party. Lisa was pleasant, articulate, educated and noncommittal about Julia and Robert's relationship. Julia was grateful for her tact. However, Lisa was the hostess and had to give all her guests equal attention. Julia felt awkward as she sat silently in the buzz of conversation. She was drinking champagne. She didn't really like champagne but had deliberately asked Lisa for it so she wouldn't be tempted to drink too much. Her glass was empty again. Lisa topped it up. Julia decided to wait ten minutes before she would start to drink the full glass. But she forgot.

Robert was talking to Donald, their voices so low that Julia couldn't hear what they were saying.

"Julia seems like a nice woman. You say she works in our legal department?" Donald asked, wiping the corner of his mouth with his napkin.

"Yes, she's been with the company six months now," Robert answered, wondering immediately what Donald was leading up to.

"And you and Dianne have officially split up?" Donald probed, with no sensitivity to the personal nature of his questions. He was used to asking what he wanted and receiving answers to whatever he chose to ask.

"Yes, we're getting a divorce, an expensive divorce at that. She never worked a day in her life, she spent my money as if it was going out of fashion and now she gets half of my assets." Robert shrugged, his wry smile cloaking a deeper resentment.

"Well, I'm glad you're getting yourself sorted out. There's been a lot of gossip about you and Julia …" Donald said, pouring himself some more red wine without offering any to Robert.

"I'm surprised – I thought we had been discreet," Robert replied, waiting for Donald to get to the point.

"I'm amazed you can be that naïve, Rob . . . you should know how much people talk . . . sometimes it's best to make things formal. That's why I married Lisa so quickly – people didn't have the chance to talk about us. It's good to be in control of your image in the company and idle gossip can be damaging . . ." Donald gave Robert a knowing smile before starting a conversation with the woman on his other side.

* * *

"Maybe we should get married," Robert said quietly. They were about halfway home and Julia was almost asleep.

She jerked upright but when she saw his expressionless face, she wondered if she had been dreaming.

"Don't you have anything to say?" he asked, giving her a tight smile.

"I thought I had misheard you. Are you serious?" She was almost whispering, terrified that he might be joking.

"Of course I am. Why wouldn't I be?" He shook his head, perplexed at her reaction.

"You – you just don't seem very – excited, I guess," she stuttered, feeling very unsure of herself.

"That's because I'm still waiting for your answer," he replied, giving her a full smile now.

She stared at him, stunned but ecstatic. "My answer is yes ... yes, I'd love to marry you," she beamed, throwing her arms around him. The car swerved.

"Julia, take it easy! I nearly ran off the road and killed us both!"

* * *

"How soon would you like the wedding to be?" she asked shyly. It was the day after the party and they were eating dinner at her apartment. Julia had made a big effort, the only light in the room coming from the romantic glow of candles. She had the table laid formally and had prepared a three-course dinner.

"How about over Christmas? My divorce should be

done by then," he suggested, unfolding his napkin.

"Robert, that's only three months away. I'd never be able to organise everything before then," she laughed at him.

"What's there to organise? A registry office . . . witnesses . . . Wayne and Cherie would be happy to do the honours. Done! Easy!" He shrugged, not noticing the smile fading from her face.

"Don't you want something more . . . substantial? I mean, a church, a reception and some guests?" she asked, sarcastic despite her efforts not to be.

"Come on, Julia! This is the second time for both of us," he said reasonably. "The fuss of a full wedding would be ridiculous, considering the circumstances."

She swallowed her response. Hurt as she was by his lack of enthusiasm, she didn't want to risk him changing his mind by being too insistent. She hid her feelings and did her best to make the meal as pleasant as possible.

"I want you to resign from Amtech," he said as she poured him his coffee.

"Why?"

"I don't think it's appropriate for us both to work for the same company, particularly so when I'm a vice-president."

It was clear that Robert wouldn't mind if she chose to be a full-time corporate wife but he knew nothing of her previous marriage. She had learned a lesson from Josh. She never wanted to experience that hopeless vulnerability again. She wanted a career and some money of her own. The following week she applied for a position at Hayes, Frank & West, a legal firm a few blocks away from Amtech.

* * *

She lost the battle on the honeymoon as well. They went to a resort only fifty kilometres from where they lived. Robert could only spare a meagre three days from his impossible schedule so it didn't make sense to go very far. She hid her disappointment well and resolved to make the very most of their time together. There was a bottle of champagne and a basket of fruit in their suite to welcome them. They drank the champagne in the private spa bath, laughing as they played silly games with the fruit. Julia's wedding ring glittered in the water. Robert hadn't suggested buying her an engagement ring so she had diamonds put into the wedding band. She loved the ring – it was the first piece of jewellery he had given her.

The next morning the familiar sound of a fax machine woke her. Robert was standing by the machine, impatiently snatching up the pages as they came through.

"Is something wrong?" she asked sleepily.

"Not really, just something urgent from work that I need to review," he answered absently.

"Work?" She sat up in the bed. "Why did you tell them where we were staying?"

"Don't be silly, Julia. I'm a vice-president of the

company . . . of course they have to be able to contact me . . . now go back to sleep for another few hours and when you wake up I'll be finished." His tone did not encourage any argument.

She lay with her eyes squeezed shut, seething. She wanted to get up now, go for a walk, breathe in the country air, not in a few hours when it suited him.

They bumped into a business contact of Robert's at breakfast. Harry Long and his wife were also spending a few days at the resort. He invited them to join him and his wife at their table. It wasn't easy to refuse the loud, red-faced Texan, just as it wasn't easy to refuse when he suggested a round of golf with Robert. Julia tried hard to be good-humoured as she drove the buggy around the course and chatted with Harry's obnoxious wife for three hours.

The argument they had when they finally got back to their room was inevitable. Julia couldn't believe they had fought in such an ugly way on their honeymoon. She wasn't sure how it had happened but blamed herself. When he stormed out, she poured herself a large bourbon from the minibar. She was shaking all over and the bourbon calmed her a little, but not enough. She didn't want to have another but still found herself pouring a second glass. When he came back she was asleep. He opened the window to clear the room of the smell of Jack Daniels.

For the rest of their stay she ignored the phone calls to work and didn't comment on the two sets of

documents that arrived by courier. She was determinedly cheerful and affectionate. She didn't drink,
deeply ashamed of her lapse on the day they had the
argument. Robert was as pleasant as she was but there
was an undeniable distance between them.

* * *

They had been married for a few months when Lisa,
Donald Skates' wife, invited Julia out for lunch. Julia
hadn't seen Lisa since the night Robert proposed. Lisa
chose a quiet café in Palo Alto. Once more, Julia was
forced to brave the suburb that held so many happy
and painful memories of Josh.

"Julia, I don't know how to say this ... and you'll
think I'm an interfering so-and-so . . ." Lisa fidgeted
with her napkin before plunging in. "Is everything OK
with you and Robert?"

"What do you mean?" Julia was immediately defensive and Lisa became more flustered.

"Donald says that Robert is not himself . . . he's not
happy . . ."

"How would Donald know if my husband is happy
or not?" Julia demanded.

Lisa put a kind hand on Julia's arm in an attempt to
calm her.

Julia shrugged it off. "I can assure you that Robert
is perfectly happy with me – tell Donald he needn't
worry."

She snatched her bag from the floor and marched
out, leaving an embarrassed Lisa to deal with the

curious stares of the other patrons.

She went to a bar across the street. She needed something strong to calm down. A double vodka.

Robert can't be unhappy. We're only just married. We're having a few teething problems, that's all.

Her hands shook and it took a few attempts to light her cigarette. She had a flashback of Josh, lying in bed, telling her it was finished. That he wasn't happy and she wasn't what he wanted. She ordered another double.

She was sick the next morning. A familiar sickness, the one she had the mornings after Josh left. She was angry with herself for getting so drunk. There had been no need; she knew Donald and Lisa had got it wrong. She was glad Robert was away on business and wouldn't see her in this state. She wondered if she should have an eye-opener, a small vodka to stop her hands from shaking. He was going to be home in a few hours and she needed to look as if nothing happened.

CHAPTER FIVE

The summer months blurred happily together: weekends away, walks on the beach, swimming in the surf
and smoky barbecues on the balcony. Claire had been
in Sydney two months. The city felt familiar, it felt like
home. The lifestyle suited her; she was happier and
healthier than she had ever been. She missed her
family, and Susan, but only a little.

Den moved out in March to live with a girl called
Jackie. Fiona didn't even know that he had been
seeing someone and Claire could tell by her expressionless face that she was upset. Claire was more than
happy to discard the draughty sunroom for Den's
bedroom. He had barely closed the door behind him
when she ran in to inspect it. The walls were a shabby
magnolia, the floorboards dull and aching for some
varnish.

"It's a bit grotty," she commented critically, "but all it

needs is a good lick of paint." She checked her watch. "If we went to the mall right now, I'd be able to get it finished today."

"I'm not really in the mood for shopping ... particularly not for paint!"

Fiona's feeble protest was squashed by Claire's determination.

"It'll do you good ... keep busy ... it's the best cure for a broken heart ... and I should know."

For a moment Fiona looked as if she was going to dispute the broken heart accusation but she let it go.

It took only an hour to choose a warm terracotta paint, a colour that would have horrified Den. She also bought a patterned rug for the floor, some new bed linen and a bedside lamp. She would have liked to get a few more things but didn't want to test Fiona's patience.

"If you think I'm going to help you paint, you're sadly mistaken." Fiona said grumpily as she flopped down on the couch when they got back.

"You don't need to worry yourself ... I know what I'm doing ... it will only take an hour or two," Claire claimed haughtily. She put on a U2 CD, turned the volume up high, and began with gusto. Two hours later she came out defeated.

Fiona was sitting in the same spot.

"I haven't even got halfway through. My neck is killing me and I swear to God I'm high from the smell," she complained, joining Fiona on the couch.

"See, it's not as easy as it looks. And this is the weekend – we're meant to be relaxing not *working*," Fiona said unsympathetically.

"What do you mean 'working'? You've been sitting on your fat bum all day. I'd be finished by now if you had helped me!" Claire was indignant.

"I would have helped only I'm very . . . fragile at the moment."

"So, you *do* mind about him moving in with Jackie," Claire didn't miss a beat.

"I know I have no right to mind. Den and I finished a long time ago . . . it was a big mistake not to make a clean break. It was comfortable to sleep with him on nights where neither of us had someone else," Fiona admitted, her voice wobbling. "I just got used to him always being there and now I feel so lonely without him.

"Poor Fi . . . OK, we have to get you a man tonight. It's the only cure! Out with the old, in with the new!" Claire made a face, trying to get her to laugh.

"What are you talking about? You haven't been with anyone since Michael," Fiona pointed out.

"As a matter of fact, I'm going on the prowl myself tonight. With this paint on my eyebrows, I've a great chance of scoring," Claire said laughing.

They ordered some take-away for dinner because Fiona declared herself too fragile to cook and definitely too fragile to eat anything Claire might concoct.

* * *

"Here." Claire handed Fiona her drink, "This should make you feel better."

The bar was packed. It was difficult to even find standing space.

"Do you think I look like a tart in this short skirt?" Claire asked in an attempt to stop Fiona from staring soulfully into her drink.

"You certainly do," Fiona answered, looking up, her face serious.

"Good, that's the look I'm trying to achieve," Claire said, smiling with satisfaction.

"What does Den see in this Jackie that he doesn't see in me? Am I fat?" Fiona demanded with a childish pout.

"No, you're gorgeous. Am I fat?"

"No, you're even more beautiful than me," Fiona said with a giggle.

"Claire?" She felt someone tap her shoulder. She turned around.

"James . . . fancy seeing you here," she said with a smile.

"I'm just enjoying a few beers on a Saturday night. Hey, this is my mate Paul . . . Paul, this is Claire, my Irish boss."

"I've heard a lot about you from James," Paul said as he shook her hand formally.

"Good things, I'm sure," Claire laughed. "By the way, this is Fiona."

"What are you girls up to tonight?" James asked,

looking from Claire to Fiona.

"Drowning our sorrows in copious amounts of alcohol," Fiona replied with a grin.

"Do you mind if we keep you company while you achieve your goal?" James asked her directly.

"Not at all."

Claire felt Paul looking at her. His blue eyes were magnified by silver-framed glasses. He was rather cute in a studious way.

Fiona eventually secured a seat and settled down to entertain James and Paul with slightly exaggerated stories of life in Ireland.

"I still have to lie to my mother about going to Mass," she complained with a long-suffering sigh. "Sometimes she phones Sunday morning just to check up on me. If I make the mistake of answering, she wants to know why I'm not at the church . . . It's Irish mothers, you see. They're a breed of their own. I could tell my mother I was pregnant before I could admit that I don't go to Mass." Fiona paused to enjoy the incredulous expressions of the two Aussie men. "My sister is married for a year now and my mother said to her last week that she hoped she wasn't using any pills to interfere with the course of nature. My sister was about to explain she didn't take drugs any more when she realised my mother was talking about contraception!"

They all laughed and Claire took the opportunity to steal a look at Paul.

It was the early hours of the morning when they

left the pub.

"Do you girls want to kick on to a club?" James asked, his hand lightly touching Fiona's waist

"Not me, I'm too tired," Claire said, "but you guys go ahead."

"I've an idea . . . why don't you come back to our humble abode to partake in a nightcap?" Fiona offered with drunken graciousness.

It was always difficult to get a taxi in Sydney on weekends. Being drunk, rowdy and uncoordinated didn't help. They fooled around until Paul miraculously secured a cab.

By the time they let themselves into the unit, Fiona was more subdued. Claire assumed the role of barmaid. When she came back with the drinks, Fiona was asleep on James' shoulder. Paul was looking through their CDs.

"Thanks." He took his beer from her laden hands. "Do you mind if I go out to your balcony for some air?"

"Sure, I'll just give James one of these beers and I'll join you." James took a beer and seemed quite content to stay on the couch with the sleeping beauty.

"What's it like to be James' boss?" Paul asked, leaning on the railing.

"He's a horror child," Claire joked, standing beside him. "Have you known him long?"

"We grew up together. James had a tough child-hood . . ."

"Did he?"

"Yeah, but it didn't stop him from being ambitious. He likes to get ahead."

James was easy-going and relaxed at work. Claire concluded that his ambitions must lie outside Amtech.

"Do you and James compete with each other?"

"Rarely. We help each other. We both want the same things out of life."

"And what's that?" she couldn't resist asking.

"To get rich quick and retire young," he grinned and she laughed with him.

James and Fiona weren't there when they went back inside. Claire felt her face colour with embarrassment.

"You look worried," Paul said with a smile. "Relax . . . nothing needs to happen if you don't want it to."

"Um . . . OK . . . I'm totally out of practice with all this," she laughed nervously.

"And why would that be?"

"I've recently come out of a long-term relationship."

"Is it OK if I put this on?" He was holding up a Van Morrison CD.

She nodded. When he sat down, he took her hand loosely in his.

"Let's just sit here and listen to some music . . ."

They fell asleep on the couch, lying lengthways, her body moulded against his. It felt nice.

* * *

What was comfortable the night before was downright agony the morning after. The couch was tiny and Paul was not small. Her face was jammed into a velvet cushion and her knees were cramped from being in the same position for hours. She couldn't speak without eating some of the cushion so she nudged Paul with her elbow to encourage him to move off her.

"Hey, what was that for?" He flinched when her elbow made contact with his stomach.

"Sorry, I couldn't breathe," she said, sitting up, taking huge gulps of air.

Her face felt red from the lack of oxygen, she was sure her hair was all over the place and her skirt was practically up her bum. She pulled it down before she stood up.

"Excuse me, I need to go to the bathroom," she mumbled, making a quick exit before he had time to see what a mess she was. The damage was worse than she expected. Her mascara was in thick black lumps under her eyes. Even though there was no lipstick remaining on her lips, there was a red smudge on her chin. She carried out some rushed repairs with the sparse cosmetics that were available in the bathroom.

"Would you like to go somewhere with me today? Maybe a drive down south?" he asked when she returned to the living-room. He was sitting up, his blond hair ruffled. He had put on his glasses.

"I'm sorry, I can't. I need to finish painting my room – I left it there half-finished yesterday," she apologised as she sat awkwardly on the arm of the couch.

"I'll help you if you promise to go out with me

afterwards," he offered.

"Do you mean it?"

"Yes."

"Really? Thank you so much! I was dreading starting it again!" She beamed at him and jumped up to show him to the bedroom before he could change his mind.

"Claire, why did you stop painting right in the middle of the wall? You'll have a line down the middle now," he scolded, a horrified look on his face as he scrutinised her handiwork.

"I've never painted before – I thought it would be easy," she replied humbly.

"Look, why don't you get ready while I finish this off? Do you have an old T-shirt I could wear?"

After Paul had finished painting and done his best to repair the damage she had done, they caught a taxi to his flat. It was in a quiet, tree-lined street in Neutral Bay. While Paul showered and changed she inspected the interior. It was rather bare, but classy and impeccably clean. She felt ashamed of her less-than-tidy dwelling. There were photos of Paul with various family members scattered around the room. Patio doors led to the terracotta-tiled balcony that had generous plants and a superb view of the city. Either Paul spent beyond his means or he had a very good job. He shared the unit with James but Claire knew that even between two people the rent would be exorbitant.

* * *

His BMW went well with the classy apartment. She looked out the window, engrossed in the busy, cosmopolitan suburbs while he concentrated on the traffic.

"So, are you going to stay here in the Great Southern Land?" he asked when they finally hit the motorway.

"I'll certainly stay for a few years," she answered, looking across at his profile as he kept his eyes on the road. "I would never get the job I have here back in Ireland."

"If you're James' boss, what exactly does that make you?"

"I'm the Finance Manager. How about you? What do you do?" she asked politely.

"I'm a Sales Manager."

She would not have guessed. He looked like he would be in a more traditional profession, like teaching. He was certainly a far cry from Frank Williams, the Sales Director at Amtech.

"I know some people in the sales team in Amtech. I've come across Frank Williams at a few of the industry seminars. Do you have much to do with Frank at work?"

She was taken aback that he mentioned Frank just as she had been thinking about him. "Yes, I know Frank quite well. I wouldn't say we are best of friends, though."

"I imagine that he would be hard to handle. All the same, he does seem to be a very smart man and he's impressive when you see him in action."

"I'll take your word for it! What company do you work for?"

"Digicom, a competitor of Amtech."

"So that's it! You're trying to extract trade secrets from me!" she teased, laughing. "I knew you couldn't like me for myself."

"*Au contraire, madame.* Trade secrets are just one of many attractions," he flattered her in an impressive French accent.

The fields were surprisingly green as they blurred past. The motorway had petered out into a narrow single-lane road that wound around the tips and dips of the gentle hills. She hummed along to the radio for a few minutes before he spoke again.

"Been to Jervis Bay before?"

"No … I've only been up north. This countryside reminds me of home," she said happily.

"Yeah, Ireland is beautiful. I was there three years ago."

"So, you've travelled a bit then?" she probed.

"Yeah, I have. I worked for Digicom in California for a few years and used it as an opportunity to see some of Europe."

They stopped for a late lunch in Huskisson's Bay. They ate in the beer garden of the main hotel, facing the startling blue bay fringed with white sand. The lazy tempo of the jazz band and the wine she had with lunch made her relax in his company. He was interesting and entertaining, and conversation flowed easily. Fiona was her only close friend in Sydney. Her colleagues at work were pleasant but they kept their distance socially. Paul filled a gap she didn't know existed before that afternoon.

She was so mellow when they began their journey back to Sydney, she drifted off to sleep within minutes. She woke with a start, looking around wildly, trying to get her bearings. Paul seemed amused by her embarrassment.

"I'm so sorry," she apologised as she sat up.

"Don't worry about it. You look cute when you're asleep."

He pulled up outside the flat.

"Thanks for a lovely day," she said.

He leaned over and cupped her face in his hands. She flinched slightly when he kissed her.

"I'll call you tomorrow," he said, his face very close.

"OK . . . bye," she muttered as she stumbled out of the car, breaking their embrace prematurely.

Fiona wasn't home and the empty silence of the flat was what she needed. She felt vulnerable. It was a long time since she had kissed someone other than Michael.

* * *

Claire arrived at work feeling unusually happy for a Monday morning. At some stage the previous night she had broken her ties with Michael. The world looked promising and exciting, and she was emotionally free to enjoy it. She worked methodically through her large pile of admin, for once not minding the monotony. She signed a large pile of invoices and then turned her attention to the sales orders that needed her approval. She checked each one carefully and signed them all with the exception of one. She could see Alan Harris from her office window as she dialled his number.

"Alan, can I see you for a minute?"

She watched him as he continued to type for a few moments before arrogantly rising from his seat, making a pathetic attempt to tuck his errant shirt into his errant trousers.

"There's a letter to this customer from Frank Williams offering ninety days' credit. Were you aware of it?" she asked, handing him the letter.

"Yeah, I am. What's the problem?" he answered, glancing at the incriminating document but not taking it from her outstretched hand.

"The problem is that neither you nor Frank have the authority to make such an offer," she informed him, annoyed that she had to spell out the obvious departure from policy. "It needs to be cleared by the treasury department in the US."

"I really don't know what you're fussing about. The customer is a low risk. There's no issue," he argued, his tone insolent.

"Alan, you know well that anything over ninety days needs corporate approval," she said, keeping her voice level with effort. "It doesn't matter how safe the customer is – you still have to document your case."

"Well, you'd better tell Frank then. He won't be pleased," he said smugly and she hid her irritation as she dialled Frank's extension.

She told him a problem had come up and asked him to come around to her office.

"What's all the drama about?" Frank asked when he arrived a few minutes later.

"This letter to Nutrifast. I can't authorise shipment to the customer until treasury clears the terms," she said bluntly.

"You can't be serious . . . the customer needs the shipment urgently." Frank's voice was raised with an instant aggression.

"Sorry . . . but you both know the rules. You shouldn't have made the commitment without getting the proper approvals," she stated, trying not to waver under his wrath.

"That's the problem with people like you!" Frank's face was an intimidating few inches from hers. "You waste my time on red tape . . . you hinder the sale process rather than help it!"

He slammed the door viciously in his wake, leaving her to deal with a smirking Alan.

"You should have known better," she said harshly. "Don't ever let something like that through again."

Shaking with anger, she took an early lunch. She wandered around the shops in Greenwood Plaza, fuming as she viciously went through the clothes on the racks. Her anger had abated when she returned to the office. She went to see Dan, anxious to get to him before Frank Williams did.

"Just the person I wanted to see . . . sit down," he said, his face solemn.

It's obviously too late. Frank must have made an official complaint already, she thought as she sat down.

"I've decided to retire. I handed in my notice to Steve today and will be leaving the end of April," he said, his serious expression transforming into a broad smile.

It took her a few seconds to absorb the enormity of his statement. When she finally did, her instinctive reaction was selfish dismay. He looked so pleased with himself, she made an effort to hide how upset she was.

"Congratulations! What are you planning to do with your spare time?" she enquired.

"Fishing and golf," he said simply.

"So what's going to happen with your position?" she asked carefully.

"David Di Gregario has put a few employment agencies on it already. I am hoping to do a full handover to my successor but Robert has also spoken to Tony Falcinella in order to have a fall-back plan should the recruitment process take longer than expected. If that happens, Tony will cover what he can from Hong Kong until the right person is found."

She hadn't met Tony Falcinella, but knew his name. He was the Finance Director for Asia. She was silent for a few moments, trying to decide if she should be open with him or not.

"You look worried," he said. "Tell me what you're thinking."

She didn't need any further encouragement.

"It's hard to imagine what it will be like here without you, Dan. I've relied on you a lot and I guess I'm apprehensive about how I'll cope without your support."

"You have nothing to worry about. I've had positive feedback from all the senior managers about you. You have their respect. I'm very confident that you will be able to manage without me – in fact, you'll soon see how dispensable I am," he said with a chuckle.

"I think you're exaggerating, Dan. Are you saying that Frank Williams has given you *positive* feedback about me?" she challenged him, with a grin.

"OK, you've caught me out. I lied about Frank."

* * *

Claire made her way home in a preoccupied daze. Her job would be very different without Dan around to support her. The phone started to ring as she trudged wearily up the stairs. She ran the last few steps, cursing as she frantically tried to fit her key in the stiff lock. She picked up the phone, breathless, to an amused Paul.

"Hi there. You're obviously just in the door!" His cheerful voice was inexplicably annoying.

"Yeah, and I must say I've had a diabolical day."

"Is it something you want to talk about? Do you

want me to come over? We could go out for a coffee or a drink."

She generally preferred to be on her own when she was in a bad mood. It seemed too soon to see him after spending all day yesterday together.

"OK," she agreed, when she had hesitated too long to be able to politely refuse.

Damn. Why didn't I say "No?" Now I have to make myself look nice.

She ran into her bedroom, threw her suit on the bed and pulled on a pair of denim shorts and a white T-shirt. When the doorbell rang twenty minutes later, she applied a light touch of lipstick and opened the door, ready to go.

"Hi," she said casually.

He kissed her – a soft, unsettling kiss.

"I know it's a corny thing to say but I've been thinking about you all day," he said as he pulled away.

She found that she couldn't return the compliment.

She suggested Tables, a popular noisy café on the main strip. They secured one of the few, more private cubicles that looked out on the street. They silently watched the passing pedestrians for a few minutes and, when their order was taken, she started to tell him about her day. He listened to her until she ran out of steam.

"Why don't you apply for Dan's job?" he asked, sipping his coffee as he looked at her intently.

"I don't have enough experience for a role like that . . . I bet you they'll give it to a man. In fact, fifty bucks says they will – they wouldn't know what to do with a female Finance Director," she said wryly.

"I'm not betting anything – I reckon you're right," he said smiling. "How do Frank and Dan get along?"

"It's hard to say. I don't think Dan lets Frank get away with much but I've never seen them have a disagreement."

"Would Dan have more authority than Frank?" Paul seemed to be extremely interested in her work life.

"Yes, Frank needs to get Dan's sign-off on customer proposals over a certain materiality level."

"What level? Half a million?"

"Enough about work, Paul. Let's talk about something else."

They made small talk for another hour before she suggested they leave.

"Do you want to go for a drink?" he asked.

"Not really – I usually like to stay at home Monday nights," she said, smiling to take the edge from her refusal. "It gives me a chance to recover from the weekend."

"OK. Can I see you tomorrow night?"

"I've got a lot of work on at the moment . . . how about we do something at the weekend instead?"

* * *

Den was there when she got back. He and Fiona were sitting on the floor, accompanied by the usual cloud of smoke and bottles of beer.

"Hey, Claire, come here and give me a hug." He stretched his arm out and hugged her legs.

"Hello, stranger. Glad to see you remembered where we live," she said as she knelt down beside him.

"I've seen what you've done to my room. That's a disgusting colour."

"What would you know about colour? You have your head stuck in black and white contracts all day, Mister Lawyer," she teased him.

"Don't call me a lawyer. I hate that," he grimaced, turning his head to puff on his cigarette.

"Tough luck. Much as you try to deny it, you *are* a lawyer. Worse still, you're a *good* lawyer. It's something you have to learn to live with, just like any other handicap."

* * *

"What time did Den leave last night?" Claire asked as she made herself some tea the next morning.

"Not long after you went to bed. It was nice to see him ... don't worry, nothing happened between us."

"I'm not sure I should believe you! How are things going with James?"

"Good. I like him. What does he do at Amtech again?" Fiona sat down with her overflowing bowl of cereal.

"He works in Accounts Payable."

"You know, James and Den are complete opposites," Fiona said, looking thoughtful.

"I noticed that."

"James is very driven – I think money motivates him. His family were poor so money was everything. Yet his chosen career isn't that well paid. Then you have Den, the corporate lawyer. He gets paid a fortune but hates material possessions and doesn't have any respect for money."

"Yes, well, you'll have to see how it goes with James . . . just take things slowly . . ."

"Hmm . . . " said Fiona.

CHAPTER SIX

Julia would be thirty-six next month and if she was honest with herself, her second marriage was heading the same way as her first. She swung into the driveway at a reckless speed, selfishly oblivious to her dangerous driving. Cherie and Wayne had an impressive house with a large garden where the children could play safely. Cherie – practical, solid and always at home on standby to deal with the crises of Julia's life.

"Julia!" Cherie's welcoming smile dissolved as she absorbed how upset Julia was. "Hey . . . what's happened?"

"It's ten p.m. and Robert still isn't home. He hasn't even called." Julia was crying loudly.

"For heaven's sake, is that all? You gave me such a shock. Come in and sit down," Cherie offered, trying to control her annoyance. Julia had really scared her. She should have known it would be something trivial.

She ushered Julia into the kitchen and closed the door so Wayne wouldn't hear the commotion.

"Robert is obviously still at work. Wayne only came home a few minutes ago," she said as she put on the kettle. Wayne had been home two hours. She was lying in an attempt to make Julia feel better.

Her efforts were wasted. Julia barged on hysterically, determined not to be consoled.

"He's having an affair! Where else would he be until this hour?"

"You're overreacting . . . just because he's late home doesn't automatically mean he's having an affair." Cherie sat down across from her.

"He works late every night and he hasn't touched me in months. It's probably his new secretary. The bitch doesn't even pass on my messages when I call!" Julia's face was contorted with an unjustified hatred.

The kettle had boiled and Cherie got up to make some coffee.

"I don't feel like coffee. Can I have a real drink?" Julia asked, taking her cigarettes from her bag. She lit one and inhaled aggressively.

"It's very late, Julia . . . and you do have to drive home . . . " Cherie hesitated. Wayne would kill her if he found Julia passed out in their living-room tomorrow morning.

"Relax . . . I'm having a hell of a time and I just need a drink."

Cherie felt a wave of pity for her and got two beers

from the fridge. She had wanted an early night and had been about to go to bed when the doorbell rang. She made a conscious effort not to think of herself and gave Julia her undivided attention.

"Julia, I really think you are overreacting. Wayne is very busy at the moment too. Amtech is doing well and everyone is struggling to keep up with the boom."

"Give me some credit – I know that something is wrong. Robert had an affair with me, remember? While he was still married to Dianne . . . so I know he is capable of being a two-timing bastard!" Julia started to cry again.

"It was different with Dianne – she and Robert were very unhappy."

"He was married when he had an affair with me, so what's stopping him from doing the same now with his secretary?"

"Well, OK . . . if you are so sure, then leave him. Maybe you'd be happier on your own," Cherie said, a hint of exasperation creeping into her voice.

"What would you know, Cherie? You've been happily married for fifteen years," Julia accused angrily. "You can't imagine what it's like to be single, what it's like to start from scratch with someone new. I don't have the energy for it . . . I've got to make it work with Robert."

Cherie had a pain in her head from arguing in circles and she was tired.

"Why don't you go home and talk to him?"

"I can't go home yet. My face is a mess. I'll have another drink . . . then I'll go. Do you have any gin?" She pushed her empty glass towards Cherie.

"I think so . . . but I don't have a mixer."

"Don't worry. I prefer it straight."

Cherie was annoyed with herself for giving in. Julia drank too much and she hated contributing in any way to her getting drunk. It was hard to resist her. Even though Julia was generally a weak person, she could be very manipulative when it came to procuring alcohol. There was an uncomfortable silence as Julia drank her gin and Cherie plucked up the courage to say what was on her mind.

"Do you think it would help if you saw someone?" she said finally, concern creasing her face into worried wrinkles. "I mean a counsellor or someone like that? You've been so unhappy and they might help you get things into perspective."

"A shrink! You're kidding, right? If there's one thing that would finish myself and Robert off, then that would. Robert despises people who can't control their emotions." Julia was looking at Cherie as if she was insane.

Cherie stared back at her, seeing her face, blotched from crying, and her eyes, glazed from the gin.

Well, Julia my dear, that's your problem with Robert in a nutshell . . . you're an emotional wreck. You're behaving like someone on the verge of a nervous break-down.

She decided to persevere, mentally bracing herself for an explosive reaction from Julia.

"What about AA? Have you ever considered going to one of their meetings?"

"Are you totally insane? You cannot be stupid enough to think I'm an alcoholic! Maybe you need to go to one of those meetings yourself and see what kind of people go!"

"All sorts of people go to AA, Julia . . . doctors, priests . . . "

"For God's sake, don't you know AA are like a sect, luring people in, shoving the Bible down their throats, depriving them of a social life?" Julia snapped, her voice raising.

"Sshhh, you'll wake the children . . . You're wrong about AA – they don't support any religions," Cherie stated with confidence.

Julia looked at her suspiciously. "You seem to know a hell of a lot about AA all of a sudden."

"Yes, I've been reading up on them. I think I have a friend who has an alcohol problem." She looked directly at Julia, challenging the denial she would make.

"I can give up drinking whenever I want. I did it before for a few months . . . it was before you knew me . . . I admit I have some problems – but they are to do with my marriage, not alcohol."

"OK, if you insist. But why not get some counselling to straighten yourself out?"

"Come on, now. You know that's not necessary."

"You said you had problems . . ."

Julia didn't know how to handle Cherie's persistence; she hadn't been exposed to it previously.

"I don't see how talking to a stranger will help me."

"It can be very powerful to talk honestly to someone you don't know."

Julia hesitated only to find herself locked in Cherie's determined stare. It was impossible not to give in.

"OK, OK. Anything to get you off my back. I'll see a shrink just for you."

"Good."

* * *

Saturday morning was crisp and sunny. Julia woke feeling more optimistic. She was disappointed to find Robert was already up.

Cherie is right, he's just busy at work. I should be more understanding, considering the pressure he's under. I'll be really nice to him today . . . we'll have a good weekend together. Everything will be fine.

She felt a wave of nausea as she pulled back the covers. She sat on the side of the bed until it passed. The nausea was happening too often.

I need to cut down, just have one or two drinks and stop at that. I'm always feeling sick these days ... I need to get healthy ...but Cherie was totally overreacting with AA . . . I can manage this myself.

She had a long shower, carefully washing away the stale smell of booze. She put on a pair of tight jeans and a white linen shirt. She tied her blonde hair back in a girlish pony-tail and leaned closer to the mirror to examine the ravages of the previous night.

I look so old – when did that happen? His secretary is only nineteen – how can I compete with her? Stop it! Stop it! Think positive. He is married to me. He must love me.

She took care with her make-up, using a concealer to disguise the shadows under her eyes and a hint of blusher to give her colour.

I've got to stop drinking ... I look pale, ill ... maybe I will see a counsellor, but I'm not going to AA.

She found him in the courtyard reading the morning paper. There was an air of tranquillity to the scene, his absorption in what he was reading, the brightness of the sun, the peaceful green of the plants. It belied the turmoil of their marriage. She admired him from the doorway. He was a very sexy man, his Californian tan looking fresh against the blue of his shirt. His hair and eyes were the same chocolate brown, a neatly trimmed beard accentuating his masculinity. She felt a sudden rush of love for him.

She kissed him on the cheek and sat down.

"Good morning, honey. Sorry I missed you last night," she smiled, resting her hand affectionately on his arm.

"Morning," he said, without raising his eyes from the paper.

"Isn't it a gorgeous day . . . maybe we should go for a

drive?" she suggested, squinting up at the sun.

"I can't. I need to go in to work for a few hours," he said, his refusal hurtfully abrupt.

"Well, maybe I could meet you for lunch then?" she persisted.

He sighed and looked up from the paper with a frown.

"OK, if it means that much to you. But only for an hour – that's all I can spare. I have a lot to do today." He folded the paper and stood up. "I'll see you at The Grill at noon."

The front door slammed in his wake. Disappointment flooded her, then anger rushed in to take its place.

That's it! Don't tell me he's going to spend all weekend working. Does he think I'm too stupid to figure out what he's up to? Well, I've had enough. I'm going to catch the bastard out.

She waited until she heard the Mercedes reverse out of the drive and speed away. She followed him in the Audi, scratching the passenger door against the gatepost in her haste. She was a fast driver and within seconds she had his car in sight.

She stayed with him, running a few reds so she wouldn't get left behind. He drove his normal route to work and his car disappeared down into the Amtech underground carpark. Julia waited across the street. The lights came on in Level 10 and she saw his silhouette moving towards his desk. There was no other woman, only his work. And it clearly took priority over his wife.

If only Robert didn't work for Amtech . . . He is so obsessed with his job, he doesn't have any time for a wife.

She saw him get up and open a filing cabinet. He took out a document and read it for a few moments before returning to his seat, his back to the window.

They would have to fire him, that's the only way he would leave. But Donald would never fire a vice-president. It would be bad publicity – he's too damned conservative. I guess if he really wanted to get rid of someone, he would pay them out. That would be good . . . I would get Robert to myself and we wouldn't suffer financially. I wonder how much Donald would pay to get rid of a vice-president.

She stayed outside thinking about it until it was time to meet him for lunch. She drove straight to the downtown restaurant. He was fifteen minutes late.

* * *

Robert sat with his back to the splendid view. It was dark outside and the lights of the other buildings glowed, giving an illusion of warmth that belied the rather cold evening it was. He was deep in conversation with Tony Falcinella, the Finance Director for Asia.

"We've interviewed twelve candidates and there's nobody even remotely suitable," Tony said, his frustration clear from his tone. He had spent the last two months in Sydney while his wife and children were in Hong Kong. Even though travel was a prerequisite for his position in the company, he was a home-bird and tried to avoid going overseas.

"Have we advertised?" Robert asked.

"Yes. Very prominent ads in the *Sydney Morning Herald* and the *Financial Review*. We're also using two of the most prestigious employment agencies. They keep telling me it's hard to get good finance people in Sydney at the moment."

Robert could hear Tony's frustration. He turned in his seat so he could look at the view. It was a rare moment that he stopped to enjoy the peculiar beauty of the concrete towers, speckled with lights.

"How are the finance team coping without Dan?"

"They're doing fine. The new finance manager, Claire Quinlan, seems quite competent but there are a few big deals on the horizon and Steve Ryan wants someone more experienced than her. She's only in her mid-twenties." Tony was fully informed, having made it his business to meet Claire as well as discussing the situation in depth with Steve on a number of occasions. He had been in favour of offering the job to her when the other candidates had not come through but Steve was adamant that she was too inexperienced.

"I know Claire – I organised her transfer from Dublin … I'm glad that she's doing well. When do you reckon she would be up to the job?"

"Well, she's certainly technically capable . . . she just needs to develop a better understanding of the business . . . maybe a year or two?"

"What if we transferred someone from San Jose on a year's assignment? Do you think that would work?" Robert spoke slowly as he usually did when his mind was running ahead with a multitude of possible solutions to a particular issue.

"Damn it, Robert, that's a good idea!" Tony said enthusiastically, a speedy return to Hong Kong now looking possible. "Then Claire should be ready to take the job at the end of the year. Do you have someone in mind?"

"I might have. I'll talk to you tomorrow," Robert said abruptly and was gone before Tony had the chance to reply.

Tony hung up the phone feeling like an office junior, not worthy to know the thoughts of the great Robert Pozos. It was an annoying habit that Tony had never quite got used to. Robert would discuss an issue in depth for hours and then reach a sudden conclusion in his own mind but wouldn't share it. It was almost as if he mentally dismissed the other party, having no use for them any longer.

* * *

Robert sat with his feet on the desk, smoking thoughtfully. It was nine thirty at night and with nobody left in the office he felt it was OK to have a cigarette. He didn't particularly want to go home. Julia was driving him crazy. He wondered who he could send to Sydney. Scott would never move his family. Ritchie was involved in a major project for the next six months.

Robert couldn't recall how many times he had been to Sydney. He did a lot of international travel and all the business trips blurred together. He had always liked Sydney. It was a beautiful city and whoever got to go would be a lucky bastard.

He left for home reluctantly, turning off the lights on his way out. Ten years ago the place would have been buzzing at this hour. The 80's, a decade of hard work and hard play. Not many new faces had joined the company since then and that youthful and enthusiastic culture had been lost. No more late nights at work or drinking beer in the bar across the street afterwards. He missed those days. His colleagues now worked 'family hours' and he felt he didn't fit in any more. He wasn't a family man and never would be. He wished he could turn the clock back.

He put on a Queen CD as he drove through the quiet suburban streets. Queen, the best band of the 80's. It was exactly ten miles from the office to their house in South San Jose. The darkness concealed the flat arid landscape and the predictability of the grid of streets. San Jose and Sydney were very different places. He knew that Tony was trying hard but, best case, the recruitment process would take at least another two months. Australia was the third largest international subsidiary in the world. It would be highly undesirable if the business had to operate without a Finance Director for a total of four months. Somewhere along twenty-minute drive home, he decided to go to Sydney himself. He reasoned that he could cover the important aspects of his current job from there whilst maintaining the Finance Director role until Claire was ready for it. It would be a convenient escape from Julia; it would be easier to divorce her from the other side of the world. A change of scene would also be good for him personally. It would get him out of the corporate rut that he was stuck in.

He was annoyed that she was waiting for him. Sitting in the living-room with no TV on, she at least appeared to be sober.

"Have you eaten?"

She jumped up eagerly and he unconsciously flinched at the possibility of physical contact.

"No … I completely forgot," he said wearily as he shrugged off his jacket and loosened his tie, moving away from her as subtly as he could.

"I'll make you something quick. You could browse through these in the meantime." She placed some holiday brochures on the coffee table. "I think we need a holiday . . . we haven't had one since our honeymoon. If you keep working this hard, you'll have a heart attack before you're fifty! Some of those islands look fantastic – you have your own private beach and they serve you cocktails . . ."

She stopped mid-stream, disconcerted by his stony face.

"Sorry, Julia, I'm going to Sydney next week."

"Sydney? How long are you going for? Maybe I

could organise some leave from work," she said, child-ishly excited at the prospect.

"Six months minimum. It could turn into a year." His answer was impersonal.

Julia felt a pang of panic and a nauseous feeling invaded her stomach.

"Are we moving there?" she asked weakly.

Finally Robert looked at her, his eyes hard, his face impassive.

"No. We're not. I think we need some space from each other . . . I have some things I need to sort out."

"What things?" she said, her voice shrill. "You can't mean I'm not going to see you for six months."

"Don't overreact, Julia. I will need to come back to San Jose a few times so that my role here isn't neglected. You'll see plenty of me."

* * *

"Are you totally crazy?" Wayne asked, obviously shocked.

"I'll have two beers, please," Robert said to the barman. "No, I'm not crazy – I just need some time out."

"But what about your job here? Don't you think Donald needs his VP of Finance on the same time zone?"

They sat at the bar. Wayne would go home after one drink; it wasn't worth moving to a table.

"Actually, Donald is very sympathetic. He's been through some rough times himself. I implied to him that I was emotionally on the edge and he couldn't do enough for me." Robert grinned. "He would have agreed had I suggested a beach in Hawaii for six months."

Wayne didn't smile. "Donald's got too soft since he married Lisa. He's too easy to manipulate."

Robert looked at Wayne critically. He wondered when his old mate had turned into a middle-aged bore.

"Wayne, listen to yourself. You sound like a grumpy old man. Leave Lisa alone. She's a great lady."

Wayne flushed and took a mouthful of beer, before asking, "What about Julia – how does she fit into all of this?"

"Julia's not coming. She's largely the reason I want to get away, so it wouldn't make sense for her to come with me, would it?" Robert was slightly defensive.

"So, you're leaving her? She must be devastated."

"I don't think she knows what to make of it. She certainly won't admit to herself that our marriage is on the rocks."

Robert took his cigarettes out. He was surprised that Wayne took one when he offered. He passed Wayne the lighter.

"Do you even know anybody over in Sydney?" It took Wayne a few fumbled attempts to light the cigarette.

"I know a few faces from my previous visits. I guess you also know some people through your role, right?"

Wayne didn't answer; he seemed to be intensely

preoccupied. Robert stared at him for a few moments and Wayne visibly jumped when he noticed.

"Some . . ." Wayne inhaled in awkward jerks. "I still think you're crazy if you believe that you can hold a vice-president's position from Sydney. It's not going to work."

Robert shrugged. "I think it *will* work, Wayne. There's no reason it shouldn't."

* * *

It was the weekend before he got to speak to Cherie.

"I was wondering if you would call around," she said when she opened the door.

"You know I would never go away without seeing you." Robert kissed her affectionately on the cheek.

"Is Wayne at home?" He followed Cherie into the kitchen. It looked as if she was in the middle of preparing dinner.

"No, you just missed him. He took the kids to the park so I could get dinner ready in peace. Would you like a coffee?"

"No, thanks for the offer but I'm a little short of time today." Robert sat on one of the wooden stools, his arms folded across the granite bench top.

"You're always short of time, Robert," Cherie said, shaking her head.

"I know. I know. I'm hoping to chill out somewhat when I get to Sydney."

Cherie resumed the food preparation, chopping vegetables with an impressive speed.

"Julia isn't taking this move to Sydney very well, Robert. She's very upset and I'm afraid that she'll go on a binge the minute you leave town."

"I think that's likely too. That's why I'm glad I've got you on your own. I wanted to ask you to talk to her about AA."

"I've spoken to her about AA already. She just doesn't want to know. I'm trying to get her to see a counsellor as a fall-back plan. She seems more open to that."

Robert gave Cherie a grateful smile. "Thank you. I really appreciate your help."

"Julia's my friend. I'm very fond of her and I want to make sure she gets some help. I'll be straight with you, Robert. I don't understand why you haven't confronted her about her drinking."

She stopped what she was doing to wait for his answer.

"Good point . . . and the answer is that Julia refuses to have an argument or a confrontation of any sort since our honeymoon. She hides her drinking and her past . . . she really believes that I don't know what's going on. I think you have a much better chance of getting through to her – at least she does confide in you to some extent. She only tells me one lie after the other."

* * *

He called Claire Quinlan when he got home from Cherie's. If his calculations on the time difference were

119

correct, it should be Monday morning in Sydney.

"Claire, it's Robert Pozos." He could hear the sound of her keyboard as she typed.

"Oh . . . hello, Robert." She stopped typing.

"How have you been?"

"Very busy," she answered frankly. He remembered the soft lilt of her voice from the last time they spoke, before she left Ireland.

"I understand . . . I do appreciate all your hard work … and I hope that I have good news for you in that help is on the way."

"Great! Does that mean you've found a new Finance Director?" she asked.

He laughed at the eagerness in her voice.

"Not quite . . . we haven't been able to attract the quality candidate that we hoped for . . . however, I do have a solution. I have decided to come to Sydney myself and do the role for six months or so."

There was silence for a moment.

"But what about your job in San Jose?" she asked.

She sounded confused and he smiled to himself.

"I can cover that from Sydney. Donald has no problem with me doing that . . . I'll be in Sydney next week . . . I'll look forward to meeting you then."

* * *

There was a large tray of unsigned cheques between Claire and Paul as they sat on the sofa. She was signing the cheques as they watched the news on TV.

"It's very bizarre that Robert Pozos is coming out

here," said Paul, turning to look at her when the interval came on. "There must be something else on his agenda."

"It does seem a little unorthodox," Claire answered absently.

"Maybe he wants to do a restructure of the senior management team," he mused.

Claire frowned at him. "Why are you so interested in Robert Pozos?"

"It's just natural curiosity. You must admit, it doesn't make sense for the vice-president of a US multinational to go to the other side of the world for six months."

"I don't understand why you care so much about Robert's reasons." Claire didn't know why Paul was annoying her.

"And I don't understand why you don't seem to care at all," he countered.

"I simply want someone in that Finance Director's role so that I can get my life back," she answered, flicking through the supporting paperwork before signing a cheque. Out of the corner of her eye she saw him pick up the next cheque in the tray.

"Put that back."

"Don't be so touchy," he chided, obediently putting it back in the tray.

"I'm not being touchy . . . those cheques are confidential to Amtech."

"Well, you shouldn't leave them where I can see them – you know that I'm a nosey bugger."

She moved the tray to her left side. "There, does that take the temptation away?" she snapped. "I don't know what you find so captivating about Amtech's vice-presidents and cheques."

"I'm only interested because you work there." He sounded hurt and she felt mean.

* * *

Steve Ryan claimed that the Australian senior management team met monthly. The secretaries did their part – they blocked out the same day and time each month for the meeting. But something always happened at the last minute and the meeting would be cancelled. They were lucky to get together once a quarter.

Steve liked to have the meetings offsite because he thought it gave him the best chance of winning the undivided attention of his undisciplined management team. The Duxton Hotel worked well – it was within walking distance of the office and offered excellent facilities for corporate meetings. The room had five chairs around a large rectangular table. Steve, Frank, Brian and David were late arriving but at least present. Tony Falcinella was back in Hong Kong so Claire was there as Acting Finance Director.

"Let's try to get this over with quickly – I've got a client lunch starting at twelve," Frank said, pouring himself some iced water.

"Frank, I'm glad you said that because it brings up a subject that I want to discuss," David said, obviously annoyed. "To be quite honest, I get the impression that this meeting isn't taken seriously. Trying to get us all together is getting more and more difficult."

"We're busy people, David," Frank responded, with an insincere smile.

"We can't be too busy for this. These meetings are about our strategic direction, how we run the company – what could possibly be more important?" David looked at the others for support.

Claire wasn't sure what input he expected her to give, if any. She watched the dynamics between the members of the team with interest.

"I agree with David," said Brian Brooker. "We're not exactly a good example to our staff. We say that tenacity is one of the company's most important principles yet we're always reneging on our commitment to this meeting." Brian looked at Steve to take up the issue.

Claire could see a split in the team, Brian and David on one side with Steve and Frank on the other. Dan would most likely have been the mediator between the two sides.

"We clearly have some differences of opinion here, but we don't have this discussion on our agenda and are already running behind time today," said Steve. "Let's park it and add it to the agenda for next month's meeting. Now, the first item here is the financials. Claire, can you run us through the final numbers for the month?"

* * *

When she left work that evening, Paul was waiting for her in the foyer to go to the gym. He was leaning across the reception desk, chatting comfortably with Audrey.

"G'day," he grinned. "Ready for a good workout?"

She was carrying a gym bag with her change of clothes.

"I don't think I'm ready for any kind of workout – I haven't been to the gym for years. You have no idea how unfit I am."

"Bye, Audrey, enjoy your weekend," Paul said and they went outside.

"You seem very friendly with Audrey – do you know her?" Claire asked.

"Not really," he said, putting an arm casually around her shoulders. "I just like chatting to people, finding out what they do. Audrey has all the company gossip – receptionists always do. Why do you want to know anyway? Are you jealous?" he teased, squeezing her shoulders.

"No, not even remotely." She shrugged his arm off. "You just seem to know the people I work with better than I do."

CHAPTER SEVEN

Emma looked very smart. Claire hadn't seen her wear the pinstripe suit before. Her make-up was noticeable only because she didn't usually wear foundation. It suddenly occurred to Claire that she may have been to an interview for another job.

"You look really nice today – is that a new suit?" she asked.

"Yep, I had a little shopping spree on the weekend and picked it up at half price," Emma answered, walking through Claire's office as if it was a catwalk. "Thought I'd wear it today for the big occasion."

"What big occasion?" Claire queried, hoping that she hadn't forgotten some important meeting.

"Robert Pozos is coming today, isn't he? That man is sex on legs," Emma said with a smitten sigh. "Did you meet him when you worked in Ireland?"

"No, I didn't. I've spoken to him a few times, but I was blissfully unaware of his alleged sexiness."

Stacey passed by the office, her perfume leaving a fragrance in her wake, her sequinned top more suitable for a nightclub than the office.

"Have all the females here dressed up for the occasion?" Claire asked with a friendly sarcasm.

"But of course."

"So, Robert Pozos has his own little fan club! Isn't that cute! Do you guys write him love letters?" Claire threw her eyes to heaven.

"Only the occasional email, but I'm sure he can read between the lines," Emma replied suggestively.

"And does he distribute posters of himself to his fans?"

"No, but there is a photo of him on our website that I have downloaded as my screen-saver," Emma improvised with a leer. They were both laughing when Steve Ryan knocked politely on her office door to announce his presence. Their jovial mood was immediately at odds with his sombre expression. The man that stood behind him could only be Robert Pozos.

"Robert, this is Claire Quinlan." Steve made the introduction awkwardly.

Claire stood up to shake his hand.

"Nice to meet you," she smiled, trying not to look at him too closely. Her conversation with Emma instinctively made her want to determine why he was so attractive to the others. She met his brown eyes for the briefest moment, registered the whiteness of his shirt across his broad shoulders. He was tall. She had looked too long and turned her eyes to Steve.

"And I believe you've met Emma before," he said to

Robert. She had never seen Steve so edgy. He fixed his tie before putting his left hand back into his trouser pocket.

"Yes, I have. How have you been, Emma?" Robert's voice was crisp, his words slow and deliberate.

"Fantastic. Loving every minute of working for Amtech."

Claire and Emma giggled. Robert smiled. Steve fixed his tie again.

"Robert only arrived in this morning but insisted on coming straight to the office," Steve said. He was obviously ill at ease and not sure how to conduct himself around Robert. It did make an interesting situation. Usually the Finance Director reported to the General Manager but in this case the Finance Director was much more senior than the General Manager and that undermined Steve's position and authority significantly.

"Gosh, I don't know how you can do it. When I got here I slept for a week," Claire said with a little laugh.

"You get used to it if you have to travel frequently. Once I can get some sleep during the flight, I find I don't suffer from jet lag." He smiled. He was looking at her. Steve and Emma didn't seem to notice the lull in the conversation.

"Have you been to Sydney before?" she asked.

"Yes, I have. It's one of my favourite cities . . . I'm looking forward to living here for the next few months."

Robert Pozos had a presence. He filled up her office, making her feel intimidated and flustered for no good reason. Her mind frantically scrambled for something else to say. Steve finally took control of the uncomfortable silence.

"Well, we better move on, Robert. There's plenty more people to meet and I'm sure you'll catch up with Claire properly later."

They left and she sat down with relief, forgetting that Emma was still there.

"Well, what do you think?" Emma startled her with the question.

"He's very attractive . . . but not my type. Too experienced . . . too smooth," she shrugged her assessment. "Anyway, he must be quite old."

"He's forty-one," Emma stated.

Claire resisted the temptation to ask how she knew his age.

"God, I hope he didn't hear what we were saying about him as he walked in . . . that would be so embarrassing I'd have to resign on the spot."

* * *

She was engrossed in work when Robert came back to her office. The Finance Department had left for the day and the buzz of voices, phones and activity had eased to a peaceful calm. She liked to work after six in the evening, her concentration not at risk of being interrupted. He had his jacket over his arm and carried a battered-looking briefcase. The worn brown leather

128

was at odds with his expensive suit. She idly wondered how long he had the briefcase.

"I thought you would have gone home long ago," she said in surprise.

"I'm just leaving now. I was hoping to talk to you earlier but it turned out to be a hectic day."

"You could say that," she agreed with a weary smile.

"We must catch up tomorrow. Can you fit a morning meeting into your schedule?" he asked. He looked full of energy as he stood in her doorway. She envied him his stamina.

"Yes, no problem. What time?" she enquired, pulling out her diary from her desk drawer.

"Does eight suit?"

"OK, see you then," she said, hoping her dismay at the early hour didn't show.

He gave her a brief nod and smile as his goodnight.

Under normal circumstances she wouldn't mind getting up early, but she had been working twelve-hour days since Dan left. She stayed back most evenings until nine and liked the luxury of starting a little later in the mornings. She and Tony Falcinella covered Dan's role between them but at the price of her social life and Tony's family life. Coming in early was a minor adjustment to her schedule but she allowed herself to be annoyed.

When she finally got home, her whole body was sagging with exhaustion and a headache was piercing relentlessly behind her eyes.

"Paul's phoned twice. He said he rang you at work as well but you never returned his call," Fiona yelled from the kitchen before Claire had even closed the front door.

"For God's sake, I do have a job to do. I can't take personal phone calls all day," she answered, irritated. She joined Fiona in the kitchen.

"Let me guess . . . you've had a hard day," Fiona commented calmly, dipping a spoon into the pot and blowing before tasting the contents tentatively.

"Right in one. Robert Pozos arrived today," Claire said and sat down with a yawn, flinging her handbag onto the kitchen table. "What's that? It smells great."

"Good old Irish stew."

"Great, I'm starving. I didn't have time for a proper lunch."

"That's really stupid. You'll get sick if you don't eat properly."

"I know, I know. Things should get better now that Robert has arrived."

"What's he like?" Fiona asked with mild interest.

"All the girls in the office are mad about him. You should have seen the style in the Finance Department this morning – I nearly choked from the whiff of perfume when I walked in." Claire smiled despite herself, remembering how funny it had been and wondering if Robert had any idea of the effect he had.

"So he's good-looking?" Fiona looked more interested now.

"You could say that. Something tells me that working for him isn't going to be a holiday – he seems to have endless energy." She leant across to the fridge and extracted a carton of orange juice without getting up from her seat. There was a comfortable silence as she drank her juice and Fiona stirred and tasted.

"Is everything OK between you and Paul?" Fiona asked after a few minutes.

"Why?"

"He rings here every evening and because you're always at work, I end up spending hours talking to him . . . he's driving me around the bend."

"You and me both," Claire said vehemently. "I've decided to finish with him. He's too intense by far . . . I can't cope with it . . . especially as I'm so busy at work."

"Are you sure about how you feel?"

"Yes, there's no spark. He's attractive, intelligent, successful . . . but the whole package does nothing to make my knees weak."

"If he leaves you cold, why did you go out with him for the last two months?"

"I was giving it time," Claire shrugged. "After being with Michael for so long, I knew I wouldn't feel any great passion straight away."

"Ah . . . so it's passion you're after!"

"That's right, I want undiluted passion. Looking back, even my relationship with Michael was too sedate. I want someone who puts me in a spin. Paul isn't going to do that."

"OK, Ms Passion . . . most girls would regard Paul as quite a catch. I just want to know you're sure before you dump him." Fiona jokingly wagged her finger in warning.

"Trust me, I'm sure . . . even little things about him annoy me ... for example – and I know you'll think I'm being petty – he's always talking about Amtech. He's totally fascinated with every little detail about my working day. It makes me mad – work is the last thing I want to talk about in my spare time."

"When are you planning to do the dirty deed?"

Claire looked at Fiona in confusion.

"You know, break it off – the dirty deed," Fiona explained.

"Oh, I didn't know what you meant there . . . I'll try to avoid him until the weekend and I'll handle it then," she said with a sigh. She didn't need any more hassles for the rest of the week. She suspected she would need all her energy to keep up with Robert.

"Why don't you unwind and watch some TV," Fiona suggested. "It'll be a while before dinner is ready." Claire obediently got up and trudged to the comfort of the couch.

"I'm going out with James tonight. I'll probably stay at his place."

She heard Fiona's voice, faint and distant as she rested her head on some cushions and closed her heavy eyes.

She woke, her back stiff and her face cold. Her sleep-clogged mind tried to remember what she was doing on the couch as her bleary eyes squinted at the clock across the room. It was seven fifteen. She was still under the happy illusion that she was waking from a little nap until she finally registered the daylight.

I have to meet Robert at eight! Oh my God, I haven't a hope in hell of making it on time.

She bolted to the bathroom, still half-asleep, jumping into the shower, the cold water drowning her disorientation. Assessing her wardrobe in panic, she chose a sleeveless ice-blue dress. It had the redeemable feature of not needing to be ironed. She was dressed in one minute. She quickly put on some lipstick and combed her wet hair back from her face. It was seven thirty when she hailed a taxi and seven fifty-five when she arrived at work.

* * *

Robert watched her rush through the office from the comfort of his leather swivel-chair. Her dress outlined her figure in a way that was almost inappropriate. Her hair was still wet and he knew she would smell of shampoo and soap. He studied her in a predatory but detached manner. She was tall. He hadn't noticed that yesterday. He thought to himself that she was quite attractive, in a natural unaffected way.

A minute later she was back. She had collected some files from her office. She placed them on his desk and sat down with a sigh of relief.

"You just wouldn't believe what happened to me this morning," she said, a little out of breath. "I fell asleep on the couch last night and didn't wake up until forty-five minutes ago . . . I can't believe I actually got here on time." She looked at her watch in disbelief.

Robert was amused by her honesty; it was refreshing, almost exciting. He didn't point out to her that she was a few minutes late and he had been waiting, punctuality being a fetish of his. She seemed to be totally relaxed in his presence. He was used to, and bored with, people holding him in awe.

"Do you normally sleep on the couch or did you have a fight with your boyfriend?" he asked, his eyes teasing her.

She resisted the lead to reveal whether she was attached or not.

"I was late home from work . . . and I was just so tired. That reminds me, I had no dinner. Ignore my tummy if it starts making rude noises," she said wryly, patting her flat stomach. He inadvertently glanced at the hand placed where the dress stretched across her shapely hips. He stood up.

"Please excuse me a moment. I need to get something before we start."

When he left she opened her files, relieved to have some time to prepare for the meeting. She wasn't sure if Robert wanted to discuss the financial results, the finance department or both. One of her files had job descriptions for each member of staff and she left it open on the table so they could access the information conveniently. She had also printed off the monthly results package in its extended form. She flicked through the pages, familiarising herself with the key figures so she wouldn't have to refer to the hard copy unnecessarily.

He returned some ten minutes later, juggling two cups of coffee and a brown-paper bag from Muffin Break.

"I can't stand hungry women! They are generally too cranky to be productive," he said, his smile dancing with charm.

She blushed, embarrassed that he had gone to such trouble. She wasn't that hungry – she had only been making conversation. "Thank you . . ." she murmured.

"Let's eat!" he said and opened the muffin bag for her.

The banana muffins disappeared in no time.

"Thank you," she said again as she cleared away the debris. "Where would you like to start?"

"How about we begin with the people. What do the finance team do, what are their strengths and weaknesses . . . and how are they perceived by the field?" he said, professional and serious without delay. The 'Muffin Man' was gone.

"I've worked closely with all of them over the last five months. I like to think that the department is held in high regard. We do have some challenges, particularly with the sales department, but who doesn't? Overall, I would say that everybody is helpful, professional and better than average at what they do."

"That's good to know. Now I need to hear about the weaknesses."

"The only negative thing I could say is that, with the exception of Emma, the others don't seem to be very ambitious. I guess that's not a true fault to find – ambition can bring its own problems." She answered him slowly being careful with her words, aware that this was his first and so most important overview of her department.

"That's an interesting theory. What kind of problems?" he challenged immediately, studying her hard. Her hair was almost dry now, it fell straight to her shoulders in a black curtain.

"If one has ambition, then you are not going to stay in your current role for very long. As a manager, it means that I have no continuity in that job. Also, if you, the employee, know that you will be leaving within, say, a year, then you don't tackle the long-term issues and you don't own the job one hundred per cent. It's almost like you are planning the day you leave from the day you start." She met his penetrating gaze squarely, fighting intimidation at his directness and intensity.

He nodded some level of agreement, his eyes never leaving her face.

"What about Alan Harris?" he flung at her suddenly,

changing direction with no warning.

"What do you mean?" She made a conscious effort not to sound defensive.

"How do you two get along?" he asked, shrugging his shoulders as if the meaning of his question was obvious.

"Well, now that you've brought it up, not very well. I don't want to be one of those women who blames all bad working relationships on the fact that males can't handle female colleagues . . . but I get the impression that Alan really can't." She was deliberately keeping her tone fair and reasonable.

"He has asked if he can report directly to me rather than through you," Robert stated in a very matter-of-fact way.

She was furious and had trouble disguising it. A mental image of Alan's smug expression made her feel like slapping him across the face. She was sure that Robert wouldn't find her thoughts very professional. It disconcerted her that Alan had approached Robert on his first day – he was obviously a lot more politically astute than she gave him credit for.

"Did he say why?" she asked, her voice controlled and hard.

"He feels that he has much more experience than you and should report to someone more senior." Robert was watching her carefully again and she didn't flinch outwardly.

"So, what did you say?"

"I told him that his reporting line wouldn't be changing and to get over it," he said, finally grinning.

The scrutiny was over, the charm was turned back on. Not usually a great admirer of charm, she found she was much happier to glow in its warmth than to endure the coldness of his scrutiny.

"I also told him that I was grooming you for Finance Director and that he'd better stay on your good side," he continued, banging the table as he laughed loudly.

She gave him a small smile, not sure if she should take him seriously.

He took Emma's job description from the file she had left open on the table.

"Emma has been with the company some time now," he commented as he read the single page.

"Ten years, I think."

"Is she happy in her role?"

"I think so. She did apply for my position when it was vacant but apparently she wasn't successful because she didn't have a formal accounting qualification."

"Do you have a career plan in place for her?" Claire was impressed with his line of thought and glad that she had a positive answer for him.

"Yes, she's now enrolled in CPA. I'm helping her with the assignments on the days we can both afford to take a lunch break."

He went back to the file, turning the pages slowly. "And James has been here a year, is that right?"

"Yes."

"I remember seeing something in the external audit report about Accounts Payable . . . I can't quite recollect the context but I do remember there was an issue . . . " He was clearly expecting Claire to supply the details that eluded him.

"That was an issue about segregation of duties. It's still a problem. James can set up vendor accounts, process invoices as well as run the payments . . . the auditors would like to see those functions split out amongst three independent staff. They do acknowledge, however, that complete segregation isn't practical for a finance department of our size."

"I remember now ... most of our subsidiaries have the same issue. We're assessing the option of centralising payables in Ireland after the Oracle upgrade is rolled out. If we decide to go ahead, it would resolve this issue."

She suddenly remembered what Susan had said about centralising IT and Finance in Dublin. It seemed like she had been on the right track.

Robert didn't give Claire the opportunity to ask for more details about the proposed centralisation and if it would mean redundancies in the Australian finance department.

"How about Stacey?"

"Stacey's great. She does the work of two people. I should tell you that I'm pretty flexible with her hours. She usually comes in at nine thirty and leaves at four thirty." She quickly looked at him for his reaction. She continued when there was no sign of disapproval. "She's got four kids. She doesn't take a lunch break and she takes work home."

"Sounds reasonable to me."

She was relieved. Flexitime was not officially endorsed by the company and he could have taken a harder line.

They spent the rest of the morning discussing the structure and productivity of the department. He was impressed that each individual had a formal development plan in place. He was keen to introduce some productivity measures for the group and asked her to think further on what would be some meaningful indicators of performance. At one she suggested a break so she could go out and get sandwiches for them both.

He was reading the monthly results package when she returned.

"Who prepares this?" he asked.

"Mostly me but I do get various people to complete the sections that are specific to their area." She put the sandwiches on the table and took hers from its paper wrapping.

"That's a good idea. I like to involve all levels of staff in reporting. Who do you distribute the report to?"

He watched her dab her mouth with a napkin. She had no lipstick left on her lips.

"The senior management team," she responded.

"Do they read it?"

"Some do. Others wouldn't read it even if I printed *Playboy* on the cover," she said with a grin.

He laughed. "Do you think there is any merit in giving a copy to each employee?"

"Maybe. I suppose I could include a glossary to help explain some of the terminology."

"Would it be a lot of extra work if you provided this report to a few hundred people?" He looked at her, waiting for her answer.

"Not really. If I could get some secretarial support it would be OK. Maybe Samantha could help."

Samantha used to be Dan's personal assistant and now worked for Robert.

"OK, let's give it a try next month and see what kind of response we get."

He was inspiring to work with. He was interested in the detail, interested in the people. At the end of the day she had a few pages of notes. He wanted her to provide extra information on a lot of the issues they had touched on throughout the day. He wanted her considered opinions on his suggestions for improvement. For the first time in a few months, she felt motivated. His energy was contagious; it steamrolled any complacency that might be lurking on the sidelines.

* * *

Robert's phone rang just after Claire left.

"Hi, honey, it's me."

"Hello, Julia . . . how are you?" He made an effort to inject some enthusiasm into his voice.

141

"I'm good . . . but I'm missing you. How's Sydney?"

"Beautiful. It's winter here so it's cool in the evenings. But the days are still in the low 20's and there's plenty of sun."

"It sounds lovely. How's the job? I hope you're not working too hard."

"Things are in reasonable shape, better than I expected considering the role was vacant for a few months."

There was a pause and he knew what she would say next.

"When can I come out to see you?"

"Now's not a good time, Julia," he responded, his voice kind to take the hurt from his words. "I've only been here a few days and there's a lot to do."

"I'm very lonely here without you, Robert." She sounded miserable.

"I know you are . . . why don't we talk about a trip in a few weeks . . . when I've settled in and have less on my mind?" He felt bad about giving her false hope but knew that it was the wrong time for the confrontation they needed to have.

"A few weeks is a long time to me right now," she whispered.

"Nonsense. You'll see how fast it will pass . . . I have to go now. Take care, I'll call you next week."

* * *

Claire wondered whether she should go home or be diligent and clear her inbox. She had received fifteen messages while she was with Robert. She noticed one was from Susan and kept that until last, dealing with the more mundane ones first.

Hi Claire,

How goes it? You haven't written to me in ages . . . I want you to know I'm taking it personally! Your replacement has fitted in well. She was fairly studious at the start and showed the rest of us up. We beat that out of her, though. I'll never forgive Mark for not taking on that gorgeous guy. I told him that it was outright discrimination against good-looking people.

I met Michael in Major Toms over the weekend. You won't believe this – the bastard is getting married. Before you ask, she isn't pregnant. He was very offended when I asked. I told him that you were having a ball in Sydney.

Write to me for God's sake. I'm bored.

Susan

It was a cruel attack on her new world, a slap in the face of her determination to prove she was over Michael. She had changed her life, gone to the other side of the globe to recover from a man who was going to marry someone else just six months later.

It was mean not to respond to Susan but she wasn't capable of even stringing some bland lines together. She shut down her PC and locked her office door, dangerously close to tears.

Robert was the last person she wanted to see but

143

there he was, holding the lift for her as he saw her approaching. She murmured her thanks and stared into space until they reached the ground floor.

"Bye, see you tomorrow," she said, her voice so subdued that he barely heard.

She was gone before he could reply. He stood for a few seconds watching her slim figure as she ran towards the train station. She seemed upset. Had something happened at work since their meeting or was it personal? He was surprised at his need to know. Maybe she was just a moody person, friendly one minute, surly the next. He was disappointed for some strange reason.

* * *

"Michael is getting married." She marched into the kitchen, her expression wobbling between rage and despair. She didn't expect James to be there.

"Who the hell is Michael?" he asked innocently.

"He's an asshole," Fiona snapped, glaring at him pointedly and he retreated to the living-room to leave them alone. "Are you serious?"

"Susan met him over the weekend. I'm so – so furious – that he fed me all that – that – *bullshit* about finding himself!" She started to cry, "What is wrong with men? Either they are lying bastards, like Michael, or they pester the hell out of me, like Paul!"

"Is she pregnant –" Fiona started.

"No, I can't even console myself with that!" She wiped her wet face with the back of her hand, streaking mascara across her cheekbone.

"So are you upset because you still have feelings for him or because he fed you bullshit?" Fiona asked gently, putting her arm around Claire as an awkward attempt to comfort her. She had never seen her so upset before and didn't quite know what to do.

"I still have feelings for him . . . I suppose I always will . . . but I'm more angry that he made a fool of me than anything. He must have been seeing Karen seriously while we were going out if they're getting – married – already!" She gulped the last few words, finding it difficult to cry and talk at the same time.

Fiona gave Claire a tight hug before extracting herself and opening their 'drinks cabinet', a long narrow cupboard under the kitchen sink.

"This should ease the pain a little," she said as she poured a generous vodka, adding only a little lemonade.

"I mean, how can he do a flip like that? One minute he's breaking up with me because he isn't ready for marriage . . . but surprise, surprise, with his *new* girlfriend, it seems like the right thing to do . . . do you have any idea how inadequate that makes me feel?"

"How did your meeting with Robert go today?" Fiona asked brightly, avoiding the open question of adequacy. Her effort to change the subject of conversation was not intended to be subtle.

Claire was glad to talk about something else and took a healthy swig of her drink, spluttering as the undiluted vodka burned its way through her system.

"God, are you trying to kill me?" she managed to laugh. "It went pretty well. I think I'm going to like working for him. What a charmer though! There were a few times when I could have sworn he was flirting with me. It's probably just my imagination – I'm sure he would go for a higher class of girl than me!"

"Yeah, you are a bit of a peasant all right," Fiona was quick to remark.

When James heard them giggling, he poked his head cautiously around the door.

"Is it safe?" he asked with exaggerated terror.

"As safe as it will ever be," Fiona answered.

"Good! Can I have one of those?" he asked, pointing at Claire's drink, the telltale bottle of vodka still on the table.

"You can, but don't expect me to make it for you," Fiona retorted.

He opted for a beer instead.

* * *

The senior management team made a more serious effort at keeping their commitment for the July meeting. After all, the form and frequency of the meeting itself was the first item on the agenda. And Robert Pozos would be there, a senior vice-president who had the ability to wipe out the entire team if he wasn't impressed by the standard of their performance.

Robert had asked Claire to go to the meeting as she

was closer to the numbers than he was. Samantha was there to minute the meeting, another change in Robert's honour.

"OK . . . good morning everyone," Steve began, clearing his throat. "I believe that we're all present . . . before I move to the first item, I would like to take this opportunity to welcome Robert to the team. Robert will assume the Finance Director's role for the next six months as our external search was not successful. Needless to say, Robert will continue to perform his vice-president's role from Sydney . . . so make sure you all take advantage of the fast track that Robert can offer to Donald Skates."

The directors laughed politely at Steve's effort at humour.

"OK, moving right along . . . David, this first item is the issue you raised last month so I'll hand over to you."

"Thanks, Steve," David said, leaning forward in his seat. "Over the last twelve months we've met a total of seven times. Of those seven meetings, there were only two where we were all present. Those statistics tell me that this meeting doesn't make it onto the priority list of the members of this team."

"I think that's a bit harsh," Steve interrupted, looking in Robert's direction to gauge his reaction to the potentially dangerous accusation.

"I don't believe so, Steve. We have no other venue to execute strategic planning. We have no other means of sharing what's happening across the business with the other team members. If we don't meet once a month, for at least a few hours, how can we possibly expect to successfully run this company?"

David sat back, finished, and waited for the others to comment. There was silence. Nobody was prepared to disagree with him in front of Robert Pozos. He smiled because he could tell there would be no absentees as long as the vice-president was around.

Claire ran into trouble when she was presenting the divisional profit and loss. Frank was smarting from his inability to challenge David on the management meetings. Claire was an easier target.

"I want to know about this 'exceptional item' that you're showing in my numbers. What is it?" he asked, staring at her from across the table with his black eyes.

"It's a bad debt, Frank. We've taken a provision against the amount we have outstanding with Nutrifast since last March," she explained.

"Why wasn't I consulted before my bottom line was hit?" His voice was angry.

She ensured her response was even, reasonable. "It's corporate policy to reserve against debts that are over three months old – it's an automatic process."

He threw his hands up in frustration. "It's – not – the – corporate – policy – that I'm questioning," he emphasised each word with contempt. "It's why I wasn't informed about it."

Tension drenched the room. She could see the others

watching her, expecting her to crack.

"Frank, can we take this off-line?" Robert asked, glancing at Claire as he spoke.

"It's OK, Robert," she said calmly. "Frank, you are right. I should have let you know in advance that this adjustment would be made in June. I apologise for surprising you."

The meeting went for five hours. It was intense and exhausting. When they finished, Claire left without delay to begin the walk from the hotel to the office. It was raining when she went outside.

"Claire, hold on." It was Robert.

She stopped and waited without turning around.

"I'm sorry that happened," he said, out of breath when he caught up.

"You've nothing to be sorry about. Frank was right to pull me up," she answered, starting to walk.

"He wasn't right to talk to you like that. It was way out of line. I'm sure Steve will speak to him about his behaviour."

"Robert . . . I'm not some little girl that needs to be protected. I can handle Frank myself. I don't need you . . . or Steve to fight my battles." She had raised her voice marginally.

He looked at her – her face was wet from the rain. He could tell she was more upset about the incident than she would admit. They walked the rest of the way in silence.

* * *

Mark called her later that evening.

"Hello, stranger, we miss you over here."

She recognised his upper-class Dublin accent immediately.

"Mark . . . hello," she said in surprise. "Long time, no hear. How are you?"

"Busy, very busy . . . and how are you? Enjoying your new role, I hope?"

"I was until today. I got a bit of a hammering this morning but I'm sure I'll get over it," she replied with honesty.

"There's nothing like a good hammering – it makes you a better, stronger person. Right?"

"Right," she agreed with a laugh.

"Now, back to business – this is not merely a social call. We're nearing the end of the Irish rollout for the Oracle Payables upgrade."

"That went by quickly. How did it work out?"

"Surprisingly smooth," Mark answered. "A few glitches but nothing major. Australia is now firmly in our sights and I wanted to talk to you about a rough timetable."

"The sooner the better, as far as I'm concerned. Our payables processes are quite weak and we're looking forward to the improvements that the upgrade will bring."

"Good. I'll forward you a timetable later today. Now, there was one other thing . . ." he paused.

"Yes?"

"I just wanted to give you a heads-up that Michael will be involved in your rollout. As you know, he is the IT implementation project manager."

"Thanks, Mark. I appreciate you letting me know."

* * *

Robert was coming to the conclusion that he didn't like the way Frank Williams operated. He displayed none of the core values that Amtech expected of its leaders across the globe. Robert wanted to confront him but he recognised that it was Steve Ryan's place to take the corrective action and not his. He would wait to see what Steve would do. He was thinking of Claire when his phone rang.

"Hi." It was Julia.

"Hello." He was unable to summon up any affection.

"You haven't called me in a week." Her voice was suspiciously uneven.

"I apologise, Julia. That was wrong of me. Sometimes when I'm working hard, I forget everything else. You should know me by now." He gave a placatory laugh.

"That's no excuse, Robert. You're on the other side of the world. I don't wake up beside you, I don't get to hear your voice. I feel as if we aren't married any more." She was drunk – there was no way she would be so confrontational if she was sober.

"Hey, calm down – there's no need to get upset."

"Don't tell me to calm down! I need to see you . . . I need to see my husband." Her angry words were slurring.

"Julia, I can't talk to you when you're like this," he said, his tone dangerously soft. "I'll call you over the weekend."

He hung up, depressed. He was married to a neurotic alcoholic. He didn't yet know the emotional or financial price of extracting himself from the marriage. He rang Tom Healy, his lawyer and old friend.

"Hello, Tom, Robert here."

"Robert, man, I thought you had fallen off the side of the world."

"I'm sorry, Tom, I should have called you to let you know what was happening . . . I needed some time to think after our last discussion." Robert's voice was subdued. The last time he had talked to Tom was the night before he left for Sydney. The topic of conversation had been divorce and Robert had taken a raincheck on the decision.

"Have you decided what you want to do?"

Robert hesitated before responding. "Yes, I've just come off the phone from Julia . . . our relationship is totally beyond repair . . . I want you to go ahead."

"I'm sorry, Robert, I truly am," Tom was sympathetic. "I'll get started on the paperwork straight away."

"I guess it will be the same process as it was with Dianne," said Robert bleakly.

* * *

Julia called Cherie straight after her disturbing conversation with Robert. Wayne answered but she didn't bother to make small talk with him.

"I've talked to Robert," she said when Cherie came on the line.

"How is he?" Cherie asked, sitting on the stairs with the phone. Phone calls with Julia were often lengthy.

"He won't commit to me coming to see him in Sydney . . . says he'll call me over the weekend . . . but I know he'll put it off again."

Cherie could hear the click of Julia's lighter and her sharp intake as she inhaled.

"It's not surprising that Rob is preoccupied – he's busy. He's doing two jobs, for goodness' sake."

"You're always defending him." Julia's tone was accusatory.

"No, I'm not. I'm giving you an independent view. Rob's a hard worker. He has to be at his level in the company. He doesn't have a nine-to-five job."

"That's absolutely true. But I *want* him to have a nine-to-five job! I want him to *leave* Amtech."

Cherie was taken aback by Julia's vehemence.

"Now you're being ridiculous."

"No, I'm not. If Amtech wasn't in the picture, we would be able to spend quality time together."

"Julia, take a reality check. Look at the house you live in . . . that's right, have a good look around . . . now, look at the clothes you're wearing . . . well-made, expensive . . . you have a lot to be thankful to Amtech for." Cherie was losing her patience.

"You're wrong. What's the point in having all these material possessions if we don't even get to see each other?" Julia was like a dog with a bone.

"Rob loves his job. There's no way he's going to leave the company," Cherie reasoned.

"Watch this space, Cherie. Watch this space," Julia said darkly and abruptly hung up.

"What was that all about?" Wayne asked, ungluing his eyes from the TV to look at Cherie as she sat down beside him.

"Just Julia . . . blaming Amtech for all her problems with Robert." She moved a toy from the sofa so she could sit comfortably.

"I'm intrigued. How has she reached that conclusion?" Wayne was sarcastic. He didn't have much time for Julia.

"She doesn't see Robert when he's here; he doesn't call her when he's away. She says he's too busy with work to have a wife." Cherie yawned. She was tired.

"Robert has always been over the top with the hours he works . . . it's all part of the image he presents to Donald. It's how he justifies his enormous salary."

"Don't be so cynical," Cherie frowned at him. "Robert has a lot of responsibility and he's very committed. How many vice-presidents are hands-on enough to take a Finance Director's role in a subsidiary?"

"That was his choice. It's the most stupid idea he's ever come up with."

Cherie was furious with Wayne for speaking about Robert in such a derogatory way but she swallowed her retort. She was too tired for an argument. They watched the news in silence for the next five minutes.

"Julia wants him to leave Amtech," she said eventually. She wasn't good with silences.

"She might not have to wait too long. We should all make the most of Robert's little visit to Sydney. Sooner or later, Donald will come to his senses and tell Robert to get back to San Jose or get out."

Wayne's jaw was rigid after his bizarre outburst. They were close to an argument so she left him to the TV and went for a bath. She didn't know what the hell was wrong with him tonight.

* * *

Paul went off to Brisbane for two weeks before Claire had the chance to speak to him. Digicom was responding to a multi-million dollar tender with the Queensland Government. Claire didn't tell Paul that Amtech was bidding on the same deal or that Frank Williams was also in Queensland. In fact, Amtech had an existing relationship with the client and Robert was confident enough to include the revenue in the quarter's forecast.

Paul called her every day while he was away and by the second week she had nothing left to say to him. She had call display on her phone and didn't pick up when she recognised the Queensland number coming through. She had a week's worth of voicemails that she hadn't listened to when he returned to Sydney.

She went around to see him after work Friday evening. As she rang the bell, she hoped he would be home now that she had psyched herself up for the long overdue confrontation. He opened the door before the bell stopped ringing. She didn't have the opportunity to avoid his embrace.

"Hi, stranger! I've been trying to call you all week . . . you've obviously been too busy to call me back!" His tone was free from accusation.

"Yeah, I had a lot of meetings and worked late most nights. That's why I kept missing your calls," she answered, hating herself for lying.

"I left you some voicemails . . . "

"I know."

"OK, I forgive you. Have you had dinner? Do you want to go out for something to eat?"

"No, I need to talk to you," she said, deliberating injecting coldness into her voice to make him realise all was not well.

"That sounds ominous," he commented lightly.

"I'm afraid it is . . . "

"Don't you want to come in? The doorway doesn't seem to be a good place to have an ominous discussion."

She didn't want to go into his living-room, sit on his sofa, drink his tea, lose her nerve.

She stepped inside the door and stood firmly in the hallway.

"Paul, I think we should stop seeing each other," she said, her words tumbling out in a rush. "I can't handle how intense you are. It's not what I want in my life right now."

"Please come in and sit down so we can at least talk it through," he said calmly. He started to walk towards the living-room. He stopped when she didn't follow.

"No, I'll lose my resolve. I've been wanting to say this for a few weeks and I'm sorry if I seem abrupt and heartless but it's the only way I can do it."

"If you want me to back off, then that's fine. But we don't need to break up to achieve that." His voice was confident, convincing. It was the first time she had seen the 'sales' side of his personality.

"Paul . . . it's not working out. Yes, I feel smothered . . . but there are other things that are wrong as well . . . it's just not working out . . . for me."

"OK then . . . if that's what you want." He was surprisingly detached and his lack of emotion confirmed her instinct that there was no special spark between them.

"I guess I'll see you around because of Fiona and James. Keep in touch," she said before letting herself out.

As she hailed down a taxi, she wondered what Paul had got out of their relationship. For someone who had been so attentive, he didn't seem very bothered that she had finished it. She felt justifiably miffed at his lukewarm reaction. Fiona wasn't there when she got home. Like most people with a life, she was out on the town, getting ridiculously drunk. Claire wondered at what point her holiday had turned into reality. It was Friday night and she was sitting at home with the exciting prospect of work tomorrow.

* * *

On Saturday morning, the brightness and energy from the morning sun made her feel better. When she got outside she was surprised to find that the sun was weak and there was a definite nip in the air. She shivered in her shorts and resolved to buy more appropriate clothes for the coming months.

It was a pleasure catching the train, not having to fight for a seat or run with the crowds as they swept impatiently through the station. She turned on the lights when she got to the office, relieved that nobody else was in, not in the mood for mindless chit-chat when all she wanted to do was work. She worked solidly for four hours, aiming to get out of the office by lunch-time and salvage something of the weekend.

"What are you doing here on such a beautiful day?"

It was Robert Pozos. He had admired her slim brown legs for a few moments before making his presence known.

She visibly jumped, not expecting to hear a voice interrupt the deathly weekend silence of the office.

"God Almighty! You scared the living daylights out of me," she squeaked.

He laughed and she swirled her seat around to face

him. Her face was bare of make-up, her black hair was tied back carelessly.

"Don't you have better things to do at weekends than hanging out at the office?" he asked. He was fishing for some information about her personal life and hoped he wasn't being too obvious.

"Not really. I broke up with my boyfriend last night . . . Coming to work is pleasant next to my miserable personal life." She gave a small laugh.

"I know how you must feel. I'm going through a divorce at the moment. I must admit that I did throw myself into work over the last few months, working weekends and twelve-hour days," he said frankly. "Now that I'm away from that mess, I must remind myself to wind down and relax a little."

He sounded lonely and she felt almost sorry for him. Knowing that he was divorcing his wife disconcerted her. She had him in the 'married category' in her mind. He was looking at her expectantly.

"I'm sorry to hear about your divorce." She didn't know what else to say.

"Thank you, but it has been a long time coming and it's certainly for the best."

She looked anxious to return to her work. He knew he should leave.

"Do you have much work to do today?" he asked, moving closer to her desk.

"A few more hours. I should have that information ready for you first thing Monday morning."

He frowned, trying to recall what she was talking about. His face cleared when he remembered.

"I didn't intend for you to work the weekend to do those reports . . . they can wait."

"It's OK . . . I only came in because I'm a little bit behind at the moment."

His eyes connected with hers. He was fascinated by their colour. They were navy against startling white, huge in her petite face.

"Well, I'd better get on with this or I'll never get out of here," she said, indicating the papers strewn on her desk to cover her discomfort.

"OK, I'll see you Monday. Have a good weekend," he smiled and left reluctantly.

* * *

Claire tried to take it easy for the rest of the weekend. She didn't go out with Fiona that Saturday night, a cardinal sin in Fiona's eyes. She was a firm believer that Saturday nights were sacred – you had to have a very pathetic life if you stayed at home. Claire somehow resisted the pressure and went to bed early with a book. She was fast asleep fifteen minutes later and didn't wake until late the next day, still tired. It was an overcast morning and she was secretly relieved. She wouldn't feel as guilty about staying at home all day. Remembering that she had brought home some two hundred cheques that needed her signature, she decided to get that particular nasty task out of the way. She put the cheques on the bed, propped up her pillows and starting signing.

She wasn't concentrating too hard on what she was doing as the cheques required two signatures and Robert had already signed. She had signed the one for DC Solutions and a few more after it before it triggered that she had never heard of DC Solutions before and the cheque was for a large amount: $600,000. She retrieved the cheque and studied the supporting paperwork. It was a commission payment related to a deal Amtech had signed during the week with Initial Insurance. It wasn't unusual for the company to pay commissions to outside parties who gave them the sales lead or helped close the deal. Claire remembered the deal being approximately $3 million, which made this commission 20% of the revenue. The usual rate was in the range of 5% to 10%. She put a Post-it on the face of the cheque to follow-up with Frank Williams the next morning.

* * *

"Hi Claire, how was your weekend?" Emma asked, popping in to say hello on her way to her desk.

"Boring wouldn't do it justice. How about you?" Claire answered, going through her mail as she spoke.

"Fantastic! Went on one last camping trip before the winter comes in. Stayed in a place called Seal Rocks . . . it was great. You'd love it there."

Emma had a very active outdoor life and frequently gave Claire welcome tips on bush walks and unspoilt beaches that were off the tourist track.

There was a red envelope in her mail that looked like an invitation of some sort.

"Oh, that's your invite to the Sales Kick-off. It's being held in Berossa House," Emma said as Claire opened it.

"Where's that?"

"On the North Shore. It's a beautiful old house. Lots of people get married there."

"Are you going?" Claire asked, quickly scanning the invitation.

"*Everyone's* going! We had the best time last year! Nobody turned up at work the next day due to severe Hangover City! And they're having it on a Thursday night again this year . . . wouldn't you think they'd have learnt their lesson?"

Emma had a pained expression on her face, presumably from the memory of how she felt the day after last year's event. Claire looked up from the invitation, just in time to see Frank Williams walking purposefully past her office.

"Frank, Frank, have you got a minute?" she yelled after him.

He changed direction and came back, his huge bulk leaning on the slender doorframe. "Yes, what's wrong?"

"It's about the payment to DC Solutions for the Initial Insurance deal. It works out at 20%. How come we're paying them so much ?" she asked, getting straight to the point. She and Frank didn't pretend to exchange pleasantries since the last senior management meeting.

"We didn't have a choice. It was a very competitive deal and DC Solutions got us in there. We hadn't a hope of winning it without them."

"I haven't come across them before . . . are they new?"

"This was our first time doing business together."

"Do we have a contract with them?" she persisted, ignoring his obvious irritation at being questioned further.

"No, we don't have a contract. It was a last-minute verbal deal. But if another deal comes up with them, I will personally make sure that our solicitors write a contract."

"Do that," she said, refusing to back down

"Is that all?" he challenged, making a move to leave.

"I suppose so."

"Touchy, isn't he?" Emma commented when he was gone.

"Frank doesn't like to be asked questions, especially not by me. Would you mind putting this cheque on James' desk as it's on your way?"

She wasn't totally satisfied with Frank's explanation but there wasn't anything else she could do. Frank was always so glib that she was never sure if he was telling the truth. She suspected that the Sales and Marketing Manager rarely had an honest moment.

CHAPTER EIGHT

Berossa House was an impressive venue for the Sales Kick-off. An expanse of immaculately manicured gardens protected it from the noise of the busy street. The old house was cloaked in soft outdoor lights, giving it a regal but welcoming aura. The four weeks that led up to the event were very busy for Claire. Robert was exacting and had endless stamina. She had prepared a lot of the financial information that he was going to present at the kick-off.

It was a full-day forum, with a series of presentations right through the day, ranging from new technical information to general strategies for the company in the coming fiscal year. The pace was fast and Claire had to listen carefully to Steve Ryan's presentation.

"To summarise, we need to do more business through our partners in the next year . . . it's the only way we'll be able to expand the company. We'll be taking on two new sales reps who will specialise in cultivating relationships with partners who have the potential to give us worthwhile sales leads. We will have standard contracts with all parties. This is an area where we have been lax in the past."

Steve switched slides to a colourful bar chart.

"One of the key assumptions behind our budgeted margin figure in this slide is a maximum incentive payment of 10% to our partners. It's important to ensure that we stay within this limit. You must remember that we will be eroding our margins with this new sales strategy. Giving more than 10% could put us in a loss."

And about time too. That should mean no more cheques like the one for DC Solutions. If we have supporting contracts and standard percentages, I'll have nothing left to argue with Frank about . . . we'll be best of friends. Claire smiled to herself.

Robert's presentation was the last one of the day. His focus was on the common weaknesses in the deals that the sales team had closed during the year. Claire had spent a few days researching the issues for him. They had worked together to narrow the list down to a few priorities he would emphasise in his presentation. He was a good presenter, his natural authority demanding the attention even of those less interested listeners. She couldn't help admiring him – his confident voice, his casual movements across the podium as he talked through the slides.

"Amtech is getting a name in the market for being a soft touch. Our customers know we will do anything to get revenue at quarter end. The deals we strike in the last week of the quarter have the worst margins and are fraught with problems. We are often forcing the customer to take software that they are not ready for. Not only is this not professional, but when we go to collect the money the customer argues that they didn't want the software until a month later . . . so why should they pay now? And their argument is valid."

His slide showed the top ten collection issues with the name of the relevant sales person beside the amount. Claire smiled to herself as she saw the embarrassed faces of those who were named. It was a good way to get action on the issues.

"Most of the problem accounts that Alan Harris is currently working on have stemmed from early delivery in the mad rush to meet quarter-end deadlines."

Claire shot a look in Alan's direction. He glowed with self-importance at Robert's reference to him.

"We've got to stop this quarter-end rush and spread our sales out evenly over the quarter. To facilitate this new initiative, we will be setting monthly targets instead of quarterly targets for our sales team. As result, our deals should be constructed better and we should also find that both our and finance staff will have a more even workload." He paused to look at his watch; they were a half hour behind schedule. "Any questions?"

Frank Williams had his hand raised before Robert

stopped speaking. One of the ushers handed him a microphone.

"No questions, Robert. I just want to take this opportunity to point out that the company will not only be setting monthly targets but as a result will also pay commissions monthly. The whole sales team will benefit from the positive cash flow of being paid commission within one month of closing the sale."

All he is interested in is how much money he gets and when he gets it, Claire thought. She knew Robert well enough to see that he was irritated by the unnecessary interruption.

"Thank you for adding that, Frank. We will be releasing a new commission plan that will spell out how it all works. We'll organise a road show to launch the new plan. Now, any more questions?"

He scanned the audience briefly.

"Never let it be said that I stood between you lot and the bar." This got a laugh, chairs were vacated with relief and a hum of conversation started as they made their way out to the foyer.

The company had booked rooms at the venue so staff could shower and change before the formal dinner in the evening. Emma, Stacey and Claire were sharing a room. Black was the theme of the night and all guests had to be dressed from head to toe in that colour. Claire's dress was a figure-hugging velvet, with slits from her ankle to knee on both sides. Stacey put her hair up for her, tendrils framing her face on both sides.

She spent quite some time with her make-up as the dress deserved it.

The night was unusually warm for July so they had the pre-dinner cocktails on the balcony. Robert was talking to Steve Ryan. He saw Claire smile and greet a number of people as she made her way to the bar. She was beautiful. He was conscious of the looks she was getting from some of the other men and he felt ridiculously jealous. He wondered if any of her admirers would get lucky with her tonight. He was immediately ashamed of his thoughts, knowing that she wasn't that type of girl. She was talking to Brian Brooker now and they were both laughing loudly. He had to restrain himself from going over and dragging her away from him.

By the time they were ushered inside for dinner, most people had downed a number of cocktails. Claire was flushed and feeling a little light-headed. All the Finance Department sat together at a large round table. Robert was sitting with the other executives. Claire, for some silly reason, had expected him to sit at their table. Watching him with the more sober executives brought home to her that she and the others were not in the same league. He was sitting next to Frank Williams. She noticed that there wasn't much conversation between them.

The mood was boisterous and an outrageous quantity of wine was quickly consumed. Whenever a table was served another bottle, someone would shout out their tally. James was determined that their table should drink the most. Even Alan Harris looked less grumpy. Claire was glad she was sitting next to James and Emma and didn't have to struggle to make conversation with Alan all night.

On the way to the bathroom after the main course, she realised she was much tipsier than she had thought. Lifting her dress to negotiate the wooden stairs was a very complicated exercise. Taking deep breaths in the privacy of the cubicle didn't help. She decided to go outside and get some fresh air.

It's so bloody hot . . . no wonder I'm a little lightheaded, she thought.

Making her way back down the stairs with a steady posture required intense concentration. She cursed the dress for being so long and awkward. She went outside, sitting down on one of the benches in the garden. Her head was spinning.

Don't make a fool of yourself. Sober up and don't drink any more. In fact, go home after the dessert.

"Are you all right Claire?"

Oh God, it's Robert. How embarrassing!

"Yes, I'm fine . . . just needed some fresh air. It's very stuffy in there," she said primly.

Then she spoilt the facade by hiccuping and they looked at each other briefly before bursting into laughter.

"OK, I'll own up. I think I had those first few drinks a little too quickly."

He sat down beside her, taking a box of cigarettes from his shirt pocket.

"Would you like a cigarette?" he asked, offering them to her.

She took one and he lit it, his tanned face and brown eyes illuminated for a second. She inhaled too deeply, choking on the smoke in a very undignified manner.

"Sorry, I don't smoke. I don't know why I took one," she explained, giggling.

Robert stood up, laughing, and took her hand.

"Come on. I'll walk you around the garden. It might help sober you up," he said.

It sounded like a sensible plan. When she was standing he let go of her hand and led her by slightly touching her elbow.

"Are you going to fire me for inappropriate behaviour?" she asked, making a funny face at him.

"You'll be getting a serious warning, young lady, but I can't afford to fire you. You work too hard."

The trees were lit with hundreds of tiny bulbs that cast just enough light on the narrow gravel path. Their feet crunched along, jointly making the only sound in the haven of stillness and tranquillity.

"How long do you plan to stay in Australia?" he asked, ruining the beautiful silence.

"I don't know. A few years. Depends on what happens at Amtech, I guess," she answered, distracted by him being so close. She didn't want him to talk; it was at odds with the romance of the garden and it made her feel even more disorientated.

"Everyone thinks very highly of you. You can go far in the company. Would you consider moving to San Jose if a good opportunity came up?" He turned to look at her briefly as they walked.

"Yes, I would," she replied, keeping her eyes down, focussing on her unsteady feet, "but I do want to stay in Sydney a while yet."

"Of course ... I was talking about a few years' time. The company likes to keep its best people and I just want you to be aware that there are opportunities for you outside Australia."

"That's good to know."

"Do you miss Dublin?" His voice was softer, less harsh against the silence.

"No, not at all. Dublin has too many bad memories for me at the moment. Maybe I'll miss it when those particular memories aren't important any more."

In the darkness, when he didn't have her face to distract him, he noticed how beautiful her accent was. He couldn't stop himself from probing further.

"Are those memories connected with your ex-boyfriend?"

He felt her stiffen. "How do you know about Michael?"

"Mark gave me some background information when he put your name forward for the role."

"How embarrassing! I could kill him for telling you that. You must think I'm pathetic ... ." She was upset.

"Not at all, Claire. I admire you for having the courage to start a new life. That's part of the reason I'm in Sydney as well." He thought Michael must be a very stupid man to leave someone like her. He wanted to say it out loud but was unsure what her reaction would be.

"You know, I visited Dublin about three years ago. Mark had just come on board and I went over there to do his induction. I remember being introduced to all his staff but I can't remember meeting you."

"I may have been on study leave. I was doing my finals about then. Anyway, there are a lot of people in the Finance Department in Dublin. I don't think you would have remembered me if we had met."

You're wrong. Again, he had to stop himself from saying it out loud.

"What about you?" she asked. "Do you miss home?"

"No. I haven't been happy in California for many years."

She didn't know how to respond to such a negative statement so she walked silently beside him until he spoke again.

"My personal life has been one mistake after another. I have a lot of regrets."

Claire was hit with the realisation that she liked Robert Pozos, his surprising lack of ego, his self-depreciating frankness.

"You work very hard. Are your regrets due to the fact you committed too much to Amtech?" She was asking the questions now – she wanted to know more about him.

"Partly. That and poor judgement in the relationships I've had."

They were almost back to the wide steps at the front entrance of the house, the brighter lights and the faint sound of music hovering too close. Robert looked down at her, his face darkened by the shadows, his eyes glittering.

"Do you feel OK to go back inside now?" he asked, almost affectionately.

His hand was on her shoulder, she felt it brush her hair gently.

"I think so. At least I have an annual leave day tomorrow, unlike some of the others who are going to be in a very sorry state in the morning . . . I'm sure we must have won the wine tally. Are you proud of the Finance Department's drinking prowess?" She smiled up at him, teasing.

"Very proud. Drinking is one of the most important skills in Finance, much more important than being numerate. That was very clever of you . . . arranging for tomorrow off. What are you planning to do ?" He was interested in how she spent her spare time.

"Sleep in. Go shopping. OK, here goes. I'm going in!" She braced her shoulders and lifted her head dramatically.

Robert leaned forward and she felt something brush the top of her hair.

Did he just kiss my hair?

She went inside, without looking back at him, knowing that he was standing there watching her movements. Nobody had even noticed she was missing and she sat down and joined in the banter easily. She noticed that he came inside about ten minutes later. He sat down without looking in her direction. She must have imagined that intimacy in the garden. It wasn't surprising, considering her advanced state of intoxication.

* * *

It hurt to move her head. She lay in bed for hours, too nauseous to get up. In addition to the dreadful headache, there was another sensation. It was almost like excitement. She compulsively replayed the scene in the garden, feeling his lips brush her hair, finding it impossible to know if it had all been in her imagination or not. She knew how easy it was to get things out of context when you were drunk. Emma phoned her at four o'clock.

"I'm absolutely dying. I've been cursing you all morning for having the day off," she complained. She sounded awful, her voice hoarse and cracked.

"You can't feel as bad as I do, believe me," Claire answered, massaging her head as she spoke. "I haven't been able to get out of bed – I've wasted my precious day off."

"Poor Stacey has spent the day in the loo, being violently ill."

"That's more than I needed to know, Emma." Claire's stomach was still very sensitive and the image of Stacey throwing up didn't help.

"James rang in sick this morning. He said to tell you that he's sorry but if there was any possible way for him to function, at any level, he would have come in. He's promised to work on Sunday instead. Some chance."

"Did Robert come in?" Claire hoped the enquiry sounded casual.

"Yeah, he was in at nine this morning and has been working like a trouper all day," Emma answered, not detecting anything unusual about the question. "He came over and asked me some questions that I actually had to use my brain to answer. It nearly killed me."

"What time did you guys finish up last night?" Claire had left straight after the meal.

"About three in the morning." Emma sounded proud.

"Really? Who was left there at that time?"

"Myself, James, Alan Harris, Frank Williams and some others from sales. The sales crowd headed off to the casino to blow their hard-earned commission so we went home. Alan followed Frank to the casino like a puppy-dog. He thinks he's part of Frank's inner circle."

Claire wanted to ask what time Robert left but didn't know how without being obvious.

She chatted with Emma for another ten minutes

175

before she told her she could go home early. She suspected that Emma had called originally with that purpose in mind. When she hung up, the inexplicable sense of excitement from earlier was dampened. She realised that she had been subconsciously hoping that Robert would call her. She knew it was stupid, but she felt something had changed between them last night. It was now five o'clock; the day was over. He wasn't going to call.

* * *

She went into work on Sunday so she could catch up on her messages. The lights were on. James was sitting at his desk, Paul standing next to him. They didn't see her approach – they were preoccupied with whatever was on the screen of James' computer.

"Hello." She stopped right beside them but James closed the window before she could see what was on the screen.

"What are you doing here, Paul?" she asked, her voice tight.

"I dropped James off."

"Yeah, my car is being serviced," James added.

"On a Sunday?" She raised her eyebrows in disbelief.

"Yes, on a Sunday . . . this is an international city," James replied, his tone defensive.

"Whatever you say," she snapped, giving him sharp look. "Paul, sorry to move you but we have a company policy that James should know about . . . only staff are allowed beyond the reception area."

"Loosen up, Claire – you know Paul. We're doing no harm." James smiled at her. Claire knew he had some games on his desktop and suspected he was showing off his prowess to Paul. She agreed it was harmless but wanted him to understand it was a serious breach of security.

"We also have a policy that stipulates that staff, and only staff, can access our internal software. James should know that as well. I don't know what you guys are doing here but you'd better get out of the system right now."

"But I came in here to do some work," James objected.

"If you do something like this again, your future will be freed up and you won't have to worry about work," she retorted.

She waited for him to log off and walked with them to the foyer.

She rang Fiona when she got back to her office.

"Hi, Fi, a quick question – is James' car in for a service today?"

"Not that I know of. He gave me a lift home this morning and didn't mention anything about it. The car does need a service, though, and he may well have booked it into the garage without telling me. Why?"

"No reason. I'll see you later. I'm going to the gym when I've finished up here so I'll be home about five."

James called her about thirty minutes later.

"I'm sorry, Claire. I'm in trouble, aren't I?"

"You certainly are."

"It wasn't as bad as it looked. We were only messing around with the games. A product of our boredom and nothing else."

She did believe him but wasn't going to let him off the hook that easily.

"That's no excuse. Paul works for Digicom. They are a competitor, remember?" she said, deliberately harsh.

"I know," he responded, subdued. "I'm feeling very sheepish right now and can only offer you the consolation that what we were doing was harmless. I *do* understand that it was totally inappropriate and it won't happen again."

"It better not."

* * *

It was two weeks since the Sales Kick-off. Robert had been in New Zealand on business. The office was different without him. It was mundane, dull. There was a video conference with Mark and Michael scheduled for 8.00pm on his first day back. She wasn't sure who she was more nervous about seeing, Robert or Michael. She was thankful that Emma was going to be there as well. She would take some of the edge off the tension.

"Let's try to wrap this one up quickly . . . I'm sure you ladies have much more exciting plans for a Friday night," Robert said, smiling at them both when they turned up at the boardroom.

"Oh . . . you know me . . . work being the most

178

important thing in my life, I turned down all the other offers I got for tonight," Emma flirted with him cheekily.

He looked at Claire briefly, expecting her to join in on the banter. She couldn't think of anything witty to say. Seeing him again shocked her. Over the last two weeks she had finally admitted, to herself only, that she did in fact find him attractive. She hated joining all the other women that swooned around him but she absolutely could not get him out of her thoughts. Fantasy had taken over and filled in the pieces of the kick-off night that she couldn't remember. The scene in the garden had about five different endings now, in a few of which they ended up making love. When reality broke through her fantasy-clogged mind, she reminded herself that she was pathetic because Robert would never be interested in someone as ordinary and inexperienced as she was.

"Does anyone know how to link up?" Robert asked, gesturing to the equipment on the table.

"I do. It's easy." Claire sprang into action, glad to have something to do. She dialled the Dublin number and Mark and Michael were on the screen within seconds.

"Good evening" and "Good morning" was said simultaneously.

"Robert, this is Michael Lehane, the IT implementation manager for the Oracle upgrade project."

Michael nodded when Mark introduced him. His

hair was shorter, his tan indicating that he had been overseas. Maybe on his honeymoon.

"Mark, Michael, let me introduce Emma Dalton, our financial accountant. At this early stage we haven't involved James Ladbrooke, the accounts payable assistant," Claire said, her words slow and clear.

"Have you had a look at the rollout timetable?" Michael asked. He seemed to be staring directly at her. Claire felt Robert glance her way.

"Yes, we have," Robert answered for her. "We have no issues with it."

"Good, that brings us to resources and travel. Will you need Michael to take a hands-on approach and go to Sydney for the rollout? Or can you drive it from your end with support coming from here?" Mark asked. He directed the question to Robert. Claire paled. She hadn't even considered the possibility of Michael coming to Sydney. Again, she felt Robert glance in her direction.

"I think we can cover it from here and save on the travel costs. We have Claire, Emma and James on site . . . they should be able to facilitate any information that Michael might need."

"Michael, can you see into the Australian accounts from Dublin?"

"Yes, but the access is slow. It would make the testing phase easier and faster if the information was downloaded from your side and sent to me by email . . . I can play around with it here until we are ready to do the live updates," Michael responded, his voice strong, his accent pronounced. It was funny how she had never noticed before how attractive his voice was. Emma looked appreciative.

"Any problems with downloading the information from here?" Robert asked Claire and Emma.

"We can get vendor details . . . and possibly the invoice and payment history," Emma confirmed. "Would that be sufficient for the testing?"

"Yes," Michael raised his hand and Claire saw his wedding ring, "that's all we will need for now."

Michael and Mark left the boardroom in Dublin and Claire switched off the screen.

"Well . . . I think I need a drink after all that . . . do you want to join me?" Robert asked as he stood up from the table.

Claire's stomach lurched.

"I could manage a drink . . . but it will have to be a quick one because I have to meet a friend," Emma agreed. They both looked at Claire and she nodded mutely.

The Greenwood was black with suited people and it was some time before Robert had success at the bar.

"That Michael was a bit of all right," Emma commented as they waited for Robert.

"Did you think so?" Claire said with a forced smile.

"You bet I did. Did you know him well when you worked in Dublin?"

"Yes," Claire's tone was ironic. "I knew him very

well . . . I went out with him for three years."

"Really?" Emma asked, her expression almost comical. Claire nodded.

"I'm sorry. Sometimes I have a big mouth . . . and a big foot."

"Sometimes?" Claire asked and they were laughing when Robert finally returned with the drinks. He chatted easily to Emma. It was too noisy for Claire to hear what they were saying so it was hard for her to join in on the conversation. She watched Emma's progress with her drink carefully, matching her pace so they could leave together.

"Claire?"

She turned around when she heard the familiar voice behind her.

"Den!" she said, beaming as he gave her an affectionate hug.

"I didn't recognise you. I've never seen you wear a suit before. You look very respectable . . . very like a lawyer."

"Now, don't start!" He threatened her with his finger. "How's Fiona?"

"She's great."

"Is she still seeing that bloke you work with?" Den was doing a poor job of sounding casual.

"Yes ... how's Jackie?"

"We finished a few weeks ago."

"Sorry."

"I'm not sorry . . . I don't know what I was thinking.

I had a great thing going with Fiona and I messed it up."

Claire didn't know what to say. She agreed with him. He had messed up.

"I'd better go – tell Fiona I said hello."

He kissed her cheek before disappearing back into the suited crowd. She turned back to Emma and Robert. Emma put down her half-empty glass.

"I have to leave . . . my girlfriend is waiting for me on her own ... I'll see you guys Monday." Claire watched her departing back in panic. She couldn't think of anything to say to fill the silence after Emma left.

"You seem to be rather subdued tonight . . . is everything OK?" Robert asked, leaning close so she could hear him.

"Oh . . . I'm just a little tired . . . I'm looking forward to a quiet weekend," she lied quickly and smiled at him to prove that she wasn't subdued at all.

"I hope you are not planning on working tomorrow." He sounded concerned.

"No. I caught up on my backlog while you were in New Zealand."

"So . . . you're more productive when I'm not around to bother you. It's nice to know you missed me in some way," he laughed. There was a lull in conversation and she was about to say it was time for her to go home, when he spoke.

"Did you enjoy your day off after the kick-off?"

She felt her face get hot.

"No. I didn't feel very well . . ."

"You went home early," he said, giving her an enigmatic look.

"Yes, I didn't want to make an even bigger fool of myself."

"Don't be silly. You were just a little wobbly ... it was cute."

Oh God! Is he flirting with me or just being friendly? she thought.

"I must say that I'm tired myself ... New Zealand was hectic and my flight was delayed by three hours," he said.

"How annoying . . ."

He paused before saying, "Is Michael Lehane the one?"

She knew what he meant and felt herself flush but still said, "Excuse me?"

"Is Michael Lehane the reason you left Ireland?" His voice was sympathetic, coaxing an answer she didn't want to give.

"Yes, Michael is my ex–boyfriend . . . it was very perceptive of you to figure that out," she said, as she took a large mouthful of wine.

"It was your body language." His calmness made her more agitated.

"Great . . . I'm totally transparent."

"No, you're not . . . I think I just know you well enough now to tell when you are on edge."

184

He waited a few moments before changing the topic. "Was that a good friend of yours earlier?"

"Den? He used to go out with my flatmate, Fiona. She's seeing James now."

"James Ladbrooke?"

"Yes. James is nice but I'm not sure if he's as right for Fiona as Den was. They were like peas in a pod." Claire was glad to be back on safer ground.

Robert nodded absently. "I'm going sailing on the harbour tomorrow," he said, his tone casual.

Why are you telling me? Are you going to ask me to come?

"Well, I had better go home . . . I don't like waiting in the train station too late at night," she said in a rush.

"Let me drive you home," he offered, finishing his drink.

"Oh no . . . I couldn't . . . it's totally out of your way," she protested, horrified at the thought of being alone with him in his car.

"It's no problem," he insisted.

They walked outside.

"Look, there's a free cab . . . I'll grab that and save you the trouble." She hailed it down frantically. "Thanks for the drink . . . have a good weekend!" She opened the door of the cab.

"And you make sure you have a rest over the weekend." He squeezed her arm lightly before walking away.

* * *

It was Monday morning and Claire was sitting in her office reading through her inbox, her nerves on edge at the thought of seeing Robert. There was a message from Tony Falcinella. She hadn't heard from him since early July, when Robert arrived. The message had been sent on Saturday night.

Hello Claire,

How is everyone in Sydney? I hope the workload has eased with Robert's arrival. I can't say the same for me. The entire Hong Kong office has been working on an applications outsourcing tender with Cathay Pacific. If we are lucky enough to win, the deal will be the second largest that Amtech has ever done worldwide. The chairman, Donald Skates, has announced that all staff involved in the tender are to make it their number one priority. Unfortunately, we are seriously short of resources and when I was talking to Robert over the weekend, he suggested that you may be able to help us out by coming up here. The tender response is due by the end of next week and I was hoping to have some help on board by next Monday. I apologise for the short notice but can guarantee that it will be great experience to contribute to a landmark deal for Amtech. Looking forward to seeing you,

Tony

PS: Hong Kong is a great city (almost as nice as Sydney).

A free trip to Hong Kong, a city she had always wanted to see! The only problem was missing a whole week of work. She thought of the tasks she had planned for next week and convinced herself there was nothing critical on the list. She presumed that she could access her email from the Hong Kong office and would be able to keep up to date with her messages at least. If she worked like crazy this week and the week after she came back, it just might be possible.

Tony,

I would love to go to Hong Kong. Should I book my flight and accommodation through your secretary or should I book it locally? Is there anything I should prepare in advance of coming?

Thanks for the opportunity,

Claire Quinlan

She had just finished typing when Robert came in, closing her door behind him.

"Claire, I need to discuss something with you."

"Hong Kong?"

"Yes, have you been talking to Tony?" He stood beside her desk, his shirt stark white against his charcoal trousers.

"He sent me a message over the weekend. It sounds like he's working around the clock on this Cathay tender."

"Can you go at such short notice?" Robert appeared

unusually anxious.

"I think so. I may have to let a few things slip but I guess they're not a priority next to this. Tony made it quite clear that this deal is number one on Donald's agenda."

"Too right it is. We badly want to get the contract before the close of the quarter. The press release would send the stock price soaring."

"That should make you rich," she said, grinning.

"Me . . . and the rest of the executive team," he admitted with a smile.

"I'm not exactly sure what Tony wants me to help with . . . his message was vague on that front." She doodled on the notepad on her desk to break away from his gaze.

"Tony is seriously short of talent up there. For the first few days I want you to drive our due diligence on Cathay . . . and towards the end of the week it will be all hands to the deck to get the pricing finalised . . . you could be doing anything from making coffee to negotiating with the third-party contractors."

"Sounds like a challenge . . . you know that I have no experience of pricing an application outsourcing deal like this one?" she said frankly, risking another look at him.

"Very few people in Amtech have the right experience. We're only just breaking into the outsourcing market – that's why Tony is so desperate for talent."

She watched him run his hand through his hair.

"I'm looking forward to it. I've always wanted to go to Hong Kong," she said to fill the small but disconcerting gap in conversation.

"It will be a fantastic opportunity and it will increase your visibility in the US. All the VP's, including Donald, have their fingers on the pulse of this deal. If we win, it will pitch the company into a market that has huge growth. If we lose, our share price will undoubtedly drop . . . we've spent millions on the pre-sales effort to get this far. The shareholders won't tolerate failure." He sounded both excited and worried.

"Is anyone else from Australia going?" she asked, tensing as she waited for his answer.

"Yes, Brian Brooker is already there and I'll be flying out tomorrow."

It was hard to stay focussed for the rest of the day. She couldn't stop day-dreaming, images of herself walking the crowded streets of Hong Kong never far from her thoughts. She didn't talk to Robert again. When she had walked past his office at lunch-time, he was on the phone. He looked busy and preoccupied but he smiled at her as she passed.

* * *

Fiona was duly impressed and envious.

"You lucky thing! What's the weather like there at the moment?"

"Dunno. Where's the paper? That should have the temperature," Claire said, looking around the room and spotting the *Sydney Morning Herald* under the coffee table.

"This is Saturday's temperature, but at least it'll give me an idea. Mmm . . . thirty-five degrees, ninety per cent humidity . . . and raining. What the hell do you wear in a climate like that?" she mused, not very happy about the rain.

"I've no idea. Lots of deodorant, I suppose." Fiona was practical, as always.

Claire, sprawled across the couch, mentally went through her wardrobe.

"I've nothing to wear. I'll have to go shopping to get some clothes . . . you know, Robert is going to be there as well."

"Are you buying new clothes to impress Robert Pozos?" Fiona asked, very quick to pick up on Claire's subconscious intentions.

Claire faltered with her reply. "I think I might be . . . I'm a nervous wreck at the thought of being in a foreign city with him."

"I thought you didn't even fancy him! Why are you acting so weird about him all of a sudden?" Fiona had been sitting on the floor. She stood up, her face serious.

"I don't know. I really don't know . . ."

"I don't want to be harsh, but the last situation you need here is the one you left behind in Dublin . . . remember what it was like to work in the same place with Michael after you split?" She sat across from Claire, waiting for reassurance.

"You're right, nothing will happen in Hong Kong . . . I'm just getting carried away. What are you doing after work on Thursday?"

"You know I hate shopping . . . and I told James I'd meet him on Thursday night." She relented at Claire's pleading look. "All right, I'll go shopping if you come for a drink with James and me afterwards."

"OK, but I can't have a big night. I'll have a busy day on Friday, trying to get everything sorted out before I leave," Claire said, frowning as she thought of all the work ahead of her.

"You're not leaving for good, you know. It's only a week," Fiona reminded her.

* * *

Claire left work early so she could meet Fiona at five. It wasn't fully dark yet and the mood of the late night Sydney shoppers was upbeat. Fiona was not a patient shopper and usually became aggravated if Claire dithered unduly over the decision to buy something.

"If you hesitate when you buy, then that means you'll most definitely never wear it," she stated, as she always did, whenever they were on a shopping spree, in case Claire should forget.

Claire suspected Fiona's advice was biased and knew she would happily skip the shopping to go straight to the pub. She found what she wanted within thirty minutes and with a minimum of fuss. She was happy with her purchases and Fiona was happy that the ordeal was over so quickly.

Her good mood evaporated when they walked into The Hero of Waterloo.

"You never told me that Paul was going to be with James. Thanks very much," she hissed angrily to Fiona when she saw that James was not alone.

"I honestly didn't know. James never told me. I'll kill him for this," Fiona replied with gritted teeth as they approached their table.

"I ran into Paul at Circular Quay and invited him to join us," James explained, looking awkward.

Yeah, sure. Claire shot James a discreet but venomous glare to show him that she didn't believe a word.

"I hope you don't mind . . . I felt like a celebratory drink. I had a big win at work today," Paul said with an engaging smile.

Claire couldn't bring herself to lie and allowed Fiona to reply, "Of course we don't mind." She resisted the temptation to ask him about his 'big win'.

"Did you girls have a successful shopping expedition and blow those credit-card limits?" James asked for the sake of conversation.

"You must be joking, not with Fiona counting every minute, her tongue hanging out for a drink." Claire's mordant response made the others laugh, even though Fiona tried to look offended. James stood up with his empty glass.

"Can I get you a beer?" he asked Claire.

"No, thanks, big day at work tomorrow . . . I'll have an orange juice, though."

"I'll have a beer," Fiona said with zeal.

"Tell me something I don't already know." They laughed again, Fiona didn't even attempt the offended look.

"Are you looking forward to your trip to Hong Kong, Claire?" Paul asked. "James told me you were going," he added when he saw her quizzical expression.

"I can't wait . . . it's an important tender for Amtech . . . it sounds as if it will be hard work and long hours but I still feel as if I'm going on a holiday."

"Who's the deal with?" His question was so fast she almost answered it without thinking.

"You know I can't tell you that," she said, with a small laugh to take the bite from her words. She saw Fiona from the corner of her eye, watching them both with interest.

"It's evidently a big tender if the company is willing to fly people up from Sydney . . . the pre-sales costs must be enormous," he persevered, his whole demeanour expecting an answer.

"Paul . . ."

He heeded the warning in her voice and leaned back in his seat to assume a more relaxed position. "How will Amtech Australia survive without you for a whole week?"

She couldn't tell from his face if he was being sarcastic or not.

"I'm sure I'm dispensable, just like everybody else,"

she replied, giving him a defiant look. James returned, leaning between Claire and Paul to put the tray of drinks on the table.

To her surprise, the initial tension dissolved. They had another round of drinks before moving to the upstairs restaurant for a leisurely dinner. Claire was taken aback to see it was midnight when she checked her watch.

"I hate to break up the party but I have to go home. I can't believe it's this late . . . I have to get up early tomorrow.' She stood up to leave.

"Hang on, I'm coming too," Fiona said, finishing her drink in a rush.

"You don't have to come . . . I'll make my own way home," Claire protested.

"I do have to . . . you're not the only one with a busy day tomorrow."

When they went outside, James and Fiona walked ahead to get a taxi.

"It's good to see you again. You're looking really well," Paul complimented her.

"Thanks, you're not looking too bad yourself," Claire answered, her tone light. They were underneath the Harbour Bridge, the steel clacking as a train went over their heads.

"You may be interested to know that Digicom won the Queensland Government deal. We signed the contract today."

So that's the 'Big Win' he was talking about.

"Congratulations . . . Frank never said anything about us losing," Claire said with a puzzled frown.

"Oh . . . the news is hot off the press, I'm sure he hasn't heard about it yet," Paul responded quickly. "Look … I'm sorry about that day in the office."

She assumed he was referring to the day she had escorted him and James to the foyer.

"You were right to do what you did," he carried on. "I hope you believe that we weren't up to any mischief?" They walked through the Rocks. People were drinking on the street outside the bars even though it was winter. A few of the bars had live music.

"I believe you . . . what were you doing there on a Sunday afternoon anyway?"

"I was bored . . . I don't have a girlfriend to distract me any more . . . I have too much time on my hands for hanging out with James . . . and I'm hoping you'll feel sorry for me and take me back."

"Sorry, Paul. I'm happy with the way things are."

"It was worth a try." His shrug was nonchalant.

Claire was piqued by such a lazy attempt on his part to get back with her. She was about to take him to task when Fiona secured a cab further up the street and shouted at her to hurry up.

CHAPTER NINE

The office was plush with soothing lemon on the smooth walls, soft thick blue carpet and patterned cushions. It made her feel healthy and nurtured just sitting there. The doctor had a strong face, chiselled cheekbones and lips. Her tan was faint enough to look healthy and her clothes were sober to prove her mind was on the job. Julia relaxed; she always felt at ease with females who were not better-looking than herself.

Dr Linda Stearman came well recommended by a friend of Cherie's. Julia had gradually warmed to the idea of seeing a shrink. She was now soundly convinced that a few sessions would fix everything that was wrong with her life.

"OK, Julia. I need to start off with some standard questions about your family and medical history. Easy stuff." Linda smiled, looking up from her notes. Julia noticed that the file in front of her was quite substantial even though this was just her first visit. She wondered what could be in it.

"Right, let's get started. Are your family living here in San Jose?"

"No. They are in San Francisco."

"Do you keep in contact with them?"

"Not much. My mother is rather overbearing. I can't meet my father without seeing her so I tend to keep my visits to a minimum."

"Do you have any siblings?"

"No."

"Do any of your family members have medical problems? You know, drugs, psychiatric, alcohol, suicidal tendencies . . . " Linda looked at Julia carefully. She noticed the tremor in her hands.

"No, nothing like that."

"How about you? Have you ever had psychiatric treatment before today?"

"No." Julia looked straight at Linda, not even flinching as she lied. She was an accomplished liar.

"Ever been in hospital?"

"Never. I'm very healthy."

"Do you drink?"

"Yes."

"How much do you drink?"

"Not much."

"How many days a week do you drink?"

"Look, I don't have any problems with alcohol. I can give it up whenever I want. I've done so in the past.

Can we move on?" Julia's smile didn't take the edge off her words.

"OK . . . are you sleeping well at the moment?" Linda had noted Julia's red eyes.

"Reasonably."

"Is your appetite normal?"

"Yes."

"At any point in your life have you ever felt so bad that you wanted to kill yourself?"

"Good heavens, no."

Linda sensed the hesitation in her response. She tried not to show her disappointment at not being able to penetrate Julia's wall of denial.

"Who do you confide in?"

"My friend, Cherie. She's the one who dragged me here today. She's waiting outside like a worried mother."

Linda smiled to acknowledge her attempt at humour. "Anybody else you talk to?"

"No."

"Tell me about your husband, Robert."

"What would you like to know?"

"Where you met him? What attracted you to him?"

"I met him at a company function. If you saw him you would understand what attracted me – he's very handsome, powerful . . . most women would kill for a husband like him."

Linda noted the jealous tinge to Julia's laugh.

"Do you have children?"

"No, Robert isn't the fatherly type."

"How do you feel about not having children? You're thirty-six, right?"

Julia nodded before responding, "It doesn't really bother me one way or the other."

"Why did you marry Robert?"

"Because he asked me . . . most women wouldn't turn down a man like him." Julia laughed again.

"How about your sex life?"

"It hasn't been as active lately as it was at the start. Robert has been working long hours."

"Do you ever take the initiative in sex?"

"Yes, sometimes."

"How long have you been married?" Linda was relentless.

Julia was tiring from the endless questions.

"Over a year – we've been very happy," she answered. Deception came easy to her; she believed that it made her more alluring to others than the plain truth. The plain truth was that she and Robert had never had a cosy relationship. They had a passionate affair, a quick marriage and Robert was distant and uninterested from that point onwards.

"Tell me, what do you think is wrong with your relationship?" Linda asked, sitting back in her seat, abandoning the file on the desk. She looked at her new client steadfastly. She strongly believed that eye contact encouraged truthfulness. She couldn't figure Julia Pozos out. All her answers to the diagnostic questions were negative but there was clearly something wrong. She was an attractive woman but Linda could see that she was taut with tension. The groomed, well-dressed look was spoilt by the unhappy aura, the red eyes, the hands she couldn't keep still. Linda suspected she had an alcohol problem but acknowledged to herself that Julia was not going to admit it at this session. Maybe she would be able to get it out of her after a few consultations.

"He loves his work more than me." Julia knew she was embellishing the truth but she didn't want Linda to think she was totally pathetic. Anyway, she couldn't quite describe precisely what was wrong with their relationship. Only Robert knew why he held himself aloof. She knew that his dedication to work was the symptom rather than the disease itself but she didn't know how to explain that to Linda. The doctor had a wedding band. She had photos of her children and husband on her desk. She wouldn't be able to understand a woman who had a husband who didn't love her.

"How hard have you tried to increase the quality time you spend together?" Linda asked. She registered Julia's confusion and rephrased the question. "How persistent have you been in making an effort with the relationship?"

Julia thought about the question carefully and her answer was slow but at least honest.

"Maybe I don't try hard enough . . . you see, Robert

can be very abrupt and preoccupied . . . when he's like that . . . I sort of . . . scurry away from him until I think he is in a good mood again. Sometimes a whole week might pass before I could approach him about something quite simple . . . "

Linda was taping the conversation so she didn't need to resume taking notes. She watched Julia's face, the hurt and insecurity written across it. She watched her hands, fidgeting, shaking.

"You seem almost intimidated by him," she said quietly.

"Yes, I often am . . . but not because he yells at me or anything . . . it's because he sometimes acts as if he can't stand to be around me . . . " Julia admitted weakly.

"Have you tried to be more assertive with him, to demand his time, to demand his attention and love? Instead of shrinking away if he is in a difficult mood . . ."

Julia shook her head.

"Have you ever said anything to him when he comes home late?"

Again, Julia answered by shaking her head.

"You seem to have difficulty expressing yourself. You should try to find your voice in this relationship. It's your life too, you should have a say in what happens."

"But I've been married before!" Julia blurted.

"And?"

"He left me." It still hurt to admit it.

"What went wrong?"

"He woke up one morning and decided he had had enough."

"How did you cope with the grief of losing him?"

"I got through." Julia shrugged.

Linda saw raw emotion on her face.

"Do you think there are any similarities between your first and second marriages?"

Julia was a little annoyed that she had to spell out the obvious.

"Maybe that I'm not very good at keeping the men in my life interested."

Linda smiled inwardly. A breakthrough. Some truth at last. Julia had a dependent personality; it was something she could work on.

"Julia, you seem to have very low self-esteem. Forget the first marriage. It's over; there is nothing you can do about it. Inject some sparkle into this one. Don't be afraid to argue in order to get your own way every now and then. Try to be stronger with him . . . "

"OK, I will." Julia gave her a tentative smile.

"I'll be honest, Julia. I think there is a lot of ground that we haven't covered today. This was almost like a 'getting to know you' session. There are other issues that we must discuss. Things we must talk about frankly. I don't think you've given much away and I can't help you until you feel confident enough to tell me the truth. I have to wrap up now as I have another consultation but I would like you to book a session with my secretary before you leave."

Time was up; there was a large clock on the opposite wall that Linda could look at discreetly. It wasn't good to check your watch in front of patients who were paying exorbitant fees for your undivided attention.

* * *

Julia left Linda's office feeling positive, hopeful. Maybe next time she would tell her a few more truths – like the affairs she suspected Robert had indulged in, the breakdown she had after Josh – to see what advice she would have to offer. The doctor was well worth the huge hourly rate and with Robert away she could see her without being secretive.

Cherie was reading a magazine in the waiting-room.

"How did it go?" she asked, looking up anxiously. Over the last few weeks she had been gradually increasing the pressure on Julia to get some help. Cherie agreed with Robert that their best chance of getting Julia to see someone was while he was out of town. Cherie had made the appointment.

"I'm truly very pleased. She told me that I possibly wasn't trying hard enough for Robert's time," Julia answered, looking happier than Cherie had seen her for some time. Cherie didn't quite understand the doctor's response but it obviously made great sense to Julia.

"Let's go for a drink," Julia suggested as she handed her credit card to the secretary. They had originally planned to go for a meal. Cherie didn't want to encourage Julia to drink but she acknowledged that it would be a long road to recovery and Dr Stearman was only the first step. Wayne was looking after the kids and she felt like a few glasses of wine. She loved her children but she rarely had time to herself. She felt giddy at the thought of a child-free evening.

"I just need to be more confident," Julia said, sliding into a seat at the bar before Cherie could suggest sitting somewhere more private. "I need to call Robert at work more often, insist that we meet for lunch, make sure we take at least one holiday a year. I have allowed work to take over his life by being too meek. That's what's been wrong. Do you know he has been in Australia six weeks and I've only called him twice? The time difference has made it hard to contact him admittedly, but for the most part I felt I was intruding when I called him. I'm his wife . . . I have a right to call him."

Cherie listened to her prattle on, remaining silent. Julia's reaction was not what she had been hoping for. She had expected that Dr Stearman would show Julia the huge cracks in her marriage and help her to realise that she needed to stop drinking before it was too late to make amends with Robert. Instead Julia was filled with optimism, believing that all she had to do was demand more of Robert's time and everything would be OK. Either Dr Stearman was bad at what she did or Julia had told her a pack of lies and put her on the wrong track.

Julia didn't want to go home to an empty house too

early and she persuaded Cherie to stay out later than she intended. Cherie knew that Julia was pathetically lonely, this probably being her only evening out in weeks. She called Wayne from the pay phone by the ladies.

"I'm going to be later than I thought," she shouted down the phone over the din of the loud music and raucous voices. "I'm at some margarita bar in South First Street!"

"OK, OK, I can hear you!" Wayne's voice was very faint. "Stay as late as you want . . . I was talking to Robert . . ."

She didn't hear the last part of his sentence.

"What did you say?" she yelled.

"I was talking to Robert . . . he told me that he . . ."

He continued to talk and she heard him mention Julia but she couldn't follow what he was saying.

"Sorry, honey. I have no idea what you're saying . . . I'm going now . . . I'll see you later!" She hung up with a crash.

* * *

Wayne grimaced as he put the phone down. He was glad she hadn't heard him. He had regretted saying it almost immediately. He got the impression that Robert wanted to keep the divorce as quiet as possible and he had nearly blundered by telling Cherie who would have told Julia for certain.

Cherie was sitting on the fence between Julia and Robert. She felt sorry for Julia and was stupid enough to believe she could reform her. She was very fond of Robert and didn't want to see his second marriage end in divorce, like the first. Cherie was too naïve to see that her efforts were wasted: Robert and Julia were doomed from the start.

* * *

"Can I buy you lovely ladies a drink?" It was another drunk businessman who thought that two attractive women sitting alone at the bar must be easy prey. That made three such offers they had received so far.

"No, thanks," Cherie declined politely.

Julia didn't even look in the man's direction. She had chosen the seat because it meant she could get served faster, not because it was a good spot to pick up men.

Cherie thought that some of the men who had approached looked decent enough but Julia was totally dedicated to Robert and the possibility of another man didn't even enter her consciousness.

"Eric's my name." He stuck his hand out. Cherie felt the sweat on his palm.

Julia continued to ignore him. She was ordering three drinks to Cherie's one. She obviously had no intention of keeping to Cherie's pace out of politeness.

"Do you ladies work around here?"

Julia did but she wasn't listening. Cherie was getting angry with her for leaving her to deal with him on her own.

"No, I don't. I'm a housewife," she said pointedly.

He eventually wandered away, his defeated

expression laughable.

"Julia, I really have to go home. Wayne will be getting worried."

"OK, OK. I'll just have one more . . . for the road." Julia made eye contact with the bar tender and he produced another margarita before Cherie could protest. She drank it in one go. Cherie felt sick watching. Tears were close. She had been looking forward to a nice evening away from anything domestic. There had been no conversation after the first thirty minutes, only with the various men who had tried to pick them up. Cherie wanted to go back to the comfort of Wayne and the kids.

"Lucky there is a taxi rank down the street. We shouldn't have to wait too long for a cab," she said as they went outside, her voice strained.

"I've got my car, silly. I don't need a cab."

"You can't drive! You've had far too much to drink."

"For Christ's sake, Cherie, stop fussing. I've only got a fifteen-minute drive and I'm perfectly in control!"

"You may think you're in control but I've seen what you've had to drink. You're way over the limit. Come on, get a cab with me," Cherie pleaded, grabbing her arm and trying to steer her in the direction of the taxi rank.

"I'm fine. I'll call you tomorrow. Bye!" Julia roughly shrugged herself free and walked away before Cherie could protest any further. She was used to large amounts of alcohol and had a high tolerance level. Her ability to drive would be better than most. She supposed there was no point in offering Cherie a ride home.

Her car was parked two blocks away. She rushed, her heels clicking, the street deserted. She got into the car quickly and locked the doors from the inside. She drove carefully, ironically a much better driver when she had been drinking than not. She turned left into the street. Their large white house was in the first block. The sound of a siren startled her out of her thoughts. There was a police-car behind her. She pulled over, parking neatly by the kerb.

"Evening, ma'am. Can I see your driving licence or registration?"

Oh shit!

She switched on the car light, pretending for a few moments that she couldn't find her licence in her bag as she desperately tried to think over her options.

"Thank you . . . Mrs Pozos," he said politely, reading her name from her licence when she finally handed it to him. "Do you know why I stopped you?"

"No . . ."

"You haven't got your headlights on . . . didn't you notice?"

"Oh . . . I'm sorry . . . I had a busy day and I guess I'm a little preoccupied," she explained with a nervous smile.

"Have you had anything to drink today, Mrs Pozos?"

He was quite young, only in his early twenties and

Julia smiled at him again.

"I had two glasses of wine about three hours ago. I sure do hope they have worn off by now." She assumed that he could smell the alcohol so it was better to appear to be honest.

"Can you step out of the car, please?"

Fuck.

"I'm going to ask you to perform a number of sobriety tests. Do you have any physical defects or medical problems that would prevent you from taking these tests?"

Think of something. Think of something.

"Mrs Pozos, can you please answer the question?"

"No ..."

"Are you comfortable doing the tests in the shoes you are wearing?"

What a stupid question!

"Yes."

"I want you to listen to the instructions first ... don't start the tests until I tell you to begin . . ."

Who the hell does he think he is? He's only a kid.

"I want you to stand with your feet together, hands by your side and lean your head . . . Mrs Pozos, please wait until I'm finished before you begin . . . "

"Sorry, I'm just nervous, I'm not used to this."

Concentrate, concentrate.

"OK, next one, see this pen I'm holding? I want you to follow the pen with your eyes without moving your head . . . look left . . . look more left . . . OK."

"Are we finished now?" Julia asked wearily. She was perspiring. He feet were aching in her shoes. Maybe she should have taken them off after all.

"I've one last test . . . put your hands behind your back, please."

She obeyed with a sigh.

"And interlace your fingers . . ."

She felt cool metal against her warm wrists.

"I'm arresting you for driving under the influence of alcohol."

"What? You can't do this to me! I'm fine, I'm perfectly sober!" she protested furiously as he opened the back door of his car.

"Please, spare me, I hear it all the time. I know a DUI when I see one. I can almost guess what your reading will be when we get back to the station."

"These handcuffs are hurting me . . . they're too tight," she complained, trying to move them so they didn't pinch her skin. They only moved marginally, exposing red marks on her wrists.

"They weren't built for comfort," he answered unsympathetically.

He made her wait in the back of his car while he filled in some forms. He didn't appear to be in any kind of hurry to complete the paperwork. He didn't care about her discomfort. Her legs were cramped; she was belted into an unyielding plastic seat. The seat was surrounded by a wire mesh. A cage.

"What do you want me to do with your car? Will I

get it towed for you?" He turned in his seat to face her through the plastic window that separated the front of the car from the back. She was so furious that she found it hard to speak to him.

"Just lock it up for me . . . I live down this street . . . what's going to happen now?"

He started the car and looked back at her through the rear-view mirror.

"We're going to jail . . ."

"You're not serious . . . I've told you a thousand times that I'm not drunk," she argued, knowing it was futile but not able to help herself.

"We'll see who's right when we do the tests back at the station," he answered. The smugness in his voice irritated her even more.

"What tests?"

"You'll be offered the opportunity for a blood or breath test. You have to go to St Vincent's Hospital if you choose the blood test . . ."

"I'm going to call my lawyer! I don't have to do any tests ... this has gone far enough –"

"When you accepted your Californian licence, for the privilege of driving in this State, you accepted that you would undertake a blood or breath test. If you don't, then you'll lose your licence straight away and there will be an additional charge against you . . . and you can only call your lawyer when you co-operatively finish our process. Understand?"

He looked at her again through the mirror. She

turned her head rudely from his stare and didn't answer him.

* * *

"How did I do?" she asked, trying to see what he was writing down.

"You're three times over the legal limit, how's that?" He looked pleased.

"Don't be ridiculous!" she snapped.

"I've taken two tests . . . you can call your lawyer now if you want." He nodded at the phones in the far corner of the room.

"Can he come and get me?" she asked as she stood up.

"No, he can't. You gotta stay here for a minimum of four hours ... until you sober up."

"*What?* Where? Here? For another four hours?" she yelled at him.

The other officers in the room looked in their direction, ready to spring into action if she got physical.

"No, not here . . . in a cell!" He smiled at her naivety.

"A *cell* . . . are you totally crazy? You're treating me like a criminal!" Her face flushed a dark purple with fury like she had never experienced before.

"That's because you *are* a criminal."

She turned her back on him and strode across the room to the phones. There were four phones mounted on the wall and they were all being used. A prostitute, her mouth full of chewing gum, finished her call and sauntered away.

Julia called Tom Healy, Robert's lawyer.

He listened to her scrambled version of events before saying, "I'm sorry Julia, he's right – you can't go anywhere for four hours."

"This is unbelievable, absolutely unbelievable!" She started to cry in frustration.

"Just calm down, lie down on the bed and sleep it off. I'll come and get you at about eleven, OK?"

"Will I have to go to court?" she asked, suddenly panicking about how she could prevent Robert from finding out.

"Yes, the case should come round in thirty days or so . . ."

"Can you represent me?"

"No, I don't do criminal law. I can find you someone suitable. Don't worry about it now, we can talk later."

Julia hung up reluctantly. She didn't follow his advice about sleeping on the bed. She guessed the thin mattress and the single blanket were filthy. She stood in the dimly lit cell for the full four hours.

* * *

Tom wasn't waiting inside the station as she expected. She was relieved to see his Landcruiser parked right outside the entrance. She hauled herself into the passenger seat awkwardly.

"This thing is too high from the ground," she complained about his vehicle and he winced as she slammed the door.

"Not for me – I love it." He looked over his shoulder

before pulling out. " I guess you've lost your licence now. How are you going to get by without a set of wheels?"

"Damn, I didn't even think of that! I suppose I'll have to get a cab to work tomorrow." She could feel her anger at the injustice surface again. They didn't talk for the rest of the fifteen-minute drive. He turned into the street, passing her car parked on the corner.

"I'll drive it down to the house for you after I've dropped you off," he offered.

"Thanks."

He pulled up outside the house.

"Well, here we are – I'll ring you tomorrow and let you know what's happening," he said, giving her a supportive smile.

Julia opened the door and turned to face him before getting out.

"Tom, don't mention a word of this to Robert. He doesn't need to know . . . If the court case happens in thirty days, it will be all over before he comes home."

Her voice was as hard as her expression. He didn't appreciate her tone.

"Oh . . . here are the keys for the car. Slip them through the letter box when you're finished." She slapped the keys into his hand.

You could say "Sorry for interrupting your night and thanks for driving me home," you selfish woman, he thought. He watched her open the large oak door of her large imposing house.

She let herself into the dark emptiness. She needed a drink. She walked over to the ornate drinks cabinet. Her hands shook as she poured herself a stiff brandy. She drank it without stopping and immediately poured herself a second. Kicking off her shoes, she sat on the warm velvet of the sofa. It had been a long day but maybe not a totally disastrous one. She relived her conversation with Dr Stearman and felt the optimism from earlier in the day return. She blocked out any thoughts of the DUI charges. She trusted Tom to make the process as smooth and painless as possible. That's what he was paid to do. Robert had known him for years and had frequently praised his professionalism and trustworthiness.

She needed to hear Robert's voice. It was so long since she had spoken to him. The warmth of the brandy gave her the courage to dial his work number, nervous anticipation making her empty stomach churn.

"Good afternoon. Samantha speaking."

Samantha was Robert's secretary. Her voice sounded youthful and Julia felt viciously jealous.

"Can I speak to Robert Pozos, please?" she asked, her tone cold.

"I'm sorry, Mr Pozos is in Hong Kong. However, I'll be speaking to him shortly and I can pass on a message."

"Tell him his wife called. I'm at home . . . I'll wait for him to return my call," Julia said with authority. She finished the bottle of brandy as she waited for him to call back.

I should call the cops over now to do a breath test. This is what drunk is . . . not what those wimps saw earlier. I'm probably fifteen times over their stupid limit by now.

* * *

Tom Healy phoned Robert from his car phone as he drove home from Julia's. Samantha answered the phone. He had spoken to her before – she sounded like a sweet young girl. She said that Robert was in Hong Kong but she could transfer the call to his mobile phone if it was urgent. Tom classified the news of Julia's arrest as urgent.

"Robert, Tom here. Isn't Sydney far enough for you? What are you doing way up in Hong Kong?"

"Keeping my hand in as vice-president – we have a big deal happening here. It's a nice city but I miss Sydney. I'm getting quite attached to it . . . If Samantha has given you this number, you must have something important to tell me." The line wasn't great – there was a disconcerting echo.

"Yes, I do . . . Julia was arrested this evening for driving under the influence," Tom said.

"For God's sake! Doesn't she have any sense? Did she hurt anyone?"

"No, I would say that she verbally abused the officer who pulled her over, but thankfully she didn't harm anybody."

"Will this count in my favour in the divorce?"

Robert's tone was even but Tom knew his mind would be racing ahead with the possibilities this new development presented.

"Sorry, man. This is a 'no fault' divorce. Alcoholism has no bearing on the case. It wouldn't matter if she was on the streets. The only way it will help is if she denies the irreconcilable differences. The judge won't be interested too much in what she has to say."

"It's a ridiculous country, Tom. In any other place in the world, having an alcoholic wife would stand for something. How did you find out she was arrested?"

"She rang me. She was outraged at the injustice of being hauled into jail. Her reading was three times the limit. She's in serious trouble and it hasn't registered with her yet." Tom was matter-of-fact in the way only a busy lawyer could be.

"Will you be representing her?" Robert asked.

"No, that's not my area. I can recommend someone – his name is Bill Carruthers."

"Good . . . will she have to go to prison?" Robert enquired thoughtfully.

"This is California, man – you could be arrested for DUI three times and they still wouldn't lock you up," Tom laughed.

"I feel like a heartless bastard for saying this, but I wouldn't mind having her out of the way for a while. I want the house and the contents professionally valued and I want to get my gear out of there."

Tom was silent for a few moments. Robert waited for

him to deliver a solution.

"Look, I might have an idea . . . I could get Bill to negotiate a term in rehab with the District Attorney . . . we could tell Julia that it's necessary unless she wants to go to prison . . . she won't know that you never get put away for a first offence."

"That sounds like a good idea. It would suit me and can only be good for her." Tom could hear Robert's approval in the warmth of his voice.

"OK . . . I need to check it out with Bill . . . as I said, I'm not an expert in this area. I'll keep you posted."

Tom turned into his drive just as Robert hung up. He went inside and watched some TV with his wife who had waited up for him.

* * *

Julia woke downstairs. The floor was hard. Her hand was at eye level. There was dried blood on her fingers. She sat up slowly. She had slept amongst the particles of glass that were all over the carpet. Where had the glass come from? She had been angry, angry with Robert for not calling back. She groaned when she remembered that it was the decanter, the one Robert had been given for his tenth anniversary with Amtech. The wall was marked from the impact. She was horrified at her own destructiveness and was sick before she could make it to the bathroom. She called work to let them know she was too ill to go in.

* * *

Julia relaxed into the soft leather with her cup of coffee. Linda also held a coffee in her strong tanned hands. Their cups were matching, pieces from a collector's pottery set, suitable for Linda's rich patients.

"Cherie told me that you were arrested," Linda said, calmly assessing Julia's deadpan face.

Only her hands trembled as she lifted the cup to her lips.

"It was the evening you had your first consultation with me, right? Let's talk about what happened after you left here."

"I'd rather not." Julia's voice was unyielding.

"OK . . . your choice . . . but it's hard for me to help you if you won't confide in me. We need some trust here if we are to get anywhere." Linda paused to give Julia time to change her mind. She put her cup down on the glass coffee table. She could tell from Julia's whole demeanour that she wasn't going to give in.

"How are things with Robert? Have you spoken with him recently?"

"Yes."

Linda sensed a lie in her abruptness. She tried not to show her frustration. "It's winter over in Sydney, right? Does it get cold?" When she was faced with a difficult patient, like Julia, she often broke the ice with some friendly but irrelevant chatter. Anything to get the conversation going. Julia's response was a shrug. Sydney was clearly a sore spot.

"Are you planning on visiting him while he's there?"

Linda persisted, staying pleasant.

"We haven't fixed a date yet. He's been busy . . . same old problem. Amtech always comes before his wife."

Some emotion at last. Linda was pleased with the breakthrough.

"Are you being fair? It's understandable that he would be a little preoccupied with this new role he's taken on."

Julia allowed herself to get angry. "This role in Australia is just a hobby for Robert . . . he's a vice-president for heaven's sake, not a finance guy in a far-off subsidiary. Disregarding all that, it doesn't matter where he is or what he's doing . . . as long as he is with that company, he'll have no time for me. Our only chance is if he leaves . . . then we could be happy."

Warning bells were clanging for Linda. She tried to diffuse Julia's hatred for the company, Amtech.

"Julia, listen to me . . . this fixation on Robert's company isn't healthy for you. You can't hang all your hopes on him giving up his job."

Julia didn't reply. There was a confidence in her smile that Linda didn't like. The session finished. Linda had an uneasy feeling when Julia left.

CHAPTER TEN

Claire's spirits were not dampened by the drudge of early check-in, mandatory for the International Terminal, or the inevitable delays before take-off. She was in a holiday mood and had to keep reminding herself that she was going to Hong Kong to work and should be taking the tender seriously.

The flight took nine hours and everyone was glad when the pilot started their descent into Hong Kong. As they broke through the dense cloud, she caught a quick glimpse of the imposing mountains that surrounded the steel waters of the harbour. Then, with no warning, the plane dropped violently. She lurched forward in her seat. As it levelled, the pilot's voice boomed over the intercom.

"Ladies and gentlemen – I apologise for the sudden drop. We are experiencing some very bad turbulence which will make our landing quite uncomfortable. I apologise in advance. Please ensure your belts are tightly fastened."

* * *

She fought her way through the thronged airport, shaky from the landing, intimidated by the crowds. She was relieved that all the signs were in English as well as Chinese – it was easy to find her bags and make her way outside to the taxi rank. The taxi driver didn't speak English but when she wrote the hotel name down for him, he seemed to understand where he was going. As the taxi sped towards the city centre, she was mesmerised, trying to take everything in. She liked Hong Kong straight away. The huge buildings conveyed a city full of zest, a city that was an unusual mix of East and West. The traffic was fast and heavy, zipping impatiently along the maze of freeways and flyovers.

The hotel was luxurious by her standards but probably nothing out of the ordinary in such an opulent city. Her room had a view of the harbour and the lights from the other buildings were glowing through the dusk and reflecting dramatically on the water in a rainbow of colours. She moved away from the hypnotic splendour and sat on the bed. It was only six o'clock but it was already getting dark. It was a daunting prospect, going out on her own in a strange city at nightfall, but it would be a dreadful waste to stay in her hotel room. The phone rang, intruding on her thoughts.

"Claire?" The voice was American.

"Yes, speaking," she answered cautiously.

"Hello, it's Tony . . . Tony Falcinella . . . I wanted to make sure you had arrived safely. Welcome to Hong Kong."

"Thank you! I've just got to my room and I'm trying to decide what to do for the rest of the evening. Do you have any recommendations?"

"I certainly do. I was also calling to see if you would like to meet me later . . . I could show you some of this wonderful city."

"Great . . . I'd like that. I need about an hour to unpack and have a shower. Is that OK with you?"

"That's fine. I'll see you in the lobby."

She arrived at the lobby just within the hour. Tony wasn't there. About five minutes later she saw his short, stocky figure approach, the toll of the last few weeks could be seen on his drawn features.

"Claire, it's good to see you again. I do appreciate this, you know." Tony was a formal man – he extended his hand for a firm shake. His severe grey suit was right for Hong Kong. She realised that her jeans weren't.

"It's no problem. It's a welcome break from the humdrum routine of my job back in Sydney."

"Where would you like to go? You're the tourist – you say and I'll lead," he said as they walked from the very cool lobby to the very humid street.

"I'd like to take a walk around the city – get a feeling for it."

The horrendous rain of the previous week had abated and the evening was sticky but dry. The chaos was charming, too many cars and too many people competing for limited space, but the overall effect was fascinating and alluring rather than oppressive and annoying. They wandered for two hours before Claire announced she would faint unless they went for something to eat. They chose an American-style steakhouse.

"This isn't very adventurous but I'm so hungry that I can't take the risk of not liking what I get," she said, sitting down gratefully and studying the menu without delay.

"You're right – you do have the rest of the week to sample the local delicacies – like cat and chicken feet." Tony kept his face straight as he waited for her reaction.

"Cat! You can't be serious? That's revolting! I'm not so sure I'm hungry any longer."

The waiter came to take their order, terminating the unsavoury conversation.

"It's nice of you to give up your family time to show me around," she said, breaking off some bread to nibble.

"My wife is very understanding. I would have liked her to come along this evening, to meet you, but being seven months pregnant is uncomfortable for her." He tucked his napkin into his shirt collar. "I haven't told her yet that I'll be working tomorrow. She won't be pleased. Sundays have been the only quality time that we've had together for the last two months."

"Do you want me to go in to the office tomorrow?" she offered, sensing that he did.

"I would be very grateful if you could." He sounded humble.

"OK, that's sorted. Is this your first child?" She moved the subject of conversation away from work. It was clear that he was under enormous pressure.

"No, I have two other children, ten and four years old." Tony looked proud.

She guessed he was tempted to show her the photos he undoubtedly kept in his wallet.

"Is your wife American?" She knew Tony hailed from Amtech in the US and she was curious about his wife.

"No, she's Hong Kong Chinese. I met her when she was studying art in California. I was working in Corporate Finance, for Robert. My wife wanted to come back to her family in Hong Kong after her graduation. We waited for almost five years until the right opportunity came up with Amtech in this region. Robert took a risk putting me in this role . . . looking back, I wasn't quite ready for it. For a man who doesn't have a family himself, he is extremely supportive of those of us who do."

It was hard for Claire to resist the temptation to grill him for more information on Robert. Tony saved her by speaking next.

"How about you? Do you have a partner?"

"Not at the moment. I was seriously involved with someone in Ireland but we split up – he needed space. He's married to someone else now. I still don't know how he changed his mind about his freedom so quickly . . . Then, I met a guy in Australia who was the exact opposite, very full on . . . I ended up begging for *my* space. I can't seem to strike a happy medium." She didn't mind telling him about her woeful love life, he was so easy to talk to.

"That's a sorry tale indeed," he laughed, his mouth full.

"Robert said that Brian Brooker was coming here as well . . . has he arrived?" Claire spoke with her mouth full too – if he didn't care then she didn't.

"Yes, Brian came on Thursday. He's been a great help . . . he's possibly still in the office now." Tony checked his watch. "I'm only sorry that I didn't ask Robert for help sooner. I thought we could manage alone – I was very wrong – completely underestimated the effort." He was tense again.

"It sounds as if you have all the right people on board now." Her tone was reassuring.

"Everybody except Frank. Robert couldn't get him to come . . . he's on vacation, I believe."

She didn't know that Frank was away. "Brian's an impressive operator and outsourcing is more up his alley than Frank's. You'll be all right." She smiled at him and he gave her a weak smile in return.

They chatted for another few hours, lingering at the

restaurant. It was after midnight when they made it back to the hotel.

"I'll pick you up tomorrow on my way to the office," he said as she waited for the lift. "What time would you like to meet in the lobby?"

"Whenever you like – I'll fit in with you." She could do with a sleep-in but knew he would appreciate an early start.

"Let's say nine, then."

"OK, goodnight. See you in the morning," she said, giving him a little wave as she got into the lift.

The combination of the journey, the heat and the late hour were taking their toll. She yawned. As she walked into the darkness of her room, she noticed the red light flashing on her phone. Turning on the lights, she picked it up.

You have one message, taken at 8.15pm, September 2. Press one to listen to the message or two to delete the message.

She followed the directions but the caller had hung up without speaking.

* * *

Jimmy Yu was the Services Manager for Amtech Hong Kong and had been in the position for fifteen years. He was impeccably dressed, his trouser creases danger-ously sharp. His English had a faint American accent, suggesting that he was educated in the US. Tony left Claire in Jimmy's hands. He was passionate in his welcoming and made very detailed enquiries about her journey and her hotel.

"This is the engine," he said as he led her into a stuffy room that had three others in it. The bid team didn't notice her – they were totally engrossed in their work. They looked as sombre as their suits. She could see why the room had been called 'the engine'. It was stifling, the air conditioning struggling to circulate sufficient cool air around the modest room. Jimmy prised each team member away from their job to make leisurely introductions. Claire was starting to understand why the tender was running close to the line on time.

"We have set up some desktops for our visitors over here . . . Brian is using this one . . . you may have your choice of the other two." There was no sign of Brian. Or Robert.

"There will be a lot of people coming and going. I hope they will not distract you too much." He smiled constantly as he spoke and she found herself smiling incessantly back at him. When Jimmy finally left, Claire sat down at her chosen desktop and logged into her mail. Brian came in about two hours later, pale and unshaven. He kissed her on the cheek, while she gazed at Robert's thunderous expression as he followed Brian into the room.

With Brian seated at his desktop, she was left facing Robert.

"Tony said he met you for dinner last night." It was a reprimand.

"Yes, we had a nice time."

"I presume he updated you on where we are at?"

"Not in any detail."

"Right," Robert said, his voice strained. "Cathay extended the scope last week, with no notice. Whilst we're happy with the increased scope of work, we need a miracle if we're going to get the pricing done by Friday."

She didn't often see this abrupt side to him. She supposed he was tired and had only a gruelling week to look forward to.

"OK, what can I do to help?"

"The due diligence must be done by tomorrow – we can't let it drag on further than that. Have you read the guidelines?"

"Yes, I read them while I was waiting for you this morning." Her response to his sharp question was calm.

"Good, you know what to do then. I'll take you over to Cathay's offices tomorrow morning." He seemed to relax a little.

"What do you want me to do for the rest of today?"

"How are your spread-sheeting skills?"

"Pretty good, I think."

"You can do some of the financial modelling for Brian."

She kept her head down for the rest of the day, working silently through the tender's worksheets, updating the changes for Brian and running some sensitivity tests. Robert was locked away in Tony's office. She was reluctant to even go for a cup of coffee in case she came face to face with him. It was easy to avoid someone in the Sydney office but the Hong Kong office was smaller and more intimate. His presence unsettled her. He looked different here, almost foreign, fitting in with the foreign city.

* * *

Robert said it would be quicker to catch the train to Cathay's head office. She followed him down the steps to the station. He stood back so she could squeeze into the packed carriage before him.

"The main thing I want you to look at today is the software maintenance contracts." His hand touched hers as they both held onto the post to keep their balance.

"OK . . . is there a particular risk with them?" Her voice was weak – his proximity was making her claustrophobic.

"Software maintenance is always something to watch for in deals like this. They have given us a register of the contracts . . . we need to ensure nothing has been left off the list. This deal has already got tight margins . . . we can't afford any material errors."

He was only talking business but the depth of his experience and knowledge made him even more attractive to her.

"Do you want me to get copies of the contracts?"

He nodded, looking down at her, his eyes penetrating.

"OK, is there anything else you want me to pay close attention to?" she asked quickly, now trapped by his gaze.

"No, just one last piece of advice: always remember that we're selling a solution to Cathay. Even though we need to perform this due diligence, I don't want it to be painful for them. I want them to be impressed by our professionalism . . . it will be another reason to choose Amtech over the competitors."

* * *

"Let's get some dinner," said Robert.

Claire hesitated. Dinner sounded far too intimate but it was a reasonable suggestion given that they had not eaten all day.

"I'll take those for you," he offered, pointing to the carrier-bag that she had filled with the contract copies. She gave him the bag and they crossed the street to a traditional Chinese restaurant. She was relieved by the glaring lights and the noise. It was hardly a romantic venue.

"Cathay want to interview Tony and Jimmy tomorrow. I hope they survive the scrutiny." Robert's face was creased in a frown as he poured two glasses of water, sliding one across the table to her.

"Tony should come across well." She hesitated to comment on Jimmy.

"It's not Tony I'm worried about. I don't think Jimmy is up to it . . . he's technically very good but, let's be straight, he's not very inspiring face to face."

The waitress put a selection of steaming dishes on the table.

"Why don't you send Brian instead of Jimmy?" Claire suggested as she spooned some rice into her bowl.

Robert was pensive for a few moments before saying, "That's an excellent idea. Cathay aren't very interested in Amtech HK. They are more interested in Amtech, the multi-national. They keep pushing for reassurance that the world-wide infrastructure will be able to adequately support them should anything happen to the HK office. I like the idea of a Sydney person being the interface . . . it sells the multinational aspect."

She felt her face go warm under his approval. The water was also warm when she drank from the glass he had poured her.

* * *

It was raining when they went outside.

"Do you want to catch a cab?" he asked, stopping to assess the rain from the shelter of the restaurant's canopy.

"Is the hotel far?"

"No, it's only a short distance away – we can walk if you don't mind the rain."

She didn't mind the rain. She walked out from the shelter of the canopy, turning her face up to meet the warm drops.

"I forgot for a moment that you're Irish! You're used to rain," he laughed at her, his shoulders stooped against the onslaught.

He was right: it was a disappointingly brief walk to the hotel. They paused inside the entrance.

"Which floor is your room on?" He ran his hand through his wet hair, the shaken beads of water landing on the tan of his forehead.

"Nine. You?" Her voice was cracked; they were on dangerous territory.

"Ten . . . look, Claire . . . I'm going to have a drink in the bar . . . would you like one?"

She could tell from his expression that it wasn't a casual invitation. This was where she had to say "No". It was hard.

"Thanks . . . but I need an early night. Goodnight."

"Goodnight."

She had walked a few steps when she heard him call her name.

"I forgot to give you these." It was the carrier-bag of contracts she had given him earlier. "I have an appointment with Cathay first up in the morning – you will need to look at the contracts when you get in." He looked as if he wanted to say something else.

She took the bag from him, flustered. "OK . . . goodnight . . . again."

* * *

She didn't see Robert the next day – he didn't come back from Cathay. He called her several times, looking for an update on the progress of the due diligence report. She had read through most of the contracts and there didn't appear to be anything serious enough to cause concern.

She went out at lunch-time so she could get some photos of the city in the daylight. The rain was still stubbornly falling and her photos featured black umbrellas and black skies. A lot of city viewing spots were redundant due to the low-lying cloud. Even though she usually hated rain, it suited Hong Kong. It made the mountains grey instead of green and the harbour grey instead of blue, giving the city an impressive aura of anger.

It was late afternoon before Brian returned from his interview.

"How did it go?" she asked him as he took off his wet jacket.

"It went quite well. I had a few tricky questions but I'm pretty pleased overall. Robert is happy too. He's a lot more optimistic about our chances now."

She called Fiona when she got back to the hotel that night.

"What's happening up there? Why haven't you called me until now?"

"I've been run off my feet. I had to work on Sunday and it was late when I got home yesterday . . . and I think the hours will get longer as the week goes on." She yawned as she spoke.

"I'm glad that you've got a good excuse . . . I was worried that you were after falling for Robert's charms."

Claire laughed as she lay back on the bed. "I'm tempted, Fi. I really am. I just hope nothing happens that will put what little resolve I have to the test."

Fiona didn't share her amusement and her response was cutting. "For God's sake, this isn't a game! If you can't trust yourself around him, then keep out of his way!"

Claire yawned again. "Yes, boss . . . enough nagging for now. Did you try to call me on Saturday night?"

"How could I call you when I didn't have your number?"

"Good point . . . somebody hung up without leaving a message . . . I wonder who it was," Claire replied, pensive.

"It was probably Robert. Asking you to jump into bed with him."

The tension melted when they burst into laughter.

* * *

Robert didn't use the provisional office that Tony had reserved for him. When he wasn't in Cathay, he sat in the engine with the rest of the team. Claire was the only non-smoker in the group. Every hour or so the team would trickle out to have a smoke in the humidity outside. It was on one of those occasions, on Wednesday afternoon, that she was left with Robert on her own.

"Have you given up?" she asked when he didn't join the others.

"Not exactly. I'm cutting back. On bids like this,

when it gets tense, it's too easy to chain-smoke. I promised myself I wouldn't fall into that trap on this bid."

She went back to the due diligence report. It was nearly complete. A clean bill of health. There were some minor points that the pricing could easily be adjusted to accommodate.

She saw him turn his head in her direction before he asked , "Any news from Mark on Oracle?"

"Not since last week. Emma downloaded the data and sent it on to Michael. I'm planning to call Ireland when I get back next week."

"Good, it sounds as if everything is on track. Ireland's role in all this will be critical in the future."

She waited for a few moments to see if he would expand on this leading statement. When he didn't, she stopped typing.

"I wanted to ask you about that. You mentioned something before about centralising Finance and IT in Ireland."

"Yes, that's still the grand plan. All transactional Finance and IT would be delivered out of Dublin. Payables would be the first function to move." It was hard to read his thoughts from his brown eyes.

"Does that mean you will be reducing headcount in Sydney?" She couldn't help being defensive.

"Not necessarily. If the natural attrition rate would not solve the problem, we would redeploy the people across the organisation."

"How can a centralisation plan work with the time

difference between Ireland and Australia?" she asked, her tone harsher than she had planned.

"We haven't worked out the details yet . . . we might put Dublin on twenty-four hours." His response was infuriatingly offhand.

"That can't be cost effective."

"Do I detect a note of resistance?" There was something like amusement in his brown eyes now.

"Yes, you do. We have only one payables person – James. How can you possibly save costs by moving the function to Ireland? Especially when you'll have to pay shift allowance over there."

Their conversation was cut off with the return of the smokers. She didn't look in his direction again as she concentrated on finishing her report.

It was late when they finished. After ten. There was only the Sydney contingent of the bid team remaining. The others had departed an hour earlier to return to their neglected families for the night.

"I'm going to have a beer back in the hotel," Brian stated, stretching as he waited for his PC to log out.

"I'll join you . . . Claire?" Robert was looking at her.

"I think I'll pass . . . I'm very tired from looking at that report all day."

She didn't even venture a glance in his direction.

The pressure came from Brian.

"Just come along for one, Claire. We haven't had a social drink all week and it will be very late when we get out of here tomorrow night . . . trust me, tomorrow will be a very hard day." She was always bad at saying 'no'.

"You guys go ahead. I'll follow you . . . I need to make a call," Robert said, waving them away.

* * *

"How well do you know Robert?" Claire asked Brian as they sat alone in the enormous but empty bar. She couldn't curb her curiosity, hoping for some insight from someone who knew him as a colleague.

"I do lunch with him every so often. He adds a lot of value – very knowledgeable about the business. I like the guy . . . and from what I hear, he's popular in San Jose also . . . especially with the ladies."

Brian chuckled and Claire felt compelled to smile.

"Apparently he's a close friend of the president, Donald Skates," Brian continued. "They socialise together. He, I mean Robert, told me that he's divorcing his wife – he says they have irreconcilable differences." Brian delivered his limited knowledge in bullet points, his male bluntness having little regard for the detail that Claire wanted.

"She's in San Jose, isn't she?" She took a sip of her wine as she spoke so that her question would appear to be casual.

"Yes. It's a peculiar arrangement with him here and her over there . . . but I guess it doesn't matter when they are getting a divorce."

She couldn't relax, drinking faster than normal, waiting for Robert to arrive with an equal mix of dread and anticipation. Brian didn't seem to notice anything out of the ordinary. He talked more to make up for her preoccupation and drank his beer quickly to keep up with her nervous pace. At eleven, she finally acknowledged that Robert wasn't going to turn up. She struggled to hide her disappointment from Brian.

When she got back to her room, the red light was flashing on her phone. A message.

Hello, Claire. It's Robert. Sorry I didn't make it tonight. My call to San Jose went on for longer than I expected. It was after eleven when I finished and I figured you guys would be gone by then. OK, I guess I'll see you in the morning. Goodnight.

Who had he phoned in San Jose? Donald Skates, the president of Amtech and, according to Brian, his close friend? Or the wife he was divorcing? She wondered if Robert had been the one who phoned her Saturday night. It hadn't been Fiona. It was unlikely to be Brian. So that left either Robert or someone who had dialled the wrong number. She lay in bed awake, upset that he hadn't turned up, happy that he had at least called her, chiding herself for reading too much into everything he did.

* * *

Brian's prediction was spot on: Thursday was a nightmare. The pressure got so bad that by midday both Robert and Claire had joined the smokers. They stood outside in the heat, kept dry from the teeming rain by the shelter outside the foyer.

"So, tell us, Tony, are you feeling bullish about the deal?" Brian asked, his eyes squinting as he inhaled deeply.

"I don't know what to think right now. When I'm rational, I believe we have a good chance," Tony replied, offering Claire a cigarette. She declined.

"All our sources inside Cathay are giving positive vibes," Robert said. "I hope it comes off, otherwise the Asia Pacific region will have a very poor quarter."

There was a tense silence after he spoke. Losing the deal after the huge investment of time and cost would be soul-destroying.

"I guess missing out on the Queensland Government deal doesn't help the results for the quarter," Claire commented, to keep the conversation alive.

Robert looked at her, his face like stone.

"What do you mean? Nobody told me that we lost it."

"Oh," Claire faltered, "Digicom won it . . . I know someone who works there." She looked at Brian to assess his reaction to the news.

"I hadn't heard either," Brian snapped. "Why the hell didn't Frank tell us before he went on holiday?"

Both Brian and Robert were glaring at her, waiting for an answer.

"Maybe Frank didn't know before he went."

"Bullshit! It's his job to know!" Brian was furious.

"There is absolutely no good reason for losing that deal. Digicom would have come in above our price. Of that, I'm certain." Robert put his cigarette out and went inside alone.

* * *

It was six in the evening. They had spent the whole day running sensitivity analyses on the pricing so that Donald Skates could get a feeling for the risk. Claire was cross-eyed from the model. She went outside to get some air. There was no air – the wave of heat hit her firmly in the face. The rain had temporarily eased and it was a balmy evening but prematurely dark because of the black clouds.

"Hi there." Robert stood beside her.

"Come down for a smoke?" Claire gave him a teasing glance.

"No, just need a break," he said, grimacing as he thought of what they had been through during the day.

They were silent for a while.

"You know, you were right yesterday . . . about the payables function," he said out of the blue.

"Was I?"

"Yes, it's not cost effective to move it from Australia to Dublin. I must have been crazy to think it was." He kicked his shoe against the concrete step, lost in thought.

"I was thinking about what you said as well," said Claire. "Maybe we should compromise – move part of the function there. The vendor set-up could be done from Dublin. It's not as time-critical as the rest of the role."

"And it means that the same person won't be setting up vendors and processing invoices. That should make the auditors happy, right?" There was admiration in his face when he looked at her.

"Right – it was one of their issues on last year's audit report."

He was still kicking his shoe against the step. She waited for him to say what was on his mind.

"That's what I like about you, Claire. Your honesty."

"Thanks," she said, her voice weak. Somehow her eyes had locked with his. His eyes were weary, the lines around them pronounced from the strain of the week.

"I appreciate your feedback," he said. "I don't often meet people who have your openness."

She didn't know how to answer him.

"I suppose you think I'm a grumpy old bastard," he smiled, shocking her by putting his hand on her shoulder.

"Just grumpy, not old."

His hand moved, his fingers stroking the curve of her neck.

"What are you two doing out here?" Robert jerked his hand away at Brian's booming voice. He took his cigarettes out of his shirt pocket, lighting one up without answering.

Claire went back inside. She was shaking, her neck blazing where he had touched it. He would have

242

kissed her had not Brian come along and ruined the moment.

* * *

Donald Skates didn't think the contingency provision was enough to cover the risk exposure. Robert was irate as he spoke to him on the phone. The team listened apprehensively, sensing another change to what they thought was a final document. They were running out of time. It was 5.00am, Friday morning. The tender was due in the offices of Cathay by nine. They had been in the office almost twenty-one hours now.

"Damn!" Robert crashed the phone down. He took a deep breath to collect himself and his voice was admirably controlled when he spoke again. "Donald won't budge. His conservative side wants to see a bigger contingency provision. But he doesn't want lower margins. Does anyone have any ideas on how to achieve this impossible result?"

He looked at the pale faces of the team. They were struggling to stay awake; bright ideas were unlikely. It was a few moments before anyone responded to his question.

"We could scale down the job grades of the managers. Make them team leaders instead, save about $20K a head," Tony suggested, flicking through the tender document to get to the relevant pricing schedule.

"Brian?" Robert was sharp as he looked at Brian for

reassurance that the delivery wouldn't be impacted by the cost-cutting.

"If Donald is adamant that he wants more contingency, then I agree with Tony: the managers' salary line is the only area where we can make a cut. It's not desirable . . . but it can be done." Brian's response was flat and totally unenthusiastic.

"Let's do it," Robert decided, "but let's get one thing straight. Jimmy, remember this: we are making these changes for the bid only. When it comes to delivery, and it turns out this idea was a bad one, then we drop it and go back to the original roles . . . got that?"

Jimmy nodded.

Claire sat down with Brian to run the new numbers through the financial model.

It was 8.00am when they finished. Tony and Robert left together to hand-deliver the tender document to Cathay. Claire caught a taxi to the hotel with Brian.

She fell into the comfort of her bed.

* * *

She was lying on her stomach. It was getting dark. The phone was ringing. She reached out her hand to pick it up.

"Claire, it's Robert here."

Robert had nearly kissed her last night. She smiled at the memory.

"Hi." Her voice was a sleepy whisper.

"Did I wake you?" His question was soft.

"Yes, but it's OK. I should be getting up anyway."

She pulled herself up in the bed, cradling his voice between her ear and shoulder.

"We're all downstairs having a drink . . . I was ringing to see if you would like to join us."

"Who's there?"

"Jimmy, Tony, Brian . . . and me."

Safety in numbers.

"OK, I'll be down in half an hour or so . . . I need to wake up and have a shower."

She wondered if she should call Fiona in order to get her feelings into perspective. A firm telling-off from Fiona might stop her from doing something stupid with Robert. She suddenly didn't want to see him. He was too vibrant, too threatening. Fiona wasn't at home when she called. She had to cope with Robert on her own.

She changed her clothes three times and it was closer to an hour before she made her way downstairs. She wore a black sleeveless top and a new silver skirt. She was tall and striking in black sandals as she walked into the lounge. It was the first time that she had seen the bar full: Friday was obviously the busiest night of the week. She made her way to the Amtech group at the far end of the room.

Robert looked handsome in beige chinos and a navy polo shirt. He beckoned the waiter so she could order a drink.

She sat next to Tony and listened to the conversation that was already well in progress.

245

"You seem to know your way around Hong Kong, Rob. Have you been here many times?" Brian asked, leaning forward in his seat, his elbows on the table.

"I don't know. Three times? Four? I've travelled so much over the last ten years that it's all a blur."

"But you enjoy it, don't you?"

"Not any more. I'm tired of it. I guess I'm getting old." Robert was smiling but Claire could see the regret on his face.

You're not old. You're the sexiest man I've met in my life . . . She met his eyes.

"So you want to cut the travel and finally settle down . . . in California, right?"

He looked away from her to answer Brian. "You know, I quite like Sydney. Watch out, Claire! You may have to work with me for longer than we both thought."

"A fate worse than death." She made a face at him.

"My wife's having our third child . . . that's settling down big-time," Tony said with a laugh.

"Congratulations, Tony! I didn't know that. I'm very happy for you both. Another regret of mine. Never had the time for kids. Now I'm wondering what the hell I was so busy with." All eyes were on Robert as he drank his beer.

"Hey, man, you sound like you're having a mid-life crisis here." Tony gave him a friendly punch on the arm.

"Maybe I am," Robert answered seriously.

Claire was happy to listen to them talk, happy to absorb the extra morsels of information about Robert's life. An elderly pianist began to play the grand piano in the corner of the lounge. His aged fingers ran agilely over the keys, the popular music filling the room and muffling the loud hum of conversation. She was busy watching the pianist, startled when Brian stood up, shrugging on the jacket of his suit.

"Where are you going?" she asked, immediately embarrassed by the shrillness in her voice.

"I've got a flight to catch . . . Tony, Jimmy, it's been a pleasure . . . fingers crossed that we'll get some good news next week." Tony stood up to shake Brian's hand. Jimmy followed suit. Brian winked at Robert and Claire.

"I'll see you both back in Sydney."

Claire knew what was going to happen next. Tony would want to go home to the pregnant wife that he had barely seen for the week. Jimmy wasn't drinking – it was almost certain he would leave with Tony. It was only fifteen minutes later that Tony checked his watch and put down his empty glass.

"I must excuse myself. I promised Joanne that we would go somewhere nice for dinner tonight. Much as I would like to invite you both along, I don't think she would be impressed."

As Claire predicted, Jimmy was also leaving for home.

"I'm afraid I must also be going . . . family

commitments, like Tony."

They departed on a wave of handshakes. She was alone with Robert. They were both standing. A profound silence stretched across what must only have been a few seconds.

She sat down.

"Would you like another drink?" he asked, sitting next to her, his beige trousers blending with the camel of the sofa.

"Yeah, why not?" she answered, with feigned indifference.

It wasn't long before the crowd started to sing along to the old favourites that were flowing from the piano. Claire felt her shyness disappear, eaten up by the haze of alcohol and the good spirits of the crowd.

"I love the piano . . . I used to play it when I was younger." She sat sideways on the sofa so she could face him. He did the same.

"Really? I'd love to hear you play some time." He instinctively looked at her slender fingers as she reached for her drink.

"I don't know if I can still play. I haven't had a piano since I moved out of home. When I buy a house of my own, it will be the first thing I get."

"He's good, isn't he?" Robert nodded in the direction of the pianist.

"Yes, he's very good. Music is a wonderful thing, it's one of the few experiences that can change your mood in the matter of seconds."

"Did it change your mood this evening?" His expression was intent.

She was honest. "Yes. I was nervous about coming here. Now I'm happy that I'm here." *Damn. I shouldn't have admitted that to him.*

"And it's changed mine also. When I was talking to Brian earlier, I was reminded of all the things I missed out on in my life . . . I was madly envious of Tony and his family. But my mood has improved remarkably. Maybe it's not just the music that is making me happy."

"Yes, there is the alcohol to consider," she said with a giggle.

"And your company," he added. His expression was sincere.

She didn't remember exactly when he put his arm around her. It was a few hours and too many drinks later. She was vaguely aware that they hadn't eaten but didn't want to suggest going for dinner. It would be unthinkable to leave the warmth of his arm and break the magic of the evening just for food. So they stayed. It was after ten when the old man stopped playing, unperturbed by the disappointment of his audience. Claire and Robert were as verbose as the rest of the patrons, begging him to play an encore. He finally obliged, the familiar notes of 'The Piano Man' enticing the crowd from their seats.

"Would you like to dance?"

She nodded and they fought for some space on the

jammed dance floor. He rested his hands loosely on her lower back. She put hers around his neck. Their bodies brushed lightly as they circled, his beard bristling against her face. When the song finished, she stayed in his embrace. He lifted her face by putting his hand under her chin. His lips met hers for a split second.

"Thank you for tonight. I haven't had such fun in a long time," he said, his tanned face inches from hers, his fathomless eyes scanning her face. She was pressed up against him in the crowd. His next kiss was deeper.

"Do you want to go on somewhere else?" he asked, stroking her face with his thumb.

"No . . . certainly not . . . if I have one more drink, I'll collapse," she laughed, falling against him as she lost her balance from the push of the dancers returning to their seats. He steadied her.

"Come to my room. I'll make you a coffee . . . it will help you stay on your feet."

He kept his arm around her shoulders as he guided her to the lobby.

Coffee. I don't want coffee now. Should I tell him? Does he really intend to give me coffee or does he want to sleep with me?

He kissed her again in the lift and she knew that he wasn't serious about the coffee.

He didn't turn on the harsh, intrusive lights. The drapes were open, creating a natural twilight in the room. Her hand was secure in his as they walked towards the bed. He sat down beside her, smoothing her hair back from her face, showering her with butterfly kisses. She leaned back so she was lying flat. He lay on top of her, his weight pressing her into the mattress. His lips moved slowly against hers. She heard herself moan. He continued to kiss her, his hands chaste against her face and hair. She moved underneath him impatiently. He held her upright and pulled her top over her head. She went to take off her bra but he stopped her.

"Leave it on. You're so sexy in it."

His hands were gentle and reverent. She forgot her impatience and adjusted her tempo to his. One of his hands slid inside the lace of her bra, stroking her pointed nipple. He pulled the material to one side so his tongue could follow where his hand had been. She felt his other hand on her panties, massaging the satin against her before slipping inside. His fingers were cool against her wetness. She took off his shirt, running her tongue over the firm muscles on his chest. He finally took off her bra so her breasts could mould against the bareness of his torso. They helped each other remove the remainder of their clothing and he finally moved inside her. The intensity of the moment made her emotional. She almost cried out his name. When he held her in his arms afterwards, it crossed her mind that she would never have guessed the dynamic and demanding Robert she knew at work would be such a gentle lover.

* * *

"Come on, lazy bones! Rise and shine!" He tickled her nose with a feather from the pillowcase. Bright morning sunlight made his face dark. A gigantic wave of panic hit as she became conscious of where she was and who she was with.

Jesus Christ, what have I done?

He saw the look of horror on her face and kissed her on the nose.

"I know what you are thinking. Just look at it like this. You may think I'm going to fire you now that I've had my wicked way with you ... but I reckon you could have me up for sexual harassment ... so we're even." He grinned, delighted with his logic.

"Robert . . . I don't believe I . . . please don't think . . . look, I'll leave right now and we can both forget it ever happened." She pulled herself up in the bed but he blocked her exit by lying on top of her.

"Sorry, I'm not letting you move until you hear me out. I don't want to forget last night. In fact, I feel very honoured to have shared something so special with you."

"This isn't right. You're my boss. What happens when . . ." She struggled for the right words.

"When what?" he asked, amused.

"Look, Robert, my last long-term relationship was with someone I worked with . . ." Her face was flaming.

"I know that. I know about Michael – this isn't the same."

"It's worse . . . you're my boss . . . I can't believe that

252

I've been so stupid."

"Claire, Claire, why are you getting so worked up?" He gazed into the navy-blue eyes that were enormous in her white face.

"I know first-hand how awkward it is when it finishes."

"Who says it will finish? Please, let's give it a go and see what happens. You make me feel different . . . I know there's something here . . . don't ignore it just because I'm your boss. I shouldn't need to say this but – your job will not be threatened if it doesn't work out." His tone was serious. His eyes were genuine. He was hard to resist.

"I've never just hopped into bed with someone like this. It doesn't seem like the right way to start a relationship . . ."

"I wish I could say I was sorry for taking advantage of you."

He kissed her deeply, his tongue exploring her mouth. Her doubts and inhibitions were discarded the minute his lips touched hers. He was more urgent and less gentle than the night before, jamming her hips with his, squeezing her breasts, invading her mouth. They made love furiously.

* * *

"When is your flight back to Sydney?" Robert said. She was curled up against him and his beard moved against the back of her neck as he spoke.

"Today. At six," she answered reluctantly. She didn't

want to think about going home.

"That's a pity. I was hoping it would be tomorrow. Still, if we ever get out of bed, we do have a few hours to go somewhere nice."

"Where do you recommend?" She turned around in his arms.

"Let me see . . . , have you seen the markets?"

"No – I didn't have much time for sightseeing, remember?"

"OK. I'm suggesting that we go to Stanley markets. They're interesting – a real Hong Kong experience."

"You've convinced me," she yawned. "Do we get a tram there?"

"I can do better than that. I have a hire car while I'm here."

She dragged herself out of bed for a long shower, grinning happily to herself as the sensuous water cascaded over her tingling skin. She came out, modestly wrapped in a soft bath sheet and picked her clothes up from the floor.

"Ugh! Smell that! Booze and cigarette smoke! I can't put those on me now that I'm nice and clean."

He lent her a pair of shorts and a T-shirt and she put her clothes in a bag. He came with her to her room.

"Can I ask you something?" she said as she opened the door and caught sight of the phone.

"You can ask me anything."

"Did you try to call me here on Saturday night when I arrived?"

"Yes . . . guilty as charged . . . I wanted to make sure you got here OK but thought that sounded silly so I didn't leave a message."

She sat on the bed and he sat beside her.

"I have another question. When you suggested to Tony that I might be available to help on the tender, did you have the ulterior motive of wooing me into bed?" She searched his face for reassurance.

"No. You've always been quite aloof with me. I got the impression that you disapproved of me in some way. Believe me, I didn't hold out any hope that this would happen. It has been a pleasant surprise." He sounded sincere.

"OK. End of interrogation," she smiled.

"Now I want to ask you something. Did you disapprove of me?"

"I certainly did. I thought you were a womaniser. I was trying not to fall for your charms."

He laughed and gave her an impulsive hug.

She changed into a white linen dress while he lay across the bed, watching her with interest. After she quickly packed her clothes and toiletries, he carried her suitcase down to the lobby. It took only a few minutes to check out.

"I don't believe it's almost midday – how long does it take to get there?" She squinted at her watch as they walked outside and fumbled in her bag to find the sunglasses that she hadn't needed all week.

"About forty-five minutes. It's a really nice ride

though," he answered, kissing her on her head. His hire car was a Porsche. She tried not to look impressed when the valet parking attendant pulled up smoothly to where they stood waiting.

Robert zipped through the crazy traffic with confidence. He knew his way around Hong Kong. He was comfortable there, just like he was in Sydney. Robert would fit in every international city around the world.

He held her hand tightly as they fought their way through the busy market crowds. The sun was hot and the dense crowd added to the unbearable humidity. The sun was searing her bare head and Robert haggled with a trader for a large straw hat. He sat it on her head and tucked her hair behind her ears.

"There . . . you look really cute in it . . . "

As they lazily made their way through the stalls, she touched the colourful goods but was hopelessly indecisive about what to buy.

"Come on, Claire. That top is $10 and the belt is only $15. Break the bank . . . buy them both! You're causing a pedestrian traffic-jam," he teased her as he shielded her from the surging shoppers.

"Oh, I forgot to convert. Am I alarming you with my innumeracy? See what happens when I leave the office . . . I become a bimbo," she laughed, giving the stall owner the cash.

"Don't worry, I have a thing for Irish bimbos." He kissed her briefly. "Come on. We'd better go and have lunch. It's getting late."

There was a restaurant at the top of the hill, looking down over the still bay and swarming crowds. Robert ordered a bottle of champagne.

"I'm not sure I can face alcohol after last night." Claire eyed the bottle dubiously.

"Have a little sip . . . it's very good." He filled her glass and held it to her lips to try.

He was right. The bubbly mixture was refreshing to drink.

"Let's toast . . . to us!" They raised their glasses and he reached for her hand across the table.

Is there an 'us'? I guess I'll find out back in Sydney, she thought.

"Did you enjoy the markets?" He let go of her hand and sat back in his seat.

"Yes, thanks for taking me."

"It was a pleasure."

Down on the bay the waves were flat as they crept unevenly into the shore.

"When do you get back to Sydney?" she asked.

"Same flight as yours next Saturday."

Are you going to call me?

She looked away from him, afraid he would see the question in her eyes. The hot breeze caressed her face and shoulders as she memorised the beautiful view. As she stared at the bay, she could feel his eyes staring at her.

They didn't talk in the car on the way to the airport, both preoccupied with their private thoughts.

"I hope you don't mind if I drop you outside – it can be quite hard to find a park here," he said as he pulled up at the Qantas departure lounge.

"No, this is fine . . . thanks for the lift." She got out of the car.

Robert took her suitcase from the boot. The queue of vehicles waiting for his car space made their farewell rushed.

"Bye, Claire. See you next week." He kissed her on the cheek rather formally.

"Bye." She felt clumsy and ridiculously emotional. She gave him a little wave as his Porsche sped off into the circus of cars.

* * *

"That's a really good way to lose your job . . . sleeping with the boss!"

Claire sat on the couch sheepishly as Fiona delivered her lecture.

"I know. It seemed so right at the time. Now I just can't believe I did it," she said feebly.

"You can't say that I didn't warn you!"

"I know. I couldn't help myself. It was inevitable from the minute I got there. Every word we said during the week was leading to it. If you saw him, Fi, you'd have to admit he's very sexy . . . he's got this . . . sort of . . . energy that bowls you over." Claire struggled to explain herself.

"It's called charm, Claire. Men like him use it to lure innocent girls like you."

"I don't think it's just charm . . . in some ways he's so down-to-earth that you'd never know he gets paid ten times our salary."

Fiona threw her eyes to heaven before asking, "Was the sex actually worth losing your job over?"

"Yes, it was hot!" Claire giggled girlishly, pulling her knees up and resting her chin on them.

Fiona allowed herself a lightning smile. "He will probably totally ignore you when he comes back. Are you prepared for that?" she demanded, stern again.

"I've got a week to get myself ready for it – he doesn't come back to work until next Monday. If he's really awful to me, then I'll just look for another job." Claire shrugged. She didn't want to tell Fiona that it wasn't just sex. What had happened in Hong Kong was more intimate than she could explain. Fiona would say she was being a fool. She only had herself to blame for Fiona's bad impression of Robert.

They settled down and watched TV for a while. Claire sat quiet in her thoughts, an unsuppressible smile playing on her face. Fiona darted a few unnoticed glances in her direction before asking, "Claire, you're not in love with him, are you?"

"Definitely not. I just lust after him." Claire looked up with a grin. "It's purely sexual!"

Fiona threw a cushion at her.

"I will not have such impure thoughts in my home! Say ten Hail Marys as your penance!"

CHAPTER ELEVEN

The only free place at the driving range was next to Martin Hayes.

"Nice evening," Tom commented as he set down his golf-bag.

"Sure is . . . it's good when you can get away from the office early on Friday," Martin answered, whipping the ball and watching it land amid the other white spots on the green. Tom and Martin knew each other casually from the golf club for many years. Their acquaintance had never progressed beyond a few pleasantries. Both men were too busy to introduce new friends into their lives – they had trouble enough making room for family.

"How's business?" Tom asked, positioning himself carefully before hitting the ball.

"Busier than ever. We're recruiting heavily . . . hard to get good people these days. How about you? Busy?"

"I sure am. I'm caught up in a few messy divorces at the moment. To tell you the truth, it's a depressing business. It's not how I envisaged my career when I left law school." Tom frowned his disappointment at a very average shot.

"Bit of an epidemic these days, Tom. People get married at the drop of a hat. I dated Edna for six years before we wed. You can't be too cautious, I say."

Martin was smug about his thirty-year marriage. Tom idly wondered how Edna Hayes felt being married to a pompous ass for a lifetime.

"That's a fair point, Martin, but the best of us make mistakes – look at Julia and Robert Pozos," Tom said absently as he braced for his next shot.

"I didn't know they were getting divorced. Julia never said anything." Martin frowned, wondering why nobody at the office had told him.

"Robert is distraught but he just couldn't stick it any longer. The best thing that could come out of this is that Julia might finally get some help."

Martin's silence gave Tom the first indication that he had made a faux pas. He peeled his eyes away from the green to look at his companion. His expression said it all and Tom cursed himself for being so indiscreet. He hoped it would take Martin a while to turn the questions in his head into words. He played a few more token shots, then he looked at his watch and packed up in a hurry.

"Sorry, pal, have to go! Must pick the kids up from basketball. See you around!"

Martin watched him go.

* * *

Martin spent the weekend wondering why Tom Healy thought Julia Pozos needed help. By Monday morning, he concluded that it must be drugs or alcohol. Both were equally unsavoury to the straight-laced managing partner at Hayes, Frank & West. Martin Hayes was a religious intolerant man who didn't drink or smoke. The immorality and bad habits of his staff annoyed him immensely. When interviewing for new staff, he was known to ask totally inappropriate questions about the candidate's religious beliefs and social habits. He asked these questions in a jovial manner and most interviewees answered frankly, having no idea of the trap they were walking into.

He was determined to watch Julia very closely for the week, despite his busy schedule. Even though they were short of staff and it wasn't a good time to lose a senior legal secretary, certain standards had to be maintained. If the worst came to the worst, they would just have to manage.

He rang for her at 9.00am sharp but was told that she hadn't arrived in yet.

"Tell her to report to my office the minute she gets here," he barked at the innocent receptionist.

Julia knocked on his door tentatively about thirty

minutes later. The receptionist had warned her that he wasn't in a good mood.

"I'm very sorry, Mr Hayes," she said, giving him an apologetic smile. "I had an accident in my car over the weekend and I'm relying on cabs until it's back on the road. Unfortunately, the one I booked this morning didn't turn up."

If her car is off the road, then alcohol could be the reason – maybe she's lost her licence, he thought to himself in disgust.

"Julia, I need you to work with me on an assignment for the week. Our deadline is Friday, so I need to be able to rely on your punctuality," he said coldly, staring at her with his watery, pale blue eyes. The assignment was partially fictitious – it did need to be done but the deadline was the end of the month.

Martin Hayes worked Julia hard, snapping his dictation at an impossible speed while she struggled to keep up. The office was stifling. She could smell his body odour worsen as the day progressed and it turned her stomach. They didn't break for lunch – he asked her to order in sandwiches. She felt he was scrutinising her every movement and she tried to maintain a professional indifference, ignoring the voice in her head that was screaming, *What the hell are you staring at, you fat pompous pig?*

By the end of the day she was drained, jumpy and flushed from the lack of air. At six o'clock, when he showed no sign of winding down his relentless barrage in his grating voice, she pointedly looked at her watch and invented some other commitment that evening. When she finally escaped his unbearable beady eyes, she resisted the urge to hurry, walking briskly down the hallway, her hands trembling as she pressed the lift button.

When she had first dated Robert, they would meet every day for lunch. After they got married he was suddenly too busy. Most days she went alone to one of the bars in the immediate area of the office. She had missed that today and needed a drink badly. She bought a bottle of vodka from a nearby liquor store and unashamedly drank from the bottle in the back of the taxi on the way home.

What's wrong with me? I've often worked harder days than today. I shouldn't feel this bad.

She absolutely dreaded the thought of tomorrow and played with the idea of calling in sick for the rest of the week. She was too tired to make herself something to eat, so she sat on the sofa with the bottle of vodka, waiting until she felt better.

* * *

Martin observed her shaking hands and lack of concentration the next morning. After a few hours of belting out dictation, he decided to allow her a two-hour lunch break. If his suspicions were correct, she would hang herself.

Julia was relieved to have such a long break. A drink would help her get through the afternoon. As usual, lunch-time in downtown San Jose was bustling with tourists, business travellers and middle-class locals. She went to Manjos and sat at the bar alone, oblivious to the curious glances of the other patrons who were happy to wait for table service. She drank only vodka so that she wouldn't smell of booze. She felt ready to handle Martin as she chewed gum on her way back to the office. The generous spray of perfume wasn't necessary but it made her feel more secure that he wouldn't smell anything.

They had been working for fifteen minutes when Martin stopped mid-sentence and looked up, his horn-rimmed glasses perched on his large ugly nose.

"Julia, have you been drinking?" he asked, his tone incredulous.

"Absolutely not, Mr Hayes. Why do you ask?" she answered, her composure perfect.

"Because I can smell alcohol and I know it is not from me. Are you aware of the no-alcohol policy of this firm during work hours?" A righteous veneer of anger clothed his hard voice.

"Perfectly aware, Mr Hayes. It must be my perfume you're smelling. Robert never did like it either," she said smiling, trying to joke but knowing it was futile with the humourless bastard.

"Don't be ridiculous! I'm not a fool. I must request that you go to the company nurse so she can verify your claim of not being under the influence whilst in the work environment," he demanded, his voice getting louder and more intimidating.

"And if I refuse?" She was defiant despite her panic.

"Then I have no option but to dismiss you. Do I take it that you are refusing?" he snapped viciously.

"Yes," she answered clearly, without hesitation.

He picked up the phone and furiously punched a series of numbers.

"Kevin, can you please come to my office – now!" A polite explanation was not Martin's style.

Julia knew Kevin Sinclair quite well. He was the Human Resources Manager, a mild-mannered but well-respected man. She waited in silence, looking out the window, refusing to look downwards as if afraid, intimidated or ashamed. She hated Martin Hayes and that helped her keep control of her emotions.

"Thanks for coming so promptly, Kevin. I need you to be a witness to the following exchange between Julia and myself," Martin said gravely, his anger now toned down to a more acceptable level.

Kevin didn't say anything. He sat down with an impassive expression on his grey lined face. Julia darted a quick glance at him, in the vain hope that he might be an unexpected ally. His eyes were firmly fixed on Martin.

"Julia, I have reason to believe that you are under the influence of alcohol. It is my wish to ask the company nurse to run some tests so that I can be hopefully proved wrong. It is against company policy to drink during the working day and also against policy to refuse to be tested by the nurse. I remind you of your contract of employment. It is not my desire to dismiss you so I ask you now, for the second time, to please undertake a breath test." Martin spoke quickly, flushed from the adrenaline of persecuting the guilty.

Julia rose gracefully from her seat and put her bag on her shoulder.

"As I said before, Mr Hayes, I refuse to be treated in such an appalling manner. I resign," she said coolly.

She was trembling from head to toe as she walked out, closing the door firmly behind her. The journey through the office and down the lift was hell. She was terrified of meeting one of her colleagues. She made it safely outside and stood for a moment hungrily gulping the fresh air, trying to get rid of the nausea.

Damn. Damn it. How can I explain this to Robert?

It just didn't make sense. She knew Mr Hayes had been lying when he said she smelt of alcohol. With the precautions she had taken, that was impossible. On reflection, she was also confused about why he had chosen her for the assignment when his usual secretary wasn't terribly busy. Something didn't gel but she instinctively knew she would never find out why.

She felt humiliated and exposed. The importance of a well-paid job was a valuable lesson she had learnt from the break-up with Josh. The journey home was a blur. She must have hailed a taxi. Sick to her stomach and with the black cloud of depression giving her a migraine, she pulled the curtains and lay on the bed sobbing. Her husband was on the other side of the world, she had no car and now no job. She wondered if she had brought her misfortune on her own head or if someone was out to get her.

* * *

"Julia, are we wasting time and money?"

Julia was startled by Linda's confrontational opening to their session.

"What do you mean?"

Linda alternated her sessions between the informal sofa and the rigidity of her desk.

This week they were at the desk, facing each other warily.

"You know well what I mean . . . you're not taking this counselling seriously." Linda's stare was fierce.

"That's not fair – of course I'm taking it seriously," Julia replied. "I thought your role is to support me, not give me a hard time." She sat upright in her seat to assume a defensive position to Linda's unexpected assault.

"As I've said previously, I can't help you until such time as you're honest with me . . . if it wasn't for Cherie keeping me in the loop, I wouldn't know what's happening in your life."

"Damn Cherie for poking her nose in!" Julia exploded.

Linda chose not to analyse her outburst.

"First you got arrested, now I hear you've lost your job – both related to consumption of alcohol."

"It was just bad luck – I'm having a run of bad luck," Julia snapped, crossing her arms in anger.

"Why can't we talk about these things calmly?" Linda was shaking her head in defeat. Julia had clearly no intention of responding so Linda attempted to get to her through an alternative line of attack. "How is Robert this week?"

"He's good." Julia reply was short but more amenable.

"Have you sorted out when you're going to Sydney?"

"Yes, I'm going at the end of the month. He doesn't know. I'm going to surprise him." Julia's smile was confident.

"Is that a good idea?" Linda queried. "Have you thought of how he is likely to react to a surprise?"

"He'll be happy once he gets over the shock. I have no choice but to be dramatic – it's the only way I can distract him from his wretched job."

* * *

"It totally beats me why you did that, Tom." Robert wasn't happy and Tom felt even worse.

"I wasn't concentrating . . . you know how absorbed I get with my golf . . . but that's a feeble excuse for speaking out of turn about you and Julia . . ." Tom was subdued. He paused to let Robert speak next.

"I shudder to imagine how Julia will react without work to keep her occupied . . . she'll hit the bottle big time," Robert said with a sigh. It was late, his head hurt after a long day of clarifying the proposal to Cathay. He was looking forward to returning to the calm of Sydney.

"I apologise, Rob, I really do . . . I was totally out of line."

"OK, Tom – she was drinking on the job anyway – it was probably only a matter of time before this happened." Robert's voice was weary.

"Do you still want to go ahead with this idea of rehab?" Tom asked.

"I think so . . . I know we are being a little underhand and I'm using it as an opportunity to go through the house . . . but she does need it . . . she needs something, man!"

Tom was reflective when he came off the phone. Something had changed with Robert. Something that would not be obvious unless you knew him well. He seemed to be more compassionate about Julia's circumstances. Tom wondered what was happening in Robert's life over in Sydney. He would take the time to talk to him properly the next time, find out about the social scene over there. This call was hardly the right time, considering the gaffe he had made.

* * *

"Julia's going to Sydney," Cherie told Wayne when he came home from work.

"What? To Robert?" Wayne scowled as he rested his briefcase on the floor of the kitchen. He always put it there and Cherie always tidied it away later.

"Who else would she be going to see but Robert?" Cherie asked with a smile, giving him a peck on the cheek.

"Well, that's a bolt out of the blue. Robert hasn't mentioned a word about it – I was only talking to him yesterday."

Cherie went back to the sink where she had a good view of the kids as they played in the garden. They were unusually quiet, absorbed with their bright plastic building blocks.

"That's because Rob doesn't know about it . . . Julia's planning on surprising him," Cherie explained.

"For Christ's sake . . . is she totally crazy?" Wayne's reaction was unnecessarily harsh and Cherie felt a rush of anger.

"What's wrong with surprising him?" she challenged, her voice raised.

"You know Robert as well as I do. What do you reckon is wrong with it? Do you think he's celibate over there? I don't think so . . . there's a good chance she'll catch him with his pants down with some girl he's picked up."

Cherie's face reddened with fury. "Don't be so crass!"

"I'm not being crass. I'm being realistic!"

"Don't you dare tell him that Julia is going." She dropped her hand to her side when she realised she was pointing her finger at him.

"I wouldn't dream of it. It will be very entertaining,

whatever transpires from this mad dash she's making to the other side of the world."

"God damn it, do you have to be so sarcastic?"

There was a yell from the garden. The solitary yell was predictably followed by a piercing scream. They both paused at the interruption to their argument.

"OK, I'll go," Wayne said and went to referee the dispute that was happening outside.

CHAPTER TWELVE

"How was Hong Kong?" Emma asked, spooning the froth from her cappuccino. The café was full inside and they were dining alfresco on the busy street. Claire had only been away for a week and North Sydney felt bewilderingly alien. She missed the bizarre routine that the bid team had fallen into in Hong Kong. The late hours, the smoking breaks, the relentless rain.

"Loved it. Didn't see much of the sights, though – we were working too hard to have any fun."

Going out for lunch with Emma was a nice break on her first day back at work. She took a hungry bite from her sandwich.

"It's been like a morgue here, with everyone away," Emma complained. "Even James was out sick for a few days."

"Oh, who did the payables while James was out?"

"Alan Harris filled in. He and James have been cross-trained in each other's roles. Did you see much of Brian and Robert in Hong Kong?"

"We were all in the same room together – working our guts out." Claire controlled the urge to tell Emma what had really happened in Hong Kong.

"Sounds boring and too much like hard work!"

"Did Michael get that download OK?" Claire changed the subject to move Emma onto safer ground.

"Yes," Emma confirmed. "I sent him all the account-detail history and the supplier master records – he's going to use it as test data on the dummy system he has over there."

Emma triggered an image of the Dublin office in Claire's mind. Some nostalgia crept onto her face.

"Robert was asking about the progress last week. I told him I would call Michael when I got back . . . " Her voice trailed off at the unwelcome thought of having to talk to Michael.

"I'm happy to call Michael if you don't want to," Emma offered quickly.

"Thanks."

* * *

The phone rang until Audrey in reception picked up the call.

"Hi, Audrey, is Frank in the office today?" Claire asked.

"No, he's on leave. He's not back for another two weeks," Audrey answered, bright but busy.

"OK, thanks."

Damn.

Another cheque for DC Solutions needed her signature. This one was for $400,000 and the invoice detailed Black & Kenny Solicitors as the ultimate customer. Again, the commission rate worked out at twenty per cent, well above the ten per cent that Steve Ryan had spoken of at kick-off. She had not seen a copy of the contract that Frank had promised to produce if they continued to do business with DC Solutions. But that didn't mean it didn't exist and she couldn't possibly hold off on the payment for two weeks until Frank returned. She eventually signed the cheque on the basis that $400,000 was within Frank's authority limits and it was possible the 20 per cent was agreed to before kick-off.

Her twenty-seventh birthday was the following week. She was going for dinner with Fiona in the evening. Celebrations were going to be restrained to a few glasses of wine because of work the next day. She picked up the Yellow Pages to book the restaurant. As she was flicking through, the computer software section caught her eye. She impulsively had a look for DC Solutions, interested in seeing their advertisement. She couldn't find them. Perplexed, she searched the white pages to see if they were there. They weren't listed. She logged onto the internet, to the Telstra home page. An online search for the company yielded no hits.

They must have a phone number. Maybe DC Solutions is just a trading name and their listing is under another name …

She pulled out the cheque from the stack that was still on her desk. The invoice was attached to the back. There was no other name on it but DC Solutions. She couldn't see a phone number.

Could Frank be involved in some kind of scam?

She carefully checked all the print on the invoice again but there wasn't a phone number.

What if DC Solutions isn't a legitimate company? Could Frank somehow have access to the $600,000 that we've already paid them?

The headed paper did have an ACN number, which at least told her that they were a registered company.

Maybe I'm jumping to conclusions about Frank too quickly . . . I guess I could get the company checked out . . . I have the ACN.

She phoned Australian Corporate Reporting.

"Hello, this is Claire from Amtech. I need a company search done, please. The company's name is DC Solutions and the ACN is 87324456."

The search was going to take a few days. She had just put the phone down when James came into her office, looking frazzled.

"Are those cheques ready for me to take?" he asked, pointing to the uneven stack on her desk.

"Yes, but I want you to hold onto the one for DC Solutions . . . I want to check something out on it."

276

"It's already a week overdue. Alan only paid the urgent stuff while I was out sick," James said as he lifted the cheques from her desk.

"Look, why don't you put it in Friday's mail rather than today's? They won't get it until the start of next week and we'll have time to cancel it if there is anything wrong."

* * *

There was a Hong Kong number showing on the display panel of her phone. The shrill ringing was demanding an answer despite her fluttering stomach.

"Claire."

It wasn't Robert.

"Hello, Tony." She couldn't disguise her disappointment.

"How are you?" He didn't wait for an answer before continuing. "I'm tying up some loose ends on the bid . . . Robert can't find where you saved the last version of the model ... he asked me to call you."

He doesn't want to call me himself.

"It's in the S drive. Version 10." She gave him the appropriate directions, her voice flat.

"OK . . . let me look while you're still on the phone . . . right, I see it now."

"Bye, then."

She was about to hang up when he said quickly, "Hold on – can you transfer me through to Frank?"

"He's still on holiday, Tony."

"Damn!" Swearing did not come naturally to Tony.

The word hung in the silence that followed.

"Why did you need to speak to him?" she asked. "Maybe someone else can help."

Tony paused before responding. "It can wait. When will he be back?"

"Not until Monday week. Are you sure it can wait?"

"It will have to." Tony wasn't happy.

Claire put the phone down with an assortment of disturbing emotions. Robert had asked Tony to call her instead of picking up the phone himself. He was avoiding her, just as Fiona said he would. Then there was Tony acting so weird about Frank. She couldn't think of any reason he would have to speak to Frank. Emma barged in on her thoughts.

"I've just talked to Michael —"

Michael is the last person I need to hear about right now.

"Things are on track on his end," Emma went on. "Testing will be finished this week. Live transfer of the data is scheduled for next weekend."

"Does Michael need us in the office over the weekend?" Claire's question came out rather absently. She was finding it hard to concentrate after her conversation with Tony.

"No, he can do it all from Dublin. He can get right into our system from there. It's very slow, though — that's why he's testing off-line. All we have to do here is get James to complete the online training and we'll be up and running."

Emma was on her way out when she stopped at the door.

"He said to say hello to you."

"James?"

"No, silly. Michael."

* * *

She was back at work a full week. She hadn't heard from Robert. There was no phone call from Hong Kong and there was no phone call when he got back to Sydney yesterday morning. And today, like an idiot, she had been waiting for him to come around to her office to say hello.

Fiona was right. I'm lucky that she prepared me for this.

She received a message from Susan just before she went home. It was Monday morning in Ireland.

Hi,

Thought I'd drop you a line before starting work (I'm really not in the mood to be here today). I met Michael over the weekend (yes, in Major Tom's again). He was with Karen. I know I'm not allowed say this, but she seemed very nice. He said that he had been on to Australia quite a bit – was that to you? I need to know if the war between you two is still on or not. I gave him the frosty treatment on Saturday night, just in case. Called in to see your mother over the weekend. She's very lonely without her only daughter. She was thrilled to see me. I even had my dinner there. I think she wants to

adopt me . . .
Take care, Susan.

Claire left for home, lost in thought as she made her way to the station. It was strange hearing from Susan that her mother was lonely. It had struck a chord, reminding her how far away she was from Dublin, and home.

Am I feeling homesick?

The city trains weren't running; there had been a minor derailment. She made her way outside to catch a bus. It was going to take forever to get to Bondi.

* * *

She arrived to work on Tuesday morning to find that Paul had sent her a dozen red roses. She put them in a vase with bad grace. His hot and cold attitude was really starting to annoy her. Emma came in to wish her a happy birthday.

"Who bought you those beautiful roses?" she asked, picking one from the vase to smell.

"Paul. I don't want them. You can have them."

"Don't be so ungrateful! By the way, this is a little something from me . . ." Emma took one hand from behind her back with a flourish to reveal a box of chocolates and a card.

"Oh, thanks, Emma!"

"Aren't you going to open it?" She was disappointed as Claire went to put the card in her bag.

"Oh . . . sorry . . . I didn't think . . . " She smiled her

apology and opened the card.

Have a swinging Birthday –
Leave your bra at home!

She laughed, her good humour restored. "Thanks a lot – it's going to get pride of place on my bookshelf."

Claire settled down and worked through the backlog that remained since her trip to Hong Kong. She tried not to think of Robert. She was packing to go home when he came in.

"You just caught me, I was on my way home." Her voice was cool and she didn't meet his eyes. He looked at the roses in her arms and the card that she was in the process of removing from the bookshelf as he walked in.

"Oh . . . it's your birthday," he stated the obvious with surprise.

"Yes."

"Happy birthday," he said, giving her an intimate smile.

"Thank you," she said primly, moving purposefully towards the door.

"Would you like to go to dinner tonight?" His voice was hesitant, finally sensing her coolness.

"I have something else planned." Her reply was indifferent. She paused at the doorway.

"Well, maybe lunch tomorrow?" he persisted, trying to make eye contact.

"I don't think so. Goodnight."

She walked away, leaving him standing alone in her

office, a bewildered air about him that would have made her laugh in other circumstances. She had been extremely rude, considering he was still her boss. She promised herself that she would look for a new job as soon as possible. It would be too hard to maintain a professional distance that denied the warmth and happiness of Hong Kong.

* * *

He waited in her office for a few minutes, foolishly expecting her to come back. He had been looking forward to spending the evening with her and cursed himself for not calling her during the week. When he thought of the roses and the fact she was meeting someone for dinner, he felt worse.

* * *

She was late for work the next morning, arriving at nine thirty, flustered from rushing. Robert was hovering in the Finance area, speaking to Alan Harris. She gave him a quick glance as she opened her office door. She had barely taken off her jacket when he came in, shutting her door behind him and pulling up a seat so that he was uncomfortably close.

"You're annoyed with me," he said flatly, searching her face for a reaction to his statement.

"No, I'm not. I have nothing to be annoyed about," she denied, looking at the picture on the wall behind him with feigned interest.

"Are you upset because I didn't call you last week?"

"That's your prerogative. I just want to get things

back on a professional level straight away," she said, playing with her pen now that she couldn't look at the picture any longer.

"Hang on a minute. I thought we left things on a positive note in Hong Kong and that we would talk when I got back. Have you changed your mind?" He was frowning now and moved back in his seat as if baffled.

"Haven't you? You don't seem very enthusiastic to me. Don't you think it's better that we just leave it?" Emotion was creeping into her voice.

"No, I don't." He leaned forward. "Claire, I have obviously done something wrong and I'm sorry." He was about to take her hand in his but saw the discouragement in her face and pulled away.

"There's no point in being sorry if you don't know what you've done," she said sharply.

"I'm sorry that I've upset you in any way. Please tell me what it is."

He was looking at her intensely and she could feel a slight weakening in her resolve.

"Robert, I'm trying not to make a big issue out of this. Not calling for ten days tells me quite plainly that you are not interested. And that's fine by me." She was pleased with her tone, it was matter-of-fact and dismissive.

"You have it all wrong. I didn't want to call you at work and I didn't have your home number. I thought about you constantly all week. You must believe that."

He sounded genuine.

She didn't answer him but he must have seen the uncertainty in her face and pressed home his advantage.

"Please, let's have lunch together so we can talk with some privacy. Can I meet you in the carpark at midday?" he asked. She nodded, feeling drained from the pressure of resisting him.

For once, lunch-time came around far too quickly. She dreaded being alone with him and wondered how on earth she had given in. It was unfair that he had caught her when she was rushed and flustered. If she had been prepared then it would have been easy to resist him.

He was waiting in his car, a convertible Saab, sleek and sophisticated, making her feel even more awkward and naive.

"Hi, there," he greeted her warmly as she got in.

She mumbled a response, immediately focussing her eyes on the dash. She couldn't talk to him, her throat clogged with a mixture of anger, nervousness and sexual attraction.

After a few minutes of silence he put on some classical music. It sounded like Mendelssohn, soothing and simple, relaxing her a little. He drove through the northern beaches and she wondered where the hell he was bringing her. He finally pulled up at Newport Beach and turned in his seat to face her.

"I'll have you know that I've done no work because of you today. I knew I would have to convince you to forgive me somehow so I brought along a picnic for the beach. I thought it would be nicer than going to a restaurant and if you start screaming and punching me, we won't get kicked out."

"A picnic? That was very thoughtful of you," she said, finally looking at him. There was a powerful silence as they looked at each other. She broke the moment by getting out of the car.

He took the picnic basket and a rug from the trunk of the car and they waded through the deep sand to the water's edge. He spread out the rug on the sand and took her hand to help her sit.

"See, a bottle of red, a bottle of white . . . " he said with a small grin as he held up two bottles of wine.

She smiled back at him, remembering the other Billy Joel song they had danced to in Hong Kong.

"What would you like to start off with ?" he asked.

"White, please."

She watched him pour the wine, trying to stay angry. He handed her a glass and changed position on the rug so he was facing her.

"I meant what I said earlier . . . about not wanting to call you at work. I thought it would embarrass you."

"Did you also think it would embarrass me if you came around to see me on Monday when you got back?" She couldn't curb her sarcasm.

"A crisis blew up with Cathay late on Friday – they were ready to pull out unless we changed one of the clauses. I spent most of the weekend and Monday on the phone to Donald Skates, trying to convince him to come to the party on something that was really only a minor change to the proposal. I even thought I might have to fly over to San Jose but we sorted it out in the end."

She looked at him. "Please don't lie to me. You don't have to. We can easily go back to the way things were before Hong Kong." She knew she couldn't but could hardly say that.

"I'm not lying, Claire. I want us to be together. For what it's worth, I did come around to see you at six on Monday, but you were already gone."

"I went home early. I was angry with my boss so I had a mini-strike."

He laughed. "I must remember that my good behaviour is directly linked to your productivity." He held her free hand loosely in his, his eyes all over her face.

"I shouldn't really drink too much wine – I have a lot of work to do this afternoon," she said, leaning back on her elbows, squinting at the sun.

"We don't have to go back . . . I told Samantha we were going to a tax seminar," he said with an expression that reminded her of a naughty schoolboy.

"What kind of tax? Fringe benefits tax, GST or income tax?" she asked, pretending to be businesslike.

"I've no idea. Let's pick income tax."

"Income tax it is," she agreed and they toasted a truce.

* * *

She lay in his arms for a long time. The sun lost its strength and started to fall slowly towards the horizon.

"Maybe we should go?" she suggested.

He sat up and took something from his trouser pocket. It was a velvet box.

"Let me give you this first. Happy birthday!" He kissed her cheek.

"Robert, you really shouldn't have! Thank you so much." She blushed.

"No problem. Open it. I can return it if you don't like it." He sounded anxious and watched her carefully as she opened the box. It was a turquoise opal pendant, simple and beautiful.

"Thank you . . . it's beautiful . . . I love it," she whispered, putting it around her neck and looking down to examine the effect as it glowed against her skin.

He fastened it for her, kissing the nape of her neck. She felt the familiar desire that flared up whenever he touched her. His lips moved down from her neck to her back and his hands moved at the same time to massage her hair. It was now totally dark and the beach was deserted. He turned her slowly until he was lying on top of her and she returned his kisses, locking her arms around his neck. It felt so good to be back in his arms, to be able to kiss him. His hands were stroking her inner thighs fervently, her skirt riding up to accommodate him. She felt his fingers inside her panties, rubbing her with a feather touch. He stopped suddenly, leaving her on the verge of climaxing, to unzip his trousers. She helped him pull them down. She was cold until he moved back on top of her, sliding into her easily, bracing himself by grasping her hips as he sought to get deeper. They kissed fiercely as they moved with each other. When it was over, the rug was by their feet and they were mostly lying on the cold sand.

She stroked his hair as they lay without moving or speaking. The warmth of his chest moving against her, the crashing waves and distant sounds of traffic, lulled her into a light sleep.

"Claire, are you awake?"

"Mmm . . ."

"I think we should put our clothes on . . . OK?" he said and she could hear the smile in his voice.

"I don't want to go home. Maybe we could sleep here," she murmured, her eyes remaining shut.

"Not very practical, I'm afraid. How about you come back to my place?"

His house was a mixture of golden wooden floors, cream walls and splashes of colour from paintings, lamps and rugs. She sat back on the luxurious sofa, her legs curled up, his arms holding her tight and they watched the mid-week movie together. When it finished she was feeling quite tired and reluctantly looked at her watch.

"I really should be getting home." She sat upright with great effort.

"Why don't you stay the night? I could drive you

home in the morning before work," he suggested, his voice light.

She hesitated for a second. The day had lulled her into a comfortable sense of lethargy and the thought of exerting herself to go home was not very appealing. And she didn't want to leave him.

"Don't you mind?" she queried, unsure if he was just being polite or if he really wanted her to stay. She didn't want to intrude into his private life; instinct told her that he liked his space.

"Not at all. Let's go to bed now – I'm quite tired myself . . . I'm not used to hanging out with twenty-something's." He was grinning as he pulled her up from the sofa, ending the debate. He held her hand as they went upstairs.

"Do you have any make-up remover?" she joked, in an attempt to ease her sudden awkwardness.

"You'll find a range of good quality cosmetics in the bathroom, madam," he quipped as he indicated the en-suite off the bedroom.

A huge wooden bed dominated the room. It was very tidy, with the exception of a pair of jeans thrown across the bed. There was a sensual smell in the room, a blend of polish and his aftershave.

* * *

She heard the phone ring in the early hours of the morning. Robert picked it up before it woke her fully.

"Tom, have you got the time difference mixed up again?" He sounded amused, as if phone calls at that hour were a regular occurrence.

Tom's voice was faint to Claire, the only word she heard clearly was "Sydney."

"Don't tell me you're calling to ask me about my social life in Sydney . . . you'll have to find a better excuse than that for waking me up!" Robert said, the bed clothes moving with him as he sat up.

Tom spoke for a few minutes and Robert listened intently.

"You're saying I have to pay her spousal support?" Robert said finally, his voice alert and hard, slicing through the peacefulness. Another few minutes elapsed, with Tom doing all the talking. Claire nearly fell back to sleep, jumping when Robert spoke again.

"That's absolutely ludicrous – we were only married for a year! Can't I file the divorce somewhere else to get out of it?"

Robert was angry. Claire was fully awake now but she didn't open her eyes.

"Tom, understand this. If I have to pay her $24,000 a month alimony because this damned software that you lawyers use says that's fair, then you'd better start getting creative with my assets. There is no way she's getting her hands on half of what I've worked hard to accumulate over the last year while she was doing her best to drink as much money down the drain as possible . . ."

Claire turned on her side, hoping her movement would remind him she was there. She didn't want to hear this ugly conversation.

"I want you to get working on an inventory of my assets to see what you can hide . . . I'm not giving her more than half a million . . . is that clear?"

Robert got up after that and Claire went back to sleep for a few hours. When she finally woke, it was with a niggling unease and it took her a while to link it to the phone call. Obviously, the conversation was about his ex-wife. Tom must be the lawyer handling the divorce. She lay there, anxiously thinking over what she had heard, trying to tell herself that it was none of her business. Trying to tell herself that lots of relationships break up on bad terms and she shouldn't read too much into what Robert had said. She suddenly felt she knew very little about him.

"Don't tell me Sleeping Beauty has still not risen?" He was carrying breakfast on an ornate silver tray. He sat on the bed next to her and kissed her forehead before balancing the tray on her knees.

"Look, banana muffins, your favourite." He broke off some, holding it to her lips.

She turned her head away.

"What's wrong?" he asked, his voice quiet.

"If I tell you, you'll only say it's nothing to do with me."

"Try me." He offered the olive branch, made it easy to ask.

"It's about the phone call . . . the one you got this morning."

"You're cross with me for waking you up?" he asked with raised eyebrows.

"No, silly . . . it's just that you sounded so angry . . . and so . . ."

"Mean? Tight with my money?" he prompted, taking her hand in his.

She couldn't find a diplomatic answer so she waited for him to explain.

"I can understand how you would think that . . . from what you heard me say to Tom." He sighed, letting go of her hand to stand up.

"I'm sorry. I shouldn't have brought this up."

"No, you should have . . . you have every right to know what a mess I've made of my marriage, what a bad judge of character I am. Julia totally duped me . . . I never had any idea she had a problem until she got blotto on our honeymoon."

"That must have been awful," Claire said, sympathetic as she watched him pace the room.

"Yes, it was pretty bad . . . but it got worse. I rang her mother after the honeymoon. I had never even met the woman – Julia told me that she had no contact with her – anyway, I found out her number and rang her. I figured that if I needed to find out about the real Julia, her mother was the obvious place to start."

He sat down again, his weight on the bed unbalancing the tray of untouched food. She steadied it.

"Her mother told me that Julia had had a nervous breakdown a few months before she met me. She had been married before – the divorce was the trigger for her breakdown. The doctors at the hospital suspected she had a problem with liquor . . . this was all news to me . . . basically, Julia lied through her teeth to reel in her new husband . . . I fell for it, hook line and sinker, fool that I am."

"You're not a fool, Robert. Everyone makes mistakes, even vice-presidents," she said, teasing him to lighten the moment.

"I can't help being bitter, and I don't believe she deserves alimony or any entitlement to my assets. That's a rather blunt but honest account of what led to the conversation you overheard."

"Thanks for telling me," she said simply.

She had a leisurely breakfast while he showered and dressed for work. She was content to watch him complete his morning routine. There seemed no need to talk after their intense conversation about his marriage.

The car phone rang while they were in transit to her apartment. She helped him put on the earpiece.

"Hello, there," he gave a friendly greeting to the caller. "It's a beautiful morning here in Sydney – blue skies, sunshine. It's good to be alive." He winked at Claire. "Yeah, I got your message. Cathay came to the table on our compromise. I thought they would. It was a good result in the end." He put his free hand on her knee while he listened.

"Yes . . . I'll make sure that it's not made public . . .

I'm glad I didn't need to fly back, I'm having far too much of a good time . . . Yeah, sure . . . Catch up with you soon."

"Was that Donald Skates?" Claire asked, curiosity getting the better of her.

"Yes, it was," Robert confirmed, taking off the ear-piece.

"You sounded as if you know him quite well," she commented.

"Yes, I do . . . We go a long way back, Donald and I."

"What's he like?"

"Donald? He's a nice man, good to work with . . . but sometimes he drives me crazy."

"Why?" she asked, laughing.

"Because he's so damned conservative . . . afraid of making mistakes . . . I keep telling him we can't learn unless we make mistakes."

"That's a good line . . . I'll say that to you the next time I muck up."

Robert didn't laugh at her joke; his thoughts were still with Donald.

"My patience with him has been stretched to new limits with this Cathay deal. He's paranoid about everything – what the press print, what they don't print . . . I'm sure the press aren't half as interested in us as he thinks."

Struggling with her key in the lock, Claire felt guilty for not ringing Fiona to tell her she wasn't coming home the night before. Fiona must have heard her trying to turn the key as she whipped the door open from the inside.

"Where the hell –"

When she saw that Claire was not alone, she altered her stance to a more hospitable one.

'I'm glad to see you weren't mugged and left for dead somewhere,' she said instead.

Robert sat in the kitchen and Fiona made him a coffee while Claire changed. She could hear them chatting easily as she threw her clothes on the bedroom floor and hurriedly changed into fresh ones.

* * *

Robert dropped her at the front of the building before parking the car. Most of Amtech's staff drove to work and they both didn't want to meet anyone in the carpark. Robert didn't live anywhere near where she did so there was no easy explanation as to why she would arrive to work in his car.

She rang Fiona as soon as she got to her office.

"I'm sorry, Fi. It was very inconsiderate of me not to call you last night to let you know I wasn't coming home," she apologised, logging onto her PC as she spoke. There was a multitude of unread messages in her inbox from yesterday afternoon.

"I was really worried. It's not like you to forget to call," Fiona answered tersely.

"I know. I know. Sorry . . . Robert sort of swept me off my feet yesterday. So, what did you think of him?" She held her breath, not wanting Fiona to disapprove but knowing that she would.

"You're right . . . he is too sexy for his own good . . . or for yours for that matter. He seemed nice . . . " She was hesitant, leaving the sentence hanging with innuendo.

"Do I detect a 'but'?" Claire prompted.

"The 'but' is that he's very charming and I'm worried you're going to get hurt," Fiona said, her voice quiet.

"I can't get hurt. I have no expectations whatsoever," Claire said firmly, her assurances sounding hollow even to herself. A message from Robert flashed in her inbox and she opened it as Fiona talked about plans for the weekend.

Would you like to go to see the Sydney Symphony Orchestra Saturday night?

She had been subconsciously afraid that he would leave things hanging like he had after Hong Kong. The message made her stupidly happy and it was hard to keep her voice normal as she spoke to Fiona.

I might do, she typed. **What's in it for me?**

She said goodbye to Fiona and did some small easy tasks, keeping a watchful eye on her inbox. He must have had a busy morning because she didn't receive his reply until midday.

Free dinner. Excellent company.

He was good company. The thought of having a proper date with him made her nervous already, even though it wasn't until the weekend. Just knowing he was in the same building made it hard to concentrate on her work. Losing half a day yesterday was bad enough without wasting the morning daydreaming. She started to go through her mail with determination.

The company search on DC Solutions had come through. She sat forward in her seat to read the soft copy report on her screen. There were no financial statements included in the report as DC Solutions satisfied the criteria of a 'small company' and did not have to file financial statements. In fact, the report was disappointingly brief. There was very little information other than the directors' names and the equity structure. There were two directors and both were citizens of the United States. The equity was fully owned by a US company called ARS Corporation.

What now? Do I waste more company money and do another search on ARS Corp or do I let it drop? Her eyes squinted as she scrolled down through the report again in case she had missed something the first time. *There's nothing out of the ordinary here. But why aren't they listed in the phone directory? And Frank was so vague when I queried him about their contract. And if they are just a 'small' company, as this report says they are, why are we paying them a million dollars? Is Amtech their only source of revenue?*

Her instincts were screaming warnings, ignoring the polite protests of the part of her that said she already had enough work to do without wasting time on another company search.

"How was the tax seminar?" James appeared

suddenly, catching her off-guard.

"What . . . oh, it was . . . good. It was more of a workshop than a seminar," she improvised, reddening marginally.

"Did they cover anything on GST?" James asked with genuine interest.

"No, it was income tax only," Claire lied uneasily.

"I'm surprised Robert went along . . . a workshop seems a bit low level for him." James was unknowingly persistent even though he was just making conversation.

"Yeah, I know. I was surprised myself. I think he got caught on the phone to one of the organisers and didn't know how to say 'no'. I don't think he'll go to another one in a hurry – he was bored out of his mind." Claire picked up the phone in an attempt to terminate the conversation before she had to tell any further lies.

"Sorry, James. You'll have to excuse me, I have to make an important phone call."

"OK . . . Before I go, have you decided what you want to do with that cheque?"

"What cheque?"

"The one for DC Solutions. I came around yesterday to ask if you wanted it cancelled but you were out . . . I think it's too late now."

Claire hesitated before saying, "I haven't really found out anything that warrants cancelling it . . . did you notice that the invoice has no phone number on it?"

"No, I didn't see that. It must be a printing error . . . I have all the right details in the system – I've had no problems contacting them."

"Who asked you to set up the vendor?" Claire asked, still holding the phone.

"I think it was Frank . . . it was a few months ago. Do you want me to check?"

"No, it's fine." She didn't want too much attention focussed on DC Solutions. Amtech was a close-knit company and it wouldn't take long for Frank to find out she was digging. She waited until James left before she dialled the number.

"Hello, it's Claire from Amtech. I need another company search. The company's name is ARS Corp., incorporated in California in June 2000."

As she said the year of incorporation, she realised the holding company was only two months old. Amtech rarely dealt with young companies; they represented too much risk for Donald Skates. As a consequence, most of Amtech's business partners were mature organisations with years of experience. She scrolled down to check the date of incorporation for DC Solutions. The company had been registered in June, the very same day as ARS.

"As the company is a foreign entity, it will take at least fourteen days before we can produce a report. Do you still want to go ahead?" the customer service officer asked politely.

"Yes, please," Claire confirmed.

CHAPTER THIRTEEN

Samantha knocked on Robert's door before popping her head inside.

"There's someone here to see you."

"I'm not expecting any visitors," Robert answered, taking off his glasses as he looked up from the document he was reading. He rarely wore them; they left a fresh red rim under his eyes.

"I know. But I think you'll be pleased to see this person," Samantha smiled innocently.

"Who is it?"

"It's your wife."

Julia was dressed up to the nines. She swept past Samantha, leaning down to smack a kiss on Robert's cheek.

He was still seated, stunned.

"Hello, honey!"

"Julia . . . what the hell . . . " Robert checked himself, remembering that Samantha was still there. She took the hint, discreetly leaving the room, closing the door softly behind her.

"Are you surprised?" Julia kissed him again, on the lips.

"Yes, yes, I am surprised." Robert was dazed as he stood up.

"Are you happy to see me?" she asked, clapping her hands together in excitement.

"Of course," he said vaguely, massaging his forehead with his fingers. He had an instant but fierce headache.

"Is that all you have to say after two months?" Julia was becoming rapidly disappointed with his lack of response.

"You've thrown me, Julia. Totally thrown me. I'm too old for shocks like this."

She acknowledged that he looked pale under his tan.

"Let's go somewhere . . . let's go to this house you're staying in." She clasped his arm, brushing her breasts suggestively against it.

"Julia, I can't just walk out of here. I've got work to do ... how long are you here for?" He was starting to gather his wits.

She shrugged as she answered, "However long . . . what does it matter?"

"It matters a lot. I can't take time off to spend with you, I have too much happening at the moment."

"For goodness' sake, you haven't seen me for months. You must be able to fit me in somewhere," she pouted, her voice getting louder. He could see

Samantha through the glass; her desk was right outside. He didn't want a scene that she could hear.

"Don't take it the wrong way . . . I just didn't have the luxury of planning for your visit," he said, his tone more reasonable.

"I know, that was very naughty of me." Her smirk was loaded with innuendo.

"And I have a golf day with some key clients tomorrow. I have to go to that . . . " Robert started to go through his schedule aloud.

"I'll come with you. I've been to golf with you before . . . it will be like old times."

Robert checked his watch. "OK, let's go. Where are your bags?"

"In reception." She linked his arm as he opened the door.

"We'll drop them off at the house . . . and then I'll show you some of Sydney."

* * *

"Do you know where Robert is?" Claire asked when she saw that his office was unoccupied.

"He's gone for the afternoon," Samantha replied, busy catching up on a stack of filing.

"He told me he wanted this report today . . . I've been working on it for the last few hours . . . I guess it wasn't that important after all." Claire went into his office to slam the report on his bare desk.

"He went off with his wife about an hour ago," Samantha said when she came out, willing to provide more information in the face of Claire's annoyance.

"His wife?" Claire was certain she looked as flabbergasted as she felt.

"Yes, she's come over to visit him."

* * *

Julia was on her best behaviour at the golf. She flirted with the clients, glowing with the status of being the only attractive female present. The spring sun glanced off her blonde hair as she mingled confidently, sipping a mineral water. The golf course was adjacent to Collaroy Beach. The green had a superb view of the coastline, warm orange sand meeting the navy water as far as the eye could see. Robert was reminded of the picnic at Newport earlier in the week. He needed to talk to Claire. He hadn't yet told her about Julia's surprise visit.

Julia was now talking to Frank, her head tilted as she looked up at his bulk. His sallow face was creased in a smitten smile.

"Your wife's very charming," Steve Ryan remarked.

"Frank certainly seems to think so," Robert said, nodding in the direction of Julia and Frank as they stood close together, away from the group.

"Yes, he seems to have a lot more to say to your wife than he has to the clients who are here," Steve answered, his sarcasm out of place in the serene setting.

"Relax, Steve. It's a social event. I'm sure he'll get to the clients," Robert said, trying to concentrate on his game. He swore when his putt rolled past the hole.

"I'm not sure how motivated he is, Robert. He's way off his quota. He won't earn any commission this year. I'm not picking up good vibes since we lost that Queensland Government deal." Something was niggling Steve but Robert wasn't in the mood to draw it out of him.

"Yes, losing that was a surprise," Robert agreed somewhat absently. His next putt went in and he smiled.

"I guess he did have the commitment to come here today, even though he's still on annual leave. That should be a good sign," Steve said, still on the subject of Frank.

"I'm sure it is . . . how about I pull my wife away from him so that he can mingle with the clients?"

"That's an excellent plan. Keep her by your side. It's where she should be." Steve flushed when he realised that his attempt at humour came out sounding inappropriately sexist.

* * *

"Julia, you're going to have to go home tomorrow." They were in the car, on their way back to the house. Robert had asked to be excused from the drinks and nibbles in the club house after the golf. As far as he knew, Julia hadn't touched alcohol since she arrived in Sydney but he wasn't brave enough to place her right in the way of temptation.

"Why? It's coming up to the weekend – you'll be off work." Julia's face was mutinous and Robert braced himself for the brewing argument.

"I won't be off work – we have a big deal happening in Hong Kong that doesn't pay any regard to week-ends." They were passing over Spit Bridge but she was blind to the splendour of the sun as it edged towards the water.

"Look, isn't that a beautiful sunset?" He took one hand from the wheel to point it out to her.

"Don't tell me that you can't make time for me after I came all this way to see you," she said, her voice a whisper as she stared ahead. The sunset was not going to distract her.

"Let's not go there – you didn't consult me before coming out – and that's the risk you took." His face was flaming hot; he must have got sunburnt in the spring sunshine. When she didn't answer, he glanced over at her to see tears weaving their way down her face.

"Give me your ticket when we get home. I'll ring the airline for you and get you on a flight tomorrow morning," he said practically, hoping she would give up the weeping when she realised he wasn't nego-tiable. Her silent tears became loud sobs. He cringed.

"Julia, don't spoil the nice time we had today and yesterday. Let's leave it on a good note . . . hmmm?"

He had planned to talk to her about the divorce tonight but she was getting close to hysterical in the seat beside him and he realised that it wouldn't be a wise move. Her reaction could be explosive and he acknowl-edged that he wasn't experienced enough to cope with it. He recalled his only conversation with Julia's mother and what she had revealed about her daughter's breakdown after her first marriage. He didn't want history repeating itself. He needed to give more thought to the best way to tell her. He might need to have a counsellor present in case she went off the deep end.

* * *

"Where's Robert?" David asked, looking impatiently at the clock on the wall of the Duxton suite.

"With his wife, I presume . . . he's possibly forgotten about the management meeting this morning," Steve replied, helping himself to a coffee. It had been a late night after the golf yesterday – he would be propping himself up with a lot of coffee today.

"If I had a wife like his, I'd certainly forget about the management meeting," Frank said with a leer.

Claire felt a twinge of jealousy. She had tried not to overreact after talking to Samantha on Wednesday, deciding she would wait to speak to Robert and hear what he had to say about his estranged wife coming to Sydney. With the whole management team discussing Julia like this, she felt her resolve to stay open-minded being whittled away.

"Frank . . . tone it down," Brian admonished, looking at Claire. She busied herself reading the agenda, furious with Frank, furious with Robert.

"It was a compliment! I found her an intelligent woman. She knows a lot about IT," Frank defended himself.

"I mentioned to Robert that she added a bit of sparkle to our uninspired golf," Steve agreed, sitting down with his coffee.

They've all met her. They like her. They don't seem to know about the divorce. They haven't said anything about her being an alcoholic. They think she's charming.

Thankfully, the conversation moved away from Robert and his wife.

"What are you doing here, Frank?" Brian asked, "Aren't you meant to be on leave?"

"I'm here to show my commitment," Frank answered, giving Steve a strange look. "Contrary to popular opinion, I do believe these meetings are important and I'm prepared to give up a few hours of my holiday for the good of the company."

Brian laughed. "That's why you're such a good sales director, Frank . . . I nearly believed you for a minute there."

Robert came in just after they decided to start without him. His white shirt was open at the collar with no restraining tie. He looked deprived of sleep.

Claire glared at him. He was clearly in a bad mood and he glared at all of them, Claire included.

"I want to discuss Queensland Government," he said, pulling out the seat opposite to Frank. His blatant disregard for the agenda made it evident that he wanted some answers.

"And what exactly would you like to know?" Frank asked, his dark eyes narrowing dangerously.

"I'd like to know why we lost to Digicom. It should have been guaranteed business."

All eyes turned to Frank for his response under Robert's aggression.

"There's no such thing as guarantees in IT, you should know that." Frank enjoyed being patronising.

Claire wasn't the only one that saw the red anger creep across Robert's skin.

"Let's park it, guys. This isn't the time or place," Steve said quickly, stepping in to prevent a nasty scene.

"I disagree, Steve. It's been over two weeks since it happened. When is Frank going to honour us with the details of what went wrong?" Robert's icy look swept past Claire before it landed on Steve.

"Are we so desperate for business that we're reduced to over-analysing what's in the past? Aren't we supposed to be looking to the future?" Frank looked at the others for support.

"Enough!" Steve was uncharacteristically authoritarian. "For once, let's stick to the agenda. David, you have something here about an affirmative action survey."

It was a clever move by Steve – David was a calming influence on all when he spoke.

"Yes, I'll be sending out a questionnaire to some of our more senior females, to assess whether we're treating them as indiscriminately as we think we are ... Claire, you'll fill out one for me, won't you?"

She looked at him without letting her eyes stray to

Robert who was next to him.

"Sure."

* * *

"We need to talk," Robert said, his voice close to her ear as they were walking out of the meeting.

"We do?" she asked, her eyebrows raised in sarcasm as she turned to face him. His grip on her arm was firm as he guided her to one side so the others could move past them.

"Yes, we do. You obviously know by now that my wife decided to come to Sydney out of the blue . . . " With his face close to hers, she could see the black semicircles of exhaustion underneath his eyes.

"Samantha was kind enough to tell me that." Claire gave him an angry smile, shaking her arm from his grasp.

"Look, Claire. It seems you're happy to jump to the wrong conclusion," he said with an impatient sigh, "but I would like to be able to tell you the full story. We can talk about it over dinner tomorrow night."

The Opera House. The symphony. Their first date.

"What about your wife? Is she coming with us?"

"For Christ's sake, Claire, Julia is gone home. I dropped her off at the airport this morning. That's why I was late. I'll put your suspicious mind at ease tomorrow night. I'll see you at Wolfies at seven, right?"

He didn't wait for her concurrence, hesitating for only a moment before striding away. Robert wasn't going to entertain any aggrieved feelings on her part.

Damn you, Robert! You can go to the symphony on your own.

* * *

Mark called from Dublin before she went home. For once, she wasn't in the mood to talk to him.

"Has Robert spoken to you about moving the Australian payables function to Dublin?" he asked, sounding enthusiastic at the start of his working day.

"Yes, we have discussed it," Claire answered cautiously, not sure where Mark was heading.

"Good, you and I can get on with the detail then. I was thinking about a November transition. Will that give you enough time to retrench your payables person over there?"

Claire paused before saying, "Hold on, Mark. When I discussed it with Robert, we came to the agreement it wasn't cost effective to move it. The only part we're going to hand over to Dublin is the vendor set-up. Didn't he tell you that?"

"No." Mark's answer was curt.

"He's had a lot on his plate with the Cathay deal in Hong Kong. Will I ask him to call you?" Claire tried to negate the sudden coldness on the line by making her voice over-friendly.

"Yes, please do. We obviously have a lot to talk about."

Claire hung up feeling perturbed. She didn't like being at odds with Mark.

Does he have a good reason for wanting the Australian

310

payables over there? Or is he just trying to build an empire?

She didn't want to talk to Robert so she sent him an email relaying the details of her conversation with Mark.

* * *

Tom called to see Julia early on Saturday morning. She was wearing a white towelling robe when she opened the door. She looked haggard.

"Want a coffee?" she offered, leading him to the kitchen where she had been having one herself.

"No, thanks . . . I'm in a rush . . . I have a few things to get done before your case on Monday."

He sat down across from her at the table. She self-consciously tucked her hair behind her ear. He wondered if she was a natural blonde.

"I just wanted to let you know about the strategy that Bill and I have decided on," he began, suddenly regretting that he hadn't taken her up on a coffee. The smell from her cup was tempting.

"OK . . . that's nice of you . . . but I trust you completely," she answered with a smile. She looked softer when she smiled. More vulnerable. He felt sorry for her. He wanted her to stop smiling at him, to stop being nice. He didn't deserve it.

"To put it bluntly, you were three times over the legal limit. That's a serious offence. To make matters worse, you've been unlucky with the judge. She's a real bitch . . . and man, she's got a hang-up about DUI." He paused for breath.

Julia looked worried. "So what are you saying?" she asked slowly.

"Bill and I believe there's a good chance that you'll get a prison sentence," he said, watching her reaction carefully.

"No . . ." She remembered the cell, the dim dirty cell they put her in the night she had been arrested.

"We've come up with a plan that we think the District Attorney will agree to . . ."

He saw hope replace the panic on her pale face.

"What plan?"

"We're going to propose that you go to a reputable rehabilitation centre for a few weeks . . . it will show them how sorry you are for the crime and should make them more lenient."

"A rehab centre? But I'm not a drunk . . . I can't agree to that ... what would I tell Robert?"

She started to cry. He felt like a bastard.

"I think I'll have a coffee after all. Do you want another?"

She nodded and he made two cups as he listened to the sounds of her weeping behind his back.

"Why don't you tell Robert that you're taking a vacation?" he suggested as he sat back down. He wanted to make her feel better. He was feeling guilty about his part in her misfortunes.

"He probably won't notice I'm gone anyway. You know, Tom, he wouldn't let me stay in Sydney more

than two days . . . after going all that way to see him."
Julia sniffed with self-pity. Her face was blotched from
crying. She took a tissue from the pocket of her robe
and blew her nose.

"He's been working very hard . . . hey, won't it make
him sit up and take notice if you disappear on an
exotic holiday with an elusive friend he has never
met?" Tom coaxed a tentative smile from her. She put
the used tissue back in her pocket.

*That is a good idea. I'll send him a rather vague email
to say I'm going on holiday and then I won't ring him for
a few weeks. He'll be insane with worry. He might even
suspect I'm having an affair and be a little jealous.*

"I'm sorry but I have to go. Do you know anybody
that can recommend a suitable centre that I can include
in my proposition to the District Attorney?" Tom got
up and rinsed his cup under the tap.

Julia nodded, thinking that Linda Stearman would
certainly know of somewhere.

"I'll call you later this morning with the details," she
said, rubbing her eyes wearily.

"OK, why don't you lie down for a while? You're
very tired and I want you to look good for the
hearing," he suggested, stopping behind her to
squeeze her shoulder.

"OK. Bye, Tom. Thanks for everything." Julia
managed another weak smile.

He let himself out.

* * *

Tom's wife hated him working on Saturdays. He had two more client meetings to endure before he could head home. He loosened his tie and hoisted himself into the LandCruiser. There was little traffic on the road. He reasoned with himself that Julia would benefit from some time in rehab but he couldn't get the bad taste from his mouth. They were playing with her to enable Robert to hide his assets. Robert would only give Julia a minimum settlement. She would be lucky to come out of her marriage with three hundred thousand dollars and her problems would eat up that sum of money in no time. She had been arrested for DUI, she had been fired from her job and now she was facing some lonely weeks in rehab. The divorce papers would be ready when she finished at the centre and Tom realised for the first time how devastated she would be.

* * *

Claire made a special trip to the hairdresser's and had subtle red highlights put through her hair before they piled it on top of her head. She spent over an hour perfecting her make-up and painting her nails the same sky blue as Fiona's backless cocktail dress. If they were going to have a yelling match in the restaurant, she wanted to look her best.

He was dark and foreign in his expensive tuxedo and the subdued lighting. He jumped to his feet as he spotted her being led across the room by the waiter.

"I wasn't sure that you would show . . . I apologise

for being so abrupt yesterday." His lips were cool as they formally touched her cheek.

"I contemplated not coming . . . but I suppose I did jump to conclusions and the least I can do is listen to your promised explanation . . . I might add that it better be good."

"Thank you. Here's the wine list. You choose, then we'll talk."

"OK, I'm listening," she prompted when the waiter left with the wine order.

"Where do I start? On Wednesday Julia turned up at work, on some harebrained scheme to surprise me. She was so excited that I hadn't the heart to disillusion her by telling her that she would be going right back to San Jose on the first available flight."

The waiter arrived with the wine. They both watched his ritual: setting up the ice bucket with unnecessary precision, moving painstakingly slowly as he uncorked the wine. Claire indicated to him that she didn't want to taste before he poured. When he moved away, she looked at Robert to continue.

"I showed her some of the sights on Wednesday afternoon. I felt she deserved that courtesy after travelling so far. I had the golf day on Thursday and I brought her along . . . "

"I heard that from Steve and Frank – they were very impressed with her." Claire's tone was sardonic.

"To be fair, she behaved very well . . . until we were on our way home. I told her that she was going back the next day. She went crazy. She started off in the car, crying her eyes out. Then she locked herself in the bedroom when we got home . . . I ignored her for the first few hours, hoping she would come to her senses. Then I started to get worried. I tried to talk to her, to get her to open the door, she didn't answer. In the end, I had to kick the door in . . . she had trashed the room."

"What do you mean 'trashed'?"

"The mirror was smashed, my clothes were ripped out of the closet . . . I can't believe I didn't hear the noise from downstairs."

"Where was Julia?"

"She was passed out on the bed. She'd finished a bottle of whiskey. I don't know where she got it."

"You had a bottle downstairs, a bottle of Jameson," Claire said, taking her first sip from the wineglass.

"I did?"

"I saw it in your kitchen – on Tuesday."

"Hell, I don't know what I have – the house is cleaned and restocked weekly." He was agitated as he poured himself a second glass of wine.

"How did you get her on the plane?" Claire asked with detached interest.

"I woke her up and spent three hours filling her with water. She was quite presentable when I checked her in."

His smile was ironic but Claire's expression remained remote.

"What's on your mind?" he asked.

"Why did your wife come to Sydney to surprise you? It doesn't sound like she thinks you're getting divorced . . . "

Answer me that, Robert . . .

His hesitation said it all.

"You're right. She doesn't know we're getting divorced . . . I haven't told her yet."

"Jesus Christ," Claire reached down to get her handbag from the floor, "I can't believe you're saying this."

He grabbed her wrist to stop her from standing up. The cutlery rattled as the tablecloth moved with his arm.

"Claire, you promised to hear me out!"

"I didn't realise that you were lying all along about getting a divorce," she hissed, conscious of the other patrons who were now looking in their direction.

"I wasn't lying . . . here," he reached into his pocket and threw his mobile phone on the table. "Call my lawyer – he can confirm I'm going ahead with the divorce. His name is Tom. Remember?"

I do remember Tom. He woke us up on Wednesday morning. To talk about alimony and assets.

"This is all too hard, Robert." She felt tears well in her eyes.

He still held her wrist, his grip relaxing a little but firm enough to prevent her from walking out.

"Please don't cry . . . Julia doesn't know about the divorce because I'm leaving it to the last possible

minute to tell her. She's not going to take it very well
. . . I may even need professional help to break the
news to her. Please don't cry."

"It's all too hard," Claire repeated, resting her head
in her free hand.

"It's not too hard, Claire. Just trust me, I'm telling
you the truth."

An emotional truce settled in. The waiter was
hovering to take their food order. Robert beckoned him
over – it was getting late.

She had had more arguments with Robert in two
weeks than she had with Michael in three years. The
mystery was that their clashes made her feel closer to
him.

"Is there something else wrong?" she asked when
she caught him staring at her while she ate.

"No, little Miss Suspicious . . . only that you look so
beautiful, I can't concentrate on my meal." He smiled,
holding her hand across the table.

"Charmer," she replied dismissively but happy that
he had belatedly noticed her efforts. She felt his free
hand stroke her inner thigh under the table. She looked
around, convinced that if the other patrons couldn't
see what he was doing with his left hand they would
surely sense the sexual tension that was totally out of
place in the formal restaurant.

"Why don't we forget about the show and go home
after our meal," he suggested impulsively.

"Don't be silly, I want to see the symphony." She

laughed but was secretly tempted to leave right then. "What did you do today?" She moved his hand from her thigh.

"I went into the office for a few hours in the morning."

"Why?" She frowned at him.

"Cathay. I thought we would have a memorandum of intent by now . . . we're getting closer but still no commitment from them . . . I wanted to call you earlier, to ask you to spend the afternoon with me. I realised that I still don't have your home number."

"That's a pity – I wasn't doing much – just went to the beach for a few hours."

"With Fiona?"

"No, on my own. I'm a big girl."

"Images of you in your bikini are not helping me to behave myself." He put his hand back on her thigh.

* * *

The day had been more like summer than early spring and it was still warm as they strolled from the restaurant to the Opera House. He stopped every few minutes to kiss her, his hands impatient as they caressed her bare back. The emotional confrontation at dinner had brought about a new level of intensity to both his touch and her response. In the darkness of the theatre the seduction continued as he slipped his hand inside her dress, his thumb stroking her taut nipple. The show finally finished and they left with ill-mannered haste, jumping into the first taxi before the crowds had even risen from their seats.

Back in his house, he playfully pulled her towards the patio-doors. "Come outside to the garden," he said.

"Why?" she flirted with him.

"The spa is heated, if you're daring enough . . . " He raised his eyebrows and leered at her suggestively, making her laugh.

"I don't think I am daring enough . . . "

"It will be fun. I'll get some champagne from the fridge."

She followed him outside. The spa was in a sheltered corner of the garden. He took his clothes off and stepped in.

"Are you going to stand there and watch or are you coming in? Don't be a chicken. The water's really warm."

He popped the champagne and the cork landed at her feet. She threw it back at him.

"It's not the water I'm worried about. It's the neighbours . . . but I suppose that's your problem and not mine."

She took off her clothes and he whistled at her naked body. The bubbles made her body weightless, the swirling water erotic against her bare skin. He handed her a glass before drawing her into the circle of his arms. They drank the champagne as the water massaged their bodies.

"This is fun," she grinned at him.

"I could say I told you so . . . we've had a fun night,

despite the shaky start."

Their eyes fastened together; his were thoughtful.

"You know, Claire, I love being with you. You're funny, intelligent, beautiful."

"Stop, you're embarrassing me," she giggled.

"I can't think why you'd want to be with me."

"Now you're fishing!"

"Let's be serious. I care about you, I want things to work out for us. Although why you want to be with an old man with two broken marriages behind him escapes me …"

"Two?" Her voice was shrill.

He saw from her navy eyes that she was distressed.

"Yes, Julia is my second wife. Dianne was my first."

"Oh."

"Do you want me to tell you about her?"

"Only if you want to." She felt herself freezing up.

"I met Dianne when I was thirty-three. I thought it was the right time to settle down. If we had met at any other time in my life, we wouldn't have married. We were together six years – bickering, driving each other crazy. Our divorce was inevitable but meeting Julia did speed up the process."

Claire was rigid in his arms. "Are you saying that you were unfaithful to Dianne . . . with Julia?"

"Yes . . . "

She took a sharp breath; his honesty was hurting her.

"Claire, I can't change who I am. I can't change my past."

321

She didn't know what to say to him. She felt strange. Jealous. Insignificant next to his overwhelming past.

"But now you know it all. I've nothing left to tell you . . . I'm not proud of my track record . . . I haven't felt like this before . . ."

A cool breeze had sprung up quite suddenly and the night was no longer balmy. Her wet hair was making her shiver.

"And why should I believe I'm different?" she challenged.

"Because you are. I can't put why into words yet. I just know you are. Why do you find it so difficult to trust me?" He smoothed her wet hair back from her face.

"Because ever since Hong Kong I don't know what to believe . . . every day there's something new, something else about you that I didn't know. It comes along and hits me left field and I'm just dazed from it."

"I'm sorry, Claire," he said quietly, "but there's nothing else for you to know, now. All my cards are on the table."

"I'm cold. Can we go inside?"

"OK, I'll get you a towel." He hopped out and went inside, totally unselfconscious.

She looked around quickly to see if any unsuspecting neighbours were looking out their window at the tall naked man walking through the garden. He came back with a large bath towel. It was soft against her skin as he dried her slowly and thoroughly. When he finished, he wrapped her in it and they went inside.

Sunday morning started with the piercing tones of the phone beside the bed. She sleepily registered that it was Donald Skates. Robert had a casual conversation with him that didn't seem to touch on business. She lay beside him, wondering why she wasn't running fast in the opposite direction from this twice-married woman-iser. She realised it was because she fundamentally believed him when he said this was different. She felt it too. It was exhilarating to rely solely on her intuition, knowing that on paper their relationship didn't look solid. They made love when he finished talking to Donald.

They spent an idyllic day together, sunbathing in the garden, swimming in the pool, floating in the spa. She borrowed one of Robert's books and read intermittently, stopping to chat every few minutes.

"I hate to talk about work, but with all that's happened this week I forgot to ask you about Oracle," he said, turning to look at her, his eyes hidden with black Raybans.

"It's all done. The live data was transferred last weekend, James has been trained and he thinks the upgrade is great," she answered, covering her mouth as a yawn escaped. Work seemed so far away.

"Well done. That went very smoothly."

"I can't take any credit for it," she said honestly. "Michael did it all from Dublin with minimal involvement from us. We didn't even need to pitch up at work when he was doing the transfer."

She had just resumed reading when he said, "The age of technology makes the world a small place . . . I guess it's on to the next project now."

"And what might that be?" She was more alert now. She realised he had something in the pipeline that he wanted to share.

"We're rolling out a new commission plan . . . the one I talked about at the Sales Kick-off. We'll need to put a road show together on the changes and run it through all the States."

"We?" She looked at him for clarification.

"I want you to do the main presentation – you'll be in the best position to explain the differences between the old plan and the new one. Frank will obviously need to be there. I'm hoping to get Steve Ryan along as well, even though it's short notice for him."

"When is all this happening?"

"Over the next two weeks. Melbourne is first, then Brisbane. We'll do Sydney last . . . Donald wants all the international subsidiaries to be compliant to the new plan by the end of the quarter . . . I'm totally to blame for the short timeframe, I knew about this weeks ago but I was absorbed in Cathay."

He ordered in pizza for lunch. They ate from the box, so there was no need to leave the garden.

* * *

"I should be going home," she said, putting the book down. It was getting too dark to read.

"Why not stay?"

324

"I don't think so . . . too much of a good thing." She smiled at him.

"OK, if I can't persuade you, I'll get my car keys. You can take the book with you if you like." He got up and stretched.

"Thanks . . . I'll give it back during the week."

The traffic was busy but he had her home in less than fifteen minutes.

"Do you want to come inside for a coffee?" she offered as he pulled up outside.

"No, thanks. I think your Fiona disapproves of me . . . maybe she thinks I'm too old for you," he answered with a wry grin.

"Don't be so paranoid. I know you're old but Fiona respects her elders," she teased.

"I'll see you tomorrow, OK?" he said, leaning across to kiss her.

"OK, thanks for a wonderful weekend," she said softly, giving him another quick kiss before getting out. She waited until the car was out of sight before going inside.

The flat had the Sunday night calmness that usually followed a busy weekend. She sat down and watched TV with Fiona.

"I'm going to Melbourne on Friday," she said after a few minutes.

"With Robert?" Fiona asked, her expression becoming wary.

"Sort of . . . Frank Williams and Steve Ryan will be

there too. We're doing a road show on the new commission plan . . . fascinating stuff . . . "

"It's just a day trip then?" Fiona's question was sharp, hitting home.

"We're having dinner with the Victorian sales team afterwards so I'll be staying the night." Claire was careful not to sound defensive.

"So what's going to happen at this dinner? Are you and Robert going to be all lovey-dovey in front of your colleagues?"

Claire was reflective for a few moments before replying, "I don't know . . . I hadn't thought of that . . . I guess I'll follow Robert's lead."

* * *

Julia was finding it hard to breathe in the stuffy room. The speaker said his name was Joe. He claimed he was a lawyer and that alcohol helped him deal with the stress of his impossible workload. Julia would have shouted out that he was a liar but for the fact it would mean she was joining in with this pathetic group of people. She studied his red face and quivering hands dispassionately. He was an ugly man. They were all ugly, with their blotched faces, their hardened lips, their dour clothes. They had no dignity, standing up in front of people they didn't know, making fools of themselves.

"I want to stop drinking, I really want to stop. I realise now that I will never be able to drink normally like other people. I'm afraid of going to the social functions at work. No matter how good my intentions are, I end up embarrassing myself, embarrassing my wife, my colleagues. My drinking does nothing but cause harm . . . I've hurt a lot of people. I have a lot of making up to do when I get out of here . . . I've got to win my family's love back . . ." He started to cry.

Julia was revolted. "As if he's a lawyer! He's a bum if I ever saw one . . ." she whispered derisively to the tiny Asian woman sitting next to her in the circle.

"And where do you think a bum would get the money to come to a place like this? Alcoholism doesn't have any respect for class or race or gender. Alcoholism is a disease, not a punishment for the 'bums' of society," the woman said, looking at Julia as if she was incredibly stupid.

Julia blushed. She should have known better than to speak to these people.

The Asian woman's name was Amy. She was pretty but worn out. She spoke well, articulate and soft. Her mother had died the previous year and she thought at the time that she had handled it well.

"I've been here before; this is my second time drying out. I was dry for five years, going to AA meetings religiously, helping other alcoholics. Then I got complacent. Forgot the AA motto of concentrating on staying sober one day at a time. Forgot that alcoholism is a disease I will carry to the grave with me and not something I'll grow out of. I started drinking again after my mother's death, just a few sherries here and there, to help me cope with the loneliness. But the loneliness got worse, not better. Ten months after her death I was struck with inexplicable grief. The emptiness inside me was unbearable. Then, two weeks ago I went on a bender, a major bender. My husband found me in the gutter, literally. I was down some alleyway, passed out. All my money was gone – I was filthy. He called an ambulance. Had to explain to the driver that the filthy person was his wife. I'll never forget his expression when I came to. The hurt. Disgust. He said that he's not sure if he could ever look at me the same way again after seeing me in that state. I knew from his face that I would lose him unless I made a dramatic and fast recovery. You know, even if I do recover, I could still lose him because I don't know if he can forget what happened, how he found me . . . so here I am, an alcoholic, and I'll never lose sight of the fact again. I'm an alcoholic for life and I'm back at my AA meetings which I now realise are the only way to keep me sober . . . I'm not capable of doing it on my own."

Julia tried hard not to listen. Amy seemed to be looking straight at her.

Stop looking at me, you stupid woman! The management of this God-forsaken place have obviously paid you some money to make up this pathetic story and make me feel bad . . . you're no more an alcoholic than I am.

* * *

Their flight was at midday and they were due at the Melbourne office thirty minutes before the 3.00pm start. Steve Ryan was giving the opening address, followed by a discussion on sales strategies by Frank Williams. Claire's presentation was on the differences between the old plan and the new one. Robert was back-up for any difficult questions that might be asked by the sales staff.

Frank, Steve and Robert were nowhere to be found at eleven so she got a taxi to the airport on her own. She had a quick look for them after she checked in but couldn't see them in any of the queues. She boarded and settled into her seat with a hard copy of her presentation to read.

"So there you are."

It was Robert. He crouched beside her.

"Why are you sitting way back here?"

"Because I'm a nobody so I get to fly economy. Executives fly business. Company Policy," she laughed, glad he had made the flight.

"But you're an executive's girlfriend. There should be special rules in the policy for that," he said, grinning.

"Well, change the policy, Mr Vice-President."

A steward stopped.

"Can you please return to your seat, sir. We're preparing for take off."

"See you in Melbourne. Wait for me this time." He kissed her forehead.

The steward had it wrong; they sat on the tarmac for another thirty minutes. They started the seminar almost an hour behind schedule. Frank ran over his time by fifteen minutes and when Claire stood up to speak, she was acutely conscious of the restless audience. She was glad that she had asked Robert's secretary, Samantha, to help her prepare an energetic PowerPoint presentation. It started off with an audio effect of the Road Runner, the sudden loud noise making her listeners sit up in their seats. She caught Robert smiling and focussed her eyes away from his direction, concentrating on delivering her slides with as much speed and clarity as possible. She was able to handle the questions without intervention by Robert or Steve.

Dinner was at an elite restaurant overlooking the Yarra river. She counted sixteen at the table.

"You know, Claire, I find it hard to believe I haven't had the pleasure of meeting you before." It was an account manager sitting on her left with an ego bigger than his sales quota.

"You must not come to Sydney very often," she forced herself to answer politely.

"I'll be coming up there for a few days next month," he said with a noticeable wink.

She cringed. "That's nice," she replied vaguely and glanced in Robert's direction for assistance. She couldn't catch his eye. He was talking to the Victorian sales manager. It looked like a serious conversation. She interrupted the conversation on her right so she wouldn't have to talk to the account manager who had moved his seat closer to hers.

When they retired to the lounge, she found herself in a different group to Robert again. He was standing apart, talking to Frank Williams and one of the female sales reps. Claire waited for him to come over, disappointed when it became apparent that he didn't intend to join her. She excused herself for the night when she saw the account manager making a beeline in her direction.

* * *

Robert knocked on her door shortly before midnight, waking her. He was making so much noise, she had no choice but to let him in.

"Hello, gorgeous." He lifted her up in his arms.

"You didn't think I was gorgeous enough to talk to all night." She was not able to contain her annoyance.

"Of course I did . . . you were so sexy giving that presentation . . . you look great in that navy suit . . . I remember you were wearing it the first day I met you," he said, showering her face with kisses.

"You remember that?" She gave him a disbelieving look.

"You bet I do! Look, honey, let's stay on here an extra night . . . we could take a day trip tomorrow, go to the casino in the evening . . . it would be fun."

"Are you drunk?" she asked, forgetting that she was annoyed with him.

"I think I may be! Come on, say yes," he coaxed, continuing to kiss her face.

"OK, you've convinced me." She hugged him and he pulled her onto the bed.

* * *

They were winning. Claire hadn't counted the chips but guessed they amounted to a few hundred dollars. Her job was to choose the numbers, Robert was handling the bets. Her face was flushed with excitement, her new dress shimmered under the glaring glitter of the lights. Robert had spotted the dress in the shop window of a small boutique in Chapel Street earlier in the day.

"Look! Is that Frank Williams over there?" she asked, suddenly seeing his large frame. He was rigid with concentration, a fine sheen of perspiration coating his forehead.

"Where?" Robert asked, looking in the wrong direction.

"There . . . straight ahead," she said, pointing.

"Yes, it is him . . . he must be staying the weekend also," Robert confirmed. "Quick, give me some numbers."

"27 . . . 36 . . . he's at the $50 table . . . he must be pretty serious about his gambling," she mused.

"Yeah ... from what I've heard, he spends most weekends at Star City running up gambling debts . . . he's always strapped for cash," Robert commented absently as he slid the chips into position on the table.

Their luck changed and they returned to their hotel soon after.

"You know that company, DC Solutions?" she said thoughtfully as she took her shoes off and sat down on the bed.

"Yeah . . . what about them?"

"Well, we don't have a signed contract with them and Frank has authorised some big payments over the last few months. I know it sounds crazy – but do you think he could be using the company in some way to pay off his gambling debts?" She felt foolish at how ridiculous it sounded out loud. He had his back to her, unbuttoning his shirt.

"DC Solutions is a US company. We may not have a local contract with them but I'm sure we have one in San Jose."

He sounded terse and she instinctively decided not to divulge to him that she had wasted money on two futile company searches. They went to bed. They didn't make love; she presumed he was tired.

* * *

Monday began with the usual anticipation at the thought of seeing him. She hummed happily to herself as she collected her mail from her pigeon hole. She had said goodbye to him at the airport yesterday morning. She couldn't wait to see him again.

"Hi, Emma, did you have a good weekend?" Claire smiled as she stopped by Emma's work station. Sunlight was streaming through the window and the shadows of the vertical blinds dashed across Emma's face as she looked up from her work.

"I had a quiet one. How about you? How was Melbourne?" she asked with friendly interest.

An image of the casino flashed into Claire's mind. She wished she could tell Emma the truth.

"It was great ... really great," she beamed and continued on to her office. She felt a pang of guilt when she saw the report on ARS corporation sitting in her inbox, recalling her conversation with Robert on Saturday night. It was more substantial than the DC Solutions report and she printed it so it would be easier to read.

She found it hard to concentrate and went to get a mid-morning cup of tea. Frank Williams was in the kitchen, clumsily making himself a cup of coffee, a task he obviously wasn't used to doing for himself.

"Did you have a nice time in Melbourne?" she enquired politely as she rinsed her cup.

"Yes ... very enjoyable ... I can't say the same about today. I still have a large number of messages since my holiday that I haven't actioned ... and my secretary called in sick this morning." His hands were unsteady as he poured the milk, spilling some on the counter.

"Well, at least you can ignore the messages I sent you ...they were just on DC Solutions."

"Why? Are you saying you don't want a contract now?" He looked at her, his black eyes impatient.

"No ... I still want it ... but it's not as urgent now that I know San Jose might have one at a corporate level," she said, squeezing up against the counter so he could move past her.

"Amtech Corp has a contract? Who told you that rubbish?" he snapped. "DC Solutions is a small Australian company – they have absolutely nothing to do with Amtech Corp."

She stared at his back in confusion as he ambled away.

* * *

Robert had signed the cheques for DC Solutions and Frank had approved the invoices. They should both know the company but they were contradicting each other on whether it was an Australian or US based company. She picked up the ARS report from the printer on her way back to her office. She read it slowly as she sat down. On page six, a Mr R Pozos was listed as one of the directors of ARS Corporation. His name danced in front of her eyes for a few moments before realisation hit.

It must be a coincidence. Pozos has to be a common name in the States. Her denial was immediate, desperate. She stared at the page. The "R Pozos" on the report was born on 14th Sept 1960. She logged into the payroll system to double-check the date against Robert's employee records. The system was slow and it took a few minutes before she could call up his details. The dates matched and she stared at the screen, feeling sick.

I know there's a perfectly legitimate explanation. Steve Ryan must be aware that Robert is connected with DC

Solutions ... there's no doubt it's all above board. Why didn't Robert tell me about it in Melbourne? Oh God, what if he comes around here right now and sees this report on my desk?

She stuffed it into her handbag – it didn't quite fit. The edges crumpled as she pulled the zip roughly.

What next? What do I do now? She shut her office door and rang Fiona, willing her to answer the phone. She answered on the second ring, businesslike and efficient.

"Fiona . . . it's me . . . will you be home tonight?" she asked, her voice strained.

"Yes. Is something wrong?"

"Just a work thing. I need your professional opinion on something," she answered, her voice marginally stronger.

"OK, sounds intriguing. I'll try to get home early but I have to run now – I should have been at a meeting five minutes ago." Fiona hung up, leaving Claire at a loose end. All the issues and tasks on her schedule for the day seemed insignificant and pointless. She somehow needed to avoid Robert until it was time to go home. She wouldn't know how to act normally around him now. He would be able to tell that something was wrong within seconds.

She organised an impromptu meeting with a busy and reluctant Emma.

"Has something happened?" Emma asked, her expression concerned as she looked at Claire carefully.

"What do you mean?" Claire countered, her tone dismissive.

"You were full of the joys of life this morning . . . and now you look as if you're about to burst into tears," she said bluntly. Claire cursed her for being so observant and wished, for the second time that morning, that she could confide in her.

"I've just got a whopper of a headache, that's all."

When lunch-time finally came around, she escaped outside with relief, her steps brisk as she put as much distance between herself and Robert as possible. She bought a sandwich and sat in the park, questions crashing ruthlessly into her thoughts, making it impossible to get away from him.

Why didn't he tell the truth in Melbourne? I asked him a direct question about DC Solutions and he could have easily told me that he was a director. Is that why we didn't make love afterwards . . . because I asked too many uncomfortable questions?

She stayed out for as long as she could without arousing suspicions, particularly Emma's. On her return she killed some time with Stacey on an issue that had just cropped up. She left just after four for a fictitious appointment with the dentist.

It took her longer than usual to get home. She wasn't sure if it was because the trains were slower outside rush hour or if it was due to the fact that she just didn't have the energy to rush like she did most evenings. Shutting the door wearily behind her, she immediately focussed on the phone. She was terrified that he would ring, even more terrified that he would call around to the flat. She waited patiently in the silence, lost in her thoughts, until Fiona came in.

"What's going on?" Fiona sat down eagerly, without taking off her shoes. She usually discarded them carelessly at the door, preferring to pad around the flat barefoot.

"I found something out at work today," Claire began, her voice uneven.

"What? What is it?" Fiona interrupted immediately.

Claire took a steadying breath, leaning forward as she carefully chose her words so that Fiona would have the full facts.

"Hold on – I'll have to tell you the whole story. In Amtech we have business partners whom we pay commission if they help us close a sale. Most of the time we have a signed contract with them. Three months ago we paid $600,000 to a company called DC Solutions. When I asked our sales director for some backup to the payment, he said that it was our first time dealing with the company and the contract wasn't drawn up yet. A few weeks ago we made another payment of $400,000 and Frank, the sales director, was on holiday. I remember it was the week before my birthday and when I was looking up the number for the restaurant in the Yellow Pages, just out of curiosity I had a look for DC Solutions' advertisement. They didn't even have a line entry, not to talk about an ad . . ." She paused.

"Yeah, go on," Fiona encouraged, impatient.

"Well, that worried me a bit so I got the paperwork for the cheque back out . . . and I noticed that their invoice didn't have a phone number on it. You know that company, Australian Corporate Reporting?"

Fiona nodded confirmation.

"I asked them to do a company search, just to put my mind at ease. It came back two weeks ago and told me nothing except that DC Solutions is a fully owned subsidiary of a US company called ARS Corporation. The directors of DC Solutions were US Citizens and I didn't recognise their names. I was going to drop it, but something was niggling me so I had another search done on the holding company, ARS corporation. I got that report this morning . . . Robert is one of the directors." Her voice broke and she swallowed before continuing. "I just don't know what to think."

Fiona didn't speak for a few moments, her face reflecting her thoughts as she digested the information. She kicked off her shoes and curled her bare toes into the carpet.

"Your Robert, as in Robert Pozos?"

"Yes, same date of birth and everything," Claire answered flatly.

"Wow! A million bucks!" Fiona was incredulous. She curled her legs beneath her on the couch.

"Yes, a million bucks. Please, Fi, help me think this through. There must be an explanation and I just can't

339

think of it," Claire said, desperately looking at her for a solution.

"Have you spoken to Robert about it?" Fiona ignored Claire's plea, immediately firing another question at her.

"I asked him in Melbourne about DC Solutions . . . on reflection, he was a bit funny with me afterwards ... I haven't told him about the company searches . . ." She rubbed her temples. Her head was throbbing both from her own endless questions and now Fiona's.

"Claire, I know that this is not what you want to hear . . . but it looks pretty black and white to me. Why would Amtech pay an executive, who is already earning a ridiculously high salary, another million bucks? And if they wanted to, then why not pay him directly through payroll instead of paying a company that he ultimately owns?" Fiona stated, her logic direct and irrefutable.

"I know, the facts are fairly damning, aren't they?" Claire was resigned, wanting to cry with disappointment but too proud to do so in front of Fiona.

"Yes, it seems so. But why would a wealthy man do such a thing? He's hardly on the breadline," Fiona mused, frowning in confusion as she rested her chin in the palm of her hand.

Claire hadn't asked herself that question but she immediately knew the answer, recalling the phone call from Tom when she had stayed over at Robert's a few weeks before.

"Because he's divorcing his wife. I overheard him on the phone to his lawyer . . . I think he wants to keep the settlement to less than half a million . . . he's very bitter about having to give her anything. Half a million US Dollars is close to a million Aussie Dollars . . . I guess he didn't want to use his own money," she finished miserably. It was the final piece of the jigsaw, giving a nice neat indisputable picture. She suddenly couldn't bear to talk about it with Fiona any longer. The betrayal was killing her and she couldn't tell Fiona who had cautioned her so many times not to get involved.

"I'm going for a walk . . . I need some fresh air," she said, standing up.

"What about dinner?"

"No offence . . . but I think I'd throw up if I saw food right now."

* * *

She was anonymous as she walked along the beach. The setting sun cast an orange hue over the crashing waves. It was a windy evening and her hair kept blowing in her face. She tried to cry quietly but couldn't help the involuntary sobs that were so loud to her own ears. All around her, happy people jogged along the water or lay on the sand watching the sun go down.

CHAPTER FOURTEEN

Julia lay in bed, awake, lonely. There was a deathly silence and she longed for some natural noise, like traffic or even children playing. It was only nine o'clock and she had chosen to go to bed rather than watch TV with the others. She could see them now, their bleak expressions, bickering over what to watch. Considering how much she had to pay to get into this place, you would expect the rooms would at least have their own TV. The décor was depressing, the staff humourless. It was hard to stay positive.

Cherie had come to visit yesterday. She brought some magazines and chocolate. Julia appreciated her thoughtfulness but she was sick of reading. Now that she had spent so much time with the dregs of society, she saw Cherie in a new light. She had always dismissed her understated good looks, her inner confidence, her happiness. She glowed against the backdrop of the drab visitors' room. Julia felt a sudden surge of envy and couldn't bring herself to talk with her. Cherie left, looking hurt, after just twenty minutes of stilted conversation.

She wondered what Robert was doing. Was he worried about her? She ached to see him, to touch him, to have the chance to obliterate what had happened on her second and last night in Sydney. She still had another two weeks to get through before she got out. She wasn't sure if she would make it intact. The pressure from the group was getting stronger. Amy was there whenever she turned around, sickeningly supportive, trying to force her to admit she was one of them.

* * *

Claire also had a sleepless night, possible explanations then painful condemnation taking turns at dominating her mind.

Maybe the company will think I've been professionally negligent and I'll get fired for letting those cheques get through. Robert knows I'm a cheque signatory … he must have been laughing at my stupidity. Did he have an affair with me so I wouldn't guess? Would he have gone that far to cover his tracks?

It was 2.00am and she was wide awake, bereft without the anticipation which had been part of her consciousness since the day they met. She felt emotionally disorientated, whipped from a relationship with no closure, whipped from happiness to despair, all without the courtesy of a warning.

Why did he do this to me? How could I be so wrong in my judgement of him? Am I totally blind? We had such a good time in Melbourne . . . how could everything go so wrong so quickly?

It was pointless lying in bed. She got up and went into the darkness of the living-room. She turned on the TV, muting the volume so it wouldn't wake Fiona.

What do I do? Who will I tell? Robert would be the first person I'd approach if this was about someone other than him. Steve Ryan is in Melbourne. I guess I could talk to David. He's the HR Director. He'll know what to do. I'll call him straight away when I get in.

The morning seemed so far away when she desperately needed the answers now. She watched the screen – the expressions of the guests on the talk show were hypnotising without the distraction of sound. When she looked at her watch again, it was 4.00am. She had to go back to bed, get some sleep.

What will David say? Will he laugh in my face and tell me I'm being ridiculous, accusing a senior vice-president of fraud? Should I tell him about my relationship with Robert?

The questions went on and on, their magnitude overwhelming. She finally drifted into a light sleep and the alarm went off what seemed like minutes later. The nausea was immediate, before she even opened her eyes. The claws of a severe headache were clamping

her forehead in their grip, making the slightest movement painful. She dragged herself out of bed, her
fingers shaking as she struggled to free two aspirin
from their stubborn container. She wanted to be clear-
headed and lucid when she spoke to David, not
nervous and tired. She was glad to leave the torture of
her thoughts behind as she focussed on getting ready
for work.

*What does one wear in a challenging situation like
this?* she asked herself with black humour as she tried
to decide what to put on. The smell of Fiona's toast
wafted through the flat and she felt her stomach
lurch.

"I'll see you later." Claire paused at the kitchen door
on her way out. Fiona was cradling her coffee,
standing over the toaster.

"What are you going to do?"

"I don't know . . . I don't know if I should talk to
Robert or David."

"Who's David?" Fiona ignored her toast when it
popped.

"The HR Manager . . . I thought I had decided on
David last night but I'm confused now again."

"What can you gain from talking to Robert? Of
course he'll deny it. You're letting your relationship
with him get in the way of your professional judgement."

Claire got to work just after nine, giving Audrey a
brisk greeting on her way in. She hurried through the

Finance Department with a busy smile, telling them indirectly that she hadn't time for the usual morning pleasantries. James wasn't at his desk when she extracted the DC Solutions invoices from his files. She ran them through the photocopier along with the reports on both DC Solutions and ARS Corporation, checking over her shoulder anxiously in case Robert should suddenly appear. Returning to her office, she put the originals in a file for David and put the copies in her bag. David's office was in the executive area and she would have to pass by Robert if she went around to see him. She couldn't face the risk of running into Robert. She booked a meeting room on the other side of the building. When she rang David's number it was engaged. She checked her voice mail for new messages while she waited for him to come off the phone. There was only one new message.

Hi, honey. It's after five. Just wondering where you got to today … I missed you …I guess you were busy…see you tomorrow.

The warmth and intimacy in his voice rattled her and she slammed down the phone in panic.

This is all a terrible mistake … how can I believe Robert would do this? He does care about me.

She sat with her head in her hands for a few moments, trying to decide what to do. Then, with trembling hands, she read through the file she had prepared for David and tried her hardest to come up with an explanation. When she failed, she dialled

David's number again.

"David, it's Claire. Can I see you about something rather urgent?"

"I'm pretty busy. Can it wait until later today?" He sounded preoccupied.

Damn, just my luck that he won't be accommodating. There's no way I can wait until later. Robert could come around here any minute.

"I'm sorry, but it's something very important and I'll try not to take up too much of your time," she pressed.

"OK . . . do you want to come around to my office?" he relented.

"I've booked the meeting room in the marketing area. I'll see you there," she said with relief.

They arrived at the meeting room simultaneously and he stood back so she could pass through the doorway before him.

"This seems very dramatic, Claire. What's the matter?" he said as he shut the door. He seemed relatively relaxed and not overly concerned about the possible reasons for the impromptu meeting. She sat down before answering, resting her hands on the smoothly polished table.

"I think I have evidence of fraudulent payments to a company controlled by one of our employees . . ." she began, her hands shaking as she opened the file and her face flushed as if she was the guilty party. There was a tense silence and she watched his expression change as he sat upright in the soft-cushioned seat.

"How much are we talking about?" he enquired gravely.

"A million dollars . . . even."

"What!" The veins in his neck protruded as his face reddened in shock. Then he visibly checked himself before asking more calmly, "And who is involved?"

"Robert Pozos," she said, keeping her eyes down as she braced herself for his reaction. Another silence, this one infinite. She wondered if he had heard her properly. She moved her eyes from the paperwork to study his face and the movement seemed to bring him out of his trance.

"That's a very serious accusation to make. I hope you can support it," he said, his voice ominously low.

"I'm not making accusations, David . . . I sincerely hope that this turns out to be a false alarm and the payments are all above board." When he didn't comment she continued, *"Prima facie* it doesn't look good and it's my job to bring it to your attention. I presume you will know how to handle it from here."

"What's in the file?"

"Supporting documents for two payments to a company called DC Solutions. The first cheque was for $600,000 and the second for $400,000. And I have company reports on DC Solutions and its holding company, ARS Corporation. Robert Pozos is a director of ARS Corporation."

She got up to stand next to his seat and she walked him through the paper trail carefully. She explained the facts to him, forcing herself not to rush.

"I'm sorry. It's not obvious to me how this is fraudulent." He seemed hostile.

"We don't have a contract with DC Solutions and we're paying them 20-25% instead of 10%. Robert is a director of the controlling company. That has to be a conflict of interest, if nothing else."

"Can I keep these documents?" he asked curtly when she finished.

"Yes, they're yours. What happens from here?" She was anxious not to be left in the dark about the outcome.

"I need to contact San Jose." He looked at his watch. "If I call straight away, I might be able to catch them before they leave for the day."

He stood up suddenly and she stepped out of his way as he hurriedly put the documents back in the file.

"David . . . just one more thing," she asked, her voice unsteady, her composure starting to slip. "I can't face seeing Robert today . . . is it OK if I go home now? This has been very traumatic for me."

"Feel free. I'll keep you informed." He nodded and left without waiting for her.

She returned to her office to get her bag and forward her phone.

"We keep missing each other!"

Her heart did a painful somersault at the sound of Robert's voice.

"Oh . . . hi . . ." She turned slowly to face him, trying

to look casual. He had both hands in the pockets of his dark trousers. His eyes were crinkled with a smile. His vibrancy shocked her as it always did.

"Are you off somewhere?" he asked, noting her bag on her shoulder and her blank monitor.

"I'm going home . . . I'm not feeling very well," she lied awkwardly.

"What's the matter? Have you caught a bug or something?" He looked worried.

"I think so . . . I feel quite sick."

"If you could wait thirty minutes, I could drive you home," he offered, putting his hand on her shoulder in concern. "I'm waiting for Tony to fax through the memorandum of intent. Cathay finally sent it to him this morning."

"Robert!" she said sharply, moving away from his touch.

"Sorry, I forgot where we were." He shrugged with an apologetic smile.

"Congratulations on Cathay . . . look . . . don't worry about me . . . I'm just fine getting a taxi," she said quickly, making a move towards the door.

"Please let me –" he began before she interrupted him forcefully.

"Really – I'm fine – just need a rest. See you tomorrow." She gave him a reassuring smile before rushing away. She wondered if she would see him tomorrow.

She walked over the bridge to the city. The furious

noise of the cars as they rattled past matched the chaos in her mind. The effect of seeing him made her feel quite strongly that he was innocent.

I may have ruined his career by jumping to conclusions . . . he will never forgive me for this . . .

It was a humid day and the light breeze on the bridge was refreshing. She stopped halfway to admire the view, a blue haze stretching over the harbour and reflecting off the whiteness of the Opera House. The sun seemed to be smeared across the sky, rather than in one circular spot. Up above her, brave tourists were climbing the steel of the bridge. She watched as a stronger wind flattened their baggy clothing. She waited until the group reached the top before moving on.

George Street was hot – it didn't have the redeeming wind of the bridge. She walked slowly to the building where Fiona worked. It was too early for lunch so she sat in the lobby reading the *Sydney Morning Herald*.

As lunch-time got closer, the lifts that opened in the lobby were fuller. The suits spilled out, brushing up against each other mercilessly as they raced to the doors. Claire grabbed Fiona by the arm.

"Hi, there ... fancy lunch?"

"Claire, where have you been? I've been trying to call you all morning." Fiona halted dramatically, almost causing a pile-up of the suits behind her.

"Oh . . . I sort of took a walking tour of Sydney . . . where will we go?"

Fiona was short of time so she suggested a small café a few doors down.

"So, what happened?" Fiona asked, eagerly leaning across the tiny table, bursting with curiosity. Claire felt a tinge of annoyance that Fiona didn't seem to register the hurt she was feeling.

"Not much. I told David and he said he'll keep me informed. Then I asked him if I could go home." Her answer was brief; she was suddenly too weary to go into any more detail.

"And how did he react to what you told him? You know, when you said you thought Robert was involved," Fiona pressed, keen to get specific.

"He was very wary of me. David is usually supportive, he's a nice man, but I think he may believe that this is all in my mind . . . I was only with him for fifteen minutes or so . . . and I spent most of that time showing him the paperwork." Claire shrugged. Her lunch made her feel sick and she pushed it away, half-eaten.

"You know, I thought I'd never say this . . . but I wouldn't mind running away from Sydney right now," she said wistfully.

"Why don't you take a holiday? Look, there's a travel agent right there." Fiona pointed across the street.

"That's what Margaret said to me when I wanted to run away from Dublin. Maybe it's not a bad idea . . . we could go together . . . could you get some time off work?" she asked, with the stirrings of enthusiasm.

"I'd love to but I'm going home for Christmas and I don't have the leave or the money for another holiday," Fiona said, looking genuinely apologetic.

"Is James going to Ireland with you?" Claire asked with casual curiosity.

"Yes . . . he is . . . actually, we're planning to get engaged . . ." Fiona revealed with a sheepish smile.

"You're kidding! Congratulations!" Claire's face ached as she smiled as widely as she could.

"Thanks ... but please don't tell anybody."

When Fiona went back to work, Claire strolled across the street to the travel agent and picked up some brochures.

The phone started to ring as she let herself into the apartment. She ignored it with difficulty as she changed out of her office clothes into a beach dress. She went out to the balcony with the brochures, shutting the patio doors to muffle the continuous ringing. She settled down on her lounger, her straw hat giving shade as she read the brochures. The phone continued to ring at frequent intervals until late afternoon.

* * *

"What happened to you yesterday?" Emma was concerned and curious about Claire's unexplained disappearance. She sat on the edge of Claire's desk, looking at her closely.

"I wasn't feeling well. I should never have come to work in the first place," she replied, her tone deliberately abrupt to discourage further questions.

"Why didn't you tell me? I didn't know what happened to you," Emma chided, blatantly perplexed at Claire's vague explanation.

"You were on the phone when I was leaving and I did tell Robert . . . I thought he would pass it on," Claire said defensively. "And I'm feeling much better today, if you're interested."

"Sorry, I'm glad to hear that you're better . . . it's just that you've been acting very strangely the last few days," Emma apologised and Claire gave her a forgiving grin.

"I've always been strange. Didn't you know that?"

She wondered if Robert was in the office. Had David spoken to him yet? Would he be angry with her? She impulsively picked up the phone and called his secretary.

"Hi, Samantha – it's Claire – is Robert in today?"

"No, he's gone back to the States. I had to book an emergency flight for him yesterday afternoon," Samantha answered.

"Oh … do you know how long he will be away for?"

"Not really. It was all such a rush, I didn't have time to ask him. I'm expecting him to call me sometime today. Do you want me to pass on a message?"

"No – not at all – it was only something small – thanks anyway," Claire said and quickly hung up the phone.

He's gone. What does that mean? Has he been fired? At

least I don't have to worry about bumping into him ...

She jumped when her phone rang.

"Claire, David here. Can you come around to my office, please?" His voice was unquestionably strained.

She suddenly didn't want to know what he would tell her and hesitated with unexpected panic before saying, "OK."

* * *

She glanced curiously into Robert's office as she walked around to see David. She could see his cleared desk through the glass window. The door was shut. His chair was pushed neatly into his desk. The files he kept on his meeting table were cleared away. There was an undeniable aura of finality.

David's expression was severe. There was another man with him that she didn't recognise as an Amtech employee.

"Sit down, please," David said briskly, indicating the only vacant seat with an impatient gesture.

"I don't believe I've met you before," she commented to the sombre stranger as she sat next to him. He had a moustache that matched his grey-black hair. His suit was an unfashionable brown.

"Claire Quinlan, this is Lee Murray. Lee regularly represents Amtech Australia in local legal matters and will be witnessing our conversation on behalf of our legal department in the Corporation," David said.

He wasn't meeting her eyes and Claire started to feel uneasy. His hands shuffled the papers in front of him unnecessarily, betraying an anxiety.

What the hell is going on? What needs to be witnessed? she wondered in confusion and she moved her chair back from the table so she could see both men clearly.

"Claire, I am sorry but the company has made the decision to let you go –" David began and paused.

She took the opportunity to interrupt him.

"What do you mean 'let me go'?" she asked in panic, looking at both of them for clarification.

"Your employment with Amtech is being terminated," David explained unemotionally.

"Why? What have I done?" Her voice was strangled with shock.

"To be quite honest, I don't know the reasons. I'm just acting on instructions. Now, moving on . . . I have here two cheques for your termination payment. One gives you your statutory entitlements, which isn't a lot of money as you've been with the Australian subsidiary less than a year." He finally looked at her, his face expressionless, before continuing, "The other cheque is for $100,000. A non-disclosure document comes with it. By signing you are agreeing not to disclose to any other party the payments to DC Solutions or the circumstances surrounding your termination of employment with Amtech. If you accept this cheque and, at a later stage, we find out that you have not abided by the conditions, Amtech will sue you for breach of contract. Lee will be able to vouch in court that the conditions of the payment were explained to you in full."

Claire glanced at Lee, who still hadn't opened his mouth to speak. There were a few moments of loaded silence as she desperately tried to organise her chaotic thoughts into concise sentences.

"David, I don't feel I can accept either cheque as I don't understand what's going on . . . I don't want to leave Amtech ... you can't do this . . . it's unfair dismissal."

"This isn't negotiable. You are leaving Amtech today, regardless of how much we pay you. At the moment I am treating your termination as a retrenchment but if you persist in making this difficult, I will handle it as dismissal due to negligence."

His threat wasn't lost on her; she had thought about that possibility last night. She squirmed in her seat, a light film of perspiration all over her body. She badly needed some fresh air.

"What has happened to Robert? Has he been fired?"

"Robert has gone back to his position in California. His wife is having some problems so he had to leave urgently," he explained, ignoring her derisive expression.

Bullshit. He doesn't care about his wife. So he keeps his job and I lose mine?

"Why do I need to leave? Are they upset that I didn't pick it up sooner? If that's the case, why are they prepared to pay me money?" she asked, trying to be calm and rational but her questions coming out emotional, bordering on hysterical.

"As I said previously, I am not privy to the reasons behind your termination. But, you must admit, $100,000 is a very generous pay-out and I think you are doing quite well," he said, a smug smile playing on his face as he leaned back in his seat. She had never seen this side to David.

It is a lot of money . . . and I don't think I want to work for this screwed-up company any longer, she thought bitterly. *I'm going to need this money while I look for another job . . . that's if I can manage to get another job after all this.*

"Will I get a reference?" she snapped at him, a reaction to his unbearable air of superiority.

"I have a written one here and if you ever need a verbal, direct the person to me and I will be happy to oblige." He smiled again, sensing victory.

"What are you going to tell my staff when I leave out of the blue without even saying goodbye?" she asked, not concealing her bitterness.

"That you were offered a job you couldn't resist with a competitor and we were unable to allow you to work out your notice." His answer was immediate, perfectly rehearsed and infuriatingly reasonable.

"Can I have a few minutes to read the legal document and the reference?"

"Of course," he confirmed, his lips twitching as if he found her request amusing.

Her innate sense of caution would not allow her to sign something she had not read. It was the last thing she wanted to do, with two hostile pairs of eyes scrutinising her as she tried to concentrate on the blurred words. She signed her name and David escorted her as far as the lifts. They miraculously didn't meet anybody on the way. As she handed over her access card, she wondered what Emma and the others would think. When she got outside, she took the cheque out of her bag. Soft drops of spring rain freckled it in seconds. It was signed by David and Steve Ryan. From her knowledge of company policy, the cheque would have to have been approved by the head of Corporate Treasury. Discretionary payments on termination were outside the authority limits of local management. She wasn't sure if she had been fired and felt foolish for not knowing this basic fact. The cheque confused their motives. The girl at the bank gave her a curious look when she saw the amount of the cheque. Claire half expected it to bounce but she was given her lodgement advice as normal.

The train station was almost deserted and it seemed to take quite a while before a train came along. She sat in a daze, staring out the window, but not seeing anything. All her previous doubts were gone. Robert was guilty.

Why else would he have me terminated? I would have believed anything I was told, I didn't need to be kicked out. He must be a lot more powerful in the company than

I gave him credit for. Not only did he manage to keep his position but he got permission from Corporate Treasury to pay out the informant. What a bastard!

Her thoughts were interrupted by the gruff voice of the guard.

"Ma'am, this is the end of the train line – you have to get off here."

She had been so preoccupied that she hadn't noticed she was home.

CHAPTER FIFTEEN

Robert tried Claire's extension from his mobile as the taxi sped away from the terminal. It was ringing through to voicemail. He hung up without leaving a message. He needed to talk to her – leaving a message would be futile. The taxi-driver turned in his seat to ask for an address. Robert didn't want to go to the house. He didn't want to stay there even with Julia away. He checked into a hotel close to the office, the mirror in the foyer confirming that he looked like shit. His eyes were an angry bloodshot, his face grey from the stress of trying to figure out how he was implicated in this debacle. The room was expensive and predictably bland. He dropped his bags at the door. The phone was by the window.

"David, it's Robert," he said, with a sense of relief at being able to talk to someone. It had been twenty-odd hours since he last spoke to David, and he was even more confused now that he had the time to think.

"Robert. You've got there OK? Seen Donald yet?" David's voice sounded weary but friendly.

"No . . . I'm literally just off the plane. I've been trying to call Claire since I landed – where is she?"

"She's gone, Robert," David said solemnly. "Donald's orders."

"What? Are you saying Donald *fired* her? *What the hell did he do that for?*" Robert heard himself yelling. He rarely raised his voice. It must have been the utter shock.

"I don't know. I'm just the messenger here. I was the one that had to tell her."

David's tone was sympathetic; it went someway to defusing Robert's anger.

"Christ, she must be devastated . . . what must she think?" Robert sat on the bed, resting the tightness of his forehead against his palm.

What a mess! What a goddamned mess!

"Yeah, she was stunned, then angry. She probably hates me now. I was as tough with her as possible. Donald's instructions were to get her out without answering any questions. She had a lot of questions . . ." David's laugh was ironic.

"Yes, Claire would . . . Damn, why didn't she just come to talk to me in the first place and none of this would have happened?" Robert muttered, more to himself than David.

"She's a very ethical lady. She did the right thing to

come to me. And I did the right thing to bring it to Donald. I knew there must be a reasonable explanation but I was duty bound to escalate it."

There was a silence as Robert absorbed and assimilated the facts. He had jumped on the plane only knowing the barest detail. Acting on another of Donald's instructions, to get back to San Jose immediately. He regretted doing it now. He should have stayed in Sydney – he had a better chance of finding out what happened from there.

"And Donald went off the deep end . . . too scared about the press to get the real facts," he said eventually, with an audible sigh of frustration.

"Yes, it was a drastic reaction from him. Claire is the last person he should have turfed out," David agreed.

David's right. She didn't deserve that.

"I agree. If it was anyone, it should have been me."

David was quick to set the record straight. "I'm not saying that. I believe that you're innocent. I'm not sure how, given the paperwork that Claire showed me, but I know you must be . . . and I trust my instincts."

"Thanks, David, for your support . . . and I do understand that you needed to escalate." Robert was about to hang up when he remembered. "David, one more thing. I don't have Claire's home number. Can you get it for me?"

David was happy to oblige.

"Sure . . . hold on a minute."

* * *

Robert decided to search the house before going to the office. He only had one theory to follow up after twenty hours of thought. It had come to him on the plane. He didn't doubt that Frank was involved. He had signed off the invoices and he had the motive, a nasty gambling habit. The question was who had helped him.

At some point I must have signed some documents to make me a director of this company, ARS. I know that I certainly didn't sign anything in Australia, at least I can remember that much.

That could only mean that, whatever he had signed, he had done so in San Jose. It also meant that Frank had an accomplice. A San Jose-based accomplice. In his role as vice-president, Robert was director of numerous Amtech companies around the world. His recollection of the full list was hazy. It was another hazy memory that had led him to his theory. It was the memory of agreeing to be a director of a small company Julia had set up last year.

The house had a stale unoccupied smell. He opened the windows to let in some air before starting with the files in the study downstairs. He flicked through them, not yet knowing what he was looking for. Julia had her own bank account. After discovering on their honeymoon that she was an alcoholic, Robert did not open a joint account. Her statements were neatly filed, the last one a month old. There were no unusual lodgements.

Finishing with the study, he went upstairs. There was a light film of dust on the banister. The bedroom looked alien; it was hard to imagine he had slept there with Julia just three months ago. He found the paperwork for Julia's small company with her personal documents. The company was a year old. The paperwork looked as if it hadn't been touched since it was filed.

What I need is a current status on this company. See if it owns shares in any other company. I'll ask Tom to check it out for me.

He shut the windows downstairs before leaving. When he was less tired, he would come back and pack his clothes.

* * *

Robert had never seen Donald so angry. If he hadn't known him for as long as he did, he might have been intimidated as Donald simmered from behind his desk.

His first words weren't promising. "You'd better have a damned good explanation for this!"

Robert sat down before answering. "I'm sorry to say I don't. I know as little as you, maybe less."

Donald's face darkened. "That's not good enough, Robert. You're a director of the company – you must know something about it. Don't take me for a fool!"

Robert met his glowering stare straight on. His tone was level as he replied, "I'd never take you for a fool. However, you, of all people, should know that being a director is not conclusive. You and I are joint directors of over thirty Amtech subsidiaries across the world. I can't remember all their names. Can you?"

Robert could see his point had hit home but Donald wasn't going to admit it.

"You've put me in a diabolical position. I'm worried about Cathay. You were so close to the deal that they'll lose confidence at even a whisper of a slur on your name. Yet this is a matter that must be investigated by the police." Donald's voice was appropriately sombre.

Robert nodded in agreement. "I appreciate that. I will fully co-operate with any police investigation. I have my reputation, and my position, to protect."

There was a brief silence, Robert knew something serious was coming.

"Speaking of your position, and considering the delicate situation with Cathay, I've decided to allow you to continue as vice-president while we investigate the fraud . . . however, I feel compelled to make it clear that under more normal circumstances I would suspend you immediately."

Robert could comprehend Donald's strategy. The CEO had a crisis on his hands, a senior vice-president of the company accused of fraud. If the scandal leaked to the shareholders, their confidence in the company would plummet. As would the share price and Donald's share options, his nest-egg for his retirement. Then there was Cathay and how they would react to the news. They were both painfully aware that they only had a letter of intent from Cathay, not a signed contract. For these reasons, Donald would want Robert to continue in his role. Donald needed to ensure that the shareholders and Cathay knew nothing of the investigation taking place behind the scenes.

"I understand." Robert stood to leave. There was a lot he wanted to discuss with Donald but now wasn't the time. Donald needed to let off steam, show that he was in charge. With that now established, Robert would be able to have a more productive discussion with him next time around.

* * *

It had been a long afternoon and Claire went to some considerable effort with dinner in an attempt to take her mind off Robert. She laid the table out on the balcony, preferring to eat outdoors. It was six when the phone rang. She did some quick calculations on the time difference: it was the middle of the night in San Jose. She only picked up the phone when she concluded it was unlikely to be Robert.

"Fiona's not home yet," she said when she recognised Den's voice.

"I guess I'll call back later." He sounded disappointed.

"Hold on. Can I ask you a work question?" She remembered that Den was a lawyer. He would know about unfair dismissal and non-disclosure statements.

"Only if you promise never to mock me again for being a lawyer."

"OK, I'll try," she smiled before launching into a

summarised version of what had happened that morning, "Amtech have retrenched me . . . at least I think they have retrenched me. They offered me a very generous termination cheque in return for my signature on a non-disclosure statement." She paused to get his reaction.

"I'm listening."

"I feel that the whole process was very unfair. I didn't want to take the cheque but they said I was being let go regardless and, if I didn't sign the non-disclosure, I would only get the minimum statutory payment."

"When you transferred from Ireland, did your contract stipulate that your period of service would be continued in Australia?" Den's words were slow and precise.

"No, I was terminated in Ireland and rehired here."

"That means your statutory payment would only be your notice period and a couple of weeks."

"That's what they said. Can I sue for unfair dismissal?"

"You could. However, the most you would get is six months' pay. It sounds as if you've got more than that already with this cheque they gave you."

She could hear some sympathy in his voice.

"Yes, you're right."

"Do you want me to have a look at the non-disclosure statement?" he offered as an afterthought.

"No, it's OK," she sighed. "It's probably best that I

walk away from all this and try to put it behind me."

"Ring me if you change your mind."

"Thanks. I'll tell Fiona you called."

Fiona didn't come in until after seven and it was dark when they sat down to eat. The balcony light was blown and Claire put a small candle on the table. It was a romantic setting and she thought of Robert despite herself.

"So, I'm unemployed, a new experience for me," she declared, with a cynical smile.

"At least you're rich," Fiona commented, the glow from the candle flickering across her face.

"I'm not sure that I did the right thing, taking the money . . . I feel as if I let them buy me out."

"Don't be stupid – if they were going to get rid of you anyway, then why not? It could take you a while to find another job," Fiona said practically.

"Yeah . . . you're right . . . I'm quite worried about finding something else."

"Did you call any of the employment agencies this afternoon?" Fiona asked, opening a second bottle of beer for herself.

"No. Despite thinking about it all day, I haven't come up with a story yet that explains my sudden departure from Amtech." Claire shrugged and looked at Fiona for ideas.

"Didn't David offer to give you a verbal reference?" Fiona queried.

"Yeah . . . but I look on that as a last resort . . . I don't trust David any more . . . I can't believe he was so callous to me."

"Do you need to tell the agencies that you've left Amtech? Why don't you pretend you still work there? Then they won't expect a reference," Fiona suggested, pushing her clean plate to the side so she could rest her elbows on the table.

"I don't think I'd be comfortable lying in my résumé about my service period with Amtech."

"I'm not sure you have a choice . . . anyway, if you get a job quickly, you'll only be lying about a few days."

They sat companionably for a while as they finished their beers. Then the phone started to ring inside the apartment.

"I'll get it," Fiona offered. Claire watched her through the patio doors as she picked up the phone. Her lips moved as she spoke, and she hung up within seconds.

"Was it Den? I forgot to tell you he called earlier," Claire said when she came back outside.

"No, it was Robert. I told him you were out."

Claire's heart raced.

He phoned. He wants to talk to me.

"What did he say?"

"Only that he would call back another time . . . I resisted the temptation to tell him to go to hell."

She didn't know whether to be angry or relieved that Fiona had taken matters into her own hands by saying she was out.

"You know, I just can't believe that Robert walked away from this without losing his job," Fiona said, shaking her head incredulously.

"Welcome to the world of corporate politics . . . if you know the right people, you can get away with anything," Claire replied, her tone absent, still thinking of his phone call.

"It seems so unfair. Don't you want to get back at him in some way?" Fiona asked, trying to read Claire's expression.

Claire didn't know what she wanted. She still couldn't believe Robert had done this. They were silent as they listened to the sounds of suburban life drifting up from the street below. A woman was having a fight with her partner. Her voice was shrill and ugly. His answers were low-toned and menacing. Another neighbour was trying to start his dead car, the engine coughing irritably until he finally gave up. At that moment, it all seemed very mundane and depressing to Claire. Her thoughts settled on what Susan had said about her mother being lonely – it had been niggling at the back of her mind for a few weeks.

"Maybe I should just go home . . ." she said, her voice quiet as she looked at Fiona for her reaction.

"Now you're being ridiculous . . . you will still have the same problems in Ireland . . . just with the extra misery of the winter."

Her bluntness made Claire smile. Fiona might not be very reassuring but she was unquestionably honest. It started to rain again, the soft drops sprinkling Claire's bare arms. They quickly cleared the table and went inside.

* * *

There was a gentle knock on her door. Julia was in bed but awake. She sat up as Amy opened the door and popped her head inside.

"Sorry to disturb you but there's a call holding for you downstairs," she said with her usual annoying smile.

"OK, give me a minute," Julia replied tersely, making a point of waiting until Amy closed the door before getting out of bed. Sudden panic struck as she put on her silk dressing-gown and went downstairs.

Please don't let it be Robert . . . he couldn't have found out I'm staying here, could he?

There was only one phone that the patients could use and it was inconveniently located in the hallway. She rudely slammed the door of the television room to block out the noise, before picking up the receiver.

"Julia? It's Cherie."

"Cherie? It's very late . . ." Julia said, her voice immediately defensive. She knew she had behaved badly when Cherie visited. She knew she owed her an apology.

"Look, I know it's late but I thought you would want to hear the good news," Cherie said, sounding excited.

"What good news?" Julia asked, her question cautious.

"Robert's back," Cherie revealed, almost triumphantly. "Wayne saw him at work."

"You're kidding me . . . really?" Julia asked, sitting down slowly on the worn armchair next to the phone stand. She tucked the smooth silk of her dressing-gown around her legs.

"Nope! Pretty sudden, isn't it? Do you think he might be jealous that his wife has gone off on 'holiday' without him?" Cherie suggested with an infectious giggle.

"Yeah, he must have been worried when I emailed him to say I was taking some time out!" Julia gave a small laugh. The sound was foreign. It seemed like months since she had laughed. "Cherie . . . I'm sorry about Sunday . . . I wasn't feeling myself. This place is enough to drive any normal person around the bend," Julia apologised awkwardly.

"It's no problem, I understand perfectly."

"OK, thanks . . . well, goodnight – I guess I'll see you soon."

"Keep your chin up. You're halfway through – I know you can survive it."

"I hope I can . . ."

"Do you want me to come and pick you up next week?" Cherie offered.

"Thanks, that would be great."

"OK, I'll get Wayne to mind the kids – he can work

from home – we'll do something nice – something to celebrate your new beginning," Cherie said enthusiastically.

Julia was grateful for her kindness, her endless support, but she didn't know how to put her gratitude into words. She went back to bed and sat up against the pillows, reliving all the good times with Robert, excited about their future. He was back. Soon she would be able to see his tanned face, touch his soft beard.

* * *

Donald acknowledged Robert with a civil nod as he shut the door behind him.

Robert sat down. They faced each other silently until Donald got up to pace restlessly around the office.

"This company, ARS Corporation . . . I vaguely remember Julia buying a shelf company last year," Robert said, moving in his seat to keep up eye contact. "I think I can remember agreeing to be a director . . . she said she wanted to start a small business . . . I wasn't listening too carefully at the time."

"Maybe you should learn to listen more carefully in the future!" Donald's words were harsh but Robert knew him well enough to detect a slight softening in his attitude since yesterday.

"Point taken," he said reasonably, watching Donald frown as he tried to work through the problem in his mind.

"Why would Julia do this?" He was standing by the

door. Robert turned in his seat to face him.

"She's an alcoholic . . . she's mentally unstable . . . to tell you the truth, she's capable of anything." He sighed, running his hand through his hair.

"Do me a favour and choose your next wife more carefully," said Donald, making a gruff stab at humour, more evidence that he had softened. Robert resisted the temptation to remind him that it was he who suggested they marry. To avoid gossip, of all things!

He could see from Donald's expression that he was still struggling to comprehend what had happened.

"I can't get this clear in my head," he said finally, his shrewd eyes focussed on Robert. "There must be someone else involved. If it was Julia, she must have had a contact in Amtech Australia to pull this off."

Robert had expected his line of questioning. He had nothing to substantiate his suspicions about Frank – however he acknowledged that Donald deserved as much information as he could give him.

"Yeah ... I've been trying to figure that one out too," he said, his response slow. "The only person I can think of is Frank Williams . . ."

"Who is Frank Williams?" Donald asked on cue.

"The sales and marketing manager."

"Why do you think it's him?"

"Don't get me wrong. I'm only guessing here . . . he signed off on the invoices from DC Solutions, he also has a gambling problem so he probably needs money . . . and he knows Julia – they were very friendly when she went to Sydney a few weeks ago . . . it's a long shot though." Robert shrugged. The connection between Frank and Julia sounded lame now that he had described it out loud.

"When we finish here, ring that HR guy in Australia and tell him to get rid of this Frank Williams immediately," Donald instructed ruthlessly.

"I have no proof," Robert protested.

"I don't care. Get him out of Amtech."

It was out of character for Donald to be so rash.

"I don't want to get rid of Frank the way you did with Claire Quinlan." Robert's voice was quietly determined.

"Who's Claire Quinlan?"

Robert realised that Donald wouldn't have bothered to commit Claire's name to his memory.

"The girl who uncovered all this and did the right thing by escalating it."

"Of course we had to get rid of her," Donald spluttered. "If this stuff leaks out, we're in serious trouble. Cathay would certainly pull the plug."

"That may be true, but I still think that terminating Claire was unethical and unfair," Robert persevered. "She's a professional – she could have been relied on to keep it quiet while we investigated."

"I don't have the privilege of knowing her personally. I had some tough decisions to make . . . it was a crisis, damn it!" Donald's face was a deep purple. Robert had never heard him swear before.

"I'm just saying you were very fast to get rid of her." Robert commented, an outrageous thought coming into his mind.

Very fast, suspiciously fast. And I'm almost certain that Frank has a US-based accomplice.

Donald didn't respond, his face still an unhealthy colour. Robert dragged his thoughts away from Frank's accomplice to say, "I've checked all our bank accounts and can't find where Julia would have lodged the money ... I'm not sure that I can retrieve it without police assistance."

Donald had to sit down on his magnificent armchair. He glared at Robert across the vast desk.

"I decide when the police get involved, not you . . . and right now I can't afford an indiscretion on their part."

"Believe me, I have the same concerns as you do about this leaking out . . . but I'm telling you we can't get the money back without the police."

"Getting it back now will risk the image of the company and that's a risk I cannot take," Donald replied with authority. "Cathay should have signed by the end of next week. The police will be informed then and no sooner. Understand?"

Robert did understand: in Donald's eyes his job was hanging by a thread. The flimsy thread of Donald's own paranoia about the scandal leaking out.

The meeting was over. Donald's shutters were up.

Robert was on his way out when Donald reminded

him, "And remember, pay this Frank Williams some money and get him out of Amtech."

Robert stopped in his tracks, his back to Donald, his stance unyielding.

"No, Donald, I will not pay Frank Williams out. If he leaves the company I have no way of finding out what happened, or clearing my name."

He continued on his way before Donald thought of pulling rank.

* * *

"I wasn't expecting you home tonight," Claire said, looking up when Fiona came in. It was late; she had spent the last few hours updating her résumé.

"You're going to kill me," Fiona grimaced as she shut the door.

"What have you done now?" Claire asked, laughing.

"I blabbed to James and Paul that you had been seeing Robert."

"You didn't!" Claire's amusement vanished.

Fiona nodded, "Sorry."

"That was really stupid!"

"I know. I know."

"James will tell everyone . . . Emma . . . Stacey . . ." Claire put her résumé to one side so she could glare at Fiona.

"He won't. I made him promise."

Claire took a few deep breaths before asking, "What else did you tell them? Did you say I was paid money to leave Amtech?"

"No . . . only that you had a fling with Robert . . . I tried to backtrack but they immediately started firing questions at me."

"Of course they would! You don't get much juicier office gossip than that!" Claire could feel herself flush.

"No, it was different. They weren't interested in the gossip . . . they were asking other stuff," Fiona said, sitting down with a guilt-ridden sigh.

"What do you mean? Was Paul jealous?"

"No . . . at least I don't think so . . . he was more interested in Robert than you."

"Charming . . . I'm not sure why Paul ever went out with me in the first place . . . I honestly believe he was more interested in everybody else in Amtech than me."

Fiona stood up again, kicking off her shoes.

"Then James started the third degree . . . David had told him you left Amtech for a competitor – he wanted to know who it was."

"What did you tell him?" Claire asked, inwardly groaning at the complex web of deceit.

"That I couldn't remember."

"Was he asking about Robert?"

"Was he what! He was trying to find out if I knew why Robert went back to California . . . and if he would be returning to Sydney . . . questions, questions, that's why I came home. I had a pain in my head from all the bloody questions."

Claire could feel the beginnings of a headache

herself. She wasn't going to get any further with her résumé tonight.

"Just make sure you tell them nothing else. It's bad enough as it is," she said, getting up to go to bed.

"Don't worry, I've well and truly learnt my lesson. Those two should apply for a job with the Gestapo."

* * *

"I've got the answer to all your problems right here," Fiona declared, waving a sheet of paper as she came in from work the next day.

"Really? That's a relief," Claire said with sarcasm. She was still working on her résumé.

"Yes . . . it's the intervention of fate," Fiona said dramatically. "I saw this internal advertisement at work today . . . it's for a project controller . . . in our Melbourne office."

"Melbourne? What's that got to do with me?" Claire asked with a confused frown.

"Well, you said you wanted to get away from Sydney. Going to Melbourne would be a hell of a lot better than running home to Ireland in defeat," Fiona stated with her usual frankness.

"But I don't even know anybody in Melbourne," Claire said with an incredulous laugh.

"I've got a few contacts in our office down there. They're really nice people." Fiona's face was earnest with encouragement.

"I've never been a project controller before," Claire pointed out. "They probably want someone with previous experience."

"But they need someone quickly and you have the huge advantage of being available immediately," she said as she thrust the printed page in front of Claire. "Have a look at the job description . . . you'd be well able to handle it."

"OK . . . it does look interesting," Claire admitted when she finished reading.

"See . . . I told you . . . give me your résumé and I'll pass it on to our HR department tomorrow."

"But I don't know if I want to go to Melbourne."

"Just give me your résumé. It won't hurt to apply. You can decide about going to Melbourne if and when they offer you the job."

The phone rang just as Claire was about to give Fiona a rude retort in relation to her domineering ways. They both knew it was Robert.

"I'll get it," Fiona said immediately.

"No, I will." Claire scrambled to the phone ahead of her. She had decided that she wanted to talk to Robert.

"Claire?"

Hearing his voice was painful. "Yes."

"It's Robert."

"I know." She waved Fiona out of the room.

"I've been trying to get hold of you for days. David told me yesterday that you were gone. I'm very sorry."

"Don't give me that bullshit. I'm not an idiot," she said, her voice level but her words severe. "I know David was acting on your instructions to pay me off."

"You're wrong. Call David and ask him. He can confirm that I didn't find out you were gone until I got back to San Jose. I've already had harsh words with Donald about it. It was bad judgement on his part."

Claire didn't answer him. It was only one sin of a long list – what did it matter if he wasn't behind her 'retrenchment'.

"You know, I was really angry with you for not talking to me before you went to David. You didn't give me a chance – you believed the worst straight off." He sounded hurt.

She was forced to protect herself.

"What did you expect me to do, Robert? You're a director of ARS Corp – it was there in black and white."

"I also admire you, for having the balls to deal with it head on. However, I only admire you when I'm not furious with you."

She knew he was smiling. Again, it was easier not to respond.

"You can't possibly think I would be involved in something fraudulent, can you?"

His question presented the perfect opportunity to tell him precisely what she thought. His response would be interesting, if nothing else.

"You tell me, Robert. You're the one who said he didn't want to pay his wife a divorce settlement . . . if I remember correctly, you said you wouldn't pay more than half a million . . . the payments to DC Solutions go a long way to meeting that sum."

"Claire, don't you know me? Don't you know that half a million is a relatively minor dent in my worth? I didn't want to pay Julia any money as a matter of principle, nothing else."

He was chipping holes in her reasoning, huge gaping holes. She had been ready to fling more accusations his way but his logic made her lose her train of thought.

"I want you to think about something," he went on. "Actually two things ... are you listening? Firstly, David said the initial payment was made at the start of July, the week after I arrived. How do you think I managed to get DC Solutions set up so quickly after I got there? Now, the second payment, that came up when I was in Hong Kong, right? Remember, I was away for the best part of three weeks. How do you think I orchestrated the payment from overseas?"

He's right. I hadn't thought of the logistics.

"I don't know."

"All I ask is that you think about those two things. I need your help to get to the bottom of this. I certainly know of one person that's involved. But I need someone in Australia to help me piece it together – I need you. I'll call you back tomorrow once you've had some time to think it over."

He's going to call me again. Would he go to all this trouble if he was guilty?

"Bye," she said, needing to get off the phone so she could mull over what he had said.

"Goodnight . . . and Claire?"

"What?"

"I miss you."

* * *

Robert felt like an outsider in the office. He was starved of social conversation. His relationship with Donald would never be quite the same. They were on speaking terms but the question mark hanging over Robert's position seemed to get bigger with each passing day. All of his colleagues were absorbed with their families, too afraid of their wives to break routine by going for a drink after work. He had been living in the hotel now for three days, making a dent in the minibar each night. He was determined not to drink alone tonight. Wayne agreed to join him for a beer.

"You look like shit," Wayne stated as he heaved himself onto the bar stool.

Robert noticed he had put on some weight. "Thanks, it's nice to see you too," he grinned.

Wayne cut right to the chase. "What the hell is happening? Why did you come running back from Sydney and why is Donald going about with a face like thunder?"

"It's a long and ugly story . . . it all started with a girl called Claire –"

Wayne guffawed. "I might have known that your libido had something to do with it."

Robert didn't appreciate his mirth. "You're wrong.

Claire's different. I think this might be the real thing – despite the fact she's got me into a helluva lot of trouble."

"Tell me," Wayne encouraged.

"Somehow or other I'm a director of a company to which Amtech Australia has made a number of suspect payments . . . I think I've been set up somewhere along the line but can't figure out where."

Wayne was immediately alert, his earlier humour forgotten. "What company?"

"I can't tell you . . . Donald would have a seizure if I did . . . he's paranoid about the scandal getting out. He's not going to stop me though – I'm going to get to the bottom of this if it kills me." Robert finished his beer and beckoned the barman.

"Want another?" he asked Wayne, knowing he wouldn't.

Wayne shook his head. He seemed ill at ease, uncomfortable with the bar or uncomfortable with Robert. Maybe both. Robert realised that Wayne had changed. He wasn't sure when it had happened but they had little to talk about these days. Wayne didn't seem to notice the frequent silences – his thoughts consumed by something else.

"Has Cherie ever heard Julia say anything . . . unusual . . . about Amtech?" Robert asked as he slid his wallet back into his breast pocket.

Wayne didn't need to think before answering. "Apparently, Julia is always going off her face about

385

Amtech. She blames all your marital problems on the company . . . in fact, she fantasises to Cherie about you leaving."

"That's interesting to know."

Their conversation died again. Wayne was frowning, his body tense as he sat next to Robert. Robert couldn't be bothered to make any further effort to distract him from whatever was on his mind. When he left, Robert had one more beer while he waded through their conversation about Julia.

Julia wants me to leave . . . she's jealous of Amtech . . . is that enough motive to set me up?

He concluded that it didn't stack up. It was a weak motive that would need an elaborate plan to ensure he was found out and fired from the company.

Robert caught a taxi back to the house. It took him a few hours to pack his clothes and possessions. He wouldn't be coming back; he intended never to set foot in the house again. On his way out, he sorted through the mail and took the envelopes that were addressed to him.

He didn't like being back in San Jose. It was stale next to the brightness of Sydney. He had an image in his mind of the special way the sun glanced off the deep blue waters of Sydney harbour. It was constantly on his mind, as was Claire's face. Her eyes, the same colour as the harbour, her smile. His comment to Wayne about their relationship being the 'real thing' had been spontaneous but spot on the mark. A few times he had attempted to test the authenticity of his feelings by trying to recall how it had been early on with Dianne and Julia. It didn't work; what he felt for Claire was incomparable. He loved her, he admired her. Being away from her gave his emotions an edge that was hurting. He decided to call her when he got back to the hotel.

* * *

"I've given you time to think . . . are you going to help me?" He hadn't intended to be so abrupt.

"I'm very confused, Robert." She sounded vulnerable.

"I wish I could give you the answers, Claire, but I know as little as you, for now at least." There was a pause and he waited for her, knowing there was something she was trying to say.

"Why did you tell me that DC Solutions was a US company when we were in Melbourne?"

"The name of the company was familiar to me. When I got back here I checked it with our payables department. It seems I was mistaken. There are quite a few companies with similar names which is possibly what put me on the wrong track." He allowed her a few moments to think; there was no rush.

"So, if it's not you, Robert, then who is behind all this?"

Now you're thinking like me . . .

"If you had to give a name, Claire, who would you think it was?"

"Frank Williams," she said without hesitation.

"Exactly. Now we're on the same page. I've gone one step further . . . I know I didn't consent to be director of any company while I was in Australia . . . that must mean I signed the paperwork in the US, before I left. And ARS is a US company, right?"

"Yes."

"So what does that mean, Claire?" He was testing the reliability of his own logic by seeing if she would arrive at the same conclusion.

"It means that Frank isn't the only one involved."

"Right again. That's why I love you – you're so bright."

She was sure that he didn't literally mean that he loved her but she couldn't stop the smile that came to her face.

"Who would help him, Robert? You know the people in San Jose. I don't."

"I've been playing with two thoughts . . . Julia or Donald Skates . . . but I now think they are both unlikely."

"Why?"

"I think Julia may have a motive – to get me fired from Amtech which she sees as the root of all our problems . . . but nothing else adds up." His words were slow coming out, his concentration deep as he tried to solve the puzzle.

"What about Donald? You can't be seriously thinking it's him?"

"I'm not. He was very quick to pay you off but I think it was just an overreaction from him. I've told you before how sensitive he is about bad press."

"So where to from here?" Her question was barely audible.

"I've been thinking about the next step . . . Frank must have communicated with his accomplice . . . there may be something in his email . . . a message to someone he would normally have no contact with."

"Can't you ask the IT Department to check his mail?"

"I could but it would certainly get back to Donald and I don't want him to know what I'm doing."

"Why?"

"Two reasons. He specifically said that he doesn't want to start the investigation until Cathay sign the contract . . . and I still have a very slight suspicion that he may be involved . . . we need to get into Frank's mail without involving IT."

"I would try it but for the fact I can't get into the office here any more. I had to hand back my access card to David." She heard the bitterness in her own voice.

"But you could ask someone, someone you totally trust . . . they could get in while he's at a meeting or something." Robert's suggestion seemed out-rageous but there were no other alternatives jumping out.

"It's a big ask," she said. "Emma is the only person . . . let me think some more on it . . ."

* * *

Claire arranged to meet Emma after work on Monday. It was exactly a week since she had first read the report on ARS. They went to the Greenwood.

"Let me get this straight: you want me to get into Frank's email without him knowing?" Emma said, her glass of red wine untouched.

"Yes."

"I could get fired for that."

"I know. You can't get caught – that's not part of the deal." Claire smiled to lighten the moment.

"Why? Why do you want me to do it?"

"Robert and I are in some trouble and we think it's because of Frank. If we could see what emails he has sent over the last few months we might be able to figure out what's happened. We're looking for messages to people outside Australia."

"Shit, this is exciting." Emma remembered her wine and took a sip.

"Will you do it?"

"Of course I will."

"Thanks." Claire gave her a grateful smile. She looked around the bar – it was very busy for a mere Monday night.

"What's happening with you and Robert?" Emma asked out of the blue.

"What do you mean?"

"Are you still involved with him?"

"How did you know?" Claire couldn't deny it. She owed Emma some truth.

"It's obvious. The Tax Seminar, Hong Kong, Melbourne . . . need I go on?" Emma was laughing but Claire's response was serious.

"I don't know where we stand . . . I don't know how he feels about me."

"He's crazy about you, silly. The first thing that made me click you were a couple was the way he looked at you."

Claire didn't allow herself to believe her. Their wine finished, they went outside.

"Emma, thanks for this. Thanks for helping me out."

"No problem . . . I'll try to do it tomorrow . . . I'll call you."

* * *

Emma reckoned that lunch-time was the best opportunity to get at Frank's mail. He enjoyed long lunches with his clients most days of the week. She confirmed with his secretary that he would be out for at least an hour. She then waited until the secretary went to lunch.

Armed with an official-looking file, she marched into Frank's office, leaving the door wide open so it looked as if she had every right to be there. She opened the file on his desk. Microsoft Outlook was open, a few unread messages in his inbox. She went into 'sent' messages and was just sorting the messages by name when Brian Brooker came in.

"Where's Frank?" he asked, giving her a curious look.

"He's gone to lunch . . . he forgot to forward me a

message that I need for quarter end . . . I just called him and he told me to get it myself . . . charming!" She did a reasonable impression of being annoyed.

"I guess he won't be back for some time then," Brian said.

"Yes, knowing Frank it will be a few glasses of expensive wine before he gets back."

They both laughed at Frank's expense and Brian went back to his office.

Emma quickly scanned the names that were now sorted in alphabetical order. After more than ten years with the company, she knew most of the names. She rang Claire.

"It's me . . . I only have two names that are based outside Australia . . . Tony Falcinella is one. I've never heard of the second. . . it's Wayne Costello. I've opened up the messages but they're rather vague . . . do you want me to read them out?"

"Where are you calling from?"

"Frank's office . . . this is fun."

"Oh my God, don't read them. The names will do! Just get out of there before you're caught!" Claire shut her eyes in panic as she visualised Emma in Frank's office.

"Calm down. Brian came in earlier and I handled him superbly, even if I say so myself . . . This was easy . . . Let me know if you need any more help." Emma closed her bogus file and marched back out with it.

* * *

Claire waited up for Robert to call. It was close to midnight when the phone rang.

"Hey, honey!" His greeting told her he was in good spirits.

"Hello."

"You got any news for me?"

"Emma found two names . . . Tony Falcinella and Wayne Costello."

Robert didn't react. His silence gave Claire the opportunity to tell him what she was thinking.

"You know, Robert, I do remember Tony looking for Frank on a few occasions . . . one day in particular he seemed very put out that Frank was on leave. I did wonder at the time what business they could have together."

"It could be anything – Tony has a lot happening in his region. Anyhow, Tony is so straight that I couldn't possibly imagine him involved in anything underhand."

Claire's perception of Tony's character was the same.

"What about this Wayne Costello – who is he?"

"He's a friend of mine. He's head of operations over here in San Jose."

"Would Frank have a relationship with him through work?"

"Not that I know of . . . but Wayne's role is very broad and it's possible," Robert replied, thinking back to the night he had told Wayne he was going to Sydney. Wayne said then that he knew a few people there. Was Frank one of them?

Claire heard Fiona's key in the lock. She had been to the movies with James. Claire didn't have to tell her it was Robert on the phone – she was sure it was obvious from her whole demeanour. It was just as obvious that Fiona didn't approve.

"Did Emma get the chance to look at the content of any of the messages to Tony and Wayne?" Robert continued, unaware that Claire now had an audience.

"She had a quick look – she said there was nothing unusual."

"Neither Wayne or Tony makes any kind of sense," Robert said. "I think we have to get creative and try some other means to get to the bottom of this."

"What do you suggest?"

There was a burst of noise as Fiona turned on the TV. She adjusted the volume.

"I don't know. I'll have to sleep on it . . . Hey, can you fax me the company search reports?" He had almost forgotten.

"On both companies?"

"Yes."

"To your hotel fax?"

"No, I won't get back here until late. Work should be OK – hold on and I'll give you the number."

She took the number down, aware of Fiona watching her rather than the TV.

"OK, got that?" said Robert. "Goodnight, love, I'll talk to you tomorrow."

Fiona didn't allow her time to think about the endearment he had used.

"I can't believe you're still talking to him!" Fiona switched off the TV for the upcoming confrontation.

"He didn't do it. We jumped to the wrong conclusion."

"Don't be so silly. He's playing with you."

"He's not. I know Robert. Every day at work I've seen his commitment to the company, his integrity when making hard decisions – he would never do something like this – and I should have trusted my instincts before assuming the worst," Claire answered, her confidence deepening Fiona's frown.

"But you have the evidence, the reports. And he needed the money for his divorce."

"You don't know the full facts."

"Well, tell me them," Fiona demanded in frustration.

"I'm sorry. I can't tell you anything right now. Only that it wasn't Robert."

Claire went to bed. An hour later, sleep was still evading her. She got dressed and went down the street to a twenty-four hour garage. She sent the fax to Robert from there.

* * *

The nurse led Robert to the visitor's room. She was professional and pleasant. So far he was impressed with both the staff and the facilities at the clinic. It was a few moments before Julia came in. She looked dreadful. He realised that the Julia he had seen in Sydney had been heavily made up to disguise the damage her addiction was wreaking on her body.

"Robert," she flung herself into his arms, emotional tears welling in her eyes. He gave her a courteous embrace before sitting her down on the sofa.

"How did you know I was here? I didn't want you to find out about this." She was uneasy, afraid of what prompted his unexpected visit.

"It doesn't matter how I know," he reassured, holding her hand loosely to calm her down.

"It was just some bad luck, Robert, bad luck with the cops . . . and the judge," Julia jumped in, her eyes pleading with him to believe her.

"Don't worry. I'm not here to talk about that. We'll talk about it another time . . . I need you to help me . . ."

"What's wrong? Are you in trouble?" Her concern was surprisingly endearing.

"Yes, I'm in trouble," he said with a sigh.

"Oh no, what's wrong, Robert? Are you ill?" She looked at him frantically, her fingers curling around his.

"No, nothing like that. It's work. Something has happened . . . I may lose my position."

"Thank heavens! Thank heavens you're not ill! It's not the end of the world if you lose your job . . . it could be the best thing that happened to us." She was suddenly excited, on a high.

He was staggered with the intensity of her reaction.

"I need you to answer some questions for me, Julia –

I need you to be honest."

"OK," she smiled at him. It was rare that Robert asked for help; it felt good.

"You know that company you bought last year, the shelf company?" He continued when Julia nodded, "Did you ever use that company?"

"No, I was going to set up a small business but I lost interest." Her answer seemed genuine.

"OK, just one more question. Did you know Frank Williams before you met him in Sydney?"

"No, why?" She looked so puzzled that Robert could only believe her.

"No reason, I must go now," he said, letting go of her hand to stand up.

"Don't go. Please stay! I haven't said 'Sorry' yet for what happened in Sydney." She was distressed, grabbing the end of his jacket as she sat on the sofa.

"It's OK, Julia. You don't have to apologise," he said, releasing his jacket from her grip. "We'll talk soon, OK? We'll talk about Sydney and some other stuff we should have talked about a long time ago."

He was trying to give her an inkling about the divorce. The joy on her face made him realise that she had completely misinterpreted what he had said.

* * *

Wayne was reading something at the fax machine when Robert got to the office.

"This was on the machine for you." He was flushed as he handed the sheets to Robert.

"Thanks."

Wayne followed him to the door of his office.

"What are you doing, Robert? You know Donald will be pissed if he finds out you are pursuing this behind his back."

"That's for me to worry about, not you."

Wayne looked as if he was about to argue the point. Robert shut the door firmly. He no longer cared about Donald. The fax pages were out of sequence; he didn't know if it was from Wayne or if it was the way they had come through the machine. There were no leads from the DC Solutions report – it was only a few pages. It was interesting that the directors of the Australian company were US citizens but their names meant nothing to him. He put the report down on his desk and started to read the ARS one. His saw his own name in the director's section. The other director was Ralph Costello.

Costello. That's Wayne's surname. This must be a bizarre coincidence.

He was frowning in concentration when his mobile rang.

"Robert, it's me, Tom . . . I've checked out that company."

Of course – Tom was checking out Julia's shelf company. There's so many companies in the ring now that I'm starting to get confused.

"Look, it's dormant, it's never been used," Tom went on to say.

"How can you tell?"

"Got a contact who's a cop – he did me a very big favour and checked to see if the company had any bank accounts or shareholdings or anything like that. All his inquiries came back negative. Don't ask me for the details – I don't want to get the guy into trouble."

"OK, thanks for that."

"Robert, I want to talk about the divorce papers. Do you have some time now?"

"Not really. I'll call you about them tomorrow."

I need to find the time to talk to Julia about the divorce.

He turned off his mobile. He needed to think without the threat of interruption.

How can I find out about Ralph Costello?

* * *

Claire called Emma first thing the next morning.

"Em, it's me again."

"Hello 007. I was hoping you'd call with another assignment."

"Not exactly an assignment, just something that has been bothering me. Do you know who has access to set up vendors in –"

"James." Emma answered before Claire finished the question.

"Is he the only person?" Claire needed to be sure.

"And Alan Harris – he's the back-up for James."

Alan Harris, Alan Harris helping Frank Williams … that makes sense … he's always been in Frank's pocket.

Emma was still speaking. "Oracle keeps a record of

all updates and logs the user name. It's a pretty good audit trail."

"So, if I want to find out who set up a vendor about four months ago, all I would have to do is look it up in Oracle?"

"Under normal circumstances, yes . . . but it's not so simple after the upgrade."

"Why?"

"Because we purged all the historical data – we didn't think it was worth transferring across."

"Surely it's been backed up?" Claire yawned – she hadn't slept much after she got back from the garage.

"Yes, but retrieving the back-up tape and reloading it would be a major task. You'd have the whole IT department involved," Emma explained.

"Damn."

Robert wouldn't want that.

"There's one other thing we could try," Emma suggested.

"What?"

"The download I sent to Michael for testing. I might still have it."

"Can you check now?"

"I'm doing it right as we speak."

Claire waited. All night she had been thinking about how Frank could have got his hands on the money. It was relatively easy for him to create a company and to sign off the invoices. It wasn't as easy to get the supplier set up in Oracle. Somewhere in the jumble of her thoughts was the previous year's audit issue regarding segregation of duties in the accounts payable area – the concern that the person who entered invoices into the payables system could also set up a vendor, making fraud all the easier. And both James and Alan were in that sensitive position.

"Bad luck," Emma said finally. "It's not here. I must have deleted it . . . but we could try Michael. He might still have it."

"I don't know," Claire said, dubious about the idea of involving yet another person.

"I would ring him for you but I have to be out of here today at five – I've got to go to the dentist." Emma misread the reasons behind Claire's reluctance to call Michael.

"It's OK. I'll ring him myself . . . but I don't want him to know I've left Amtech." She knew he wouldn't be able to find her on the global mailing list; she would be deleted by now. "If he has the file, I'll ask him to send it to you. Is that OK?"

"No problem. I might drop in when I'm finished with the dentist to see if he's sent it . . . of course, that's dependent on how much pain I'm in."

* * *

Cherie answered the phone. It was three in the afternoon and Wayne was at work.

"Hello there," Robert said. His friendliness wasn't forced – he was very fond of Cherie. These days he had much more in common with her than he had with Wayne.

"Robert! About time! I was wondering if you would ever call me," Cherie scolded.

"I'm sorry – I had a lot on. But that's no excuse, I know."

"Wayne said you had some trouble at work. Is everything OK?"

"Yes, it was just a misunderstanding. I'm getting it sorted as we speak." He didn't mind her asking – it was only because she cared.

"Good."

"Cherie, I had another reason to call . . . it's coming up to Wayne's tenth anniversary with the company –" he began.

"So it is . . . doesn't time fly?"

"We're planning a few things for him, maybe a big party."

"Oh, how exciting. He'll be so pleased!"

"I need you to help me. I need a list of all the people he knows, friends, family . . . don't hold back, because it will be a big function."

"OK, I won't."

If this turned out to be a false lead, he resolved that he would have a party for Wayne – it would go someway to relieving his guilt at lying to Cherie like this.

"And I need a copy of his birth cert . . . "

"Why on earth do you need that?" Cherie was understandably curious.

"Can't tell you. It's a surprise . . . and I need all this as quickly as you can get it to me."

* * *

Claire thought about ringing Mark to see if she could get the file from him rather than Michael. Then she remembered that she wasn't on the best of terms with Mark – she was an obstacle to his empire building plans. Michael's phone rang for a while before it was picked up.

"Michael?"

"Yes . . . "

"It's Claire." Her voice was professionally cool.

"Hello, Claire. I should have recognised your voice. It's been a long time."

"Yes, it has. How are you?" she asked graciously.

"I'm grand . . . marriage must agree with me."

She felt detached. There was no jealousy. There was a pause and Claire used it as an opportunity to move from the personal to business.

"Michael, we need your help with something . . . we're looking for a copy of the download that Emma sent you for testing."

"Why? Have you had a system crash?" He was instantly alert.

"No, nothing like that. We're just doing an internal audit on the transition from the old system to the new one." Claire had her explanation well rehearsed. It came out sounding reasonably plausible.

"OK. I'm a magpie, I keep everything, so I should

have it somewhere – I'll send it to you in a few minutes."

"No, send it to Emma. I've been having some problems with my PC."

* * *

It was after eight when Emma called.

"The bastard took my tooth out! I can't feel the left side of my face" she moaned, her voice muffled.

"Poor you!" Claire's sympathy was rushed. "Did Michael send the file?"

"Yes. What vendor did you want me to check?" Emma had the file open, ready to run a search.

"DC Solutions . . . it should have been created around May or June."

It took a few moments for Emma to look it up.

"It's here . . . it was set up . . . at the end of June . . . James was the user," Emma said, her response coming bit by bit as she read the record.

"What about Alan? Does he use James' password?"

"No, he has his own password. He didn't set this vendor up."

James. Was it James who helped Frank?

"Claire?" Emma prompted when there was silence.

"What other details are on the file? Is there a phone number?"

"No, no phone number."

James said there was a phone number in the system. He said he had no problems contacting DC Solutions.

"OK, thanks, Em . . . and keep this quiet, OK?"

"You don't need to tell me that." Emma was rightfully offended.

"Sorry, I'm just paranoid."

"Are you ever going to tell me what's going on?" Fiona asked when Claire came off the phone. Her open expression was devoid of the disapproval she had shown the previous night. If anything, she looked hurt at being excluded from what was consuming Claire.

"I can't . . . I'm sorry, Fi. I would tell you if I could." Claire gave her a tentative smile as she sat next to her on the couch.

"OK, I suppose I have to accept that," Fiona shrugged but returned her smile. "Our HR manager wants to interview you for that role in Melbourne."

"I can't make any decisions like that right now . . . Can you tell him I'm away for the next week or something?"

Fiona nodded.

"What are you doing there?" Claire asked, noticing the notepad on Fiona's lap. It looked like she was making a list of some sort.

"It's a wedding list."

Shit, I forgot about you – you're marrying James.

"How many people?"

"Looks like over two hundred." Fiona was embarrassed.

"That's a big wedding."

You always said you'd elope rather than have a tradi-

tional wedding. But that was when you were with Den.

"James said not to hold back – we can afford to splash out."

"You can?" Claire stared at her. She knew Fiona for nearly eight years. Fiona lived life to the limit – savings weren't high on her agenda.

"Not me – James is the one with the money."

What money? He's on a basic wage.

* * *

Cherie sent the information by courier the next day; it got to Robert just before five. She must have spent the whole day on it, a consequence of being at home with the children. Any distraction was welcome. The copy of the birth certificate wasn't good quality but the name was clear.

Ralph Wayne Costello.

Robert was stunned. Deep down he hadn't expected the match. Wayne, of all people, was the other director of ARS. Robert had known him for ten years but he never knew that Wayne was just his middle name.

Cherie had handwritten the list of friends and family. It was a considerable list, over a hundred names. But he found what he was looking for.

Luca Domingo, Liam Metcalf.

Cherie had listed them as friends. They were also the directors of DC Solutions. It was coming together for Robert. Wayne's bizarre preoccupation the night he told him he was going to Sydney. Wayne's advice not to pursue his investigations on DC Solutions, leveraging off Donald's disapproval. Wayne, Head of Operations, setting up a new subsidiary.

ARS, ARS . . . A for Amtech . . . R . . . R for Resources . . . no, R for Regional . . . S for Services. Amtech Regional Services.

Robert now remembered. Amtech Regional Services was a special-purpose subsidiary for outsourcing services on the East Coast. At least, that was what Wayne said the company was for when he asked Robert to sign the paperwork before he left for Sydney.

His phone rang. It was Tony Falcincella, calling from Hong Kong. Robert knew from his voice that something was wrong.

"I need to talk to you about a rather delicate matter," Tony began, bypassing the usual pleasantries.

"OK, shoot," Robert said, wondering what else the day was going to spring on him.

"A few weeks ago I had a call from an old colleague – he works in Sydney, in Digicom. He told me that sensitive information about Amtech was being discussed at board level in Digicom. He suspected that someone in Amtech was leaking the information. Lucky for us, my colleague has strong principles of fair play and he called me."

Robert sat up at the mention of Digicom, immediately thinking of the Queensland Government deal.

"Go on," he encouraged.

"I thought it would be courteous to talk to Frank Williams before talking to you. I called him a number of times, leaving explicit messages about what I wanted to discuss."

"And what did Frank have to say?"

"He hasn't returned my calls." Tony lowered his voice. "To be honest, I'm starting to suspect he has something to do with the leak."

"And I suspect you're right," Robert spoke slowly. "It explains something that happened with a deal we had in Queensland."

"I was afraid you would think I was jumping to conclusions too quickly." Tony sounded relieved.

"Not at all – it makes sense. I think Mr Williams won't be working for Amtech much longer."

"Right, Robert, I'll leave it in your hands. I have a file note of my conversation with my friend from Digicom – let me know if you want to see it."

"Thanks, I have all I need for now."

Robert hung up. More evidence proving Frank's corruption. He was nowhere near his quota – he would earn zero commission from Amtech for the year. It would certainly be more profitable to pass information to Digicom and get paid under the table. It also explained the unexpected loss of the Queensland Government contract to Digicom.

Frank was the ideal Australian contact for Wayne. Wayne must have realised the opportunity the night Robert said he was going to Sydney.

Robert typed a message to David Di Gregario.

Where did Frank Williams work before Amtech?

His secretary knocked on the door. She had her jacket on, ready to leave for the day.

"Tom Healy has been trying to contact you – he left a message for you to call him."

"Thanks, will do."

Robert called Tom but his line was busy. He clean forgot to try again.

* * *

Claire waited until lunch-time to call Robert. It would be late evening in San Jose; it was difficult juggling the two time zones.

"I've had an interesting development," she began, anxious to get her suspicions concerning James off her chest.

"So have I – but you go first." He sounded distracted.

"I went off on a tangent," she said, "trying to figure out how Frank got DC Solutions set up as a vendor in Oracle – I found out that James set it up at the end of June."

"Doesn't he set up all the vendors?"

"Most of them. Alan Harris also has access but only as a back-up. James set this one up . . . The auditors weren't happy about the accounts payable clerk having access to set up vendors . . . They considered it a control weakness . . . Do you remember?"

"Yes, I remember talking to you about that," he said. "It was the day after I arrived, our first meeting."

She knew he was smiling at the memory. She

continued, "The real anomaly is that James told me a few weeks ago that he had a phone number on the system for DC Solutions . . . Emma looked it up last night and there's no number – he lied."

She paused to take a breath and Robert said, "Maybe he got confused . . . "

"No, he was adamant that he never had any problems contacting them – and there's something else that supports my suspicions . . . "

"And what is that, my little sleuth?" Robert couldn't resist teasing her.

"Fiona told me that she and James are planning this huge wedding. She said that James has the money, but you and I know that his salary isn't great . . . " She was speaking quickly in her haste to tell him her thoughts.

"Maybe he has money in his family," Robert suggested.

"No, Fiona told me before that his family are not well off."

They were both silent for a few moments. Robert spoke next.

"Well, it looks like we have a circle of three, then. Frank, James . . . and Wayne."

"Do you mean Wayne Costello?" she asked, remembering that Wayne was Robert's friend.

"That's where I've been expending my energies since we last spoke: Mr Ralph Wayne Costello." His sarcasm did not hide his disappointment.

"Ralph Costello – he's a director of ARS!" Claire said,

ecognising the name from the report.

"Correct – and Wayne has friends who happen to be he directors of DC Solutions," Robert said flatly.

Claire tried to piece it together.

"So Wayne set up the companies, Frank signed the nvoices and James paid the money . . . is that how it vorked?"

"I think so." Robert yawned and lay back on the hotel bed.

"But why did Wayne involve you . . . why did he make you a director?" Claire's mind was fresh, working through the puzzle.

"I have no idea. Maybe he figured I would be first in he firing line if his scheme was ever found out. He would be long gone by the time the police had finished vith me and turned their attention to the other director. Nobody in Amtech knows that Wayne's first hame is Ralph . . . I've been his friend for ten years and didn't know . . . and I was also blissfully unaware hat he knew Frank." Robert thought again about the hight he told Wayne he was going to Sydney. Looking back, he should have registered that Wayne's behaviour was out of the ordinary. Robert was starting to blame himself. He was too tired to think rationally.

"How did he get your signature to be a director in he first place? Don't you have to sign some documents or the SEC?" Claire asked, in an attempt to bring him back on track.

"That would have been easy for him – I'm director of

over thirty different Amtech subsidiaries – I usuall
trust those around me to ensure there's nothing unto
ward in what they give me to sign. I'll know better i
future," he replied with an audible sigh.

"So what now, Robert?"

"I don't think you and I can get any further on thi
We take what we have and give it to the police . . . the
should be able to find the missing pieces."

What does it mean for us, Robert?

"I want you to come over here, Claire, while I get thi
sorted out," he continued without any expression i
his voice.

"I have this interview coming up, for a job i
Melbourne." She said it to test him, to flush out when
he was really at with their relationship.

"Please come over, just while I sort it out, then we'
go back to Sydney together."

"Together?"

"Yes, unless you don't love me like I love you . . . I'v
never asked you . . . Do you love me?"

The time of truth.

"Yes."

CHAPTER SIXTEEN

Cherie was waiting for her in the foyer. Julia put down her suitcase to give her an impulsive hug. She signed out, the attending nurse watching her with the cynical belief that this particular patient would be back in a few months. Maybe the next time Mrs Pozos would be more receptive to dealing with her problem.

As Julia turned around, she spotted Amy coming down the corridor, presumably to say "Goodbye." She rushed Cherie outside so she would not have to make introductions.

They were mostly silent on the drive into town.

"I've booked us both into the hairdresser's this after-noon . . . after that I thought we might do some shop-ping," Cherie said as they sat down at a tiny table in an overcrowded restaurant.

"Sounds good to me – I badly need a makeover,"

413

Julia replied, touching her hair as she spoke, drawing Cherie's attention to the dark roots. Cherie thought she looked different, not just her hair, which was usually impeccable, but her face. She looked drawn, tired. The three weeks had obviously taken a lot out of her.

"Have you seen Robert recently?" Julia asked after the waiter brought the menus.

"No, I haven't . . . but I did talk to him yesterday. Maybe now that you are both back in town you could come over for dinner some evening."

"Thanks . . . you know, I'm really nervous about seeing him." Julia smoothed her napkin against the cold marble of the table.

"Oh, he'll be the same . . . Don't be worrying," Cherie said with a reassuring smile. She was unaware that Julia had already seen him at the clinic.

"Want some champagne? Oh, sorry, I shouldn't have said that!" Cherie put her hand over her mouth in embarrassment at her own tactlessness.

"Don't be silly. Of course I can have champagne. Honestly, Cherie, if you saw the people in that place you'd quickly realise that I do *not* have an alcohol problem." Julia laughed and signalled the waiter.

"Julia, please don't," Cherie said quietly.

The waiter came and Julia gave him the order.

"Please don't ruin everything you've achieved over the last few weeks," Cherie tried again.

When Julia didn't answer, Cherie stood up, putting on her jacket as she spoke.

"I'm not going to sit here and watch you do this."

She walked away just as the champagne arrived.

* * *

Claire tried Den's work number. When he didn't pick up, she tried his mobile. She was about to give up when he answered.

"Thank God I've got you," she said with relief.

"Claire? What's wrong?" She could hear the background noise of traffic – his voice was uneven as he walked.

"Den, I have to go to California. I'm at the airport right now."

"A holiday?" he asked with friendly interest.

"Not exactly, more like a mission . . . look, something is going to happen, something that will affect Fiona." Her words tumbled out when she saw that her flight was boarding.

"What? Is she all right?" His concern was genuine. She knew she had been right to call him.

"Yes, she's OK now, but something bad is going to happen with James in the next few days."

"What do you want me to do?" He didn't waste time; it was the lawyer in him that she had never seen.

"I won't be here. She'll need someone – she'll be devastated – can you make sure she's all right?"

"Of course I can, Claire, but tell me what's happening – are you OK?" he asked urgently.

"I can't tell you what's happening, Den. But I'm fine. Just keep an eye on Fiona for me . . . I've got to run, they're doing a final boarding call." She ran through the gate, the last passenger to board.

* * *

They were leaving Sydney behind. From this height the Harbour Bridge was a small black arch, the harbour itself seemed nothing more than a river. It was a beautiful day. The city sparkled. The orange beaches joined the city and the water as they flew East.

Something was niggling Claire. The connection between Frank and James was grating away, opening up new possibilities.

Frank and James. James and Paul. Frank, James, Paul ...

She was too tired to think it through. She put back her seat and shut her eyes.

* * *

Julia was terribly disappointed that Robert wasn't there when she got home. She called out his name as she closed the front door only to be met with a resounding silence. She kicked the mail that was on the floor out of her way. She called his name again.

Well, how was he to know the exact time I would come in? she reasoned with herself as she brought her bags upstairs. *He couldn't stay at home all day waiting for me.*

The house seemed bare. It was probably because she had been away for a while and was now seeing it with new eyes. Coming back downstairs, she picked up three weeks of mail from the floor, shaking her head at the fact that Robert had not dealt with it. He must have been very busy.

The doorbell rang. Her chest felt tight with anticipation. It wasn't Robert. She should have known it wouldn't be – he had a key. It was an elderly man. His pale eyes twitched and his scrawny hands fidgeted with the envelope he was holding. She regretting opening the door in such haste.

"Are you Julia Pozos?"

"Yes, I am."

"I have some papers for you." He thrust the envelope at her.

She had no option but to take it.

"What . . . " She started to question him but he was gone, scurrying down the driveway in his battered loafers.

She went to the conservatory, checking her reflection in the mirror on the way, wanting to look perfect should Robert come home. She had gone to the hairdressers without Cherie and loved the elegance of her new haircut. The girl had also gone over her black roots with fresh highlights. Satisfied with her appearance, she sat down and opened the old man's envelope.

Family Law ...

She had only seen divorce papers once before. She stared at them in shock before smiling weakly.

Robert is having a joke on me. I'll kill him for giving me a shock like this when he comes home.

She put them down on the coffee table without reading any further. Her hands shook as she went through the rest of the mail.

* * *

"I thought you were going shopping with Julia," Wayne said when Cherie came home prematurely.

"Don't ask . . . " Cherie replied, her face flushed with disappointment.

"What's she done now?"

"I don't want to talk about it . . . "

Wayne was feeding their two-year-old. They were both making a mess. Cherie took the spoon from Wayne and coaxed Max to open his mouth.

"I was talking to Robert on Tuesday – I forgot to tell you he called me," she said, calmed by the routine of feeding Max.

"Why did he call?" Wayne's voice was tense and she looked up from Max to check what was wrong with him.

"Just to say hello . . . I asked him about this trouble you said he was in . . . "

"What did you do that for? I told you it was confidential." His rebuke seemed over-the-top to Cherie.

"Because I was worried about him . . . anyway, he said that he's getting it all sorted out now." Max started grabbing the spoon and she resumed feeding him.

"What did he mean by that?"

"I presume he meant exactly what he said: he's

getting it all sorted out."

Wayne went outside, the only place where he could be alone to think without the children climbing all over him.

Damn Robert, why can't he just drop it? He needs something to distract him, something to take his mind off playing Sherlock Holmes.

His mobile was in his shirt pocket. He rang Julia from the peace of the garden.

"Hello, Julia, it's Wayne."

"Hello." He heard surprise in her voice. Wayne rarely spoke to Julia unless it was a necessity. Even she knew that he disliked her.

"Julia, I've something to tell you . . . It's about Robert . . . He's been having an affair . . . with a girl in Sydney called Claire Quinlan . . . She works for him . . . Everybody knows about it. I thought it only fair that you should not be the last one to find out."

There was no reaction on the other side. He was left with the dialling tone when she hung up. He smiled. She would go crazy. That would keep Robert busy for a while and it gave Wayne time to think about the best way to stop Robert from progressing his enquiries. The frustrating thing was that Donald was perfectly happy to forget about the matter. Robert was the only problem. Wayne looked at his watch. Now that Cherie was home early, he could go back to the office for a few hours.

* * *

David Di Gregario had responded to Robert's message overnight.

Frank's previous employer was Zenith Systems, in California.

Robert rang Cherie. He hung up when Wayne answered. He waited an hour before trying again.

"Hi, Rob." Cherie sounded tired. "I sent your stuff by courier. Did you get it?"

"Yes, thanks. I was just looking at the list for the party. Did you remember to include some of Wayne's friends from his last job?"

"The crowd from Zenith? That was a long time ago, Wayne hasn't kept up contact with them."

Zenith! Zenith Systems is the connection between Wayne and Frank. That's how they know each other.

"Sorry, Cherie. I have a call coming through – I need to go." Robert wanted to get off the phone so he could think.

All this effort and risk for one million Aussie dollars. Why would Wayne bother?

Robert suddenly realised he was missing the obvious. Claire was the only reason the scam stopped at a million. If she hadn't cottoned on as early as she had, the dollars involved would have been a lot more.

* * *

Julia sat in stunned horror, her perfectly made-up face and newly styled hair sagging simultaneously. When she looked up she noticed that half of the CDs on the CD rack were missing. She swung around wildly to find that most of the books on the bookshelf weren't there, the remaining few lying flatly without the others to prop them up. He had moved out; his things were gone. That was why the house seemed bare.

The bastard, the fucking bastard! How could he do this to me? Who the hell is this Claire Quinlan? An Australian slut, probably half his fucking age!

It was some time later when she pulled herself up from the sofa. She walked numbly from the conservatory to the living-room. She emptied the drinks cabinet of its contents, cracking the glass as she slammed the door. She lowered herself onto the soft thick carpet, surrounded by the bottles of vodka, bourbon and wine. Opening all the bottles at once, she drank without a glass, carelessly spilling the liquid on herself and the cream carpet in her haste to take the edge off the pain. All elegance was gone, her face distorted by bitterness, hatred in her half-shut eyes.

The fucking bastard! I hate him! I fucking hate him!

She emptied the contents of her bag on the floor, desperate to find the packet of Asprin she always carried with her. There were only a few tablets left. She gagged as she tried to swallow them together. Then she drank until a furious calmness descended.

* * *

Claire woke, the conundrum of Frank, James and Paul immediately bombarding her consciousness. An image of Paul at James' desk flashed into her mind. It was the day she had got angry with James for breaching security regulations. She had assumed they had been playing computer games. Was it possible they had been in Oracle? In the Sales Orders module?

Paul in Queensland. Paul and Frank in Queensland at the same time. Amtech losing the Queensland Government contract . . . to Digicom.

She knew a significant portion of Paul's salary was commission-based. Winning the Queensland Government contract would have meant a big pay cheque for him. Now that she thought about it clearly, any information that Paul could glean on Amtech would give him a competitive advantage not only on the Queensland Government deal but any other tender where both companies were bidding. She realised that Frank had no commission to lose by passing on pricing information as he wasn't going to meet his quota for the year. Frank would have signed a confidentiality declaration when he joined Amtech, just as she had. Would a flimsy declaration be enough to stop him from passing information to Paul? Was Paul paying him under the table for the privilege?

She recalled Paul's incessant questions about Amtech, his obsession with everything she did at work.

Why did he date me? He didn't seem to care that much when I broke it off.

There seemed to be only one answer: he wanted information on Amtech. Considering he had two other sources of information in James and Frank, he must have felt that he had all bases covered. She would tell

Robert when she got to San Francisco. They would figure it out together. She looked at her watch: only two hours to go. Robert was going to meet her off the plane. She couldn't wait to see him.

* * *

"I thought I made it perfectly clear that I didn't want you to pursue this any further," Donald said, his tone dangerously cold.

"And I thought I made it perfectly clear that I would clear my name," Robert retorted. He was standing in Donald's office – it was an advantageous position for the inevitable argument.

"You're saying that Wayne Costello is behind this? It's ludicrous, Robert. You're totally losing your sense of reason." Donald tapped his pen impatiently on his desk as his voice rose in volume.

"I think I have enough evidence to give the police a damn good start at piecing the whole scam together," Robert replied confidently.

"I said I didn't want the police involved at this point!" Donald's pale face was getting darker with anger.

"I know what you said – you're forgetting that I'm also an officer of this company – I have the same responsibilities as you and I'm not going to side-step them in order to save face for the company." Robert was a brick wall of determination.

Donald changed hats from the bully to the negotiator.

"At least wait until Cathay sign the contract . . . it's only a matter of days now." Donald stood up so he was at eye level with Robert across the desk.

"Sorry, Donald. You're too late. I spoke to the police this afternoon. I obviously asked them to be discreet. I'm sure you will be pleasantly surprised by their ability to keep it under wraps."

* * *

Julia's movements were controlled and deliberate as she went upstairs. When she went into the bedroom, she felt the bareness again, his personal things noticeably missing. She didn't understand how she had not seen it when she came up earlier. Sitting on the bed, she opened the bottom drawer of the bedside locker. The gun was there as it always was, despite the fact she had begged Robert on a number of occasions to get rid of it. Having a loaded weapon in their bedroom used to make her nervous. He would be sorry that he hadn't listened to her. It was heavy in her hand. She fired it at their wedding photograph to see if it was working. She missed and the bullet bedded in the timber wall.

It was raining solidly when she went outside. Her suit wasn't much protection, the water darkening the light pink within seconds. She was oblivious as the rain streamed down her face and flattened her hair. She knew where to find him: he would be in the damned office.

* * *

Robert was drained when he got back to his office. There was a handwritten note on his desk to ring Tom. He remembered that he also owed Tom a call from yesterday. He dialled his number before sitting down.

"Robert, where the hell have you been?" Tom sounded frazzled.

"I've had a lot of shit happening. Sorry it took me so long to ring you back."

"I was calling to remind you about the divorce papers – they were due to go to Julia today," Tom explained.

"Christ, I totally forgot!" Robert swore in annoyance at his own forgetfulness.

Damn. Damn.

"I thought you might have – that's why I've been trying to contact you. I guess it's no big deal . . . she'll have them by now anyway," Tom replied, a trace of *fait accompli* in his tone.

"It *is* a big deal, Tom. With all that's going on, I didn't have the chance to speak to her about the divorce . . . she's going to get a nasty shock."

"Shit, man, I can't believe you haven't told her!" Tom was amazed.

"I know, I know . . . maybe Donald is right and I *am* losing my senses."

Robert sat still for a few moments after the call, trying to collect his wits.

Fuck. How could I have forgotten that today was the day?

He checked the Waterford Crystal clock on his desk, a gift from Julia. It was almost five. He didn't have enough time to call around to see her now. Claire's flight was due in soon and it would take over an hour to drive to San Francisco to meet her.

* * *

The pilot circled San Francisco, waiting for a landing slot. It was raining, just like it was the morning Claire arrived in Sydney. She stared out the window at the thick grey cloud, her stomach churning with a cocktail of emotions. So much had happened in the nine months she had lived in Sydney. Michael was a vague memory now, that pain replaced with the rollercoaster ride with Robert. She realised she had no doubts about following Robert to California. Despite all the ups and downs and twists and turns of the rollercoaster, she had come out the other side with supreme confidence about their future. If it had been nine months ago she would have fallen off at the first dip.

* * *

The traffic screeched to a halt. Burning rubber mingled with the streaming rain. Pedestrians scurried in all directions. Those who had lived in California too long watched from what they judged to be a safe distance.

It took only a few seconds for the deafening noise of rush-hour traffic to be replaced with a tense silence. Julia stood unsteadily in the middle of the street, her hair sticking to her wet face, her suit crumpled, angry blots of red wine on the jacket. She pulled the trigger,

aughing hysterically when she heard glass smashing.
She fired at the building again, screaming a torrent of
hatred as she stumbled across the street, oblivious to
he crouched drivers of the stationary vehicles.

The lift opened in the lobby, filled with a sea of
weary faces holding bulging briefcases, escaping home
o complete the work they hadn't managed to finish
within the constraints of the working day. It amused
her to watch their expressions graduate from preoccupied to terrified. They didn't run as she expected, but
remained frozen, their eyes fixed on her, waiting for
her instructions.

"Get out of my fucking way . . . "

They bolted, heads down, bodies stooped, selfishly
pushing each other as they made their way to safety.
She smiled, walked leisurely into the empty lift and
pressed the button for Level Ten. The ride was smooth
and uninterrupted. She was prepared for the threat of a
pre-alerted security guard as the doors opened slowly
at the tenth floor. She came out cautiously but the
reception area was deserted. She walked past the
empty offices holding the gun rigidly out in front of
her.

Someone was walking towards her, his head down,
reading. He didn't see her, didn't see the gun.

"Julia!" He looked up as they passed each other. It
was Wayne. "What the hell . . ." He noticed the gun
and jumped backwards, dropping the document in his
hand, his arms stretched in front of him, palms flat, as

if they could protect him.

"Shut the fuck up!" she hissed, putting the coo
barrel of the gun against the sweat of his forehead
"Get down on the floor and if you fucking move, I'l
blow your head off . . . "

She hated Wayne; she knew he would have taken
great pleasure in telling her about Robert's slut. It wa
good to be able to hit back.

Donald was in his office, reading the evening paper.

"Julia, how nice to see you . . . " She had the pleasur
of watching his phoney smile slip as his eyes focusse
on the gun.

"You bastard . . . it's all your fault . . . this compan
took my husband from me!"

He wasn't responding, wasn't contrite. She fired th
gun at the window behind him, to give her accusation
weight. The rain immediately soaked the papers on hi
desk and the light coloured carpet. There was glas
everywhere, some pieces large and jagged, others tin
and glistening. Donald scrambled to the floor, seekin
protection from the solid mass of his desk, his fac
whiter than the icy gleam of his perfect hair. She left hir
there. He was too pathetic to waste any more time on.

* * *

Exhaustion crept over Robert. His eyes watered. Hi
head hurt. But soon he would see Claire. He logged o
and shrugged on his suit jacket. It was pouring rai
outside and he remembered that he had an umbrella i
the closet. As he walked out, he saw Julia. She wa

soaked, her blonde hair dark from the rain. Even the gun she was pointing at him was wet.

"My, my – it's only five o'clock – aren't you leaving early today?" she said sarcastically. His face whitened under his tan but he didn't flinch at the gun.

"Aren't you happy to see your wife, honey? Did you miss me? Or were you too busy with that Australian slut?"

He didn't answer. She couldn't find emotion on his face. His self-control was freaking her out.

"*Answer me, you fucking bastard! Did you think you could just discard me like that? Well, I'm sick of your shit . . . I won't be thrown out like a piece of trash!*" She was screaming and his continuing silence was making her angrier.

"*Say something . . . say something, or else . . .*" she threatened hysterically. "*Will you fucking say some-thing?*"

"What do you want me to say?"

She heard contempt in his voice. "Say you're sorry. Say you're sorry!"

"Put the gun down, Julia. You're only making this worse for yourself."

He wasn't going to apologise. He didn't leave her a choice. She watched in shock as the vibrant red spread across the pristine white of his shirt. He slumped to the floor and the gun slipped from her limp grasp as she was struck by the horror of what she had done.

* * *

"I'm Officer Tim Hurst. What's your name?" He looked old, too old to be in the police force.

"Julia."

"What's happened here?" He was softly spoken, a nice old man.

"I've hurt him," she whispered.

"You fired the gun?"

She nodded. When she looked down she saw blood on her jacket – Robert's blood had splattered her jacket.

"Put your hands behind your back . . . "

She had heard that before, a lifetime ago.

"You have the right to remain silent . . . "

The paramedics came. They surrounded Robert. She couldn't see his face any more.

"Anything you do or say may be used against you in a court of law . . . "

They were pumping something under his legs with air. She caught a brief glimpse of his face again as they put on an oxygen mask. His face was grey.

"You have the right to consult an attorney . . . "

They took Robert away.

"Do you understand?"

Donald was standing outside his office, an officer busily writing notes as he spoke. There was no sign of Wayne.

"Do you understand?"

She nodded.

She was oblivious to the sirens and the rotating blue

lights reflecting on the wet street in front of her. For an old man, Tim Hurst had an iron grasp. She didn't resist, her silence almost demure. When they reached the car, he put paper bags on her hands, sealing them with rubber bands on her wrists. It was an odd thing to do and she smiled. He put her in the cage at the back of the car. She remembered the cage. The officers left behind had a hard time moving spectators out of the way as the car crept cautiously forward.

* * *

Claire waited for Robert, watching the teeming rain through the glass front of the arrivals lounge. She felt conspicuous, people swarming around her as she stood close to the main entrance.

Don't panic. Trust him. Something must have happened to delay him.

She waited for an hour before she tried his mobile. An unfamiliar voice answered after a few rings, a man, stating his name – all she could make out was "officer".

"I'm looking for Robert Pozos. I thought this was his number," she said, starting to feel desperate.

"Who's speaking?" The voice was clipped and authoritative.

She was hesitant to give her name to a stranger.

"I'm a police officer – it's safe to tell me your name." The voice had softened.

"Claire Quinlan."

Where is Robert? Why does a police officer have his

mobile phone? Claire felt herself fill with dread.

"Are you a relative of Robert's?" the officer enquired.

"No . . . I'm his . . . girlfriend."

"Where are you calling from?" he asked, his tone now urgent.

"I'm at the airport – in San Francisco – he was meant to pick me up – do you know where he is?" Panic was making her stutter.

"There's been an accident, Claire. Now, I don't want you to worry. Robert will be OK – stay where you are and we'll send a car to pick you up."

* * *

The station was an ugly place at night: bright glaring lights, abusive foul-mouthed drunks, bad-tempered surly officers. They brought Julia to a small room away from the chaos of the reception area. Tim pulled out a seat for her. A few other officers had followed them to the room but she just focussed on Tim. He was a kind man. She could tell that. He crouched behind her as he removed the rubber bands and unlocked the cuffs on her wrists.

"Hold your hands out straight."

"What are you doing?" she asked.

"Testing for gunshot residue on your hands . . . Hold still . . . This won't hurt. It's just sticky . . . "

Tim was wearing rubber gloves and he was repeatedly stamping her hand with a plastic disc. He looked funny in the gloves. She smiled at him. He smiled back as he put the disc into a clear plastic bag. He handed it to one of the other officers who immediately left the room.

"OK . . . that's over with . . . What's your surname, Julia?"

"Pozos."

"And age?"

"Thirty-six."

"Next of kin?"

She paused.

"My husband, Robert," she answered, her voice strangled.

Tim took hold of her hand again. She held her fingers rigid thinking it would make it easier for him to take the prints.

"Relax. Don't try to help me. I've been taking prints for years . . . I'm an old hand at this, if you'll pardon the pun." He gave her another nice smile.

"I've had this done before," she confessed, wanting to help him.

"I know," he replied simply. "We'll be taking a breath test next – it will be just the same as the one you had the last time."

Tim went away and she was left alone with a female officer whose grey hair was drawn severely back from her face. She wasn't as nice as Tim.

"Empty your pockets," she instructed, her voice was as hard as her face.

"I have no pockets," Julia pointed out.

"Take off all your jewellery." Julia hesitated before

slipping off her wedding band.

"Bra and panty hose, now . . . we don't want you doing anything silly in that cell."

* * *

Julia didn't know how long she had been in the cell. They had taken her watch. There was a lot of noise with the angry drunks shouting abuse at the officers and picking fights with each other. She lay on the bed. She was tired. It was surprisingly comfortable. She was almost asleep when they came to get her.

Detective Sarah Dawson watched Julia with a mixture of intrigue and pity. Her suit was a good cut, her hair had subtle highlights that were the product of an expensive salon. Sarah had seen it all before, middle-class women going over the edge and, in one moment of madness, ruining the rest of their lives. She always felt helpless and depressed with cases like this one. Sarah nodded at the officer to leave so she could talk to Julia alone.

"Hello, Julia, I'm Detective Dawson. Call me Sarah. We're here because of what happened today," she began.

Julia was looking around the room in bewilderment. Sarah couldn't blame her. The acoustic ceiling and neon lighting were pretty dramatic.

"Before we go any further, I need to read you your Miranda rights again . . . "

Julia looked at Sarah as she recited the mantra. Sarah was older than her. Her grey suit looked dull. She needed to wear some make-up to give colour to her drawn face. She would be quite striking if she made the effort.

"Knowing and understanding your rights as I have explained them to you, are you willing to answer my questions without an attorney present?"

Julia decided she liked her so she said, "Yes".

"I'd like to find out more about you, Julia . . . How long have you been married to Robert?" Sarah's pen was poised to start writing.

"Just over a year."

Sarah didn't write it down.

"Do you have kids?"

"No." Sarah's pen still didn't make contact with the blank pad.

"What happened between the two of you today?" Sarah's expression was sympathetic. She was her friend.

"I found out he was having an affair," she said, her voice subdued.

"That must have hurt you . . . "

"Yes . . . he's divorcing me . . . " Julia started crying. Shock had cocooned her from emotion until now. Sarah was making her remember things. "I don't know what I was thinking . . . I got really drunk, you see . . . I was upset . . . You can understand why I'd be upset." She looked at Sarah through her tears and Sarah nodded her affirmation.

"I didn't mean to hurt him, though . . . I just went a

little crazy . . . I still love him . . . "

Sarah was writing in her notebook now.

"What am I being charged with?" Julia asked, her body taut with delayed panic.

"I don't know yet . . . It depends on whether Robert dies . . ." Sarah's words were followed by a fatal silence.

"Where did you get the gun?" Sarah asked, her eyes drilling through Julia.

"We had it at home."

"Are you familiar with guns? Do you practise at a driving range?" Sarah's questions were getting more determined and less gentle. Julia could feel her panic getting out of control.

"I don't want to talk any more," she said suddenly. "I want an attorney."

Sarah looked disappointed but her voice was kind.

"That's fine, Julia . . . The interview is over . . . Thank you for being so helpful."

The phone rang. They looked at it simultaneously. It was a dirty beige colour. Sarah answered it.

"OK . . . when? Right."

She put the phone down. Julia could read nothing from her expression before she said, "You're one lucky lady . . . They say he's going to make it . . . "

* * *

It was close to midnight when Claire got to see Robert. His face was ashen. Long spaghetti-like tubes

436

connected his body to the machines around him. The bullet had been removed a few hours earlier and the surgeon was pleased with his condition. Claire held his hand in hers and eventually fell asleep in the armchair next to his bed.

She woke when he increased the pressure on her limp hand. His brown eyes were alert. He slid the oxygen mask down.

"Hey." It was a croak.

"Robert, you shouldn't . . . please put it back on!" She was terrified that he wouldn't be able to breathe.

"Don't worry. It's only oxygen." He was finding his voice.

A nurse came in, throwing Claire a filthy look as if she was responsible for the misplaced mask. Claire went outside to give Robert some privacy. The windows were high up but they told that dawn was breaking outside. The surgeon passed her in the corridor, acknowledging her with a nod before following the nurse inside. It was thirty minutes before they finished and she could talk to him again.

"I'm so glad you're here." He clasped her hand as tight as he could manage.

"I'm so glad you're alive . . . The police told me that Julia did this," Claire answered, her voice as broken as his.

"Yes . . . but I'm also at fault . . . The divorce papers were served on her . . . I forgot about it, with all that was happening, I clean forgot . . . I intended to tell her well before she got the papers." His speech was laboured.

"The officer said that she'll go to prison, for at least a few years."

Robert nodded. His face had a raw sadness.

"I must be insane to feel sorry for her . . . I must have a hell of a lot of drugs in me."

They smiled at each other.

"I was thinking on the plane about something . . . about Frank and Paul," Claire said, remembering her flight to San Francisco as if it was from a different life.

"Paul?"

"My ex-boyfriend, the one who works in Digicom . . . He lives with James. I think it wasn't a coincidence that we lost Queensland Government to Digicom."

"I already know that Frank was leaking information to Digicom. I found out yesterday."

"Did you know about Paul?"

"Only Frank . . . the police can check Paul out . . . I'm tired of it all." Robert looked as weary as he said he was.

"I'm sorry. This is hardly the right time to talk about it."

"Don't be sorry . . . I just want to forget about the whole fiasco," he said.

She could see the resolve on his grey face.

There was a knock on the door. It was Donald Skates, casual in a pair of jeans.

"Excuse me, I hope I'm not interrupting." He threw

Claire a curious look.

"Donald, this is Claire, Claire Quinlan," Robert said hoarsely and Claire handed him a glass of water.

Donald looked befuddled; he had obviously forgotten who Claire was.

"The surgeon updated me on my way in. He's happy with your progress." Donald stood awkwardly, his hands clasped behind his back.

"Yes, it's good to be alive. Attempted murder makes one see life in a new light." Robert's grip on Claire's hand tightened. Donald seemed uncomfortable with their intimacy.

"Wayne was taken in for questioning last night. The police know of Ralph Costello – he was implicated in a swindle at his last job."

"Convicted?" Robert asked.

"No, not convicted. Police in Australia are also questioning the individuals over there." The specific names clearly escaped Donald.

"Good," Robert said with a slight nod.

There was a small silence.

"I wanted you to know what was happening. I'm personally ensuring that the police get all the assistance they need." Donald sounded as if he was seeking Robert's approval. It was the closest he would get to an apology.

"I should get going. I'll drop by later tonight." Donald shot Claire another confused look before taking his leave.

"What happens now?" Claire asked, the emotion in the small room intense.

"You tell me, honey. You were struggling to cope with two ex-wives. Now corporate fraud and attempted murder have been added to the mix! What are you feeling?" Robert was grinning but serious.

"Surprisingly confident about us. I'm trusting my instincts – they're all I have to rely on with you. For some reason, they think that ex-wives, fraud and murder are minor obstacles."

They both laughed, giddy from the elation of making it through the last few weeks.

"How about you?" Claire kept smiling, "Tempted to go back to Julia?"

Robert was solemn when he answered, "I'm leaving Amtech, Claire. Going to Sydney and meeting you has been an eye-opener for me. I can see clearly what I was missing from my life and what I need to do to be happy."

"And what's that?"

"I need to buy a house on Sydney Harbour . . . oh, and I need to ask a beautiful Irish girl if she'll live there with me."

THE END